SRA Open Court Reading

ESL
Visual Glossary

A Division of The McGraw-Hill Companies

Columbus, Ohio

SRA/McGraw-Hill

*A Division of The **McGraw·Hill** Companies*

Copyright © 2000 by SRA/McGraw-Hill.

Send all inquiries to:
SRA/McGraw-Hill
8787 Orion Place
Columbus, OH 43240-4027

Printed in the United States of America.

ISBN 0-02-661089-2

3 4 5 6 7 8 9 VIC 04 03 02 01 00

ESL Visual Glossary

Introduction

The ***ESL Visual Glossary*** is a unique reference manual compiled from abstract English words found in the ***Open Court Reading*** series. It has been designed to assist the ESL student, or any teacher, in explaining the meaning of these English words. It is filled with suggestions in the forms of pantomimes, demonstrations, explanations, drawings, and student participation that will help to explain these English words.

English-speaking students and second-language students alike can benefit from learning the meaning of abstract words that form the backbone of English sentences.

About the Visual Glossary

- The *Visual Glossary* contains many of the words found in the ***Student Anthologies,*** and the *Blending* and the *Word Knowledge* sections of the Teacher's Editions of ***Open Court Reading*** Grades K-6.

- It is not a dictionary. It does not contain every word or word form in the English language.

- Explanations of words are determined by the reading selections. Not all meanings for each entry word have been supplied.

- Many suggestions provide sample sentences, as well as suggestions for pantomime or demonstration.

- Most word forms are compiled under the base word. This should assist teachers in quickly locating the word or words that they need to explain. These compilations also will assist the teacher in explaining the various forms of the word. There may be occasional exceptions to these base-word compilations, as in the words *is* and *was*.

- If a word that you need to explain does not appear in this ***ESL Visual Glossary***, look for synonyms or antonyms of that word.

- These words can also be found in the specific grade level ***ESL Supplement.***

1881 ➤ Use a time line to help show *1881*.

1973 ➤ Use a time line to help show *1973*.

a ➤ Pick up *a* book and say "*A* book." Then pick up *two* books and say "*Two* books." Lead students in finding *a* thing and then *two* things. Lead students in sentences. If it will be helpful, explain that *a* means "one."

aah ➤ Pantomime saying "*aah*" while looking surprised.

abandoned ➤ Toss a puppet aside and walk away from it. Say "I have *abandoned* [Patches]."

able ➤ Pantomime not being *able* to do various actions and then explain, "I am not *able* to _____." Contrast this with being *able* to do something and explain, "I am *able* to _____."

aboard ➤ Show a picture of a train or ship. Have a puppet *try to* get on a train or ship; tell students that the puppet is going *aboard*. Have students pantomime going *aboard* a train or ship. —*all aboard*, once you have explained the individual words in this phrase, you can explain that people know when to get on a train or ship because they will hear someone call "*All aboard.*" Draw a picture of a ship on the chalkboard with people waiting to board. Call out, "*All aboard!*" Erase the people waiting to board and draw them on the ship.

abolish, abolition, abolitionist ➤ Draw a "No Pushing" sign on the chalkboard (one child pushing another with a diagonal line through them). Have the students pantomime pushing. Point to the sign on the board and say "No pushing allowed in school!" "Our rules *abolish* pushing in school." "We enforce rules for the *abolition* of pushing in school." "I am an *abolitionist*. I enforce rules to get rid of pushing in school."

about ➤ **1.** Hold up a book and say "The book is *about* _____." Repeat with other examples, such as television shows or movies. **2.** Make sentences, such as "How *about* reading a story" and "What *about* having lunch? I don't know *about* you, but I'm hungry." **3.** Open a book to the last few pages. Then say "I have read this much of the book. I am *about* finished with the book." **4.** Tell a puppet, "Look *about* the room and tell me what you see." Then have the puppet look around and list a few things that it sees. Repeat with students.

abrupt ➤ Play "Simon Says" where students must come to an *abrupt* stop.

absolute, absolutely ➤ **1.** Have a puppet tell an *absolute* truth about its actions over the past few moments. For example, have a puppet sit on a desk and say "I sat on a desk." Contrast by having the puppet sit on the desk and say "I jumped on the desk." **2.** Have one puppet ask the other, "Do you like chocolate?" or other similar questions. Have the other answer, "Yes, *absolutely!*" Explain that *absolutely* means "Yes! Yes! Yes!"

absurd ➤ Have a puppet say something silly, such as "I can fly!" Then make the puppet fall down. Say "It is *absurd* to think a puppet can fly like a bird!"

abundant, abundantly ➤ Tell students, "We have a lot of food." Then tell them, "We are *abundant* with food." Finally, tell them we are *abundantly* fed. Repeat the series with other examples. Lead them in sentences.

accelerating ❧ Have students pretend to drive around the classroom, slowly at first, then gradually moving faster and faster. Say "You are *accelerating*."

accents ❧ Say, good morning to the students using a variety of *accents*, such as British, French, Spanish, New York, Texan, etc.

accident ❧ Bump into something or drop something and describe these actions as an *accident*.

accomplished, accomplishing ❧ **1.** Have students name people who are very good at what they do. Say, for example, "[Michael Jordan] is an *accomplished* [basketball player]." **2.** At the end of a school day, say "We *accomplished* a lot today." **3.** Help students through an assignment. While they are working, say "We are *accomplishing* lots."

accord ❧ —*on own accord*, have a puppet erase the chalkboard for you without your telling it. Then have the puppet clean up a mess on your desk without your saying anything. Use as many examples as needed. Say "It is cleaning on its own accord."

according ❧ Have students move their hands *according* to your directions.

accounting ❧ Show a page from your checkbook register or do some simple *accounting* on the chalkboard.

accurate, accuracy ❧ **1.** Ask a student to walk to your desk while two puppets watch. Ask each puppet to tell you what it saw. Have the first puppet give an *accurate* account. "Jose got up and walked to your desk." Tell the puppet, "That is *accurate*." Have the second puppet say "Jose walked over to the bookshelf." Tell the puppet, "That is not *accurate*." **2.** Draw a bull's-eye on the chalkboard. Have students throw wadded paper at the center. Praise *accuracy*.

accusing ❧ Have a puppet *accuse* you of taking something from it. Say "Why is [Fluffy] *accusing* me?"

ache, ached ❧ **1.** Used as a metaphor meaning "strong but frustrated desire," it combines the feeling of pain from an *ache* (pantomime a stomach*ache*) and the feeling of wanting something badly (pantomime strong desire, perhaps using a puppet to show the feeling). Give sentences, such as "I *ache* for a good friend," using body language for emphasis. **2.** Show an old injury and explain that the injury hurt; it *ached*.

achieve ❧ Pantomime a scene of a puppet climbing a mountain. When it reaches the top of the mountain, explain to the class that it *achieved* its goal.

acknowledge ❧ Ask a student to say something to you. Answer him or her. Then say "When I answer you, I *acknowledge* you."

acres ❧ Show students pictures of farms of varying sizes. Estimate for them the *acreage* of each. If this is not sufficient, have them measure the size of the playground and tell them how much *acreage* that is. Then help them figure out how big ten acres would be and so on.

across ◆ Walk *across* the floor. Have students walk *across* the floor. Draw a circle on the board and demonstrate moving *across* it. Have students push a pencil *across* their desk.

act, acting, acts, actor ◆ **1.** Do some *acting* out of words, such as *sad* and *happy*, and explain that this is *acting*. **2.** Have students *act* out roles in a short pantomime. Explain that they are *acting*, and that they are called *actors* when doing so. Ask who watches T.V., and explain that *actors* play those roles. Give examples of *actors* students may be familiar with. Ask students to name other *actors*. **3.** Explain this sense of *act* by having one puppet exclaim to another, "We'll miss our ride! *Act* fast!" Have the second puppet urge "*Act! Act!*" until the first runs or does some other action.

action ◆ Have students perform various *actions*, such as putting away their pencils, standing up, sitting down, running in place, etc.

actual, actually ◆ **1.** Have each student hand you an item of his or her choice. Contrast by drawing an enormous version of each item on the chalkboard. **2.** Hold a small object behind your back. Have students guess what it is. Then tell them what it *actually* is. Repeat this with various objects.

adapting ◆ Give each student a manila folder. Explain that its original purpose is to hold sheets of paper. Have students roll the folders into tubes and use them as telescopes or megaphones. Say "We are changing our folders into other things. We are *adapting* them for other uses."

add, adding, added, addition ◆ **1.** Place a few paper clips in a pile and invite students to *add* another one. **2.** Lead students in *adding* piles of paper clips. Help them make past tense sentences. **3.** Demonstrate an *addition* problem. Have students recite simple *addition* facts.

adequate ◆ Distribute a pile of paper clips to each student. Have them take turns filling a paper cup with paper clips. When the cup is full, say "That's an *adequate* number of paper clips to fill the cup." Then give students an *inadequate* number of paper clips to fill the cup.

adjustable, adjust, adjusts ◆ **1.** Demonstrate with a belt. *Adjust* the belt to different circumferences by moving the buckle to different holes. Say "This belt is *adjustable*, so it can fit people; I can *adjust* the belt to fit different people." **2.** Read a passage very softly. Ask how many students could hear you. *Adjust* your reading volume until they can hear you easily. Say "I needed to *adjust* my voice so you could hear me better."

administration ◆ Have students work in committees to plan something for the class. Each committee can select a person to be in charge. Say "[Tuan] is in charge of *administration* of this committee."

admire, admired, admiring, admiration, admirer ◆ **1.** Go about the room and *admire* students' displayed work. **2.** Say to a student, "I like your picture." Say to the class, "I am *admiring* her picture," and "I *admired* her picture." Have students imitate. **3.** Show *admiration* of the artwork done by some of your students. Say to the class, "I love this picture. I *admire* it. I am showing *admiration* for it."

admit ❖   Walk by your desk and nonchalantly knock a book off. Act surprised and say "Who knocked my book off the desk?" When students accuse you, say "You're right! I *admit* I was the one who did it."

adobe ❖   A structure made from sun-dried clay and straw. Show students a picture of an *adobe* and a picture of a traditional house.

adopt, adopts ❖   **1.** Show a picture of a baby and say that it has no mother. Explain that you wish to be its mother and that you will *adopt* it. Pantomime filling out forms, talking to people, and then taking a baby home. **2.** Pick up a doll or stuffed animal and say to it, "I am going to take this baby home to live with my family." Then say to students, "This is how the teacher *adopts* the [baby]."

adore ❖   Describe people or things you like, love, and *adore*. For example, say "I like my neighbor; I love my mother; I *adore* my son." Use body language to emphasize *adore*. Ask students for examples.

advance ❖   Ask for a few volunteers to help you. Divide them into two groups, and have one small group *advance* while the other *retreats*.

advantage ❖   Ask students to tell you good and bad things about dodgeball. Write them down on the chalkboard in columns labeled "*Advantages*" and "*Disadvantages*." Offer a few examples if students have difficulty. Then go through the list saying, "Dodging the ball is an *advantage*" and "Getting out is a *disadvantage*." Repeat for the rest of the list. Have students repeat the sentences with you. Tell students that *dis-* means "not."

adventure, adventures ❖   **1.** Show pictures of skiing, riding a roller coaster, or other acts that students might think of as an *adventure*. Have a couple of puppets go on an *adventure*, perhaps hiking up a trail and seeing a rabbit. Make it exciting and fun. Tell students that the puppets had an *adventure*. Ask students if they have ever had an *adventure*. **2.** Pantomime looking around the classroom for danger, as if you were walking through a haunted forest. **3.** Show pictures of people hiking, exploring caves, climbing mountains, or on other *adventures*. Lead them in plural sentences.

advice ❖   Have a puppet tell you it wants to start a business. Say "Well then, let me give you some *advice*. Here's what you should do… ."

afford ❖   Have one puppet give another puppet a dollar for a box of cookies. Say "The puppet can *afford* the cookies."

afraid ❖   Hold up a toy snake, spider, or other "scary" object. Lead students in pantomiming being *afraid* by shaking and shrinking from it. Contrast this with acting *brave* and approaching it.

after ❖   Line students up to take turns at making a mark on the chalkboard. Explain repeatedly, "[Yen] is *after* [Ana]." See *before*.

afternoon ❖   Draw a clock on the chalkboard with the hands set at 12:00 P.M. Explain that the time in the middle of the day, lunchtime, is called "*noon*," and

ESL Visual Glossary

that the time *after* lunch and before dinner is called *afternoon*. Have students recite 12:00 noon, 1:00 P.M., 2:00 P.M., etc. up to 6:00 P.M.

afterthought ❖ Tell students the agenda for today's lesson, leaving one item out. Then say "There's one more thing. I *thought* of this after I told you the rest of the plan. This item is an *afterthought*."

afterward ❖ Have a puppet write it name on the board. Then have the puppet go to visit another puppet. Tell the class, "[Sparky] wrote his name on the board; *afterward* he went to play with [Fluffy]."

again ❖ Have students raise their hands. Then have them raise their hands *again*.

against ❖ Place one object *against* another. Tell students, "The eraser is *against* the scissors." Lead students in placing one object *against* another.

age ❖ Ask a student how old she is. Prompt as needed. Then say "Your *age* is ____." Repeat with another student. Then change the question to, "What is your *age?*"

agent ❖ Set up a scene in which one student is a movie star, another student is a movie producer, and you are negotiating on behalf of the movie star. Pantomime the salary negotiation with the producer. Say "I am the *agent*. It is my job to get the best deal for my client."

aggravate, aggravation ❖ **1.** Have one puppet *aggravate* another. **2.** Pantomime looking for a particular book on your bookshelf and getting annoyed when you don't find it. Say "I really needed that book, and it wasn't where I put it. This is an *aggravation*, because I couldn't find it."

aggressive ❖ **1.** Show a toy animal ready to attack. **2.** Hold up a dollar bill. Say "Who would like this dollar?" When a student comes forward to get it, say "[Jorge] came right up and got what he wanted. His *aggressive* action got the reward."

agitated ❖ Have a puppet come and tell you some bad news. Act *agitated* and tell the class that you are *agitated* over the puppet's bad news.

ago ❖ Explain that *ago* means "before." Have students practice with sentences, such as "Yesterday was one day *ago*," "Saturday was ___ days *ago*," and "Independence Day was __ days *ago*." —*long ago*, say "The dinosaurs lived *long ago*." Show pictures of prehistoric humans.

agree, agrees, agreed, agreeable, agreement ❖ **1.** Have two puppets *agree* about what to do at recess. **2.** Have one puppet say things, such as, "It is hot" and "It is cold." A second puppet *agrees* with everything said; it acts very *agreeable*. **3.** Write 2 + 3 on the board and have the puppets reach an *agreement* about the answer. Make them say "We are in *agreement* about the answer." Lead students in past tense sentences.

ahead ❖ **1.** Show on the chalkboard one racer far *ahead* of another. **2.** Have one student walk *ahead* of another.

aid ❖ Have one puppet give *aid* to another that is hurt or ill.

ailment ❖ Cough. Say "This cough is a terrible *ailment*." Scratch your skin. Say "Another *ailment!* Itchy skin!"

aim, aimed ➤ *Aim* for the wastebasket as you toss a wadded-up piece of paper into it. Have students do the same. Lead students in past tense sentences.

ain't ➤ A shortened informal form of *am not, is not, are not, has not,* or *have not.* Lead students in sentences, such as "She is not there; she *ain't* there." (Although *ain't* is used orally, it is never used in formal writing, such as most school assignments. Please note that it is used in dialogue.)

air ➤ Have students puff out some *air* and feel it with a hand. Have them wave their hands around in the *air* so that they can feel the *air* move. Have them feel the *air* by breathing it in and out.

airstream ➤ On the chalkboard draw an airplane wing showing the *airstream* going over it.

aisle, aisles ➤ Walk down the *aisle* in the classroom if your furniture is arranged this way. Otherwise, draw an aerial view of a supermarket showing the *aisles*.

alarm, alarming ➤ **1.** Suddenly act very frightened or startled. **2.** Set up a scene where a puppet is in bed and the *alarm* goes off. **3.** Have a puppet balance precariously at the edge of a tabletop. Have it almost fall. Tell the class, "That was *alarming!*"

alignments ➤ Drop a handful of pencils on your desk. Ask students to arrange the pencils in straight rows along the edge of the desk. Show them the *alignments* they made.

alive ➤ Have students touch things that are *alive*, such as people, plants, and pets. Then, have them touch things in the room that are not *alive*, such as desks and chairs.

all ➤ **1.** Put a group of paper clips on your desk and knock *all* of them off. Contrast that with knocking *some* of them off. Do other similar examples. **2.** Check that students understand the meaning of *all*. Then make sentences, such as "*All* we ate was candy" or "*All* we saw was white." **3.** Show *all* of a piece of paper and then *part* of a piece of paper. —*after all*, have two puppets dramatize this expression. One offers the other a piece of candy and then drops it on the ground. The second says that he or she doesn't want it *after all*. Have the first puppet offer a ride on his back and give a very rocky ride. The second decides that he or she doesn't want a ride *after all*. —*at all*, makes the sentence stronger. Give example sentences, such as "I have nothing" and then more expressively, "I have nothing *at all*;" "I am not angry," and more expressively, "I am not angry *at all*." Have students repeat and use other examples.

allergic ➤ Show students a picture or toy kitten. Put your face close to it. Sneeze, and say "I am *allergic* to kittens."

allow, allowed ➤ **1.** Have a puppet try to pick a fight. Tell the puppet to stop as you do not *allow* fighting. Contrast with something that you will *allow*. Lead students in making sentences: "The teacher does not *allow* fighting; he/she does *allow* reading." Tell the puppet that fighting is not *allowed*, but sitting is *allowed*. **2.** Instruct students to ask you if they may do something. Say to each of their questions, "Yes, it is *allowed*," or "No, it is not *allowed*."

allowance ❯ Have a puppet do chores for its "mother." Have the mother give it an *allowance*. Tell the class, "The puppet empties the garbage every day for its *allowance*."

almost ❯ Show students all of the crayons and contrast with *almost* all of the crayons. Repeat with other examples.

alone ❯ Show some paper clips. Take away all but one and point out the one that is *alone*. Do a similar demonstration with a group of students. Ask one child to sit *alone*. —*leave alone, left alone*. Put out some paper clips on a table. Put a few aside and say that you are going to *leave* those *alone*. Hand out the others. Point out repeatedly that you are going to *leave* one pile *alone*. Have two puppets *leave* one by itself and say that they have *left* Fluffy *alone*. Contrast that with having puppets play *together*.

along ❯ **1.** Draw a road on the chalkboard and show things that are located *along* the road. **2.** Show the difference between walking in place and walking *along* or forward.

alongside ❯ Draw a line on the chalkboard. Draw another line *alongside* the first one. Have students do the same. Place a stapler *alongside* a book. Repeat with other objects.

alphabet ❯ Point to *alphabet* bulletin board strips, if available, or have students sing their A-B-Cs.

already ❯ List things that the class has *already* learned or *already* done that morning. Then mention things that you have not *already* done.

although ❯ Point to something you are wearing. Say "I bought this one, *although* there was a [blue] one I also liked."

altitude ❯ Draw a mountain on the chalkboard and point to low and high *altitudes*.

always ❯ Mention things that the class *always* does. Perhaps the class *always* does reading in the morning, *always* does math after recess, *always* does art on Fridays, and so on. You can point to a calendar or class schedule as you explain. Ask if students *always* do certain jobs or do certain activities for their birthdays or other celebrations.

am ❯ Lead students in making sentences while pantomiming: "I *am* [Carlos]," "I *am* a student," "I *am* in America." —*I'm*, show on the board the words *I* and *am* and then squeeze them together to make the word *I'm*. Lead students in using *I am* in sentences, such as "*I am* a student," "*I am* American," and so on. (See *I* and *am*.)

Amanda's ❯ Make examples of possessives using student names, such as *Maria's* jacket, *Min's* lunch box, and so on. It may clarify to point to *Maria*, for example, and say "*Maria*." Then hold up her jacket and say "*Maria's* jacket."

amazed, amazing, amazement ❯ Show *amazing* pictures, such as a huge anaconda snake or a huge bear. Lead students in pantomiming their *amazement*. Help students make past tense sentences, such as "I was *amazed* by the picture of the snake."

ambiguity ◆ Tell the class, "After John and Joe finished lunch, he went away." Then ask, "Who went away?" Student answers will vary. Explain that this is what we call *ambiguity*. Give and get other examples.

amend, amendment ◆ **1.** On the chalkboard, write the sentence, "The birds fly." Ask students to *amend* the sentence in some way, such as, "The big birds fly." Give example sentences using *amendment*. **2.** Show the Constitution. Point to the original paragraphs and then the *amendments*. Explain that each time we make a change, we do it with an *amendment*.

American Sign Language ◆ Comprised of hand shapes and movements, ASL is the primary language system of the American deaf community. It has its own unique syntax and is not merely translated English. Show students the ASL sign for "I love you." Hold up the thumb and index and pinkie fingers of your right hand. Have students imitate. Say "This is one of thousands of signs used by deaf people in *American Sign Language*."

American, Americans ◆ **1.** Show *America* on a map or globe. Tell students that things from the country America are called *American*. Give examples, such as *American* cars and *American* movies. **2.** Explain that people from *America* are called *Americans*.

amiss ◆ Do something silly, such as wear your glasses upside down. Ask students if there is anything *amiss*. Adjust your glasses. Reply, "Yes, something was *amiss*. I had my glasses on upside down."

among ◆ Sketch some plants on the chalkboard. Show a mouse *among* the plants. Sketch a forest of trees. Show animals *among* the trees.

amply ◆ Fatten a puppet up by stuffing paper around your hand and then putting the puppet on over it. Say "This puppet has been *amply* fed."

amuse, amused, amusement ◆ **1.** Pretend to be *amused* by something you are reading. Have students tell you about things that *amuse* them. **2.** Lead students in past tense sentences. **3.** Any of the activities that *amuse* are *amusements*. Have students tell you some of their favorite *amusements*.

an ◆ Lead students in phrases using the word *an*. Show pictures of things that one would use with *an*, and model the words "*an* egg," "*an* apple," or "*an* elephant."

analyzing ◆ Demonstrate *analyzing* a science experiment. Say to the class, "I am *analyzing* what made this experiment work."

ancestors ◆ Help students write the names of their parents and grandparents on a family tree. Tell them that the persons before their grandparents are their *ancestors*.

anchor, anchored ◆ Show a picture of an *anchor* and explain that sailors use an *anchor* so their boat will not float away. Draw a picture of a sailboat floating near a beach with an *anchor* hanging deep in the water from a chain. Explain that the boat is *anchored*.

ancient ◆ **1.** Show students *ancient* things, perhaps pictures of pottery from archaeological digs. Contrast with modern things. Tell them, "These are *ancient*, and these are modern." **2.** Show a picture of a very old person and another of a baby.

and ◆ **1.** Hold up small objects in sequence. Each time you add one to what you are holding, say the word *and*. Say "A book *and* a stapler *and* a paper clip…." **2.** Lead students in saying *and* pantomiming phrases, such as "pencil *and* pen," "Jose *and* Maria," or "crayon *and* pencil."

anesthesia ◆ Show a picture of a patient receiving *anesthesia*, or pantomime putting something over your mouth and going to sleep.

anew ◆ Explain that *anew* means "doing something again." Give examples by repeating a sentence.

angel ◆ Show a picture of an *angel*. Explain to students that *angels* are supposed to be good. If somebody says that you are an *angel*, you are being good.

angle ◆ Draw a series of *angles* on the chalkboard.

angry, angrier, angriest ◆ **1.** Draw *angry* and *pleased* faces on the chalkboard. Lead students in pantomiming these emotions. Make *angry* faces and fists. **2.** Have puppets dramatize being *angry*, *angrier*, and *angriest*.

animal's ◆ Make examples by pointing to a picture of an *animal* and saying: "The *animal's* tail, the *animal's* head," and so on.

Ann ◆ Explain that *Ann* is a girl's name. Ask for corresponding first-language names, such as *Ana*.

announce, announcing, announcement ◆ **1.** *Announce* something to the class. Then explain that you were *announcing* it. **2.** In a loud voice, say "*Announcement*." Repeat until you have student attention. Tell them what they are going to do the rest of the day.

annoy, annoys ◆ **1.** Ask a student to pretend to read. Begin to *annoy* him or her by talking or making loud noises, etc. **2.** Have students chatter while you work at your desk. Pantomime irritation and say "All this noise *annoys* me." Make an unpleasant squeaking sound on the chalkboard and say "That sound *annoys* me."

anomalies ◆ Have students draw pictures of a thing, and of an unusual version of the same thing, such as a normal car and a car with wings.

anonymous, anonymously ◆ **1.** Point out a poem that has no author listed. Explain that there was an author, but we don't know the name. He or she is *anonymous*. **2.** Pretend to find a thank-you note on your desk. Read it aloud and let the note praise you for doing something nice. Show that there is no signature. Give example sentences using *anonymously*. Say "Somebody *anonymously* wrote this note."

another ◆ **1.** Make a pile of paper clips. Add *another* paper clip. Then add *another*. **2.** Using the books in the class, point out one, *another*, and *another*, etc. Point out chalk and desks in this way. —*another one*, ask students to find pencils and place them on your desk. Every time a pencil is produced, say "Here's *another one!*"

answer, answered, answering ❧ **1.** Have one puppet *ask* a question. Then have the second puppet *answer*. Tell students the puppet *answered*. Then lead students in *asking* and *answering*. **2.** Show a picture of a telephone; identify it. Dramatize *answering* the phone after it rings.

anthropologist ❧ Show pictures of *anthropologists* at work. Give example sentences.

antibiotic ❧ Show pictures of typical medicines. Explain that when we get sick with certain diseases, these medicines, called *antibiotics*, can help us get well.

antibodies ❧ Divide the class into two groups. Tape signs with "V" for Virus on the chests of one group, and "A" for *Antibodies* on the other. Have the "A" group stand in strong stances while the "V" group pretends to attack them. Have the "V" group fall down when they meet up with the "A" group. Say "Our bodies make *antibodies* to fight viruses that can make us sick. *Antibodies* help keep our bodies healthy and strong."

anticipate, anticipates, anticipating, anticipation ❧ **1.** Ask students what they will be doing the rest of the day. Say "[Jai] *anticipates* the rest of the day." **2.** Set up a scene where a puppet is looking at and wondering about the contents of a birthday present. Have the puppet question how much longer it will be until it can open the gift. Have the puppet portray excitement and *anticipation*. Tell the students that the puppet is *anticipating* opening its gift.

antislavery ❧ Write the word *Slavery* in a circle and draw a slash through it to indicate no *slavery*. Lead students in sentences using *antislavery*. Explain, if necessary, the circumstances of the Civil War.

anxious, anxiously ❧ Pantomime waiting *anxiously* for a train to arrive, perhaps because you are expecting an old friend who is quite ill. Ask students if they have ever been *anxious* about something, such as starting a new school year.

any ❧ Closing your eyes, choose from among a group of books. Say that you will read *any* book. Pick out a paper clip without caring which one. Say that you will take *any* paper clip. Do the same with pencils or pens.

anybody ❧ Say "*Anybody* can hold the chalk." Close your eyes and choose a student at random. Repeat this method of choosing with other things.

anyhow ❧ Have one puppet put a silly hat on, such as a paper cup, and have another one say "You look beautiful *anyhow*." Make up other similar sentences.

anymore ❧ **1.** Give a student a pencil. Then give him or her more pencils. Give him or her all the pencils and say "I don't have *anymore* pencils." **2.** Ask a puppet to do something for you—perhaps sharpen the pencils. When the puppet is done, tell it that it doesn't need to do that *anymore*. Then ask a student to do the same thing; tell him or her that he or she can stop—he or she doesn't need to do that *anymore*. Repeat with other examples. **3.** Draw a picture on the chalkboard and stop. Say "I don't feel like drawing *anymore*."

anything ❧ Have a puppet claim that it is so hungry that it will eat *anything*. Have it eat paper clips, pencils, erasers, and so on.

anywhere ◆ Pick up an object and place it in various locations in the classroom. Say "Where should I put this? I could put it here, or there, or *anywhere*." Call upon students to put a pencil *anywhere* in the class. Repeat as needed.

apart ◆ **1.** Show two puppets *together* and then *apart*. **2.** Ask one child to sit *apart* from the others.

appealing ◆ Have students work together to draw an ice-cream sundae on the chalkboard. Admire it and say "What an *appealing* sundae you've made!"

appear, appeared, appearing, appearance ◆ **1.** Make something *appear* from behind your back. **2.** Demonstrate *appearing* and *disappearing* with a puppet. **3.** Show pictures of older actors and actresses wearing makeup that makes them look younger. Say "This [actor] is [65 years old]. The makeup he is wearing gives him the *appearance* of looking younger."

appetite ◆ Have each student draw a picture of his or her favorite food and pantomime eating it hungrily. Say "You were really hungry for that food. You have a good *appetite*."

applaud, applause ◆ **1.** Have one puppet *applaud* the other. **2.** Have a puppet perform a short tune. Then ask students to give *applause* to the puppet. Model as needed.

apply, applied, application, applicants ◆ **1.** Show a student how to work out a math problem. Have the student *apply* what you demonstrated. **2.** Lead students in past tense sentences. **3.** *Apply* some glue or paint to a piece of paper. **4.** Explain that you *applied* it. **5.** (See *interviews*.) Continue with the interview scene and say "You are all *applicants*." **6.** Have students fill out a sample *application*.

appoint, appointed, appointment ◆ **1.** *Appoint* different students to routine tasks for the classroom. **2.** Point to a day on the calendar that has been designated for a certain event. Say, for example, "[Thursday, March 3] is the *appointed* day for our [school picnic]." **3.** Give a student the *appointment* of being your helper for the day.

appreciate ◆ Ask students to tell you something they value. Lead students in making sentences using *appreciate*.

apprehension ◆ Make a list of things students do not like to do. Lead them in sentences using *apprehension*. Say "I feel *apprehension* if I ride in a car with my seat belt unbuckled."

apprentice ◆ Choose a student to be your *apprentice* for the day.

approach, approached ◆ **1.** Have a puppet *approach* another puppet. Repeat with students. **2.** Demonstrate coming closer to a student. Say "I *approached* Juan." Lead students in *approaching* each other.

appropriate ◆ Put scissors, tape, and a stapler on your desk. Pick up a piece of paper. Look over the tools and select the scissors. Say "Scissors are the *appropriate* tool to use for cutting paper."

approval ◆ Act out with a puppet. Have the puppet ask you for permission to do something, such as make a craft project. Answer, "Yes, you may [make a mask]; you have my *approval* to [make a mask]."

April ◆ Show a calendar and the months. Then show *April* as well as pictures of spring. Contrast with other seasons if necessary.

apt ◆ Have students come up with names they feel best describe themselves or someone they know. Say "That is a very *apt* name."

archaeology ◆ Show students pictures of ancient buildings, tools, dishes, weapons, etc. Say "This study of ancient things is called *archaeology*."

arcs ◆ Draw a series of *arcs* on a sheet of paper to demonstrate the shape. Say "These are *arcs*."

are ◆ Lead students in making and pantomiming sentences, such as, "My hand *is* on my desk" and "My hands *are* on my desk." Lead students in making sentences about themselves, such as, "We *are* Americans," "We *are* in the class," "Shoes *are* on the feet," and so on. Explain that the word *are* is like the words *is* or *am*. —*you're*, show how the words *you* and *are* are squeezed together to make the word *you're*.

area, areas ◆ **1.** Point out the main regions of the United States on a map. Say "This *area* is called the Northeast; this *area* is called the South," and so on. **2.** Write the word *Mathematics* on the board. Explain that there are many different things to learn in mathematics. List some students will be familiar with, such as arithmetic, algebra, and geometry. Explain that each is an *area* or part of mathematics.

aren't Show how the words *are* and *not* squeeze together to make the word *aren't*. See *are* and *not*.

argue, arguing, argument ◆ **1.** Have two puppets *argue* with each other. **2.** Show two puppets *arguing*. Explain that the puppets are having an *argument*. —*good arguments*, an *argument* tells why you should do something. *Good arguments* are good reasons for doing something. Have students tell you why the class should have a pizza party. Tell each student who gives a reason, "That's a *good argument*."

armed ◆ Have students help you make a list of Superman's special powers, such as X-ray vision, flying, etc. Say "Superman has many special powers; he is *armed* with these qualities, so he can help people."

aroma ◆ Bring in some strong-smelling spice. Tell the students, "The room is filled with an *aroma* of spice."

around ◆ **1.** Tell a puppet, "Look *around* the room and tell me what you see." Then have the puppet look *around* and list a few things that it sees. Repeat with students looking *around*. Name the things that you see *around* the room. Then have students name things that they see *around* the room. **2.** Have students walk *around* another student or a desk. Lead students in putting their arms *around* their desks or themselves. **3.** Move *around* from place to place like a rabbit might. —*'round*, explain that this is short for the word *around*. Show paper clips *around* a book or *'round* a book. Have them place objects *'round* a pencil.

aroused ❯ *Arouse* a puppet from sleep. Have the puppet gradually wake up.

arrange, arrangement, arrangements ❯ **1.** Give a student a few pencils. Ask him or her to make the shape of a square with them. Repeat, this time asking him or her to *arrange* the pencils into a square. Tell the class that [Jose] made an *arrangement* with the pencils. Show pictures of a flower *arrangement*. **2.** Have two students make an agreement about something— perhaps who will sharpen pencils for the teacher over the next few days. When they are finished, have them shake hands and tell the class that they have made an *arrangement*. **3.** Ask students to help you make a list of all the things that need to be done to set up a field trip. Say "These are all the *arrangements* that need to be made to get ready to go on a field trip."

arrest, arrested ❯ Pretend to *arrest* a puppet.

arrive, arrived, arrives, arrival ❯ Leave and enter the classroom. Say that you have *arrived*. Ask a student to go into the hall and then *arrive* in the classroom. As the student *arrives*, announce his or her arrival.

art, artist ❯ **1.** Show paintings, drawings, sculptures, or book illustrations. **2.** Explain that an *artist* is someone who makes *art*. The illustrators of stories are *artists*, as are the people who made the fine *art* in the Fine *Art* sections. If there is time, have students draw a picture and tell them that they are *artists*.

as ❯ Have students clap their hands *as* they tap their toes. Have students tap their toes *as* they sing a song. Have them do other simultaneous activities to communicate the idea of *as*. —*as* ____ *as*, show items that are *as* big *as* each other. Contrast those with items that are *as* flat, round, or straight *as* each other. —*as if*, have a puppet mimic what you do. Say "It is *as if* [Fluffy] is me today."

ascend, ascent ❯ **1.** Draw a staircase on the chalkboard. Have a puppet walk up the stairs. **2.** Draw a mountain on the chalkboard and make your fingers make the *ascent*.

ashamed ❯ Have a puppet take something, and then admit that it did it. Have it hang its head and say "I am *ashamed* of myself." Have one puppet turn in its homework and another say it forgot its homework. Have the second puppet act *ashamed*. Lead students in pantomiming looking *ashamed*. Give examples of reasons to feel *ashamed*, such as, "Be *ashamed* of yelling at your friend."

aside ❯ Have a student stand in your path. As you approach the student, say to the class that you will step *aside*, and do so. Tell the class that you will set the book *aside*, and place it next to you.

ask, asked ❯ *Ask* a student a question, such as his or her name, and have him or her answer it. Explain "I *ask* a question" and "The student answers the question." Repeat with different questions. For past tense, explain, "I *asked* a question" and "The student answered the question." Repeat with different questions.

asleep ❯ Show a picture of a *sleeping* person, or have a puppet be *sleeping*. Tell the class, "She is *asleep*." Contrast with being *awake* by showing people who are *awake*. Have the puppet *wake up* and tell the class that it is *awake*. Lead students in a pantomime of being *asleep*. —*fall asleep, fell asleep*, have a puppet *fall asleep*, then wake up and say "I am sorry; I *fell asleep*." Lead students in pantomimes of *falling asleep*, waking up, and saying, "I *fell asleep*." —*fast asleep*, demonstrate with a puppet. Have the puppet be *fast asleep* and attempt to wake it several times. Tell students, "This puppet is hard to *wake up*, because it is *fast asleep*." Contrast with a puppet *sleeping* lightly.

aspects ❧ Show photos from a trip you have made or photos of some experience. Tell students these are different *aspects* of your trip.

assault, assaults ❧ Have a puppet repeatedly *assault* another. Give example sentences using *assaults*.

assemble ❧ **1.** *Assemble* students at the front of the classroom. *Assemble* students into two or three orderly rows. Have students *assemble* to play a game or sing. **2.** *Assemble* a Lego kit or something similar.

asserting ❧ Act out by asking two puppets what they would like for lunch. Have one act shy and say "I don't know; whatever you want." Have the other say boldly, "I would like a peanut butter sandwich. Mom says I'll get what I want by *asserting* myself."

assess ❧ Write "Poor" and "Excellent" on the board. Then ask the class to help you *assess* the puppet's skills in exercising. Have a puppet do some various exercises, either poorly or excellently, and have students *assess*. Make a slash mark in the appropriate column on the board.

assignment ❧ Give students their *assignment* in a particular subject.

assist ❧ Attempt to gather a large armload of books. Say "These books are heavy. I need some help. Could one of you please *assist* me?"

assume, assumed ❧ Tell students something they will like to hear, such as that there's no homework today. When they respond positively, say "I thought you would like that. I *assumed* that would be good news!"

assure ❧ —*be assured*, place one puppet on your desk. Have another puppet visit with a student. Make the second puppet say "Where is the other puppet? Is it still there?" Encourage the student to reply, "*Be assured* that it is still there." Repeat this with several students.

astronomical ❧ Ask students to give you really large numbers until you get into the trillions. Say "Anything more than this would be *astronomical*."

astronomy ❧ Show pictures of star systems and the solar system. Say "*Astronomy* is the study of stars."

astuteness ❧ Have a puppet work a word puzzle and find all of the answers. Say with amazement, "I've never seen such *astuteness* for solving word puzzles!"

at ❧ Have a puppet look *at* a book, be mad *at* another puppet, or throw a ball *at* the other puppet. Lead students in sentences.

ate ❧ Show pictures of people *eating*. Pantomime *eating* something. Then say that you *ate*.

atop ❧ Place a book on your head. Say "This book is *atop* my head." Have students imitate.

attack, attacked, attacker, attacking ❖ **1.** Have students make balls out of crumpled sheets of paper. Invite them to throw their balls at a thief that you've drawn on the board. Say "Go ahead and *attack* the thief." **2.** (Specialized poetry definition) Explain that this *attack* means the wheels are hitting the track hard and show pictures of trains on tracks. **3.** To explain what an *attacker* is, you can have one puppet *attack* another and give example sentences using *attacked* and *attacker*. Explain that *attacking* is a bad thing.

attempt ❖ Have students *attempt* to do various things, such as touch the ceiling while standing on the floor. Then have them do things that they can succeed at, such as sit in a chair or write a sentence.

attend, attendant, attendants ❖ **1.** Explain that when you go to school, you *attend* school. **2.** Have a puppet *attend* to your every wish. **3.** Set up a scene where two students are the king and queen and others are their *attendants*.

attention ❖ **1.** Have a puppet pay *attention* to another puppet and then pay no *attention*. **2.** Use puppets and/or dolls and have them give excess *attention* to one among them. Then have them give it no *attention*.

attitude ❖ Have students ask a puppet to do different fun things. Have the puppet always say "No." Have students ask another puppet to do the same things. Have that puppet always answer cheerfully, "Yes." Describe the *attitude* of each respectively.

attract, attraction ❖ Demonstrate using a magnet and a paper clip. —*gravitational attraction*, pick up something and drop it. Say "The *gravitational attraction* of Earth made the [book] fall to the floor." See *gravity*.

auction ❖ Show pictures of an *auction*, and tell the class that the person who offers the most money will get to buy the thing being sold. If there is time, *auction* off a few pencils and erasers (using play money) to the class to help them understand the process.

authentic ❖ Contrast *authentic* and *fake*, perhaps by showing a picture made by a student, and then by making another one similar to the student's and saying that it was made by that student.

authoritative, authority ❖ Demonstrate by saying in an assertive tone of voice, "'No running in the halls,' said the school principal." Have students imitate an *authoritative* tone of voice. Show students a picture of an auto mechanic and say "He is an *authority* on automobiles."

autograph ❖ Have a puppet play the role of a celebrity that students know. Have another puppet ask for its *autograph* and receive it. Then have the puppet excitedly show students the *autograph* it received. Have students repeat the pantomime with each other.

automatic ❖ Contrast a picture of a person washing laundry with a picture of a washing machine. Contrast washing dishes *by hand* with using an *automatic* dishwasher. Explain that *automatic* means "moving by itself." Ask students to name other *automatic* things. If you have an *automatic* stapler or pencil sharpener, show these and compare to ones that are not powered.

autumn ➠ Show pictures of the seasons and identify each one.

available ➠ Point to objects that student use in the classroom. Say "I have six pencils *available*. Who needs one?"

avaricious ➠ (See *greedily*.) On the board, draw a person with huge stacks of money around him or her. Give example sentences using *avaricious*.

avoid, avoided ➠ **1.** Demonstrate with a toy car and doll by having the toy car *avoid* the doll. Then show students how you can *avoid* walking into someone by heading toward him or her and then veering out of the way. **2.** Use a puppet to pretend that it is upset with a student. Every time the puppet sees that student, it turns and goes in the other direction. **3.** Have one puppet *avoid* another because it is wearing red (or some other absurdity), then say "*Avoid* puppets wearing red." Lead students in sentences. Pantomime walking toward someone and then veer around. Say "I *avoided* you." Invite a student to *avoid* you.

awake, awaken, awakened, awoke ➠ **1.** Pantomime *sleeping*. Contrast that with a pantomime of being *awake*. Go back and forth between *sleeping* and *awake*. **2.** Have a puppet be asleep. Tell the class not to make a noise because you do not want the puppet to *awaken*. **3.** Pretend that a puppet was *sleeping* and a noise *awakened* it. Tell the class, "That noise *awakened* the puppet." Lead students in similar pantomimes and sentences. **4.** Show a puppet *sleeping* and then wake it up. Tell the class, "The puppet *awoke*."

aware ➠ Ask students today's date. When they respond correctly, say "You know what day it is. You are *aware* of today's date."

away ➠ **1.** Lead students in pantomiming jumping *away* from a toy snake. Contrast this with walking *to* the snake. Have them walk *away* from a wall. Contrast with walking *to* a wall. Have one student walk *away* from another. Then have students throw something *away*. **2.** Pantomime playing "hide and seek" with a puppet. Have the puppet hide but giggle from the hiding place. Say "You gave yourself *away*."

awesome ➠ Explain that people like to say this to show how much they like something; similar to *neat* or *cool*. Give example sentences, such as "Your writing is *awesome!*"

awful ➠ Write your name in a messy way on the board and say "That looks *awful!*" Write it nicely and say "That looks *great!*" Sing terribly and say "That sounds *awful!*" Sing nicely and say "That sounds *great!*" Ask students about things that taste *awful* and things that taste *good*.

awhile ➠ Have students talk to each other for *awhile*. Contrast by having them sit quietly for a longer period of time (perhaps talking for a minute and sitting for a minute and thirty seconds).

awkward ➠ Contrast by walking across the room *gracefully* and then *awkwardly* while saying, "I am being *graceful;* I am being *awkward*."

awry ➠ If you have a doll or puppet with hair, mess it up so that it is all *awry*. Otherwise, draw this on the chalkboard.

axis ◆ Show students a globe; spin it on its *axis*. Draw a globe on the chalkboard with a vertical line running through it from the north pole to the south pole.

B.C. ◆ Draw a horizontal line on the chalkboard. In the center write, "before Christ." Label the left side *B.C.* and the right side *A.D.* Give examples of things that happened *B.C.*

babybuggy ◆ Explain that this is a made-up word for a *baby bug*. As needed show pictures of *bugs* and *babies*.

bachelor ◆ Give an example of someone who is not married—perhaps a movie star. Say "He is a *bachelor*."

back, backing, backed ◆ **1.** Demonstrate the *back* of the room, the *back* of a book, etc. Contrast with *front*. **2.** Begin to write a sentence on the chalkboard. Stop to do something else—perhaps answer a puppet's question. Then tell students that you must get *back* to writing the sentence and do so. Lead students in similar demonstrations. **3.** Ask a student to come to you. Then ask him or her to return to his or her seat. Then ask the student to come *back*. Repeat with several students. **4.** Have students step *back*. Contrast by having them step *forward*. **5.** Take books out and put them *back*. Take things out of your desk drawers and put them *back*.

backup ◆ Show students a picture of a radio receiver. Draw a second one. Say "This second one is our *backup*."

backward, backwards ◆ Walk *backward*. Have students imitate. Have students lean *forwards* and *backwards*.

backyard ◆ Use a picture of a *backyard*, or point out the *backyards* of houses near the school.

bad, badly ◆ **1.** Show pictures of *good*, hardworking people at work and *bad* people, such as robbers and thieves. **2.** Show or give examples of *good* and *bad* weather, such as a sunny day versus a hurricane. **3.** Write a sentence on the board *badly*. Contrast by writing the same sentence *nicely*.

bade ◆ Lead students in *bidding* each other hello and good-bye. Then help students to make both present tense and past tense sentences.

bail, bailing ◆ Pantomime being at sea in a boat and *bailing* water.

bake, baking ◆ Show a picture of an oven. Or, take students to the school kitchen and show them the oven. Explain that when you cook in the oven, you *bake*. Say "When I put the cake into the oven to cook, I am *baking* the cake."

balance ◆ Have students stand on one leg and maintain their *balance*.

balk ◆ Draw a picture of a baseball diamond on the board. Have a puppet walk up as if to bat and then *balk*. Say, "[Muffin] feels unprepared because she did not practice. She is not sure she wants to bat.

ballots ◆ Show the class two pictures, and give each picture a number (one and two). Tell the class to write the number for the picture they like best on a piece of paper. Collect their *ballots*, saying to each student, "The *ballots* show that ten like picture number one and five like picture number two."

bandits ◆ Pantomime a robbery with puppets. Explain that the puppet who robs is a *bandit*.

bang ◆ *Bang* a book on a table.

banked ◆ Demonstrate by imitating a bird in flight with arms held out straight. "Fly" around the room. Then tip right arm down and left arm up, turn to the right, and say "The bird *banked* to make a right turn." Have students do the same.

banner ◆ Draw a *banner* on the chalkboard, .

barely ◆ Stuff foam peanuts into a cup so they *barely* fit. Try to fit your hand into the other hand, which is cupped. Have it *barely* fit.

bargaining ◆ With a puppet, pantomime a sale where the two of you are *bargaining* with each other.

bark, barked, barking ◆ *Bark* like a dog. Lead students in *barking* and past tense sentences.

barrier ◆ Form a line of chairs across a natural pathway in the classroom. Ask students to find a way around the *barrier*.

barter ◆ Have students pretend to exchange things. Explain that to *barter* is to exchange.

baseball ◆ If students do not know this game, get a ball and bat to show them.

based ◆ Have a puppet be friendly, kind, and polite to students. Explain, "Its actions are *based* on doing good to others."

bashfulness ◆ Pantomime *bashfulness*.

bask ◆ Show a picture of a lizard *basking* in the sun. If not available, show illustrations of animals or people who are *basking*.

bath ◆ Either you can show pictures of a *bathtub* and explain, or you can show an illustrated picture book for small children to explain.

bats ◆ Have students pantomime *batting* a ball. —*at bat*, have students line up at an invented home plate and take turns being *at bat*. Include a pitcher who pantomimes throwing a ball.

batter, battered ◆ **1.** Show a picture of *batter* and then a cake or pancake. Explain that the *batter* is put in the oven and makes a cake. Or, make cake *batter* from a mix. **2.** Show a picture of a baseball *batter*. **3.** Lead students in past tense sentences. **4.** Show pictures of buildings or objects (such as pans) that have been *battered*. Pantomime *battering* something, perhaps by hitting it with a stick.

battle ◆ Pantomime fighting a fire. Explain that you had to *battle* the fire to put it out. Lead students in similar pantomimes.

bawl ◆ Dramatize *bawling* and have students join you.

bay ◆ Show oceans and *bays* on a map.

be ◆ **1.** Help students make sentences, such as "You must *be* quiet while the teacher reads [connects *you* and *quiet*]" or "I want to *be* a fireman [connects *I* and *fireman*].” Explain that *be* has little meaning but puts two things together. You can also write these sentences on the board and draw a chain between the parts that the word *be* connects. **2.** Give examples, such as, “We will *be* going to recess soon,” “The book may *be* on the shelf,” and “Will you *be* at my party?” —*be off*, explain the individual words as needed. Tell students this means “leave” or “to leave quickly.” Lead them in sentences, such as, “I must *be off* now,” and have them walk away. Or, “I will *be off* before you,” and begin to run.

beam ❖ Darken the classroom and turn on a flashlight. Use the *beam* of the flashlight to spotlight various objects in the room.

beans ❖ If possible, show students real *beans*. If not available, show them a picture of *beans*.

bear's ❖ See *animal's*.

beat, beating ❖ **1.** Have two puppets run a race. Say of the winner, “[Rabbit] won the race! He *beat* [Tortoise]!” Explain that *beating* others in a race means “winning.” **2.** Tap out different rhythms. Let students improvise and then say “I like that *beat*.” *Beat* on your desk or a table with your hands or a couple of pencils. Lead students in *beating* on their desktops. **3.** Pantomime a heart *beating*.

beautiful ❖ Show a *beautiful* picture. Play *beautiful* music.

because ❖ Lead students in familiar examples, such as, “I am tired *because* I ran hard,” “I am sweaty *because* I ran,” or “The child was crying *because* she fell down.” —*'cause*, explain that *'cause* is a fast way of saying *because*.

become, becoming, becomes, became ❖ **1.** Have students rub their hands together quickly so that their hands *become* warm. Then, when they stop rubbing their hands, ask students if their hands are *becoming* colder. Lead them in past tense sentences, “First our hands *became* warm, then they *became* cold.” **2.** Have a puppet tell you that it is studying so that it can grow up to be a doctor. Tell the class, “The puppet wants to *become* a doctor.” Ask what individuals in the class wish to *become*. **3.** Compliment a student's outfit. Say “That dress *becomes* you.”

beeps ❖ Lead students in making various types of *beeps*. Try to imitate some of the different *beeps* that you've heard.

before ❖ **1.** Make sentences that reflect your actual daily schedule, such as “Now it is *before* lunch; it is *after* recess” or “We do reading *before* lunch and singing *after* lunch.” Show the minutes *before* midnight on a clock. **2.** Show students things they've done in the past, such as books that they've read or writing that they have done. Lead them in sentences, such as “You have read this book *before*” and “You've written your name *before*.” Contrast with things they have not done *before*.

beg, begging, begged ❖ Have a puppet *beg* for something from another puppet. Lead students in *begging* like a dog. Lead students in past tense sentences. —*beg pardon*, have a puppet bump into another puppet and *beg* its *pardon*. Have a puppet interrupt you when you are talking and then *beg* your *pardon*. —*begging your pardon*, see *I beg your pardon*. Give example sentences using *begging your pardon*. —*I beg your pardon!*, walk across the room and pantomime bumping into one student. Say "Oh, *I beg your pardon!*" Explain that *pardon* means "to forgive," and that this is a very polite phrase.

begin, beginning, begins, began ◆ Explain that *begin* means "start." Do quick activities, such as coloring a small area, taking a step, or clapping your hands. *Begin* the activity and finish the activity. Once done, list the activities that they *began*. Draw a line on the board and show students where it *begins*. *Begin* to read. Tell students, "I am *beginning* to read to you." Lead them in *beginning* to do things.

beguiled ◆ Have a puppet demonstrate its charming ways. Act completely taken in or enchanted by the puppet. Tell the class, "The puppet fascinates me; I am *beguiled* by it."

behind ◆ Put an object *behind* another. Have one student stand *behind* another.

believe, believing ◆ **1.** Ask a student to tell you something that he or she did that morning, such as "I rode the bus to school." Say "I *believe* you." Have a student tell you an obvious lie. Say "I don't *believe* you." **2.** Have a puppet walk around and say things that are true, such as "This is a desk; I *believe* that." Tell a puppet an obvious lie. Have the puppet look at you in a skeptical manner. Tell the class, "This puppet is not *believing* me." **3.** Have a student hold something secretly in his or her hand. Tell the other students what you know about the student, and what you *believe* is in his or her hand: "I know that he or she is wearing shoes" or "I know that he or she has two legs"; "I *believe* that he or she has a pencil in his or her hand" or "I *believe* that he or she has a paper clip in his or her hand."

bellies ◆ Pantomime chewing, then swallowing. Pat your stomach; have students imitate. Say "When we eat, the food goes in our *bellies*."

bellow, bellowed ◆ Deepen your voice and *bellow*. Explain that you *bellowed*. Contrast with hollering so that students can hear the deeper sound of the *bellow*. Have students *bellow*.

belong, belongs, belonging, belongings, belonged ◆ **1.** Show books that *belong* to you. Say "These are my books. They *belong* to me." Ask students what items *belong* to them. Say "This *belongs* to me," and point to something of your own. Repeat for items *belonging* to others, such as, "That book *belongs* to him." Show pictures of items, such as might be found in a museum, that *belonged* to someone who has died. Give example sentences. **2.** Show students some of your *belongings*, and invite them to show you some of their *belongings*.

below ◆ Have students reach *below* their desks and then *above* their desks.

bend, bending ◆ **1.** Draw a path on the board. Say that a curve or change of direction in the path is a *bend*. **2.** Lead students in *bending*.

beneath ◆ Have students put their hands *beneath* their desks. Tell students that their feet are *beneath* their desks. Point out other things that are *beneath* something.

benefits ◆ Make two columns on the chalkboard and head each respectively "Company A" and "Company B." Make a list of extras that come with a job at

"Company A," such as health insurance and paid vacation time. Say "Look at all the extra things you get when you work at "Company A." "Company A" has good *benefits*!"

bent ❖ Lead students in *bending*. Help students make past tense sentences.

berate ❖ Have one puppet *berate* another. Give example sentences.

beside ❖ Put two small items *beside* each other. Ask students to stand *beside* each other and then behind one another. Ask students to place their hands *beside* each other and then behind one another.

besiegers ❖ Have students form a circle around a puppet and not let the puppet pass. Lead students in sentences using *besiegers*.

best ❖ **1.** Have a puppet choose between two or three items. Ask the puppet, "Which one do you like the *best*?" Have the puppet answer, "I like this one *best*." Repeat with students. **2.** Pantomime doing a task in a sloppy manner, then doing it the *best* you can.

bet ❖ **1.** Dramatize. Have a mock race with two puppets. Ask students which one they think will win. **2.** Say sentences in a challenging tone, such as, "I *bet* I can write a very long sentence" or "I *bet* I have something in this hand."

better ❖ **1.** Show two paper clips, one in good condition and one bent. Point out the one that is *better*. Do this with clean and dirty paper, a good pencil and a pencil stub, and so on. Have students contrast sentences, such as, "This bread tastes good. This bread tastes *better*." **2.** Demonstrate with a puppet first getting sick and then getting *better*.

between ❖ Place an item on your desk *between* two other items. Tell students that the item is *between* the other two. Lead students in sentences.

bewilderment ❖ Write a complicated arithmetic problem on the board. Look at it with *bewilderment*.

beyond ❖ **1.** Place something out of reach. Say "It is *beyond* me." **2.** Draw a country on the chalkboard. Then use your fingers and "walk" *beyond* the boundaries of that country. **3.** Say "*Beyond* [Sarah] is [a poster, a bookshelf, a window]." Repeat the sample sentence using another student and then see if a student can create a new sentence using this model.

bid ❖ *Bid* a student good-bye. *Bid* another student hello. Have students *bid* each other good-bye or hello.

big, bigger, biggest ❖ **1.** Draw a *little* spot and a *big* spot on the board. Have students do this on paper. Contrast *big* and *little* things. Have students show you things that are *big* and *little*. **2.** Demonstrate with books of various sizes: *small, smaller, smallest* and *big, bigger, biggest*. —*great big*, contrast *big* and *great big* things for students. Then have them find things that are *big* and *great big*.

bill ❖ On the board, draw Congress. Draw a *bill* going to Congress and show it coming out a law. Give example sentences.

billion ❖ Give each student some scratch paper. Ask students to tear the paper into tiny bits. Have all the students bring all the bits to your desk and place them in a container. Tell students there might be one hundred bits in the container and that they need more. Repeat the process several times, each time saying how many pieces might be in the container, and that they need more. When the container is overflowing, say there are still not a *billion* pieces. Say that many, many more containers would be needed to hold a *billion* pieces of paper. —*half-billion*, Show students a container of sand with its many particles. Explain the enormity of *half-billion*. Write the number 1,000,000 on the board and explain it is a *million*, then write 1,000,000,000 on the board and explain that the zeros make it a *billion*.

binding ❥ Demonstrate by *binding* pencils together with a rubber band or string.

biography, biographies ❥ Show a number of written *biographies* and explain that they are true stories about a person's life or work. Have students make sentences, such as, "This is a *biography* about Benjamin Franklin" and "There are many *biographies* about Abraham Lincoln."

biology ❥ List the subjects students study on the board. Say, for example, "You study many things in [sixth grade]: science, reading, etc. When you get to high school, you will study plants and animals and the way they grow in *biology*."

birthday ❥ Write the *birth date* of one of the students on the board. Write the first anniversary date, the second, and so on. Explain that each of these dates is a *birthday*.

bit ❥ A small piece. Show a *bit* of paper and then a big piece. —*a bit*, look *a bit* sad and then, in contrast, very sad. Look *a bit* happy and then, in contrast, very happy. Pantomime doing *a bit* of work; contrast with *a lot* of work. Tear *a bit* of paper from a large piece. Break *a bit* of chalk off.

bit, bite, biting ❥ *Bite* an apple and lead students in pantomiming *biting* an apple. Help students with past tense sentences.

bitter, bitterly ❥ **1.** Show students pictures of the arctic tundra or similar scenes. Explain that these are very hard, or *bitter*, places for people to live. Lead students in sentences. **2.** Have two puppets talk *bitterly*. Say "The puppets are talking *bitterly* to each other."

black ❥ Ask everyone to hold up something *black*.

blackout ❥ Draw a picture of house with *black* windows on the board. Explain that during WWII in England, all the lights were turned off so the enemy could not find them from their airplanes. Give example sentences using *blackout*.

blame, blaming, blamed ❥ Have a puppet knock something over and *blame* another puppet. Explain that it *blamed* the other. Have the other puppet speak up and say that the first puppet is *blaming* it when it did not do it.

blank ❥ Show students a piece of paper. Explain that nothing is on it; it is *blank*. Contrast with a *printed* piece of paper.

blares ❥ Turn the volume up high on a radio, and explain that the sound *blares* from the radio.

blast ➡ **1.** Show pictures of an explosion. Make a noise like a *blast*. **2.** Show students a picture of a boy playing the tuba, and explain that a loud noise from the tuba is a *blast*.

blemish, blemishes ➡ Draw two faces on the board, one clear and one with acne. Point to the *blemishes*.

blend, blends, blended, blending ➡ **1.** Show an illustration of an animal that *blends* with its environment because the animal's colors match those in the environment. Point out how the animal is *blending* in with the background. **2.** *Blend* two colors of chalk on the chalkboard. Say "The colors have *blended*." Invite a student to do the same. Say "We are *blending* the colors."

bless, blessed ➡ **1.** Show pictures of religious leaders, such as the Pope, *blessing* people. Say "The people *bless* others." **2.** Describe or show pictures of beautiful places and say "These are *blessed* places."

blind ➡ Pantomime being *blind* by walking with your eyes closed.

blink ➡ *Blink.*

bliss Show a puppet experiencing extreme pleasure, perhaps over a new toy. Explain that it is *blissful* or experiencing *bliss*. Ask students if they have ever felt *bliss*.

block, blocking, blockade ➡ *Block* the light. *Block* a student's path to your desk. Have students stand in a line side by side with their arms linked at the elbows. Pantomime trying to push through the line. Lead students in sentences using *blockade*.

bloodthirsty ➡ Show pictures of ancient and fierce warriors, perhaps Atilla the Hun or the Vikings. Say "I hate to see people fight and get hurt. I am not *bloodthirsty*."

bloom, blooming, bloomed ➡ Show students pictures of trees and flowers that are *blooming* in spring, and tell them, "The trees and flowers *bloom* in the spring" or "These trees and flowers are *blooming*."

blossom, blossomed ➡ Show a picture of trees and flowers in *blossom*. Tell students when the flowers have come out, the trees and plants have *blossomed*. Contrast with pictures of plants and trees that have not *blossomed*.

blow, blowing, blew, blown ➡ Have students *blow* out air from their mouths. Lead students in *blowing* out air against a piece of paper. Lead students in past tense sentences. Hold a piece of paper lightly in your hand and *blow* it away. Say "The paper was *blown* from my hand."

bluff ➡ Have two puppets argue. Have one say "My dad is bigger than your dad." When it says that, shake your head "no" and say "That is [Fluffy's] *bluff*."

blush ➡ Draw a child on a sheet of white paper. Ask students to give the child a compliment. Fill the face in, from the neck up, with a dark pink crayon. Give examples sentences using *blush*.

boast, boasted ➡ Have a puppet walk around saying things, such as, "I'm great, wonderful, and beautiful." "Say [Rabbit] just *boasted*."

Bob ⇨ Explain that *Bob* is a boy's name. List boys' names including *Bob*.

body ⇨ Show students pictures of some of the planets in our solar system, and explain that *body* is the word used when we talk about the planets. Explain that it means "the whole thing." Compare with human *bodies*, animal *bodies*, or *bodies* of water.

bog ⇨ Show pictures of a *bog*. Explain that a *bog* is a wet, muddy area.

boil, boiling ⇨ Draw a stove with a pot of bubbling water on the chalkboard. Say "I *boil* water for my coffee." Show pictures of *boiling* water. Lead students in sentences.

bold, boldly ⇨ **1.** Ask for a volunteer to work a simple math problem on the board. When the student comes up, say "He or she is *bold*." **2.** Walk *boldly*, then walk *timidly*. Lead students in sentences.

bomb ⇨ Show a picture of a *bomb*. Help the students to understand that it is a very bad thing. —*giant bomb*, draw an enormous *bomb* on the board and say "I have drawn a *giant bomb*."

bombard, bombardment ⇨ **1.** Have students make balls out of crumpled sheets of paper. Invite students to throw their balls at a chair. Lead students in sentences using *bombardment*. **2.** Set up a scene where a puppet is a soldier in a war. Have it hiding behind a tower of blocks while students *bombard* it with bits of paper. Have the puppet shout out, "Stop the *bombardment!*"

bonus ⇨ Pantomime a scene of hiring a puppet to clean your desk. Tell the puppet that it can receive extra money if it does a good job. Have the puppet do the job, pay him, and give him a *bonus*. Say "This money is a *bonus* because you did a good job."

boo ⇨ **1.** Have one puppet perform a trick poorly, such as standing on its head. Have a second puppet *boo* the first one. Have the first puppet perform a trick well, and have the second puppet *applaud*. **2.** Show a picture of a Halloween ghost and say "*Boo!*" Have students pretend to frighten one another by saying, "*Boo!*"

booby-trapped ⇨ Work with students to create a *booby trap* and test it. You might place a book on top of a door that stands partially open and wait for someone to open the door fully. Say "We *booby-trapped* the door."

boo-hooing ⇨ Pretend to cry. Give example sentences using *boo-hooing*.

bookkeeper ⇨ Write on the board how much you spent to buy a tractor, and how much money you made selling eggs. Then announce how much money is left. Tell students, "A *bookkeeper* writes down in a book all the money that is spent or earned." Lead them in a similar pantomime. Perhaps they can buy and sell pencils to each other and keep the *books*.

boom, booming ⇨ **1.** Drop a book on the floor and say "*Boom!*" Show a picture of an explosion and say "*Boom!*" **2.** Demonstrate a *booming* voice.

boost ⇨ Have a puppet attempt to get onto the seat of a desk. Have the puppet ask for a *boost*. *Boost* the puppet up.

borders ⇨ Use a map to show the *borders* around states or countries.

bore, bored, boring, boredom ◆ **1.** *Bore* a hole in a piece of clay with a pencil. Show students the hole. Explain that *bore* means "to make a hole." **2.** Lead students in pantomiming *bored* by glancing around randomly and sighing. Contrast that with being very attentive and *interested* in a particular thing in the room. **3.** Hold up some toys or books and act as if they are *boring* (look around aimlessly, yawn). Say that the objects are *boring*. Then, in contrast, become very *interested* in them and say that they are *interesting*. Have students repeat. **4.** Ask a student to read a passage aloud. Pantomime apathy: yawn, lean heavily on your desk with your head in your hand, and fidget. Then say "I have no interest in this lesson. I don't like this feeling of *boredom*."

born ◆ Show pictures of a pregnant woman and then a *newborn*. Tell students, "When the baby comes out, it is *born*." Explain that when a baby is *born*, it starts life. If available, show pictures of *newborn* babies or animals as well.

borrow, borrowed ◆ **1.** Have a puppet ask to use a pencil belonging to another puppet. The second puppet can say "Yes, you may *borrow* this." Then have the first puppet return it. Lead students in similar demonstrations. Ask to *borrow* a student's pencil. Use it and return it. Say "I *borrowed* a pencil from Lynn." **2.** Ask students to laugh like a comedian or a particular character on TV. Say "You *borrowed* that laugh from [Jim Carrey].

boss, bossy, bossed ◆ *Boss* a puppet around. Then have the puppet say "You are *bossy*!" Let students be *bossy* with the puppet. Give sentences using *bossed*. —*bossed around*, *boss* a puppet *around*. Then have the puppet say "I do not want to be *bossed around*!"

both ◆ Point to your eyes and say "*Both* of my eyes are brown." Point to your shoes and say "*Both* of my shoes are white."

bother ◆ Pantomime a bug *bothering* you. Swat it away saying, "You *bother* me."

bottom ◆ Point out the *bottom* of a jar and, in contrast, the *top* of a jar. Show a picture of a bed. Point to the *bottom* of it.

bottomless ◆ Show a container with no *bottom*. Explain that it is *bottomless*. Demonstrate how things will not stay in it.

bounce, bouncing, bounced ◆ Lead students in *bouncing* a ball. Tell them to *bounce* the ball. Help with past tense sentences.

boundaries ◆ Draw a house with a fence around the yard. Pointing to the fence, say "These are the *boundaries* of this person's property."

bounds ◆ Draw a circle on a large sheet of paper. Stand in the center. Show students the *bounds* of the circle.

bow, bowing, bowed, bows ◆ Demonstrate by *bowing*. Say "I am *bowing*." *Bow* three times and say "I *bowed* three times. Lead students in *bowing*. Have a student *bow*. Say "[Ana] *bows*."

box ◆ Show students a *box*. —*deposit box*, draw a large sign on the board with the word BANK on it. Below that, draw a sign that says "Closed." Place a *box* on a desk below the sign. Have students put play money in the *box*. Say "When the bank is closed at night, you may put money in your bank account by using the *deposit box*."

boxed ◆ Pantomime *boxing*. Lead students in *boxing* pantomimes and sentences.

boycott ◆ Pantomime a scene with puppets. Have one puppet be a storekeeper that is selling lollipops for two dollars. Have other puppets or toy animals *boycott* his store because the price of lollipops is too high. If time permits, allow students to do a similar enactment.

boyhood ◆ Show pictures of people at different ages. Explain, "This is an adult; he or she is in his or her *adulthood*," "These are children; they are in their *childhood*," "She is a girl; she is in her *girlhood*," and "This is a boy; he is in his *boyhood*."

Brad ◆ Explain that *Brad* is a boy's name. Write a list of boys' names including *Brad*. Ask students about boys' names that they know. —*Brad's*, make examples of possessives using student names, such as *Maria's* jacket, *Min's* lunch box, and so on. It may clarify to point to *Maria* and say "*Maria*." Then hold up her jacket and say "*Maria's* jacket." Emphasize the difference between *Maria* and *Maria's* as you say the two words.

brag, bragging ◆ Have a puppet *brag* to another: "I run fast," "I'm smart," "I eat fast," and so on. Tell the class, "The puppet is *bragging*."

braided ◆ *Braid* three pieces of string. Lead students in past tense sentences.

Braille ◆ Show something written in *Braille*. (Some dictionaries and encyclopedias include examples.) Elevator buttons are labeled with *Braille*. Then make tiny holes on a piece of paper, and show how you can feel the bumps on the other side. Explain that *Braille* is how a blind person can read and write.

brake ◆ Sit in a chair and pantomime driving a car. Pantomime hitting the *brake*.

branches ◆ Show a variety of trees and their *branches*. Compare with limbs. (Limbs are large *branches*.)

branding, branded ◆ On the board, draw a fire, a *branding* iron, and a cow. Pantomime heating the iron in the fire and then *branding* the cow. Say "I *branded* the cow."

brandishing ◆ Show a picture of someone *brandishing* a sword, or pantomime *brandishing* with a piece of rolled-up paper.

bravado ◆ Have a puppet swagger and say "I'm not afraid of lions or tigers." Continue with other similar statements. Yell, "boo." Have the puppet tremble. Or, set up a scene where a puppet has to fight a dangerous toy animal. Have [Fido] tell the class that he's scared. Then have another puppet come up to [Fido] and ask if he's afraid. Have [Fido] put on an air of *bravado* and answer, "Me? Afraid? No, I fight dangerous animals every day."

brave, braver, bravest, bravery ◆ **1.** Lead students in pretending to be *afraid*, and then contrast that with acting *brave*. Tell them that they are full of *bravery*. **2.** Have three puppets talk about jumping from one desk to another. Have them all express *fear*. Let one decide not to jump. Let another make a small jump. Have the third puppet make a big jump. Say "The first puppet was *brave*, the second puppet was *braver*, and the third was the *bravest*."

braying, brayed ◆ Show a picture of a donkey. Make a *braying* sound. Tell students that you *brayed* like a donkey. Lead students in *braying*.

brazen ◆ Have a puppet walk up to your desk and take something while you are watching. Give example sentences using *brazen*, perhaps, "That is a *brazen* puppet!"

break, broke, broken ◆ **1.** *Break* a pencil or show one that is *broken*. *Break* a piece of chalk. Tell students that you *broke* it. **2.** Have students make codes. Let the other students *break* them. **3.** Say "You have been working hard. Let's take a *break*." **4.** Pantomime a scene of a puppet *breaking* into a locked closet or desk drawer. Tell the class that the puppet *broke* into it. —*break open* a nut. —*broke ground*, on the board, write the number "1." After it, draw a picture of someone *breaking* the *ground* with a shovel. Write the number "2." After it, draw a picture of a building. Say "Today we will *break* new *ground* by [doing some new activity]. *broke up*, look very solemn and then begin laughing loudly.

breakable ◆ Demonstrate with a paper cup and a piece of brittle candy, such as peanut brittle or a candy cane. Drop the cup, pick it up, look at it, and say "It did not *break*. It is not *breakable*." Drop the candy on the floor, pick up the pieces and say "It *broke*. Peanut brittle is *breakable*." Name other things that are *breakable*, such as a glass. Ask students to name some more *breakable* things.

breathe, breathing ◆ Lead students in *breathing* in and out.

breathlessly ◆ Have a puppet jog around the perimeter of a tabletop or desk. Then have the puppet say to the class *breathlessly*, "I'm all out of *breath*." Have a student jog around the perimeter of the classroom and then speak *breathlessly*.

breeds ◆ Have a puppet show pictures of purebred puppies and pictures of the owners. Say "[Fluffy] owns [Trixie] and [Frederick], and these are their babies. [Fluffy] *breeds* dogs."

breeze, breezy ◆ **1.** Blow at some loose papers so that they move gently. Tell students that when the wind blows just a little, it is a *breeze*. Ask who has seen leaves on a tree blow in the *breeze*. **2.** Fan yourself with a folder and say "What a nice *breeze*." Have students do the same, and say that it is *breezy* in the classroom.

Bremen Town ◆ The name of the town in the story, "The *Bremen Town* Musicians." —*Bremen Town Band*, once students understand *band*, tell them that this is the name of the *band* for *Bremen Town*. Make other similar examples of the names of familiar towns.

bribe ◆ Have a puppet give you some candy and ask for an "A."

bridge ◆ Show pictures of *bridges*.

brief ◆ Contrast *brief* and *lengthy* sentences. Ask students to sit for a *brief* moment and then stand for a *longer* period of time.

bright, brighter, brightest, brightly ◆ **1.** Write three arithmetic equations of increasing difficulty on the board. Solve the first one yourself and have each of the puppets solve the other two. Say "I am smart; I am *bright* enough to solve this hard problem. [Pumpkin] is *brighter* than I am; she solved a harder problem. [Muffin] is the *brightest* of all; she solved the hardest problem."

2. Draw on the board a picture of the sun with clouds in front of it. Shade the sky in lightly to show that it's not *bright* and sunny. Then draw another picture with no clouds to show a *bright*, sunny day. **3.** Show bright and dull objects. Show the *bright* light in the classroom and contrast against the *dim* light of the hallway. Show things that are *bright* and contrast with things of a *mellow* color. **4.** Show a ring or something that can be polished. Say that it is shiny. Polish it, and say "Now it is *brighter* than before." **5.** Lead the class in saying things *brightly*.

brimming ❖ Show a *brimming* glass of water.

bring, brings, bringing, brought ❖ Ask a student to *bring* a book to you or another student. Lead them through the action of *bringing* it if needed. Say "[Sarah] *brings* the book to [Fernando.]" *Bring* a book to a student and explain that you *brought* him a book. Repeat with other objects. Then say "The sun *brought* warmth; snow *brought* cold." Then have students create sentences, such as "Her smile *brought* happiness." Ask students to think of other examples.

brink ❖ Push a book to the edge of your desk. Say "The book is on the *brink* of falling."

brisk, briskly ❖ Walk *briskly*. Contrast by walking *slowly*.

brittle ❖ Explain that glass breaks into small pieces because glass is *brittle*.

broil, broiling, broiled ❖ Show a picture of meat that has been *broiled* or is *broiling* in an oven.

brooded ❖ Tell students you have lost something. Pantomime worrying. Say "The teacher *brooded* over the loss of [her] [purse]."

brother ❖ Show pictures of a family and point out the *brother*. If not available, draw a family in stick figures on the board. Have students tell about any *brothers* they have. —*little brother*, draw figures on the board to represent two children: the *big sister* and the *little brother*. Ask students if any of them have *little brothers* or *sisters*.

brow ❖ Place your hand on your forehead. Explain that this is your *brow*. Have students touch their *brows*.

brush, brush off ❖ Have students *brush off* their desks.

brute ❖ Show pictures of characters, such as Brutus from the Popeye cartoons or comics. Explain that he is strong as you point to his muscles. Also explain that he is mean. Tell the class that people like this are called *brutes*.

bubbles, bubbling ❖ Demonstrate with soap *bubbles*. Tell students, "The soap is *bubbling*."

buckles ❖ Draw a horizontal line and then a bump. Say "This is the flat earth and this is where the earth *buckles*."

budge ❖ Push on something heavy to move it slightly, or *budge* it. Show something that is fixed in place (perhaps a pencil sharpener that is bolted down) and demonstrate trying to move it. Explain to students that it will not *budge*. Contrast with things that will *budge*. Have students find things in the classroom that will and will not *budge*.

bug ❖ Draw or show illustrations of various *bugs*. Say "A bee is a *bug*, an ant is a *bug*, a fly is a *bug*, and so on."

bugging ❖ Demonstrate with puppets. While one puppet keeps talking to another puppet who is trying to read, the other says, "You are *bugging* me."

build, built, building, buildings ❖ *Build* a block tower. Ask students to help you *build* a block tower. Lead students in *building* a block tower and using past tense sentences. Show pictures of a *building* or *buildings*.

bulldogged ❖ Use a toy animal to demonstrate seizing a calf by its horns, twisting its neck, and throwing it to the ground. Lead students in past tense sentences.

bump, bumping, bumped ❖ **1.** Demonstrate by having one puppet or toy animal *bump* into another. Demonstrate by *bumping* into a desk; say that you *bumped* into it. **2.** Put a book behind your back and let it fall. Ask students if they heard the *bump*.

bundle, bundles ❖ Pantomime rolling up some clothes or fabric into *bundles*.

burdensome ❖ Have the puppet tell you its troubles. Act sad and say "Oh, [Shaggy]. It's hard for me to hear this. It is really *burdensome*."

burial, buried, bury ❖ **1.** Have a puppet die. Have another puppet place him in a casket and *bury* him. Tell students, "After the puppet died, they had to *bury* him." Then pantomime performing a *burial*. Tell students, "The puppet died, so his family gave him a *burial*." **2.** *Bury* a small object, such as an eraser, in a flowerpot or under a pile of paper or books. Say "The eraser is *buried*."

burn, burning, burned ❖ Show a picture of a fire, and say "Fire makes things *burn*." Light a candle and explain that the fire is *burning*. Show pictures of things that have been *burned*. Explain that they were *burned* by fire.

burn down ❖ Show pictures of houses on fire and houses that are *burned down*.

burrow ❖ Show a picture of animals, such as rabbits, moles, or gophers, in *burrows*.

burst ❖ **1.** Blow up a balloon and *burst* it. If not available, draw a balloon on the board and talk about what would happen if you broke it with a pin or scissors. Dramatize the bang it would make. **2.** Pantomime *burst* by making a fist and opening up your fingers suddenly in a dramatic version of the way that a robin *bursts* out of its shell.

bushes ❖ Show pictures of *bushes* or draw them on the board.

business ❖ Try to engage a puppet who is studying in some idle chatter. Have the puppet say "Leave me alone. This work is serious *business*." —*none of your business*, have one puppet ask personal questions; have the other respond, "That is personal. I don't want to answer that; it is *none of your business*."

bustling ❖ Get students *bustling* about the classroom and quickly cleaning things up. Explain to them that they are *bustling* to clean up the classroom.

busy, busier, busiest ◈   **1.** Have students pretend to be drivers by moving around the room making car engine and honking horn sounds. Say "Look at all these cars! This is a *busy* road!" **2.** Have students take out a lesson and begin to work on it. Tell them they are *busy*. Then have them put their work away and do nothing. Tell them they are not *busy*. Repeat as necessary. Divide the class into three groups, and lead each group in a higher level of activity, showing *busy*, *busier*, and *busiest*.

but ◈   Use *but* to contrast ideas. Pantomime sentences, such as: "I dropped a penny, *but* I still have a nickel" or "I hurt my toe, *but* it only hurts a little."

butted ◈   Demonstrate a stuffed animal *butting* some object.

buy, buying, bought ◈   **1.** Play a game of *buying* things with the students. Set up a little store on your desk using toys from the classroom and pennies. Give each student a few pennies, and let them *buy* things from you. With each thing that they *buy*, use the word *buy*. If needed, demonstrate with a puppet making a purchase from you first. **2.** Sell a paper clip. Say "It costs a nickel." Have the student give you a nickel and say that you sold the paper clip, and the student *bought* the paper clip.

buzz, buzzing, buzzed ◈   Show pictures of bees. Lead students in making a *buzzing* sound. Help them to make past tense sentences.

by ◈   Demonstrate a paper clip *by* a book and not *by* a book. Demonstrate it being *by* and not *by* other objects. —*by and by*, explain that this means "after a while." Give examples, such as, "We were walking down the road and *by and by* we came to a river." —*by heart*, say a rhyme or phone number *by heart*. Explain that you did not need to read it because you know it *by heart*. Have students say something that they know *by heart*, perhaps the alphabet. —*by herself/himself/myself*, show some paper clips together with other paper clips. Pretend that the clips are children, with one paper clip off *by herself/himself*. **1.** Stand *by* yourself and say "*By myself*." Stand among students and say "Not *by myself*." Have individual students practice this. **2.** Have a puppet brush his teeth, getting help from his mother. Contrast with a puppet brushing his teeth independently. Then have the puppet say "I can brush my teeth *by myself*." Ask students what they can do *by themselves*.

byte ◈   Show a picture of a computer and explain that computers store and process information in a form called a *byte*.

byway ◈   Draw a road on the board, and then draw a second road running alongside of the first. Explain that this second road is called a *byway*.

caboose ◈   Show pictures of trains. Point out the last car or *caboose*. Contrast it with the engine.

cackle ◈   Show pictures of chickens. Encourage students to *cackle* like chickens. Say "You *cackle* like a chicken!"

calf ◈   **1.** Show students the *calf* of your leg. **2.** Show pictures of a *calf*.

call, calls, calling, called ◈   **1.** Pantomime *calling* a name, and then just saying it. *Call* a puppet; then have a puppet *call* you. *Call* to a student and have the student come. Have students *call* to the puppet, and have the puppet go to the student. Each time the person or puppet arrives, have him or her say "You *called* me." **2.** Say "We *call* this a chair," "This student is *called* ___." **3.** Imitate various animal *calls*, such as quacking, mewing, barking, etc. —*call-up*, show pictures of soldiers. On the board, draw a building that says, "U.S. Army, Air Force, Navy, and Marines." Have a puppet receive his *call-up* notice and report to the building.

calm ◆ Explain that *calm* means "quiet and with no excitement." Have a puppet be *calm* and then *noisy* and *excited*.

campaign ◆ Explain *president* if needed. Set up a scene in which one student is running for class president. Have the other students make signs that say "[Marta] for class president." Have them march around the room chanting, "[Marta] for president!" Say "Marta is *campaigning* for president."

can, cannot, can't ◆ Reach for something and explain, "I *can*." Pantomime not being able to do various actions and then explain, "I *cannot*." For example, try unsuccessfully to reach various objects. Explain that *can't* is a fast way of saying *cannot*. Or, show on the board how *cannot* squeezes together to make *can't*. Contrast with *can*.

candidate ◆ Set up a scene in which one student is running for class president. Say "[Jesse] wants to be your class president. He is a *candidate*."

cannibals ◆ Have students pretend to eat each other for lunch. Say "People who eat people are called *cannibals*."

cap ◆ On the board, draw a mountain with an ice *cap*.

capable ◆ Ask a student volunteer to read a familiar passage. Then say "That was good, [Carla]. You read that very well. You are a *capable* reader."

capacity ◆ Test the *capacity* of a sponge to hold water.

cape ◆ Show pictures of *capes*. Show how a *cape* extends out into the water.

capital ◆ See *excellent*.

capsizing ◆ Draw a picture of a boat on the board. Then draw a huge wave on the board and make a rushing sound. Next draw a picture of the boat upside down. Explain that the boat tipped over. Say "The giant wave knocked over the boat; it is *capsizing!*"

captain ◆ Divide the class into two groups for a spelling bee. Appoint a *captain* for each team.

captivity ◆ Show a picture of an animal at a zoo. Say "This animal is in *captivity*."

capture, capturing, captured ◆ Have a puppet hop around the room. Catch it and say "I *captured* the [rabbit]!" Have a puppet *capture* a toy animal or whale. Explain that the puppet *captured* the toy or whale.

care, caring, cared, careful, careless, carefully, carelessly ◆ **1.** Show stepping with *care* and then stepping without *care*, or handling something with *care* and then without *care*. **2.** Take *care* of a doll or a stuffed animal by feeding it and holding it. Explain that you are *caring* for it. **3.** Set up a scene where a puppet is sick in bed. Worry over the puppet and tend to its needs. Tell the class that you *care* about the puppet. Lead the class in past tense sentences such as, "I *cared* about the puppet when it was sick." **4.** Tell the class that you must decide if you want chocolate or chicken for lunch. Then say that you don't *care*. You will have the chocolate because you like it best. Contrast by repeating the above and giving *careful* thought to the choice. Tell the class chicken is better for you than chocolate, etc. Choose the chicken. Have students pantomime a *careful* and *careless* decision about what to wear to school. **5.** Fill a cup to the brim with water. Ask a student to carry it a few steps. Say "*Careful!* Don't spill it!" **6.** Have a student carry a glass of water *carefully* so as not to spill it. Have students walk *carefully* or touch something breakable *carefully*. **7.** Throw a book onto your desk. Say "I threw that *carelessly*." Then place a book *carefully*. Say "I placed that book *carefully*."

carefree ❧ Skip lightly around while looking happy.

cargo ❧ Load a *cargo* of paper clips onto a toy truck or wagon. Point to the paper clips and say "This is the *cargo*."

carpenter ❧ Draw the frame of a house on the board. Have each student draw and cut out a tool (i.e., hammer, saw, drill, etc.) and pantomime using it to build the house. Say "A *carpenter* uses tools to build a house."

carry, carrying, carried ❧ Lead students in *carrying* things. Ask students to *carry* things. Lead students in past tense sentences. —*carried off*, have a puppet *carry off* a few items.

cartwheel ❧ Ask if anyone can demonstrate. Or, draw a picture on the board of a *cartwheel*.

carve, carving, carved ❧ **1.** Pantomime *carving* an apple with a plastic knife. **2.** Using a bar of soap, *carve* a few shavings with a plastic knife. Tell students people *carve* with wood and stone too. Show a *carved* figure or a picture.

cast, casting ❧ **1.** *Cast* something into the trash. Tell students that *casting* is another word for *tossing* and demonstrate. **2.** Dramatize a scene with students and a puppet, where the puppet is the director. The director can watch student performances and *cast* them for roles in his upcoming play, "Puppet Goes to School" (or some other title that students would enjoy). —*cast off*, toss various items off your desk. Say "I am going to *cast off* these things I don't need."

cat ❧ Show a picture of a *cat*. —*Cat got your tongue?*, ask a puppet many questions but have it give no answers. Ask, "*Cat got your tongue?*" Explain that this means, "Can't you talk?" —*cat's*, see *animal's*. —*cat's cradle*, this is a traditional Native American game and can be found in anthologies of those games. Find a student who can teach the class this game, in which string is looped over the fingers in various designs and passed back and forth between players.

catastrophe, catastrophes ❧ Show pictures of various types of *catastrophes* or natural disasters.

catch, catches, catching, caught ❧ **1.** Ask a student to throw a ball to you so you can *catch* it. Then, throw it back and say "*Catch*." Toss an eraser to a student and tell her to *catch* it. Tell the class that she *caught* the eraser. Have

two students toss a ball back and forth, and explain that they are *catching* it.
2. Use a toy fishing pole and fish to demonstrate how to *catch* a fish. Let students *catch* a fish. Pantomime a hook with one finger and a fish's mouth gulping it down. Now the fish is *caught*; it wiggles, but it can't get off the hook. **3.** Set up a scene where a puppet sheriff *catches* some toy robbers. **4.** *Catch* your finger with your other hand and say that it is *caught.* —*caught up*, act out with puppets. Have two puppets run a race, with one taking the lead. Have the lagging puppet move up even with the leader. Say "[Tiger] *caught up* with [Rabbit]."

cause, causes, caused ◆ **1.** Explain that a *cause* is something that a person believes in. Give examples, such as saving the whales or cleaning up pollution. **2.** Lead students in making sentences, such as, "Exercise *causes* sweat," "Tiredness *causes* sleep," "Food *causes* smells," or "Fun *causes* smiles." **3.** Lead students in making sentences, such as, "The exercise *caused* me to sweat," "The food *caused* me to become hungry," "Rain *caused* the flowers to grow," and "The mother leaving *caused* the child to cry."

caution, cautious, cautiously ◆ **1.** Show looking under a book with *caution*. Contrast that with lifting the book without *caution*. Lead students in opening their desks or books with *caution*. **2.** Act out by casting one student as Ronny *Reckless*, another as Cathy *Cautious*, and the rest as drivers. Have the drivers race around the room. Have Ronnie *Reckless* run into the traffic without looking and crash into the cars. Have Cathy *Cautious* cross safely. Say "Ronny was *reckless* and crashed into the cars. Cathy was *cautious* and crossed safely." **3.** Pantomime looking *cautiously* both ways before crossing a street, and *continue* to watch carefully as you cross. Say "I crossed the street *cautiously*."

ceiling ◆ Point to the *ceiling*.

celebrate, celebrating, celebration ◆ **1.** Have puppets *celebrate* a special day, such as Thanksgiving. Have them bring food, sing, visit old friends, etc. Tell students that the puppets *celebrate* Thanksgiving. Ask students what they *celebrate* with their families. Lead them in sentences. **2.** Show pictures of a birthday party. Ask students to tell about other times when people *celebrate*. Show pictures of people *celebrating*. Explain that a party is a *celebration*. Have students pantomime a *celebration* in the classroom, perhaps a birthday party.

celestial ◆ Show students pictures of some of the planets and constellations. Explain that the stars, moons, and planets are in space, and when we talk about them, we use the word *celestial*. Give examples, such as, "The moon is a *celestial* body, Jupiter is a *celestial* body, and the sun is a *celestial* body."

cellar ◆ Draw a house with a room underneath. Lead students in sentences using *cellar*.

center ◆ Draw a circle on the board and put a dot at its *center*. Have a student stand in the *center* of the room.

century, centuries ◆ Show students the classroom calendar. Say "One year." Tell them, "One hundred years makes a *century*." On the chalkboard, write *century* = 100 years. Have students tell you what year it was 100 years ago, 200 years ago, and three *centuries* ago.

ceremonies ❯ Show pictures of *ceremonies*, such as weddings, graduations, etc.

certain, certainly ❯ **1.** Hold something while saying you are *certain* that you will not drop it. Contrast by holding something in an *uncertain* manner. **2.** Say "There are many students in the class, but there is one certain student who ___." Describe a particular student using hair and eye color, clothing, and so forth until everyone knows which student you are describing. **3.** Act out with a puppet. Have the puppet ask you to go to the movies. With exaggerated assuredness, say "I *certainly* will!"

chafing ❯ Pretend that your shoe is *chafing* your ankle. Show students the sore spot and demonstrate the *chafing* action.

challenge ❯ Have one puppet *challenge* another in a race or a game of checkers.

champions ❯ Compare to winners in a sport. If needed, hold walking races and announce the *champion* of each race.

championship ❯ Have students line up and hop across the room on one foot. Of the winner, say "[Consuela] is the winner! [She] has won the *championship!*"

chance, chances ❯ **1.** Have a puppet come to the board and write its name. Then ask individual students if they would like a *chance* to write their name on the board. Pantomime a scene with a puppet going through a door. Have the puppet tell the class that it cannot open the door itself, and as soon as somebody opens the door, it will have a *chance* to go through it. **2.** Play jump rope with students. Ask individual students to jump in; give them *chances* to jump rope.

chandeliers ❯ Show or draw pictures of *chandeliers.*

change, changed, changes ❯ Ask two students to *change* places. On the board, draw an ice cube, a puddle of water, and the sun shining above. Say "When ice gets warm, it *changes* into water." Show students a piece of paper, tear it, and tell them that it has *changed.* Find a couple of other objects that can easily be *changed.* —*change hands,* draw a house on a sheet of paper. Pantomime selling it to a puppet by having the puppet hand you one dollar and you handing the house to the student. Give example sentences using *change hands.*

chant, chants ❯ Lead students in a *chant* that they would be familiar with. Divide students into two groups. Have one group pretend to be onlookers of a sport and *chant* at the other group playing the sport. Let the two groups trade roles and repeat. Ask students if they know any *chants.* If not, sing them, "2, 4, 6, 8, Who do we appreciate?" or another *chant* you know.

character ❯ Ask each student to name one thing each believes makes him or her unique. Give example sentences using *character.*

charge ❯ Yell, "*charge!*" Have students *charge* forward. (This is best done outside.) —*in charge of,* appoint a student to be *in charge of* picking up assignments, cleaning the board, etc.

charm ❯ **1.** Smile and ask students to do something in an appealing way. Say "I used my *charm* to get you to do the math problem." **2.** Show pictures of *charms* or show actual *charms.*

chase, chased ◆ Have a student *chase* after a rolling ball. Have one puppet *chase* another. Explain that cats *chase* mice. Ask if students *chase* each other on the playground. Lead students in past tense sentences.

chat ◆ Have two puppets *chat*. Ask students to *chat* for a moment.

chatter, chattered ◆ *Chatter* at students. Have students *chatter* with each other. Once done, explain that they *chattered*.

cheap, cheaper, cheapest ◆ Draw something on the board with a price tag attached. Say "This does not cost much. This is *cheap*." Show three objects: the first, *cheap*; the next, *cheaper*; and the last, *cheapest*.

cheating ◆ Have a puppet participate with students in a mock spelling test. Have the puppet look for answers on another's paper. Say "That's *cheating!*"

check, checking ◆ Go to a piece of equipment or a student's workbook and *check* it. Lead students in *checking* things around the classroom, perhaps *checking* that all the books have been put on the proper shelves.

cheder ◆ Yiddish word pronounced: *KAY-der*. Make a broad gesture indicating the classroom. Say "*Cheder* is a Yiddish word meaning 'room of learning.'"

cheer, cheering, cheered, cheerfully ◆ Divide students into two groups. Have one group pretend to be onlookers of a sport and *cheer* the players on. Let the two groups trade roles and repeat. Or, lead students in a pantomime of *cheering* on a track-and-field performer. Help students with past tense sentences. Walk around the classroom in a *cheerful* manner and greet the class *cheerfully*. Contrast by speaking to the class *gloomily*.

Cherokee ◆ Native Americans who now live in Oklahoma, Tennessee, Alabama, Missouri, Arkansas, and North Carolina. Show a picture of a *Cherokee* person. Explain that *Cherokee* is also the name of their language.

chew, chewing ◆ Lead students in *chewing*.

chief ◆ **1.** Ask each student what extracurricular activity he or she likes best. Say, for example, "[Manuel]'s *chief* interest is [soccer]; [Gabriella]'s *chief* interest is [karate]." **2.** Once students understand *clan*, explain that the leader of all the families is called the *chief*. (See *clan*.)

childhood ◆ See *boyhood*.

childish Ask a couple of students to crawl around the floor and whine. Say "They are being *childish*. Babies crawl; we don't because we are older."

chill ◆ Shiver as if you were cold. Say that you have a *chill*. Lead students in a pantomime and have them repeat the sentence. —*chilled to the bone*, check that students understand the individual words in the idiom. Show a picture of a skeleton and identify the bones. Tell students, "When you are very cold, even your bones feel cold. You are *chilled to the bone*."

chimney ◆ Show pictures of houses with *chimneys* on them. Students may not know what *chimneys* are for. If so, draw or show a picture of a fireplace or a wood-burning stove. Ask if students have seen a fireplace or a wood-burning stove. Explain as needed. Draw on the board to explain how the smoke goes up the *chimney* so that the air in the house doesn't get smoky—*chimney's*, see *animal's*.

chin ❖ Point to your *chin*. —*chinny-chin-chin*, check that students know what their *chin* is. Then explain that *chinny-chin-chin* is a fun way to say *chin*.

Chinatown ❖ Show a map of San Francisco or some other large city. Mark one small area as *Chinatown*. Explain that this is a section where mostly *Chinese* people live.

chip ❖ Show a *chipped* surface. —*chip in*, give all students play money. Ask them to *chip in* for a pizza.

choice, choicer, choicest, choose, chose, chosen ❖ **1.** Lay a few pencils on your desk and say to a puppet, "*Choose.*" Have the puppet *choose* one. Display a few pencils to a student and say "*Choose.*" Announce to the class, "[Erica] has *chosen* a pencil." Repeat with several students. Lead students in sentences, such as, "I like her *choice* in pencils," "That was a good *choice*," or "Did you see the pencil she *chose*?" **2.** Have students name good, better, and best products in a category, such as brands of athletic shoes. Say "This is a *choice* brand, this one is even *choicer*, but this one is *choicest* of all."

choke ❖ Pretend to be eating and have the food get caught in your throat. Cough and pat your chest. Say "That is how you *choke* on your food."

chomp ❖ Pantomime *chomping* on your food. Lead students in similar pantomimes.

chop, chopping, chopped ❖ Draw some vegetables on the board. Pantomime *chopping* vegetables for salad or stir-fry. Then draw the same vegetables in small pieces. Lead students in past tense sentences.

chore, chores ❖ Ask students if they have things that their parents tell them to do each day, such as empty the garbage or make their bed. Explain that these are *chores*.

chowder ❖ Show students a picture of *chowder*, and explain that it is a seafood soup. Explain that it is also the name of a clown they will be reading about. Have students make sentences for both meanings.

chronological ❖ List the birthdays of some of the students on the board. Then have the students list them in *chronological* order.

chuckle, chuckled ❖ *Chuckle* for the students and lead them in past tense sentences.

chug ❖ Puffing sound made by a steam engine. Have the students form a train by lining up and holding on to the person in front of them. Have everyone move around the room saying, "*Chug, chug, chug.*"

chunks ❖ Slice a crayon. Say that now you have *chunks* of crayon. Give other examples, such as *chunks* of chocolate, *chunks* of clay, etc. Lead students in sentences.

cinders ❖ Draw a fire made with logs. Erase the fire to show that it has gone out, and then draw in little *cinders*.

circle, circling, circled, circles ❧ **1.** Draw a *circle* on the board. Have students draw *circles*. **2.** *Circle* your desk. Have students *circle* their desks. Lead students in past tense sentences. **3.** Make a sign that says "Saturn." Have other students make signs that say "Moon." Holding their signs, have them walk around "Saturn" in a *circle*. Using a ball and a globe, demonstrate how the moon *circles* Earth.

circuit ❧ **1.** Draw a circle on the board indicating its beginning and ending points. Explain that a *circuit* is a path that something can travel on. Show an electrical *circuit* from a science book. Have students form a circle and pass a pencil around their *circuit*. On the board, draw a lightbulb with a *circuit* to a battery. —*closed circuit*, demonstrate an *open* and *closed circuit* by turning on a lightbulb and saying that we have a *closed circuit*; then turn the lightbulb off and say that we have an *open circuit*. —*open circuit*, show an *open circuit* from a science book. Contrast with a *closed circuit*. **2.** Plug a lamp into an electrical outlet. Dramatize smelling something burning. Say "I smell something burning. I think it is this outlet or cord. There must be a *short circuit*."

circulate, circulation ❧ **1.** Have students stand up and spread out around the room. Walk around the room, weaving in and out among the students. Say "This is how I *circulate* through a group of students standing around the classroom." **2.** Distribute "Weekly Readers" or another student publication. Give example sentences using *circulation*.

circumstances ❧ Describe the events that led to your becoming a teacher. Then say "These were the *circumstances* that made me a teacher."

circus ❧ Show photos, drawings, or toys representing *circus* acts, clowns, and so on.

citizen, citizens ❧ **1.** Point to a country on the world map and say that if you were born in that country, you are a *citizen* there. **2.** Explain as members of a town or country. Have students divide into two groups. Give each group a name for their town. Say "You are the *citizens* of [Berryville], and you are the *citizens* of [Brownsville]."

city ❧ Show pictures of *cities*. —*inner city*, use a map to show students a large *city*. Have students stand in a group in the center of the room, crowded closely together. Explain that the *inner city* is the older part of the *city*, in or near the center, that is usually overcrowded and in bad condition.

civil, civilized ❧ **1.** Have two puppets argue. Intercede to settle it. Say "This is a *civil* matter." Pantomime going to court with a judge. **2.** Have a puppet be rude to another, and then have the puppet be *civil* to another.

civilians ❧ Show pictures of the military and *civilians*.

claim ❧ Show pictures of miners from the California gold rush or homesteaders in Native American Territory. On the board, show how stakes marked a *claim*. Have students stake a *claim* in the classroom or on the playground.

clan ❧ Draw a picture of related families all living together in a *clan*. Show the brothers and their wives, the sisters and their husbands, etc. Explain that they are all related.

clang ◆ Demonstrate the sound of a *clang* by hitting a metal table or chair leg with a spoon or other metal object.

clap, clapped, clapping ◆ Show students how to *clap*. Lead students in *clapping*. Say "We *clapped*."

clarify ◆ Choose a word that is hard to *clarify*. Say "I can *clarify* the meaning of the word by showing you a sample of the real thing." Then show them a sample.

clashed ◆ Say something and have a puppet always say the opposite. Give example sentences using *clashed*.

class ◆ Divide the *class* up into different groups and give each group a non-inflammatory title, such as the walking *class*, the sitting *class*, and the standing *class*. Help them to understand that *class* means "group."—*first class*, on the board, draw an airplane showing *first class* and *coach*.

clatter, clattering, clattered ◆ Demonstrate the sound of a *clatter*, perhaps by tossing a set of keys onto a desk. As the keys land, explain that they are making a *clattering* sound. Lead students in past tense sentences.

clause ◆ Explain to the class that this is a word used to help in teaching how to write sentences in English, which they will learn more about later.

clay ◆ Show classroom *clay* if you have it. Show illustrations of pottery. Explain that the pottery is made out of *clay*.

clean, cleaning, cleaned ◆ Lead students in dramatizing *cleaning* by pantomiming dusting, sweeping, and so on. Say "We are *cleaning* the classroom." Lead students in past tense sentences.

clear ◆ *Clear* off a table or desk.

clench, clenching, clenched ◆ *Clench* your teeth. Lead students in *clenching* their teeth. Help with past tense sentences.

clever ◆ Write a math problem on the board that students would consider hard. Solve it quickly, and explain that you are *clever* at math. Write the same problem on the board and have a great deal of trouble solving it. Explain that you are not *clever* at math.

click ◆ *Click* a retractable pen. Let students *click* it as well.

clickety-clack ◆ Have students tap their shoes on the floor to make a *clickety-clack* sound.

cliff, cliffs ◆ If available, show pictures of *cliffs*. Draw two mountains on the board—one with a gradual slope and the other with a vertical face. Explain that a straight up-and-down face in a mountain is called a *cliff*.

climate ◆ Show illustrations of various *climates*, such as the desert, the tropics, or the arctic.

climb, climbing, climbed, climbable, climbers ◆ 1. Using a toy animal, demonstrate how it can *climb* up something—perhaps a chair leg. Ask students if they have ever seen cats *climb* trees. Show a toy bird, stuffed animal, or kite *climbing* up into the air. Lead students in past tense sentences. 2. Draw a hill and an impossibly steep mountain. Lead students in sentences using *climbable*. **3.** Show pictures of mountain *climbers* and explain that they are called *climbers*.

cling, clinging, clings ❖ *Cling* to a doll or toy animal and tell students you do not want to let it go. Have students *cling* to a doll or toy animal. Pantomime *clinging* to something. Demonstrate with dolls. Say "The baby *clings* to her mother."

close, closer, closest, closely ❖ **1.** Show things that are *close* and *distant*. Place a stapler *close* to a book. Have students place their pencils *close* to paper and then far away from their paper. Place three objects *close*, *closer*, and *closest* to a book. **2.** Have a puppet follow another around *closely* and then from a *distance*.

close, closing, closed ❖ *Open* and *close* books, desktops, doors, and drawers. Have students do the same. Lead students in *closing* a book. Say and demonstrate these sentences: "This book is *closed*. This book is *open*."

close-knit ❖ Divide students into two groups. Have them assume family roles (mother, father, etc.). Have one group stand apart from one another, arms crossed and back to back. Have the other group act lovingly toward one another. Say "There are different kinds of families. Some don't get along; others do. This happy group is a *close-knit* family."

closeness ❖ Demonstrate the concept of *closeness* by using two puppets who get along very well, agree upon things to do, and generally enjoy the time they spend with each other. Contrast by having them be disagreeable and miserable in each other's company. Explain that the puppets are *distant*.

close-up ❖ Draw a camera on a sheet of paper. Pantomime using it to take pictures of students. Move in real *close* for a *close-up*.

clotted ❖ Demonstrate with glue. Squeeze some glue out of the bottle and show students how it flows easily. Wait a few moments and show that it is beginning to *clot*. Explain that it has *clotted*.

cloudy ❖ Have a puppet show you a new math problem. Look puzzled and say "That problem is very *cloudy*."

club ❖ Show pictures of *clubs*. Explain that people who get together and do special things as a group are a *club*. Ask if any students are or have been in *clubs*. Or, mention *clubs* that students may be familiar with, such as *Pep Club* or *Math Club*, or any *club* you have at your school. Find out if any of the students are members of *clubs*. If available, show a picture of a *clubhouse*.

cluck, clucked, clucking ❖ Draw or show a picture of a hen. Make *clucking* sounds. Have students imitate. Lead students in past tense sentences.

clue, clues ❖ **1.** Remind students of the game they play with *blending words* in which the teacher gives them *clues*. **2.** Tell students that you have hidden a pencil and that you will give them *clues* to find it. For example, "Your first *clue* is that it is yellow" and "Your second *clue* is that it is in a box."

clumping ❖ Walk with the heavy, dull sound characteristic of *clumping*. Have students go *clumping* around the classroom.

clumsy, clumsily ⟶ Act out by carrying something across the classroom, stumbling and dropping it. Walk across the classroom *clumsily*.

clunked ⟶ Explain that this is a noise. Bang a piece of metal or a book on a desk to demonstrate.

cluster ⟶ Ask students to spread out around the classroom. Then ask them to move together to form a tight bunch.

coach, coaches ⟶ **1.** Explain that a *coach* helps the players on a team to play. Ask if students have had experience with a *coach*. **2.** Have students pair up to learn spelling words or math facts where one student *coaches* the other.

coaxing ⟶ Set a bowl on the table and place a puppet a foot or so away. Stand near the bowl and use gestures and a high-pitched voice to *coax* the puppet to come and eat. Say "I am *coaxing* the puppet to come and eat."

cobbler ⟶ Explain that a *cobbler* makes shoes. If available, show a picture of the *cobbler* in the story "The Elves and the Shoemaker."

cock-a-doodle-doo ⟶ Demonstrate crowing. Lead students in *crowing*.

code ⟶ Have students create their own *codes*.

coil, coiled ⟶ Draw a *coil* on the board. Make a *coil* with modeling clay. Show a snake *coiled* up.

coincidence ⟶ Ask a student to name his or her favorite color. Say "Really? That's my favorite color too! What a *coincidence!*"

cold ⟶ Have students feel their warm foreheads and contrast this with a *cold* metal surface. Pantomime *cold* by shivering and holding yourself as if *cold*. Say "Brrr, I am so *cold!*"

collapsing, collapsed ⟶ If possible, demonstrate with a folding chair. Otherwise, build a tower out of blocks and place a heavy book on top so the tower falls. Demonstrate the action by having blocks *collapse*. Lead students in past tense sentences.

collar ⟶ Point to a *collar* on a shirt or coat. Show a dog *collar*.

collecting, collected ⟶ Walk around the classroom, collecting papers. Say "I am *collecting* your papers." Lead students in past tense sentences.

college ⟶ Review *high school* if necessary. Then tell students that they will go to *college* when they have finished high school. If possible show pictures of a high school and high school students, then pictures of a *college* and its students.

collide, colliding, collided ⟶ Have two toy cars *collide*. Say "They *collided*." Act this out with the puppets. Say "Watch [Fluffy] *colliding* with [Bear]."

colonial ⟶ See *colonist*. Explain that we use the word *colonial* when we talk about that time in America, or things from that time. Make example sentences, such as, "This is a *colonial* dress" or "These are pictures of *colonial* America."

colonies, colony, colonial, colonist, colonists ⟶ Show pictures of *colonies* and *colonists* from *colonial* America. Explain that people who came from England were called *colonists*, and that America was a *colony* of England. Show students the globe, and have them trace with their finger the route from England to America. Lead them in pantomimes of coming across on a boat and starting their own *colony* as *colonists*.

color, colors, coloring, colored ◆ **1.** Display a number of sheets of construction paper, each a different *color*. Point to each and say "*Color*." Make a sweeping gesture over them and say "*Colors*." Lead students in sentences with individual *colors* and many *colors*. **2.** Lead students in *coloring* a picture. Help students make past tense sentences.

colossal ◆ Compare the size of a student with the size of a puppet. Have the puppet say "You are *colossal!*" Show pictures of large objects, particularly ones that dwarf people. Use the words *enormous*, *giant*, *gigantic*, *monumental*, *prodigious*, *stupendous*, *titanic*, and *tremendous* to describe the object.

column, columns, columnist ◆ **1.** Write a *column* of numbers on the board. Compare with a *row* of numbers. **2.** Show students a newspaper. Point out the long sections of words lying side by side on the pages. Identify these as *columns*. Then point out the author's name at the top of the article. Say "A person who writes articles like these is called a *columnist*."

comb, combed, combing ◆ *Comb* a puppet's hair. Pantomime or demonstrate *combing* your hair. Lead students in past tense sentences.

combination ◆ Show a *combination* lock and how it works. Write a *combination* of words on the board to create a sentence. Ask students what they wear on their feet (a *combination* of shoes and socks).

come, comes ◆ Ask a student to *come* to the front of the room. As he or she is walking, say "He/she *comes*."

coming, came ◆ Say "[Angelina] is *coming* to my desk." Then say "She *came* to the front." Repeat with other locations. Walk over to a student's desk and say that you *came* to it. Toss a ball to a student. As it is sailing through the air, say "Here it *comes!*" Ask a student to walk to another student. As he/she approaches, say "Here he/she *comes!*" — *came along*, explain that this is something we say in English. Using puppets, pantomime sentences that express the meaning of "showing up" or "appearing": "*Along came* a puppet," "*Along came* a friend," or "A stranger *came along* and wanted to play." —*comes forth*, with a puppet, demonstrate *comes forth*. Have students *come forth*. —*come along*, Motion for students to *come along*. Lead them around the room as you say "*Come along*." —*come ashore*, have puppets get off a boat that has docked. Tell students, "The students have *come ashore*." Lead them in pantomimes. — *come closer*, have a student walk toward you, one step at a time. After each step say "*Come closer*." —*come for*, have one puppet *come for* another puppet and then go off with it. —*come off*, erase the board and show students how the chalk will *come off*. Have students wash their hands. Tell them the dirt will *come off*. —*come on*, have a puppet wave to another to *come on*. Have the other puppet follow the first. —*come or bring to a head*, tell a puppet in a very strong voice that it must really start being nicer to the other puppets or it won't have any puppet friends. Have the puppet look sad. Give example sentences using *bring to a head.*

comfort, comfortingly ◆ Ask a female student to volunteer to act upset. Put your arm around her shoulder and speak soothingly to her. Say "[Claudia] was upset, and I tried to *comfort* her." Have a puppet or doll "bump itself" and then *comfort* it. Show a puppet rocking a doll and say "It rocks the baby *comfortingly.*"

comfortable ◆ Sit on a chair and pantomime being *uncomfortable.* Make yourself *comfortable* and say "Now I feel *comfortable.*"

command, commanded ◆ Have a puppet *command* another puppet to come and then, in contrast, *ask* the puppet. Pantomime a scene where you are the king or queen and you *command* your royal subjects (students). Help them to make past tense sentences.

comment ◆ *Comment* about a student's artwork in a complimentary way.

commercial, commercials ◆ Mention *commercials* or ads that students may be familiar with. If you have access to a television, show them an actual *commercial.*

commitment ◆ Examples might include a man and a woman who make a *commitment* to stay married, or a mom and a dad who make a *commitment* to take care of their children.

committee ◆ Organize students into *committees* for a class party. Lead students in sentences using *committee.*

common ◆ Point to *common* things in the classroom. Contrast with things that are *uncommon.*

commonplace ◆ Show things that are *commonplace*, such as a yellow pencil and contrast with something more *extraordinary*, such as a novelty pencil.

commotion ◆ Use puppets to create a *commotion.* Ask students to create a *commotion.*

communicate, communication, communicated ◆ Have two puppets say "hello" to each other. Write today's date on the board. Say "I *communicated* to you that today is (date)." Have students write brief notes and exchange them with one another. Ask each one, "What did you *communicate*?"

community, communities ◆ Show pictures of *communities.* Have students tell you about their *communities.* Give example sentences using *community.*

commutes ◆ Demonstrate traveling from home to work and back with a toy car.

compactness ◆ Demonstrate by showing a dollhouse or photographs or tiny apartments.

companion, companions ◆ Have a puppet read a book with you. Say "This puppet is my *companion.*" Ask a student to walk to the door alone. Ask the same student to return to the door with two *companions.*

compartment ❯ Show a wallet with different *compartments*. Give example sentences using *compartment*.

compass ❯ Draw a *compass* on the board, or show a compass.

compassion ❯ Show a picture of a sad person. Pantomime showing *compassion* by giving the person a hug and a smile.

compensate, compensation ❯ **1.** Have two large students pull one end of a rope. Place a small student at the other end. Have them pull the rope. Get other students to help the small student. **2.** Set up a scene in which students are your employees. Have them build a castle out of blocks. Hand them each some play money. Lead students in sentences using *compensation*.

compete, competition ❯ Using examples from the sports page of the newspaper, lead students in sentences using *compete*. Have two dolls or puppets *compete* in terms of how strong they are by having them lift various small objects. Have students *compete* in walking races across the classroom. Hold jogging or walking *competitions*.

complain, complaint, complaints ❯ **1.** Set up a scene where students run a restaurant, and you are the patron. When they bring you your meal, say "I hate to *complain*, but this food is cold" or "I cannot eat this meal. This food is cold. What can you do about my *complaint?*" **2.** Tell students you do not feel well and list your *complaints*.

complete, completed, completion ❯ **1.** Contrast *complete* and *incomplete* sets of crayons or markers. Say a *complete* sentence and contrast with an incomplete sentence. **2.** Add the final piece to a simple puzzle. Show work that has been *completed*. Show students things that have reached a point of *completion*, and show things that have not.

complex ❯ **1.** Draw a *complex* maze on the board. Contrast with a *simple* maze. **2.** Work through a *complex* grammar exercise. Contrast it with a *simple* one.

complication ❯ Show a puppet lying in a bed. Explain that it is in the hospital, and you are the doctor. Tell the class the puppet is very sick with the flu, but that you believe it will get better. Then pretend to run a few more tests on the sick puppet and say to the class, "This puppet is sick with something new— pneumonia." (See *pneumonia*.) "He has a *complication*."

compose, composing, composed, composer, composition ❯ **1.** Write some notes on the board and explain that they are musical notes. Explain that when you are writing a song, you are *composing*. Lead students in sentences with *compose*. **2.** Explain that the person *composing* the song is called a *composer*. **3.** Point to your notes on the board and explain that the song you wrote is called a *composition*.

composed, composition ❯ **1.** Divide students into two work groups. Say "This team is made up of you three: Team A is *composed* of [Alejandro], [Teresa], and [Dong]. Team B consists of you three: Team B is *composed* of [Jorge], [May], and [Consuela]." **2.** Hold up a pencil and tell students what it is *composed* of (wood, graphite, and rubber). **3.** Hold up a pencil and say "The *composition* of a pencil is graphite, wood, and rubber."

composure ◆► Draw a burning building on the board. Have a puppet calmly call 911 for help. When it hangs up the phone, have it start screaming and hopping around anxiously. Give example sentences using *composure*—perhaps "The puppet has lost its *composure.*"

compromise, compromises ◆► Make two puppets argue about using a computer. Each puppet wants to go first and not give the other a turn. Say "You must *compromise* so that it's fair for both of you." Resolve the dispute in an equitable way. Say "I will toss a coin to see who goes first. That's a good *compromise.*" Make *compromises* with students on some assignments. Give example sentences.

compute, computation ◆► Show a calculator and demonstrate a mathematical operation. Say that you can calculate or *compute* with the calculator. Demonstrate a mathematical operation on the board and then on the calculator. Say that the calculator is good to calculate. It is good for a *computation.*

comrades ◆► Show pictures of people with their arms around each other, or demonstrate with puppets. Give example sentences using *comrades.*

concave ◆► Draw a bowl on the board. Show how the inside of the bowl is hollow and rounded out. Say "The inside of the bowl is *concave.*"

conceive, conceived ◆► **1.** Ask students what kind of ideas they can think of or imagine. Say "Can you *conceive* of a space alien?" **2.** Have students work together to organize a surprise party for their classroom teacher. When they tell you what their scheme is, say "You have *conceived* a good plan."

concentrate, concentrating, concentrated, concentration ◆► **1.** Pantomime *concentrating* on something you are doing while a puppet makes a lot of noise next to you. Write an arithmetic problem on the board. Study it with exaggerated attention. Say "If I think really hard, I know I can figure this out. It will take a lot of *concentration.*" **2.** Have students stand spread out around the classroom, pretending they live in a rural area. Then have them stand in a cluster, pretending they live in a crowded city. Say "The people who live in the countryside are spread far apart. In cities, lots of people are *concentrated* in a small area" or "There is a heavy *concentration* of people in this small area."

concern, concerned ◆► Pretend that you have lost something. Have a puppet be *concerned.* Have a puppet show *concern.*

conclude, conclusion ◆► Explain that *conclude* means to bring something to an end. Give examples: "We *conclude* our school day at 2:00 P.M." or "We will *conclude* the story that we have been reading tomorrow." Read the *conclusion* of a story to the class and say "This story had an interesting *conclusion.*" — *jump to conclusions*, draw a door on the board with a plume of smoke curling up from under it. Pantomime feeling the door to feel if it is hot. Lead students in sentences using *jump to conclusions.*

concoctions ◆ Have students work in groups or committees. Give each group pieces of fruit, such as raisins, grapes, orange slices, etc., to put together to eat. When they have finished, let everybody sample the *concoctions*.

condemnation ◆ Have a puppet be a leader of another country. Show a picture of poor people. Then say that the leader will not help the people. Have another puppet tell the class, "This leader is bad. We *condemn* him. We give him our *condemnation*." Have the puppet say to the leader puppet, "You are a bad leader!"

condensation ◆ If time permits, fill a cup halfway with water. Put a square of plastic wrap over the top and place the cup in a sunny window. After a while, show students the droplets of water clinging to the underside of the plastic wrap. Otherwise, illustrate the concept on the board.

condescending ◆ Talk "baby talk" to a puppet. Pat it on the head and say "What a good little baby!" Give example sentences using *condescending*.

conference ◆ **1.** Call a *conference* with students. Decide what game to play at recess. **2.** Schedule a *conference* with each student to discuss a particular assignment or how well the student is doing in school.

confess, confesses, confession ◆ **1.** Have two puppets argue over the correct answer for a simple math problem. One puppet has the correct answer, and the other does not. Have the puppet with the wrong answer say "I *confess*, you're right." **2.** Have a puppet take a pencil from your desk. Tell the class that a pencil has been stolen, and that you will not let anyone leave today until the person *confesses*. Pretend that time has passed. Tell the class that it is almost 3:00 P.M. and you still want to know who took the pencil. Finally, have the puppet say that it did it. Tell the class, "The puppet has made a *confession*."

confidence, confident ◆ **1.** On the board, draw a picture of one person giving another a hundred dollars. Draw a second picture of the same person coming back, and tell the class that it is now one week later. Show that the other person still has the hundred dollars. Say "He has *confidence* in his friend, because his friend kept his money safe." **2.** Have two puppets running for class president. One says to the class, "I know I will win!" The other says, "I don't think I will win." Say of the first, "This puppet has *confidence*" and "I am *confident* it will win." Say of the second, "This puppet does not have *confidence*."

confine, confined ◆ *Confine* a puppet by placing it in your desk drawer. Explain that the puppet is *confined*. Show a picture of animals in a zoo.

confuse, confusing, confused, confusion ◆ Act out with puppets. Have one puppet tell another how to get to the shopping mall. Have the second puppet shake its head, show confusion, and say "Wait. I don't understand what you're telling me. I am so *confused*," or show a look of *confusion*.

congratulating, congratulations ◆ **1.** Put a blue ribbon on a puppet and *congratulate* it for winning a contest. **2.** Show pictures of a wedding or a graduation. Pantomime *congratulating* a puppet. Give your *congratulations* to the puppet.

connect, connected ◈ *Connect* and *disconnect* a power cord from a wall outlet. *Connect* and *disconnect* a zipper. Ask students for ideas of other things that can be *connected* and *disconnected*.

conquered ◈ Use pictures of historical defeats. Lead students in sentences using *conquered*.

conscious, consciousness ◈ Show two puppets roughhousing. Have one puppet get knocked out. Tell the class, "This puppet is *unconscious*; this puppet is *conscious*." Ask who is *conscious* in the class. Lead students in sentences using *consciousness*.

consecrate ◈ On the board, draw a picture of a church being built. Explain dedicating the church using *consecrate*.

consequently ◈ Add two rocks to two rocks. Say "*Consequently*, we get four."

conserving ◈ Have a pile of little candies on your desk. Eat one and put the others away. Say "I am *conserving* my candy."

consideration ◈ Set up a scene where a puppet does not want to finish the assignment because it feels sick. Say to the puppet, "I will take your feelings into *consideration*."

console, consoled ◈ *Console* a crying puppet. Say "I *consoled* [Fluffy]."

constantly ◈ Ask the class about things that they do each day. Each time students suggest something, such as reading or writing, answer, "Yes, we do reading *constantly*."

constellation ◈ Draw or show a picture of a *constellation*, such as the Big Dipper.

consternation ◈ Look in your bag. Say "I'm looking for my money. I can't see it." Look really confused. Have students imitate. Say "Those are really good looks of *consternation*."

construct, constructed, construction ◈ Show a picture of a *construction* site. Explain that buildings are built, or *constructed*. Have students *construct constructions* with blocks.

consumed ◈ Drink a glass of water. Say "I *consumed* the water."

consumptive ◈ Make a puppet cough and get weaker and weaker. Say "It is very sad. The puppet is *consumptive*."

contact ◈ Pantomime placing a phone call and waiting for someone to pick up. Finally have someone answer. Say "We finally made *contact*."

contain, contains ◈ Put some paper clips in a *container* and explain that it *contains* paper clips. Repeat with other objects. Ask several students, "What does your bag *contain*?" Have them reply by producing one object and say "My bag *contains* . . . ."

contempt ◈ See *thief*. Pantomime *contempt* for the *thief*.

content, contented ◈ Contrast with puppets. Have one puppet happily playing with its things. Show it being happy to have those items and talking about how it doesn't need anything else. Have another puppet be *unsatisfied* with its toys, wanting more, and becoming angry that it does not have more. Make contrasting sentences; for example, "It is *content* with its toys" and "It is not *content* with its toys."

content, contents ❖ Fill a ceramic cup with various small items. Have students guess its *content*. Ask students what the *contents* of their desks are.

contest ❖ See *spelling bee.* Let students have a contest in spelling or math.

continue, continued ❖ **1.** Lead students in walking around the room; stop, then *continue*. Do this several times. **2.** Draw a cloud and raindrops on the board. Using a calendar, point out several days of a week and say "It rained on Monday and *continued* to rain on Tuesday and Wednesday." **3.** Have a student read a sentence from a book. Tell them to *continue* and have them read another sentence.

continuity ❖ On the board, draw a short line. Ask a student to *continue* it. Give example sentences using *continuity*.

contract, contracts ❖ Write a simple *contract* for a student, such as, "John will pass out paper on Tuesday." Have the student sign the *contract* to show it's agreed upon.

contradict, contradicting, contradicted ❖ Act out with a puppet. Talk with the puppet, and have it *contradict* everything you say. Say to students, "[Pumpkin] did not agree with me at all. She *contradicted* everything I said." Have pairs of students practice *contradicting* each other.

control, controls, controlled ❖ **1.** Carefully pick up a pen and move it to another spot. Contrast this with having no *control* by dropping the pen or missing the spot. *Control* the movements of a puppet. Lead students in past tense sentences. **2.** Play a short game of "Simon Says" and then say "Simon has *control* in that game. Whatever Simon says is what you do. Simon *controls* you in that game." **3.** Draw or show a picture of a panel of knobs and levers that operates a machine, such as an airplane.

controversial ❖ Ask, "Who likes beauty pageants? Why and why not?" Encourage the expression of opposite views and say "This subject is *controversial*."

conveniences, convenient ❖ Talk about new inventions that make life easier. Say "Telephones, computers, and microwaves are *conveniences*." Place paper, pencils, and an eraser on your desk. Tell students you are going to write a story, and that having everything there makes it *convenient*."

conversation ❖ Talk with one student, taking turns in a two-way dialogue. After a minute, say to the class, "We are having a nice *conversation*."

convert, converted ❖ *Convert* ice into water. Give sentences using *converted*.

convex ❖ Draw a baseball cap on the board. Show how the outside of the hat curves outward. Say "The outside of the hat is *convex*."

convince, convinced ❖ **1.** Have one puppet *convince* another puppet to read a certain book. Let that puppet say "You *convinced* me. I will read it." **2.** Have a student tell the class he or she just won a million dollars. Ask the class if they believe him or her. Ask them if the student *convinced* them.

cooking, cooked ◆ Pantomime *cooking* food on a stove. Tell students that you *cooked* the food. Lead students in pantomimes of *cooking*.

cool, cooler ◆ **1.** Have students feel something *cool*, such as *cool* water from a tap. **2.** Put some *warm* water in a container. Have students feel the water. Then have students *cool* the water by adding *cold* water. **3.** Explain that *cool* means "very good or great." Admire various shoes or clothing and say: "You have *cool* shoes," "You have a *cool* shirt," and "That is a *cool* dress." **4.** Have students warm their hands by rubbing them and then letting them *cool*. Have them touch something *cool* like a piece of metal. Ask them which was *cooler*—their hands or the metal.

copy, copied ◆ **1.** Ask a student to make slow gestures and movements. Mimic everything the student does, explaining that each of your actions is a *copy* of one of the student's actions. **2.** Write something on the board; have students write it on a piece of paper. Say "You *copied* my words." **3.** Say something and have students repeat your words. Say "You *copied* my words."

corner, corners ◆ **1.** Draw an aerial map of some roads intersecting. Mark each *corner* with an "X." Ask students to put a finger on a *corner*. Then ask students to stand in a *corner*. Ask students how many *corners* there are in the room. **2.** Have students feel the *corners* of their chairs or desks.

cornerstone ◆ Show students a photograph of the *cornerstone* of a large building. Lead students in sample sentences using *cornerstone*.

cornhusking ◆ Show *corn* with the *husk* on. Tell students, "This is the *corn*; this is the *husk*." Then tell them, "When you take the *husk* off, you are *cornhusking*."

cornier ◆ Draw a heart on the board and show February 14 on a calendar. Say "On Valentine's Day, we send greeting cards to people we love. Some are serious, some are funny, and some are *cornier* than others, such as: 'Roses are red, violets are blue, sugar is sweet, and so are you.'"

corridors ◆ Show students the *corridors* outside your classroom.

cost, costly ◆ Play "store" with students (where you are the shopkeeper and they pretend to buy things from you). Each time they want to buy something, tell them, "That will *cost* a nickel." Have students give you the nickel in exchange for the item. Occasionally say "This [pencil] is very *costly*; it will *cost* a dollar."

costume ◆ Engage students in conversation about school-play *costumes*. If at all possible, show a picture of a *costume*.

cottony ◆ Show *cottony* fabrics and contrast with polyesters or wools.

cough, coughing ◆ Demonstrate *coughing*.

could ◆ Explain that *could* is like the word *can*. Give examples: "I *can* walk. Yesterday, I *could* walk" or "I *can* run. Yesterday, I *could* run." See *can*.

couldn't ◆ Show on the board how *could* and *not* squeeze together to make *couldn't*.

council ◆ Select a Class *Council* to help you resolve classroom issues such as tidying, project boards, computer time, etc. Describe other types of *councils* that exist.

counsel ➧ Have a puppet come to you for advice on how to complete his or her homework assignments in a timely fashion. *Counsel* him or her on good homework habits.

count, counting, counted ➧ Lead students in *counting* various items. Lead them in past tense sentences.

countdown ➧ Write the numbers ten through one in a column in descending order. Draw a rocket on a sheet of paper and hold it up, ready to launch. Say "Do the *countdown* with me."

counteract ➧ Push a toy car forward with one hand. Use the other to *counteract* the motion.

countless ➧ Have students flip through their textbooks. Ask them how many words they think are in the book. Say "Too many words to *count*. There are *countless* words in your books."

courage, courageous ➧ Have one puppet apologize to another. Say "It takes *courage* to do that." Draw a picture on the board of a burning building. Say "Firefighters have to be very brave to save people from burning buildings. Firefighters are *courageous*." Talk with students about other people who are *courageous*.

course ➧ Clear everything off a desk. Pour a small amount of water across it and let the water take a natural *course*. Have students fly paper airplanes. Talk about the *course* each airplane took. —*of course*, *of course not*, lead students in saying "*of course*" to questions that you ask, such as "Did you come to school today?" "*Of course.*" Have one puppet ask the other, "Do elephants fly?" The second puppet answers, "*Of course not.*"

courteous ➧ Model *courteous* behavior. Lead students in sentences using *courteous*.

courtship ➧ Act out with a puppet. Have the puppet bring you a bouquet of flowers and ask you for a date. Look starry-eyed and say "[Fuzzy] and I are sweethearts; we're falling in love. He is asking me to go out and giving me flowers and candy. I like our *courtship*."

cousin, cousins ➧ Draw on the board two families. Explain that the children in the families are *cousins*. Ask students if they have *cousins*. Ask for their first-language word for *cousin*. Ask children to name their *cousins*.

cover, covering, covered ➧ **1.** Draw a planet on the board. *Cover* it with a thick layer of clouds. Show a picture of snow *covering* the ground. **2.** Safe place. Have students pantomime running to get out of the rain and ducking under their desks. Say "It's raining! Run for *cover!*" **3.** Show the class a jar with a *cover*. Have students place their hands over small objects, and point out that they have *covered* the objects. **4.** Place a *covering*, such as a blanket, over a doll or puppet.

coward ➧ See *brave*. Pantomime being a *coward* and then being *brave*. Lead students in similar pantomimes.

coy ◈ Have a puppet act *coy* (shy and flirtatious) in response to questions asked by another puppet.

cozy, cozier ◈ Show pictures of animals or babies sleeping in a *cozy* place. Explain that *cozy* means "warm and comfortable." Ask students to draw an even *cozier* place for the animals.

crab cakes ◈ Small, fried patties of *crabmeat*, mixed with chopped onions, eggs, bread crumbs, and spices. Show or draw pictures of *crab cakes* or similar dishes, explaining what they are.

crabby, crabbier, crabbiest ◈ First, explain *crabby*, which means the same as *grouchy*. Have a puppet talk in a slightly *crabby* way to another puppet. Then have the second puppet be even *crabbier*, and the first puppet then be the *crabbiest*.

crack, cracks, cracked ◈ **1.** Show a *crack* or *cracks* in a wall, door, or desktop. **2.** Show pictures of train tracks and point out the space between the ties. Explain that the train is going over those *cracks*. **3.** *Crack* a pencil. Explain that it is *cracked*. —*cracked up*, use slapstick humor, such as pretending to trip or walk into something, to get students to laugh. Say "That made us laugh. It really *cracked* us *up*."

craftsmen, craftsmanship ◈ **1.** Invite students to pantomime making things by hand, such as shoes, pottery, glassware, rugs, jewelry, etc. Say "People who make things like these are called *craftsmen*." **2.** Show items with good *craftsmanship*.

cramped ◈ **1.** Have students attempt to climb into a small space, such as under their desks. Say "That is a very small space for you big kids. It is *cramped* in there." **2.** Walk across the room and suddenly start limping. Say "My leg just *cramped*." On the board, draw a picture of a muscle with a knot in it.

cranky ◈ Have a puppet act *cranky* by complaining about the weather or something it is eating. Have it bother another puppet. Comment on how *cranky* the puppet is.

cranny ◈ Show nooks and *crannies* in the classroom.

crash, crashes ◈ **1.** *Crash* two toy cars or other objects together. Show a picture of a meteorite *crashing* into Earth. Demonstrate the sound of a *crash*, perhaps by knocking over a metal wastebasket. Cover your ears and make a face. Ask students if they heard the *crash*. **2.** Make a paper airplane. Make it fly and then *crash*. As it *crashes*, say "The airplane *crashes*!"

crater ◈ Show pictures of *craters* on the moon.

crawl, crawling, crawled ◈ Demonstrate *crawling* with a puppet or toy animal. Ask if students have ever seen a baby *crawl*. Lead students in past tense sentences.

crayon, crayons, crayoned ◈ **1.** Show *crayons*. **2.** To color with *crayons*. Make sure students know what *crayons* are; then have them *crayon* something for you.

crazy, crazier, craziest, crazily ◈ Take your hand and move it in a forward, circular motion a few inches from your ear. Say "*Crazy*." Make a *crazy* or silly face. Ask students to make *crazy* faces. Say "This is a *crazy* face, this one is *crazier*, and this one is the *craziest!*" Have a puppet act *crazily*.

creaked, creaking ❧ Open a door and pantomime a *creaking* sound. Then say "The door *creaked*."

creasing ❧ Lead the class in folding and *creasing* a piece of paper.

create, creating, created, creative ❧ *Create* a picture. Lead students in *creating* a picture with crayons or colored pencils. Draw a picture on the board. Tell the student to look at what you *created*. Have each student color a picture, using many colors and designs. Compliment their work and express how *creative* they are.

creatures ❧ Point to pictures of animals and say "These are *creatures*."

credit ❧ Set up a scene in which you are a bookstore owner. Have a puppet return a book to you. Hand the puppet a slip of paper that says "*Credit*: $10.00." Say "I can't give you your money back, but I can give you this *credit* slip for $10.00 that you can use to get another book."

creeping, crept ❧ Demonstrate *creeping* in the sense of walking stealthily, slowly, and quietly.

creepy ❧ Show a picture of a *creepy*-looking house. Pantomime feeling *creepy*. Have students pantomime feeling *creepy*.

cremated ❧ Show pictures of funeral pyres. Give example sentences using *cremated*.

crew ❧ Show a picture of a *crew* of a boat, a plane, or a fire truck.

crime ❧ Have a puppet commit a *crime* such as theft. Tell students that the puppet committed a *crime*.

criminology ❧ Demonstrate with two puppets. One is a *criminal* and the other is studying him. Explain that there are people who study *criminals*. They are trying to learn how to stop *crime*.

crinkle, crinkled ❧ *Crinkle* a piece of paper. Have students *crinkle* paper. Lead students in past tense sentences.

crisp ❧ Show a picture of a breakfast cereal, such as corn flakes. Ask if students have ever seen or eaten it. Explain that it is *crisp* until you pour milk on it, then it is *soggy*. Pantomime munching on a *crisp* flake, then pouring milk over the flakes and eating *soggy* ones. You could also demonstrate by breaking *crisp* crackers or potato chips.

crisscrossed ❧ Draw *crisscrossed* lines on the board.

critic, critics, criticized ❧ Have students portray roles in a short pantomime. Pretend to be a *critic* and rate their performances. Ask each student to comment on what he or she liked and disliked about one of the readings. Give example sentences using *critics*. Lead students in sentences using *criticized*.

critters ❧ Show students a few animal pictures. Tell them, "These are *critters*."

croak ❧ Draw or show a picture of a frog. *Croak* like a frog. Have students imitate.

crooked ➠ Draw two lines on the board: a straight one and a *crooked* one.

croon, crooning ➠ *Croon* to a doll or toy animal. Lead students in *crooning*.

crops ➠ Show pictures of *crops*. Have students name some *crops* grown in the region where they live.

cross, crossing, crossed ➠ **1.** Have students *cross* the room or other spaces. Lead them in past tense sentences. Draw a bridge over a river on the board. Have a puppet *cross* the bridge. Say "The puppet is *crossing* the river." **2.** Have one puppet be *cross* with the other. —*crossed out*, write words on the board. Have students *cross* them *out* with a line through them. —*cross-section*, show or draw a *cross-section* of a tree or plant.

crouching, crouched ➠ Lead students in *crouching*. Lead them in past tense sentences.

crowd, crowded ➠ **1.** Show a picture of a *crowd* of people. Or, have a group of students *crowd* together. **2.** Have students all *crowd* into the front section of the classroom. Tell them, "It is *crowded* here." Then have them spread out and say "Now it is not *crowded*."

crucial ➠ Show pictures of emergencies. Ask students to suggest the next course of action. Give example sentences using *crucial*—perhaps "It is *crucial* to put a bandage on the wound."

crude ➠ Make a *crude* drawing of a stick person on the board, then show a very refined drawing of a person. Make a *crude* knot, then show a well-made knot. Show pictures of *crude* houses or clothes and then very *refined* versions of the same things.

cruel ➠ Have a puppet do something *cruel*, such as take another puppet's book. Then have the puppet say it's sorry and do something *kind*, like help the puppet with its homework.

crumple, crumpled ➠ *Crumple* a piece of paper and say that it's *crumpled*.

crunching ➠ Make a *crunching* noise by *crunching* down on dry toast, dry cereal, dry leaves, or walking on some gravel.

crusade, crusading, crusaders ➠ Explain that there are many people who spend their lives working to save something, such as the whales. They are called *crusaders*. They are *crusading*, or on a *crusade*, to save the [whales].

crush ➠ Take a hammer and *crush* some ice.

cry, cried, cries, crying ➠ **1.** *Cry* out with surprise or emotion. Contrast by *saying* the same thing. *Cry* out, "Why do you sit in your chair?" Contrast it with *asking* the same thing. **2.** Lead students in pantomimes of *crying*. Start them by saying, "*Cry*." Stop them and say "You *cried*."

crybaby ➠ Have a puppet whine every time you ask it to do something. Have another puppet say "You are such a *crybaby*!"

cuddle, cuddling ➠ Demonstrate by *cuddling* a doll. Lead students in sentences.

cue ➠ Have one puppet tell another to pop up every time that it gives the *cue* "Pop!" Demonstrate giving the *cue* and having the puppet pop up. Repeat with other *cues*. Give students a *cue*, such as raising your hand and saying, "When I go like this, I want you to stand up." Try various *cues* so that students understand that a *cue* could be many different signals.

culprit ◆ Act out with puppets. Have one puppet cry. Say "Who took [Fuzzy's] book? Come on! Who is the *culprit?*" Have another puppet admit being guilty of the crime and say "I am the *culprit*. I did it."

cultivate ◆ Give attention to a real plant or a drawing of a plant. Pantomime watering and pruning it. Say "I like to *cultivate* plants."

culture ◆ Ask students about special things that people from their family do, have, or believe. Explain these as the things that make up a culture. Talk about your *culture*.

cupful ◆ Show students a *cupful* of paper clips.

curds and whey ◆ If possible, show milk and cottage cheese or fresh feta in whey. Explain that when milk is becoming cheese, part of it turns into *curds* (as in cottage cheese) and part into *whey*. Explain that *whey* is like milk, but more watery and clear. Farmers take the *curds* from the milk and turn them into different kinds of cheeses including cottage cheese.

cure ◆ Have one puppet be a doctor and the other be a sick patient. The doctor gives the sick patient a *cure* (a bottle of medicine).

curious, curiosity ◆ Pick up a backpack. Say "I am *curious*. What do you have in here? Can I look inside? I am so *curious!*" Repeat. Have the puppet try to pry its way into your desk drawer and ask you what's in it. Say "[Muffin], you are so *curious!*" Give example sentences using *curiosity*.

curl, curls ◆ Draw two heads on the board, one with straight hair and the other with *curly* hair. Show the *curls* in the hair. *Curl* a strip of paper with scissors.

curled up ◆ Pantomime rolling yourself up. Say "Now I am *curled up*." *Curl up* a piece of string. Ask students to *curl up* like cats.

currents ◆ Draw a river on the board with various curved lines indicating changes in the flow of the water. Draw a boat on a sheet of paper and make it travel on the river, following in the direction of the curved lines. Say "The boat is moving with the *currents*."

curriculum ◆ Make a list of all the things that students will study in school. Lead students in sentences.

curse, curses ◆ Have one puppet *curse* another, avoiding offensive words. Example *curses* might be, "Phooey on you" or "Darn!"

customer, customers ◆ Set up a scene where you are starting an ice-cream company. Pantomime selling ice-cream cones to each student. Say "I am the store owner; you are the *customer*." Give sentences using *customers*.

customs, customary ◆ **1.** Show pictures of *customs* from other countries. **2.** Ask students to tell you what things the class usually does. Say "These are our *customary* activities."

cut, cutting ❖ *Cut* some paper with your scissors. Lead the students in *cutting* paper. Pantomime *cutting* paper or steak.

cute ❖ Show pictures of *cute* babies or animals.

cycle, cycles ❖ Show students different types of *cycles*; for example, the life *cycle* of an insect, the water *cycle*, and the *cycle* of the school day.

dabbing ❖ Lead students in *dabbing* a paintbrush into some paint.

dabble ❖ Let students *dabble* in some paints and make a picture of a garden.

dainty, daintiness ❖ Describe and show pictures of things that are *dainty*, such as lace handkerchiefs, small flowers, porcelain teacups, or ballerina dolls. Show *dainty* things and animals, such as mice, cats, teacups, tiny toys, etc. Indicate that each thing is *dainty*. Then lead students in sentences: "The *daintiness* of the mouse makes her hard to hear when she walks" or "The *daintiness* of the teacup makes it hard for a big man to hold." Pantomime sentences as needed.

damaged ❖ Use a broken toy, scuffed shoe, or torn paper. Explain that it is *damaged*.

damp ❖ Moisten a paper towel and explain that it is *damp*. Compare with dry and wet paper towels.

Dan ❖ Explain that *Dan* is a boy's name. Write a list of boys' names and include *Dan*.

dance, dancing, danced ❖ *Dance*, and invite students to join you in *dancing*. Then have everyone sit down and say "We *danced*."

danger, dangers, dangerous ❖ Give examples, such as a busy street, hot stove, electrical outlet, etc. Say "You know it is safe to cross the street at a green light. It would be a *danger* to cross when cars are coming. Ask students for other examples. Show illustrations of *dangerous* situations, such as being in a lion's den or on the tracks with a train coming. You can describe *dangerous* actions, such as walking on the train tracks or crossing the street without looking both ways.

dangling ❖ Hook a pen onto a large rubber band. Hold it up so the pen hangs down. Say "The pen is *dangling* from the rubber band."

dare ❖ Act out with a puppet. Have the puppet challenge you to walk across the room with a book balanced on your head. Do it. Then say "I accepted [Fluffy]'s *dare*." —*How dare you!*, check that students understand the individual words in the expression. Have one puppet bump into the other. The first says very indignantly, "*How dare you* bump into me!" Create other similar scenes with lines, such as, "*How dare you* insult me!" "*How dare you* step on my foot!" "*How dare* you take my food!"

dark, darkness ❖ Point out things in the room that have *dark* colors; contrast these with light-colored things. Show pictures of a *dark* night. Give examples of *dark* and *light*: at night it is *dark*, and during the day it is *light*. Turn off the lights. Show pictures of a *dark* night. Show a picture of a cave, and point to the *darkness*.

darn ❖ Drop a book on the floor and say *"Darn!* I dropped the book."

dash, dashing ❖ Mark off a length for students to run. Have them run as fast as they can. Give example sentences using *dash.*

data ❖ Have students list all the planets in our solar system. Have them collect information about butterflies, cats, or dogs. Say "These things are *data."*

date ❖ *—dates,* ask each child to write his or her *date* of birth on the board. Say "I see a lot of *dates."* Point to different *dates* on the calendar.

daughter ❖ Show a picture of *parents* and their *daughter.* Explain that females are *daughters* of their parents and males are *sons.* Draw a *daughter* with her *parents* and a *son* with his *parents* on the board.

daughter-in-law ❖ Draw a family tree on the board. Explain that a *daughter-in-law* is the wife of a mother/father's son.

dawdle, dawdling, dawdled ❖ Tell a puppet to follow along, and have it do so in a *dawdling* manner. Tell the puppet not to *dawdle* and have it follow more swiftly. Have students pair up and repeat. Lead students in past tense sentences.

dawn ❖ Show pictures of the sun rising and explain that this time of day is called *dawn.*

day ❖ Show pictures of *day* and *night.* Explain that now it is *day,* and that at bedtime, it will be *night.* Explain that we go to school during the *day,* and we sleep at *night.* Explain that Monday, Tuesday, and so on are *days.* Show a *calendar.*

daydream, daydreaming ❖ Draw on the board a stick figure with a cartoonist's balloon connected to it. Draw something that the figure is *daydreaming* about, perhaps a football or a doll, inside the balloon. Explain that when you are thinking about something that you wish for, it is called a *daydream.*

dead ❖ Have a puppet die melodramatically. Tell students that the puppet is *dead.*

deaf ❖ Have students plug their ears and whisper something so they can't hear you. Say "People who are *deaf* can't hear anything."

deal ❖ **1.** Ask a student to carry a large stack of books across the room. Say "Can you handle all those books? That is a lot of books to *deal* with." **2.** *Deal* cards in a game of Go Fish. *—great deal,* check that students understand the individual words in the expression. Then show students a *great deal* of pencils, paper clips, or paper and contrast by showing small amounts of the same.

dear ❖ Hold a doll and call it *dear.* Make clear the meaning of *dear* as "beloved" and "cherished." *—Oh dear!,* lead students in dramatizing being upset and saying, *"Oh dear!"*

debris ❖ Show pictures of *debris* from hurricanes, tornadoes, or other natural disasters. Give examples sentences.

deceit, deceived, deceitful ❖ Have a puppet steal something from another puppet. Then have the thief say that it didn't do it and pretend to help it find it.

Tell students, "The puppet is showing *deceit*." Lead them in similar examples and sentences: "The puppet is *deceitful*." "The puppet *deceived* me."

decent ◆ Use puppets to demonstrate *decent* acts, such as helping somebody to cross a street or holding a door for somebody with packages. Have them take turns performing *decent* acts for each other.

decide, decided, decision ◆ Offer a student a choice of pencils. Ask him or her to *decide* which one he or she wants. Once the student has chosen, tell him or her, "You *decided* on this one." Repeat with other things, such as colored paper or erasers. Talk about *decisions* that students have made. Tell them about *decisions* you have made. If needed, pantomime a puppet making a *decision* over which pencil or pen to use for his lesson or where to go for a vacation.

decipher ◆ Write something illegible on the board. Say "Can anyone figure this out? Can anyone *decipher* it?"

decode ◆ Write something on a sheet of paper with reversed letters. Ask students whether they can read it. Say "We need to figure out how to read this. Aha! I know how to *decode* it! We'll hold the message up to a mirror and read the reflection." Demonstrate.

decorate, decorating, decorated ◆ Help students to *decorate* a piece of paper with glitter or other art supplies. Explain that *decorating* a room means "to make it look nice." Talk about how you have *decorated* the classroom. Point out clothes that are *decorated* with designs or glitter. Contrast with *plain* clothing.

decreased ◆ Put a pile of pencils on your desk. Invite each student to take some. Say "I had a lot of pencils. After you took some, my number of pencils *decreased*."

decree ◆ Pretending to read from a large sheet of paper, give students simple commands to execute, such as, "Sit down," "Stand up," and so on. Explain that you have given them orders. Explain that a *decree* is also an order, normally written down. Give examples of classroom rules and explain that these are similar to a *decree* because they are your orders written down.

dedicate, dedicated ◆ **1.** See *consecrate*. Set up a space for display of student work. Give example sentences using *dedicate*. **2.** Show students an example of a poem in their textbook. Ask them to pretend they had written it, and ask them to write down the name of someone they love to whom they would want to address their poem. Say "To show your love and honor for this person, you have *dedicated* a poem to [her]." Suggest other things that can be *dedicated* (songs, stories, performances, etc.).

deduction ◆ Write a pattern, such as "2, 4, 6, 8, __, __, __" on the board. Have a puppet solve the problem by filling in "10, 12, 14" in the blank spaces. Say "That was an excellent *deduction*."

deed, deeds ◆ Have a puppet help a blind person across the street. Tell students that it did a good *deed*. Show other examples and lead students in sentences. Ask students to name things that would be nice to do for others, such as holding a door open, picking up something that dropped, or giving someone the first turn at something. Then say "Yes. Those are nice things to do for other people. Those are good *deeds*."

deep, deeper, deepest, deeply, depth ◆ **1.** Draw on the board containers that are *shallow*, *deep*, *deeper*, and *deepest*. **2.** Reach *deeply* into a box. **3.** Place water in a glass and measure its *depth*.

defeat, defeated, defeatist ◆ **1.** Ask for two volunteers. Have them pantomime a short game of "trash can ball" (tossing a balled-up piece of paper into the trash). Announce the winner and loser. Explain that the winner had to *defeat* the loser to win. Repeat, but this time have students reverse roles so that each gets to be a winner. Challenge a puppet to an arm wrestling match. When you have won, say "I *defeated* the puppet." **2.** See *attitude*. Use the first puppet as an example.

defending, defensively ◆ **1.** Use pictures from history of *defending* armies. Lead students in sentences. **2.** Have one puppet greet another pleasantly. Have the other respond *defensively*.

defiance, defiant ◆ Ask a puppet to do something. Have the puppet say "no" very *defiantly*. Act out a scene in which you are enforcing a rule and students resist and oppose you. Say "The students were *defiant*."

defining ◆ Explain to students that when you teach them a new word, you are *defining* it.

degree ◆ Take a magnifying glass and have students look at different objects. Tell students that how big or little something looks indicates the *degree* of the magnification.

delay, delayed ◆ **1.** Divide students into two groups. Give them an assignment. Have one group begin immediately, and *delay* the other for a count of ten. **2.** Pantomime a scene where students are waiting for a bus that has been *delayed*.

deliberately ◆ Have a mess on your desk. Pantomime getting an idea. Walk *deliberately* to your desk and clean up the mess.

delicious ◆ Show pictures of a cake and pantomime eating it. Tell them, "This tastes very good. It is *delicious*."

delight, delighted, delightful ◆ Lead students in looking as if they feel *delight*. Have students say things that they are *delighted* to do; for example, "I am *delighted* to help my mother cook." Lead students in looking *delightful*. Show them pictures of things that they would consider *delightful*. With each picture that you show, say "This is a *delightful* picture of snow" or "These kittens are *delightful*."

delirious, deliriously ◆ Show a puppet sick and with a high fever. Have the puppet mumble things *deliriously*. Explain to the class that it is making no sense because it is *delirious*.

delivery, delivering, delivered ◆ **1.** Ask a student to take a paper clip to another student. Say "[Anabel] *delivered* the paper clip" and "[Tran] is *delivering* the paper clip." **2.** Show an illustration of a *delivery* man. Demonstrate *delivering* something by bringing toys, books, or papers to each student. Say to each recipient, "Here is your *delivery*."

demand, demands, demanding, demanded ◆ **1.** Hold up a desirable item, such as a sticker. Say "Who wants a sticker?" When students indicate their desire for stickers, say "You each want a sticker. There are [5] of you, and I have only [3] stickers. Your *demand* for stickers is greater than my supply." **2.** Make some *demands* of students. You can begin by saying, "I am *demanding* . . . ." *Demand* something and contrast that with asking politely. Lead students in past tense sentences.

democracy ◆ Pantomime *democracy* (where students vote for a president and vote on a few laws for their country).

demons ◆ Draw or show pictures of *demons*.

dent, dents, dented ◆ Show a *dented* soda can. Point to each *dent*.

deny ◆ Have one puppet accuse the other: "You took my book!" Have the other puppet *deny* it. Repeat with other accusations.

department ◆ Draw the floor plans of a grocery store on the board. Have students help you name different kinds of food. Write the *department* names in squares on the floor plan. Lead students in sentences.

depend, depending, depended ◆ **1.** Engage students in a discussion of what they need from their parents, such as love, respect, encouragement, food, shelter, clothing, etc. Say "You need your parents for all these things. You *depend* on your parents to give you what you need. I *depended* upon my parents for the same things." **2.** Tell students that they are *depending* on the weather to be sunny so they can go outside, or that they are *depending* on the teacher to help them understand the lesson.

depression ◆ Make a nest out of some clothing or use modeling clay. Make a *depression* with your fist. Say "I made a *depression* in the clay with my fist."

deserts, deserting, deserted, desertion ◆ Set up a scene where puppets or toys are soldiers in a war and one of them *deserts*. Say "The soldier *deserted*." Or, show pictures of battles. On the board, draw a person *deserting*. Give example sentences using *desertion*.

deserve ◆ Have a puppet help you clean your desk. Give it a sticker and say "You *deserve* this."

design ◆ Show a *design* for a house. Ask each student to make a *design* for a dream house.

despair ◆ Use one of your toy soldiers to show this concept. Have it be surrounded by enemy soldiers. Have it first try to fight back and then give up in *despair*.

desperate, desperation ◆ **1.** Draw a picture of the sun on the board. Pantomime being really thirsty. Act *desperate* for a drink. Have a glass of water. **2.** Tell students that out of *desperation* to win the game the player threw the ball the full length of the field.

destination ❖ Show students on a map the starting point and end point of a trip you took. For example, say "Last summer I traveled from Los Angeles to Mexico City. Mexico City was my *destination*."

destroy, destroyed ❖ Have a puppet *destroy* a piece of paper. Then say to the puppet, "Do not *destroy* the paper." Build a tower out of blocks. Have a puppet knock it over. Say indignantly, "[King Kong]! You *destroyed* my tower!"

details ❖ Show the *details* in some illustrations. Have students help you inspect something closely, perhaps a painting, and lead them in finding *details* in it.

detain ❖ Ask a student to pantomime making a trip across the room to the door. Stop the student about halfway to the door. Say "I need to stop you on your way to the door. I must *detain* you and ask you a few questions."

detect ❖ Ask a student to hide something from your desk while your back is turned. Then examine your desk and *detect* that something is gone.

deter ❖ Have a puppet run toward the door. *Deter* it.

determine, determined ❖ **1.** Write an arithmetic problem on the board. Say "I'm having trouble with this; who can help me *determine* the answer?" **2.** Have a puppet try to push something larger than itself up an incline. Have it have a difficult time, but continue pushing until the object is at the top. Give example sentences. Pantomime a scene with a puppet struggling to write his name on the board. Tell the class, "This is hard for the puppet to do, but it is *determined* to do it." Have the puppet complete the task.

detract ❖ **1.** Draw a house and lawn on the board. Invite students to draw things that would add to its beauty, such as flowers. Then invite them to draw things that would *detract* from its beauty, such as weeds, garbage, etc. Give example sentences. **2.** Lead the class in a short discussion about what they will do at recess. Have a puppet offer negative comments that *detract* from the discussion.

develop, develops, developing, developed, development ❖ **1.** Show *development* sequences. Show illustrations of how a seed *develops* into a plant, a baby *develops* into a person, and so on. Show pictures of baby animals *developing* into adult animals. Lead students in past tense sentences. **2.** Point out countries on the globe that are growing and changing. Say, for example, "[names of countries] are growing and improving. They are *developing*."

devise, devised ❖ Divide students into groups. Ask each group to *devise* plans for getting their homework done for a week. Lead students in past tense sentences.

devote, devoted, devotion ❖ **1.** Have a puppet *devote* itself to an activity such as reading. Demonstrate how *devoted* the puppet is by calling upon students to ask the puppet to join them in something else. Each time the puppet can respond that it wants to read. Explain that the puppet wants to *devote* himself to his reading. **2.** Ask students about something they really like to do more than anything else. Lead students in sentences using *devoted*. **3.** Give each student a puppet or doll and ask them to act out how they show love to friends and family members.

devoured ➡ Have a puppet eat some paper clips on your desk. Then have the puppet *devour* the paper clips on your desk. Lead students in past tense sentences.

dialing, dialed ➡ Show a rotary-*dial* telephone. Pantomime or demonstrate *dialing* a telephone. Lead students in past tense sentences.

diameter ➡ Draw a circle on the board. Draw a horizontal line through the center of the circle. Point to the line and say "*Diameter.*" Have students imitate.

dickory ➡ Explain that *dickory* doesn't mean anything, but it sounds fun.

did ➡ **1.** *Did* is the past tense of *do.* Lead students in making sentences such as "I *did* not talk" or "You *did* not give me a present." Make example sentences, such as, "I *did* a dive," "I *did* a spin," and "I *did* a jump." **2.** Ask students questions using *did,* such as," *Did* you eat?" or "*Did* you read?" Lead them in asking such questions. —*did it,* have one puppet try to reach something repeatedly and finally *do it.* Have another puppet say "You *did it!*" Repeat with various other efforts, such as lifting a book or throwing a paper into the waste-paper basket. —*didn't,* show on the board how *did* and *not* squeeze together to make the word *didn't.* See *did* and *not.*

die, dying, died ➡ Use dolls or puppets to dramatize *dying.* —*die out,* review *extinct* and explain that *died out* is another word for *extinct.*

dietician ➡ Tell the students that a *dietician* is a person who is in charge of planning proper meals for people. If possible, introduce the class to the school *dietician.*

difference ➡ Contrast. Place your two hands on a desk: one, palm up; the other, palm down. Say "What is the *difference* between my hands?" Repeat with other items, such as pencils, books, etc.

different, differently ➡ **1.** Ask students to give you a book. Then, ask for a *different* book. Show students some crayons and tell them that each one is *different.* Show them shapes or draw shapes on the board and tell them that each one is *different.* Then, show them crayons and shapes that are the *same.* **2.** Have students find things that are *different* and the *same.* **3.** Ask a student to stand on one foot. Explain to the class that you will now have him or her stand *differently,* and ask the student to stand on two feet.

difficult ➡ Write a word that is *difficult* to pronounce on the board. Contrast with one that is *easy* to pronounce. Write two arithmetic problems on the board—one very simple, the other complex. Say "This arithmetic problem is *easy*; this one is *difficult.*"

diffusion ➡ Mix salt into a glass of warm water. Show the *diffusion* of the salt into the water.

dig, digging, dug ➡ *Dig* a hole in a flowerpot. Lead students in pantomiming *digging.* Show a picture of a hole in the ground and a shovel. Pantomime *digging* a hole with the shovel. Have students do the same. Help students to make past tense sentences. —*dug up,* bury an eraser in a flowerpot or under a pile of paper or books. Then *dig* it *up.* Lead students in past tense sentences.

dignity ❯ Read a poem in a silly way. Then read the same poem with *dignity*. Give example sentences.

dilemma ❯ Give students two equal choices about something pleasant, such as choosing whether to have an ice-cream party or a pizza party. Give example sentences using *dilemma*.

dim, dimming ❯ Hold up a coat toward the light source and say "This will *dim* the light and make it less bright." Say "I am *dimming* the light."

diminished ❯ Have a full glass of water. Drink some and say "The water has *diminished*."

din ❯ Have students pound on their desks and yell or act this out with a puppet.

dining, dined ❯ Show people *dining*. Use *dined* in sentences.

dinner ❯ Show puppets having *dinner*. Tell students that *dinner* is the largest meal of the day.

dip, dips, dipping, dipped ❯ **1.** Lead students in standing and *dipping*. Have a student *dip* and say "He or she *dips*." **2.** Demonstrate *dipping* a pencil into water. Lead students in past tense sentences.

direct, directs, direction, directions ❯ *Direct* students around the room. Play "Simon Says." After a few turns, say "Simon *directs* your movements." Give students a series of *directions*. Have students walk in different *directions*. Each time say "You are walking in the *direction* of the [door]."

dirty, dirtied ❯ **1.** *Dirty* your hands with chalk. Lead students in sentences, such as, "I did not want to *dirty* my hands" or "Did you *dirty* your shoes?" Lead students in past tense sentences. **2.** Show students *clean* and *dirty* things.

disadvantage ❯ See *advantage*.

disappear, disappearing, disappeared ❯ Make pencils or erasers *disappear* off your desk. Demonstrate *appearing* and *disappearing* with the puppet. Show something to students, then quickly hide it. Say that it has *disappeared*. Repeat with *disappearance*. Make a puppet *disappear*. Then, ask students to help you find him. Explain that his *disappearance* has worried you.

disappoint, disappointment ❯ **1.** Draw a can of soda on a sign with a line through it. Give a student a can, look at the sign, and then take the soda back and say "I am sorry to *disappoint* you." **2.** Pantomime excitement about an envelope with your name on it. Open it and find it empty. Pantomime *disappointment*.

disapprove ❯ Have two puppets engaging in a loud conversation. Frown and shake your head "no." Say "I *disapprove*."

disaster ❯ Show pictures of *disasters*. Point to each and say "This is a *disaster*."

discomfort ❯ Have a puppet sit in *comfort*, perhaps on your lap. Contrast by having the puppet sit on something *uncomfortable*, perhaps the stapler. Then have the puppet say "I am not *comfortable*; I am sitting in *discomfort*."

disconnect ❯ See *connect*.

disconsolate, disconsolately ◆ Have a puppet be very sad over a loss of a toy or other item. Explain to the class that it is *disconsolate* or very sad. Speak to the class *disconsolately*. Have students speak to you *disconsolately*. Contrast by speaking *ecstatically*.

discontented ◆ Have one puppet happily playing with its things and talking about how it doesn't need anything else. Have another puppet be unsatisfied with its toys, and angry that it does not have more. Make contrasting sentences: "It is *contented* with its toys" and "It is *discontented* with its toys."

discontinue ◆ Once students understand *continue*, begin to read to them, and then tell them that you must *discontinue* reading. Then have a puppet play with toys and say to the puppet, "You must *discontinue* playing with toys at school." Ask a student to tell a story, and mid-story ask him to *discontinue* it. Remind students that *dis-* means "not."

discord, discords ◆ **1.** Set up the scene where students are to place their desks in a circle. Have them work against each other, creating *discord*. **2.** Have students voice their opinion on a given topic loudly, continuously, and all at the same time to create *discords*.

discouraged ◆ Demonstrate trying unsuccessfully to do something, such as whistling. Say "I just can't whistle. I'm feeling *discouraged*."

discover, discovered, discovery, discoveries ◆ *Discover* something in your desk drawer and act surprised at your *discovery*. Have students *discover* something new that they haven't noticed before in a picture. Lead students in past tense sentences. Have a puppet make *discoveries* about how something works. Perhaps a puppet could explore a pencil sharpener or stapler.

discredited ◆ Act the role of the astronomer Copernicus. Draw the solar system on the board and explain that the planets orbit the sun. Have students shout, "No! The sun orbits the planets!" Then say "For a long time, nobody believed Copernicus; they *discredited* his theory."

disease, diseases ◆ List some of the *diseases* that students may have heard about: cancer, heart *disease*, diabetes, etc. Explain that sometimes people die of these *diseases*, and sometimes they can survive with them or be cured of them.

disguise, disguised ◆ *Disguise* yourself by putting on a hat, glasses, etc.

disinfected ◆ Have each student draw and cut out a germ. Spread the germs on a desk. Draw a bottle of bleach on the board. Pantomime pouring bleach on a sponge and wiping down the desk, knocking the germs to the floor. Say "I wiped the desk with bleach and got rid of all the germs that could make us sick; I *disinfected* the desk."

disintegrate ◆ Dunk a tissue in water. Show students how the paper falls apart. Lead students in sentences using *disintegrate*.

dislike ◆ Hold up something that you *like* and something that you *dislike*. Pantomime your *like* and *dislike*. Lead students in pantomiming their *like* and *dislike* of various things.

disloyal ◆ See *loyal*.

dismayed ◆ Ask students to describe examples of bad news, such as a house fire, a car accident, or a death in the family. Say "Yes. That would be terrible news. I would feel *dismayed* if that happened to someone I know."

dismissal ◆ Draw a bell. Pretend to ring it and make a ringing sound. Say "Did you hear the *dismissal* bell? You are *dismissed*. Good-bye!"

disobedience ◆ Tell a puppet to sit down and make the puppet *disobey* you. Give example sentences using *disobedience*.

disown ◆ Have one puppet drop a piece of paper. Have a second puppet pick the paper up and try to give it back. Have the first puppet act like it has never seen it.

dispatch ◆ Ask a student to deliver a note to the main office. Say "I need to send [Alex] out quickly to deliver this message to the office. I need to *dispatch* [Alex] to deliver this message."

disperse ◆ See *gather*.

displace, displaced ◆ Show a picture of people leaving their ruined homes because of war or natural disaster. Explain that the people were *displaced* because of this.

display, displayed ◆ *Display* a variety of pictures to students. Have students *display* the contents of their desks or pockets to each other. Lead students in past tense sentences.

disprove ◆ Have a puppet *disprove* something that you said, perhaps an incorrect hair color.

dispute, disputed ◆ Have puppets *dispute* over who knocked down the tower of blocks. Tell students, "The puppets *disputed* over the blocks falling down." Lead them in sentences.

dissatisfied ◆ See *discontented*.

distant ◆ Place some items *close* to you and others far away. Say "These objects are *close* to me. Those are *distant*."

distinctly ◆ Contrast using puppets. Have one puppet mumble, and the other puppet speak *distinctly*. Ask someone to take off his or her eyeglasses. Say "Can you see me *distinctly*?" When the student has replaced the eyeglasses, ask the question again.

distraught ◆ Pantomime hunting for something that you have lost and feeling *distraught* because you can't find it.

distress ◆ Have a puppet pantomime *distress* over taking a test. Have the puppet say "Taking tests causes me *distress*."

disturb, disturbing, disturbance ◆ Using puppets, have one *disturb* the other. Say that one is *disturbing* the other. Lead students in creating a *disturbance* in the classroom (noisy chatter, walking around, etc.).

ditch ◆ Show students a picture of a *ditch*, or draw one on the board. Demonstrate the concept further by having a toy truck drive into an imaginary *ditch*.

dive, diving, dives ◆ Draw a pool of water on the board. Pantomime *diving* into the water. Say "The teacher *dives* into the water." Have students pretend to *dive* into water.

diverse ◆ Contrast with two puppets. Have one tell of its *diverse* hobbies, while the other tells about the only hobby it has.

division ◆ Demonstrate a *division* problem on the board. Have students recite simple *division* facts.

divorce ◆ On the board, draw a groom and a bride. Draw a line from each one going in the opposite direction. Lead students in sentences using *divorce*.

dizzy, dizzier ◆ Ask a student to twirl around until he or she becomes *dizzy*. Then have him or her twirl a bit more, so that he or she becomes *dizzier*.

do ◆ Have a puppet ask the other, "*Do* you like cake?" The second answers, "I *do!*" Continue asking similar questions that can be answered with, "I *do!*" —*do the trick*, snap a pencil in two pieces and say that you will fix it. Use some scotch tape and tape it back together. Tell students, "That will *do the trick*." Repeat with other examples. —*does*, *does* is a helping verb. Have students practice sentences, such as "The clock *does* not work" or "Where *does* your father work?" —*done*, draw a heart or other shape on the board. Explain that you are starting to draw it. Then when you finish it, say that it's *done*. Have students draw shapes on paper and raise their hands when they are *done*. Pick up some books and put them away. Say "*Done.*" Repeat for other items that need to be put away. Have students join in.

dock ◆ Show a picture of a boat and a *dock*. Explain that after the boat comes up to the *dock*, it has *docked*. Compare to the concept of parking a car if needed.

documented ◆ Ask two students to pantomime shopping at the grocery store. Follow along, taking notes of all that they bought. Explain to the class that you *documented* their trip to the store.

dodge ◆ Have students toss wadded bits of paper at a puppet or toy animal. Have the puppet or toy animal *dodge* the wadded bits by moving quickly out of the way. Pantomime with a puppet or doll *dodging* out of the way of a crumpled paper ball.

does ◆ *Does* is a helping verb. Have students practice sentences, such as, "The clock *does* not work" or "Where *does* your father work?" Also, see *do*.

doggoned ◆ Ask student volunteers to tell you something they think you don't know. Act surprised and say "Well, I'll be *doggoned*. I never knew that!"

dog's ◆ See *animal's*.

dolly ◆ Show a picture of a *dolly* and explain that it is used to help move things, such as refrigerators. Show a refrigerator if needed.

domestic, domesticated ◆ 1. Ask students to help you make two lists of work they do: one comprised of chores they do at home, the other of school or other outside work (such as a newspaper route or baby-sitting). Say "Things like emptying the trash are jobs you do at home; they are *domestic* chores."

2. Have students help you make two columns of animals: one wild animals, the other pets or *domesticated* animals."

dominance ◆ On the board, draw a hierarchy of governments in this country with the federal government on top, state governments underneath, and city governments underneath the state. Label each level. Say "The federal government has *dominance* over the other two."

donated ◆ Have students help you make a list of the things they would give to a homeless person. Say "We *donated* many useful things to the homeless people."

donkey's ◆ See *animal's.*

doom, doomed ◆ Show pictures of marching soldiers and explain that they are going to fight, and they may die in the fighting; they are walking to their *doom.* Pile up a lot of books. Say "I have to read all these today. I am *doomed* to fail. I cannot read that fast."

dope ◆ Have a puppet walk into a wall or bookshelf. Say "Only a *dope* would do that!"

dot, dots ◆ Make some *dots* on the board, and have students make *dots* on paper.

double, doubled ◆ Make a pile of paper clips on your desk. *Double* it. Say "I *doubled* the paper clips."

double take ◆ Walk by a student's desk and glance at him or her nonchalantly. Then stop suddenly and turn your head sharply to look at the student a second time. Say "When I saw [Tran]'s [red shirt], I did a *double take!*" Have students imitate.

double yuk ◆ —*double yuk,* have students help you make a list of foods they dislike and a list of foods they hate. Write "*Yuk*" on top of one list; "*Yuk Yuk*" on top of the other. Say "You don't like [lima beans]. *Yuk!* But you hate [brussels sprouts]. *Double yuk!*" Have students imitate.

doubt ◆ Have a puppet stand on the edge of your desk. Have him hesitate and say "I *doubt* if I can make it," while getting ready to jump to the closest student desk.

dough ◆ Show pictures of different types of *dough.*

down ◆ **1.** Contrast *up* with *down,* pointing or reaching *up* and *down.* **2.** Draw a line on the board to represent a track. Explain that toward the end of the line is *down* the track. **3.** Demonstrate walking *down* the mountain with your fingers. —*down,* draw a picture of a road on the board and have a toy animal walk *down* the road on the board. **4.** Show how a pencil stood on end or other objects can be knocked *down.* **5.** Show pictures of the soft feathers of a chick and explain that this is *down.* Explain that big birds have short, soft feathers called *down* under their bigger feathers.

downcast ◆ Contrast examples of praise and criticism. Praise a puppet and have it show the class that it feels good. Criticize the puppet and have it show a *downcast* mannerism. Identify each emotion as the puppet displays them.

downstairs ◆ If the building you are in has *stairs,* show students the *downstairs* area. If you are not in a building with *stairs,* show pictures of *stairs* or draw them on the board and explain.

downtown ❖ On a city map, show *downtown*. Contrast with *outskirts*.

downwind ❖ Have students gather to one side of the drawing and blow to create "wind." Stand on the other side. Sniff as if smelling something, and say "I can feel the wind because I am standing *downwind*."

drag, dragging, dragged ❖ *Drag* a book across your desk. Lead students in *dragging* a book across their desks. Have a student *drag* a chair across the room.

dragon ❖ As you show a picture of a *dragon*, explain to students that *dragons* are supposed to be brave. If somebody says that you are a *dragon*, then you are being brave.

drama, dramatize, dramatically ❖ **1.** Give examples of *dramas* on TV. Ask students to name *dramas* they have seen. **2.** Have students pretend to be actors performing in a play. Explain to them that plays are also called *dramas*. Show pictures of people on stage. **3.** Divide students into two groups. Ask one group to write a word. Ask the other group to *dramatize* the meaning of the word. **4.** Pantomime expressing yourself *dramatically*.

drastic, drastically ❖ Make a tiny cut on a piece of paper, then make a *drastic* cut. Write a sloppy letter on the board; follow it with a *drastic* improvement. Make a quiet sound; then make that same sound *drastically* louder.

Drat! ❖ Have a puppet fall down or drop something and say "*Drat!*"

draw, drew ❖ Have students *draw* a few shapes or a picture. Contrast with having them write their name or a short sentence. *Draw* a picture on the board. Tell students that you *drew*. Ask them to *draw*. When they are done, admire their work, saying, "Look at what you *drew*."

dread, dreadful ❖ **1.** Bring pictures of monsters, such as Frankenstein or Godzilla. Pantomime *dread* and lead students in sentences using *dreadful*. **2.** Contrast with *good* or *wonderful*. Show a student a nice drawing; say it is *wonderful*. Hastily scribble a drawing, and tell students, "This is *dreadful*." Repeat with other examples, such as pictures of *wonderful* and *dreadful* people, a *wonderful* countryside and a littered landscape, etc.

dream, dreams, dreamers ❖ **1.** On the board, draw a picture of someone sleeping. Draw a bubble above the head with a dog or cat in it. Explain that *dreams* are stories you see when you are asleep. Explain about seeing pictures and stories when one sleeps. Ask students if they have *dreamed*. **2.** Explain that *dream* also means "an idea that one has when one is awake." It is something one really wants. For example, a child might have the *dream* of getting a bicycle for Christmas. Parents might have the *dream* of a nice house. Ask a student if he or she has a *dream*. Have one puppet talk to another, telling it what it wants to do when it grows up. Have the other puppet answer, "You have nice *dreams*." Repeat this dialogue with students. You may want to tell students your *dreams* too. **3.** Lead students in a discussion of wishes and *dreams*. For example, say "We wish nobody would ever have to be hungry, cold, lonely, or without a home. These are some of our dreams for the people of the world." Explain that when you *dream*, you are a *dreamer*.

drench, drenched ➧ *Drench* a paper towel or sponge and explain that it is *drenched.*

dress, dressing, dressed ➧ **1.** Show a picture of a *dress.* **2.** *Dress* a puppet. Explain that you are *dressing* the puppet. Lead students in past tense sentences. **3.** Describe how you and the students are *dressed.*

drift, drifts, drifted ➧ **1.** Place a scrap of paper in a shallow container of water. Gently blow on the paper and show students how it *drifts.* Lead students in past tense sentences. Have students draw and cut out leaves. Have them hold their leaves up high and drop them. Say "Look at the way your leaf *drifts* to the ground." **2.** Show snow *drifts. Drift* around the classroom. Explain that when someone *drifts,* he or she is not headed in any direction. This is why mounds of snow are called *drifts.* The wind pushes the snow, and the snow stops when the wind stops.

drills ➧ Have students do math fact *drills.*

drink ➧ *Drink* from a glass. Lead students in sentences and pantomimes.

drip, dripping, drips ➧ *Drip* some water from a glass. Turn the tap on so that it *drips.* Explain that the water is *dripping.*

drive, driving, drove ➧ **1.** Draw or show a picture of a car. Pantomime *driving* it, and explain that you *drove* it. **2.** Have a puppet *drive* another puppet away. Explain that the puppet *drove* it away.

droning ➧ Repeat the following sentences in dull monotone: "I'm so tired. I need to sleep. I am *droning* on and on."

drool, drooling ➧ Show pictures of dogs and babies. Point to their mouths and describe *drool,* unless you can find a picture of a *drooling* dog or baby. Tell them that dogs and babies *drool.* Ask if any have seen this.

droop, droopy ➧ **1.** Have your hand *droop* down. Lead the children in making their arms *droop.* **2.** Show pictures of animals with *droopy* ears or trees with *droopy* limbs. Contrast with pictures of animals and trees that do not *droop.*

drop, dropping, droppings, dropped ➧ **1.** *Drop* a pencil. **2.** Have a puppet tell a second to *drop* something that it is holding. Lead students in past tense sentences. **3.** Lead students in *dropping* something onto their desks. **4.** Show *droppings* from a classroom pet if you have one. —*drop in,* pantomime going to visit a friend, saying that you *dropped in* to say hello.

drought ➧ Show pictures of deserts and explain that they are dry because there is very little or no rain. Explain that when other places get very little rain, people say they are having a *drought.*

drown ➧ Explain that to *drown* is to die from breathing water and not having air.

drowsy, drowsily ➧ Have a puppet be *drowsy.* Tell students that it is *drowsy.* Repeat with students performing the pantomime and saying sentences.

drudge, drudges ➧ Set up a scene where students are menial laborers in a rock quarry. Explain that people who do this type of labor are called *drudges.*

drum, drummed ❖ Have students *drum* their fingers on their desk. Lead them in past tense sentences.

dry, dried, drier ❖ **1.** Touch your tongue. Say "*Wet*, not *dry*." Touch lots of *dry* things and say "*Dry*, not *wet*. **2.** Free from moisture. Get a cup of hot water, coffee, or tea and show students the steam rising from it. Explain that this makes the air *wet* or humid. Explain that when there is not a lot of water in the air, we say that the air is *dry*. Point to *dried* flowers or herbs. **3.** *Wet* something with water and then *dry* it with a paper towel. Show students that first it was *wet* and now it is *dry*. **4.** Demonstrate with water and construction paper. Sprinkle a lot of water on one sheet of paper, a little on a second sheet, and leave one sheet dry. Say "This sheet of paper is very *wet*; this one is a little *drier*; and this one is *dry*."

ducking, ducked ❖ Have puppets *duck* as you toss a wadded piece of paper their way. Help students to make past tense sentences using *ducking* and *ducked*.

due ❖ Have one puppet tell a second puppet that homework is *due* today, library books are *due*, or money is *due*, and have the second puppet deliver what is *due*.

duet ❖ Sing a song by yourself. Say "I am singing by myself. I am singing a *solo*." Then ask a student to sing with you. Say "The two of us are singing together. We are singing a *duet*."

duke ❖ Show an illustration of a *duke*. Explain that a *duke* is like a prince.

dull, dullness ❖ **1.** Show a shiny surface, then a *dull* surface, and say "This is shiny." "This is *dull*." **2.** Turn off the lights in the room and say "The *dullness* of the light in the room makes it hard to read."

dump, dumps, dumping, dumped ❖ **1.** Show the wastepaper basket. Explain that it contains trash, and that the place where we put all the trash collected from buildings and homes is called the *dump*. Show pictures of a *dump* if possible. **2.** *Dump* some paper clips or pencils out of a container. Lead students in *dumping* something from a cup or other container. Help them with past tense sentences. Use a toy *dump* truck and show how it *dumps* things.

durable ❖ Show students something you have had for a long time that has withstood a lot of wear and tear. Say, for example, "I have used this [briefcase] every day for a long time, and it's still as good as new. This is a very *durable* [briefcase]."

during ❖ Discuss different things that students do *during* recess or lunch. Contrast and compare with *before* and *after*.

dust, dusty, dusting ❖ **1.** Wipe a *dusty* surface with a white paper towel. Show the *dust*. Show a picture of a *dusty* road. If not available, draw a stick figure walking down a road. Draw little clouds of *dust* near its feet. **2.** Demonstrate *dusting*.

Dutch ❖ On a globe, show Holland. Say "People from Holland are called *Dutch*."

duty, duties ❖ **1.** Explain *duties* as those things that a person must do: "It is my *duty* to help you learn." "It is your *duty* to learn." Use other examples and sentences. Ask students to tell about a *duty* they perform at home. **2.** Give examples of your responsibilities as a teacher, such as cafeteria *duty*, bus *duty*, and so forth. **3.** Mention or show some *duties* of a student, such as the duties of a paper monitor or other positions within the classroom.

dwarf ◆ Draw or show a picture of a *dwarf* rabbit, a common white rabbit, and a giant rabbit.

dwell, dwelling ◆ **1.** Ask students to say where they live. Have them reply, "I *dwell* at [address]." **2.** Draw a house on the board and describe its features as you add windows, a door, and a chimney. Say "A *dwelling* is our house."

dye ◆ Put ink on a piece of wool. Explain that *dye* is used to give color to things.

each ◆ Give *each* student a paper clip. Then have some students give theirs back so that *each* student no longer has a paper clip. Pantomime this with other objects.

eager, eagerly ◆ **1.** Color as if you were *eager* to do so. Then color as if you are unwilling to do so. **2.** Demonstrate doing something *eagerly*, such as coloring. Then do the same thing against your will. **3.** Have a puppet tidy up your desktop *eagerly* and then *begrudgingly*. **4.** Pantomime looking outside *eagerly*. Say "I am *eagerly* waiting for recess."

early, earlier, earliest ◆ **1.** Give examples to reflect your actual schedule: If students come to school at 7:45, they would come *early*. Or, if they left school at 1:30, they would leave *early*. **2.** Use an alarm clock and set the alarm to go off at a specific time. Have three students arrive at your desk *early*, *earlier*, and *earliest*. Demonstrate with *puppets* if needed. **3.** Write a column of centuries on the board: 2000, 1900, 1800, etc. Draw a line under the *earliest*.

earn, earning, earned, earnings ◆ **1.** Have students pretend to work, perhaps washing their desks. When they are done, tell them they *earned* a sticker. **2.** Discuss with students jobs that they have done to *earn* money. Use the word *earn* to describe this activity. Give example sentences for *earning* and *earned*. **3.** Hand out pennies to students and set up a pretend lemonade stand. Have students buy cups of lemonade. Count your pennies. Say "I have taken in 23 cents with my lemonade business today. My *earnings* for the day are 23 cents." **4.** Have students create a little bazaar, selling items to each other with play money. Then have them count their *earnings*. Lead them in sentences.

ears ◆ Have a puppet tell you some exciting news. Act happy and incredulous. Point to your *ears* and say "I can't believe my *ears*."

earshot ◆ Have puppets close by. Tell the class you have a surprise for the puppets. Begin to talk, hesitate, and say "The puppets are in *earshot*, so I can't tell you now." Move the puppets further away and say "The puppets will get new clothes."

earth ◆ **1.** Show pictures of *soil*. Tell students that it is also called *earth*. **2.** Show students a globe and have them touch *Earth*.

earthquake ◆ Dramatize being rocked and shaken in an *earthquake*. Show pictures of *earthquake* damage.

ease, easy, easier, easiest, easily ◆ **1.** Skip with *ease*. **2.** Draw a lit candle and a running faucet on the board. Touch your finger to the flame and mime burning your finger. Say "Ouch! That hurt!" Pantomime quickly plunging your hand into the running water. Say "Ah! That feels better. Running cold water on a burn is a great way to *ease* the pain quickly." **3.** Have students do things that are *hard*, then do things that are *easy, easier*, and *easiest*. Perhaps you can have them hop on one foot, then hop on two feet, then walk, and finally, sit. **4.** Show moving something *easily* and then moving something with *difficulty*.

eat, eating, eaten ◆ Pantomime *eating*. Lead students in making sentences with *eat, eating*, and *eaten*.

echo ◆ Have students copy everything you say. After a few turns, say "I hear an *echo*" and "I hear *echoes*."

ecology, ecological ◆ Show pictures of animals in their natural habitat. Explain that *ecology* is learning about how to keep these animals—how they live and how we live—so we can all live together. Then show pictures of a planet that has not been well cared for, and explain that the people who were there did not learn *ecology* and destroyed the land for people and animals. Lead students in sentences with *ecology* and *ecological*.

economic ◆ Ask students if they get an allowance or earn money for odd jobs. Ask them to plan how they will spend the money. Lead students in sentences using *economic*. Say "I like your *economic* plan."

ecstasy ◆ Draw an elaborate ice-cream sundae on the board. Have students join you in "eating" the sundae. Pantomime *ecstasy!*

edge, edges, edged ◆ **1.** Show the *edge* of a hillside. **2.** Show the *edge* of your desktop. Have students show you the *edge* of their desktop. Show the *edges* of desks, books, chairs, or doorways. **3.** *Edge* a piece of paper with a border and explain that you *edged* it.

edible ◆ Show pictures of *edible* and *inedible* things.

edit, editor, edition ◆ **1.** Write something on the board and then *edit* it. **2.** Take a student's paper [from someone else's class]. Have students help you *edit* it. Lead students in sentences using *editor*. **3.** Show books of varying *editions* and explain that each time the book is changed or rewritten, it is a new *edition*.

education ◆ **1.** Ask students if they are learning a lot at school. Have them list things they have learned in school. **2.** Ask students why they come to school. When they answer, "To learn," tell them that learning gives them an *education*. Have students give examples of different subjects they study to get an *education*.

eerie ◆ **1.** Show pictures of things you think are *eerie*. **2.** Have a puppet dress in black and move around the room in a sneaky, *eerie* manner. Give sample sentences.

effects ◆ Show the *effects* of different actions, such as a tornado or hurricane.

effort, efforts ◆ **1.** Lift something with *effort*. **2.** Ask students to help you tidy the class. Thank them for their *efforts*.

eight ◆ Lead students in counting *eight* objects. Ask students to show you *eight* objects.

eighteenth-century ◆ Use a time line to illustrate the *eighteenth century*. If possible, show pictures of people and things from this period.

either ◆ Using the word *either*, offer a student the choice of two books or two of something else.

ejected ◆ On the board, draw a pilot *ejected* from his or her plane.

elaborate ◆ Draw a simple design on the board. Draw another simple design and begin to make it more *elaborate*. Continue until it is very *elaborate*.

eldest ◆ Draw three children on the board: one tall, one medium-sized, one small. Write their ages above their heads, i.e., 17, 10, and 3. Point to the one that is 17 and say "This is the *eldest*."

elections ◆ Use any current *elections* as an example, or use the closest presidential *election*.

electric, electricity ◆ **1.** Turn the lights on and off in the classroom. Use other *electrically* run equipment. Show students where these plug into the walls. Contrast *electric* equipment with manually operated equipment, such as a pencil sharpener, a candle, and a stapler. Have students look through pictures and identify things from both categories. **2.** On the board, draw a picture of a lightbulb. Draw a line to it to show the *electricity* coming in. **3.** Show things that use *electricity* and things that do not use *electricity*.

elegant ◆ Show pictures of *elegant* birds, homes, or parties. Contrast with pictures of *plain* birds, homes, or parties.

elevation ◆ Show different mountains and indicate their height or *elevation*.

eliminate ◆ Write a "To Do" list on the board and then *eliminate* one item. Say "We don't have time to do that one, so I can *eliminate* it."

eloquence, eloquently ◆ Contrast using puppets. Have one speak haltingly. Say "His speech is awkward and clumsy." Have the other puppet speak with *eloquence*. Say "She speaks with *eloquence*" and "She speaks *eloquently*."

else ◆ **1.** Give students several books. Take one and look dissatisfied. Ask, "What *else* do you have?" Have him or her show you other books. Repeat with different colored papers. Explain that *else* means "another thing." **2.** Say "I want to go on a picnic. What will I need?" After the first answer you can ask, "What *else*?" Continue building your picnic supplies list in this manner. Say "I want to go to the back of the class. How can I get there?" Continue the list using "How *else*."

elsewhere ◆ Lead students in going *elsewhere* in the building. Repeat if needed.

emancipated, emancipation ◆ **1.** Make paper chains and link students to one another by their wrists. Then free them by tearing their chains apart. Say "You have been *emancipated*." **2.** Show pictures of African Americans as slaves and as professionals. Give example sentences using *emancipation*.

embarrassing, embarrassed, embarrassment ◆ **1.** Catch a puppet doing something that students would find *embarrassing*—perhaps taking somebody's pencil without permission. Have the puppet act *embarrassed* about being caught. **2.** Act out a scene in which you felt ill at ease and flustered, such as spilling something on yourself. Say "That accident caused me great *embarrassment*."

embattled ◆ Give a puppet a sword. Say "The *embattled* [Fluffy] goes off to war."

embed, embedding ◆ *Embed* various objects (especially the ones mentioned in the sand-casting project) in sand. Lead students in *embedding* things in the sand.

emblem, emblems ◆ Show the American flag, and say "The flag is an *emblem* of the United States." Show pictures of state birds or state flowers as *emblems* of the states. Scout badges can also serve as examples of *emblems*.

embrace ◆ Have two puppets *embrace*.

emergency, emergencies ◆ **1.** Engage students in a discussion of things that require immediate action, such as fire, robbery, heart attack, car accident, etc. Draw a telephone on the board and write 911 above it. Say "When something like this happens, we call 911 to get help. We tell them, 'This is an *emergency!*'" Have students imitate. **2.** Show pictures of *emergencies*. Have a puppet fall and break its arm. Race it off to the hospital. Have the hospital fix the puppet's arm. Ask for examples of *emergencies*.

emigration ◆ Ask how many of the students' families left their country to come to this country. Then tell them, "Leaving your country and going to a new country is called *emigration*." If needed, demonstrate with puppets. Have puppets pack their belongings, say their tearful farewells, and board a boat or plane. Draw a border and signs labeling the two countries. Once they have crossed it, tell students, "The puppets *emigrated* from (Italy) to America."

emotion, emotions, emotionally ◆ **1.** Lead students in pantomiming different *emotions*, such as love, joy, fear, surprise, anger, boredom, etc. **2.** Lead students in reading *emotionally* various sentences from stories that they have read.

employ, employing, employed, employer ◆ Pantomime an *employment* situation with several students. Explain that you need to *employ* people to work for you in your ice-cream store. Interview and *employ* a couple of students. Discuss their pay and hours as language skills permit. Allow them to pantomime selling ice cream to other students. Lead students in sentences for *employ, employing*, and *employed* at the correct times in your pantomimes.

empty, emptier, emptiest, emptiness ◆ **1.** Draw a square on the board. Fill it with circles. Erase some circles and say that the square is almost *empty*. Erase more and say that the box is *emptier*. Erase more of the circles and explain that the box is *emptiest*. **2.** Fill a container and then *empty* it. **3.** On the board, draw a circle with nothing in it. Point to the inside and say "This is *emptiness*."

enables ◆ Write a column of numbers on the board and have a puppet laboriously add them up. Then use a calculator to add them up quickly. Say "This calculator *enables* me to add them quickly and easily."

enchantingly ◆ See *magically*.

enclose ◆ *Enclose* a piece of paper in an envelope. *Enclose* some pencils in a box.

encourage, encouraging, encouraged ◆ **1.** Pantomime with a puppet. Have a puppet undertake some task and then tell you that she cannot do it.

Encourage the puppet to complete the task. Lead students in sentences using *encouraged*. **2.** While a puppet tries to write, be *encouraging*.

end, ended, endless ❖ **1.** Have students find the *end* of a story or book. **2.** Read a short story or poem to students. When you are done, close the book and tell students the story has *ended*. Lead them in finding other things that have *ended*, such as, "When recess is done, it has *ended*" and "When school is done for the day, it has *ended*." **3.** Draw a short line on the board and indicate its *end*. Draw another one, slowly taking it to the edge of the board. Explain that if there were another board, the line would continue onto it. Then say that the line has no *end*; it is *endless*.

endure, endured ❖ **1.** Have students build a tower out of blocks. Proceed to place a heavy book on the tower. Say "Let's see if the tower can *endure* having this book on top." **2.** Have a puppet climb a mountain. While it is climbing, have it shiver with cold. Have the puppet keep climbing until it reaches the top. Tell students that the puppet *endured* many things to climb the mountain.

enemy, enemies ❖ **1.** Have one puppet act like the *enemy* of another by attacking it. **2.** Show toy soldiers and explain that they strongly disagree; they are *enemies*. *Enemies* fight each other. **3.** Show pictures of *enemies* in a battle. —*enemy territory*, refer students to the two opposing countries in your war scene with the toy soldiers.

energy, energetic ❖ Have a puppet act lethargic. Have the puppet eat lunch so that it has *energy*. Once the puppet has eaten its lunch, have it be *energetic*. Have students pretend to be cars, some with gas and some without gas. Tell the cars with gas to drive and the cars without gas not to drive. Explain that gas is *energy* for cars just like food is *energy* for people.

enforced ❖ Have students help you list some school rules. Have a puppet break one of the rules. Issue a punishment, such as time out. Say "By punishing [Spot], I have *enforced* our school rules."

engineers ❖ Show pictures of *engineers*.

England, English ❖ Help students find *England* on a world map. Tell them that people and things from *England* are called *English*. Give examples and lead them in sentences.

enjoy ❖ **1.** Pantomime eating a piece of candy. Display your pleasure and tell students, "I like this candy; I *enjoy* it." Lead students in similar pantomimes and sentences. **2.** Draw a happy face. Pantomime being happy and say "I *enjoy* walking. I *enjoy* coming to school in the morning." **3.** Have students pantomime taking great pleasure in eating their favorite dessert. Say "The students are *enjoying* their dessert."

enlarge ❖ If you have a computer in your class, show students how you can *enlarge* letters or windows or graphics. Otherwise, write letters on the board and then *enlarge* them.

enlightening, enlightened ❖ Tell students that when you teach them, you are *enlightening* them. Have students show you how to work a math problem. Say "You *enlightened* me."

enlisted ◆ Show students a picture of an army recruitment poster, with Uncle Sam pointing, and say "The people who joined the Army or Navy *enlisted*. They are soldiers or sailors now."

enormous ◆ Show students big things and *enormous* things, perhaps with drawings on the board. Have students show you things that are big and *enormous*.

enough ◆ Ask for noise and then say "*Enough* noise!" Pat your stomach and say "I have had *enough* to eat!" —*I've had enough!*, have students all start speaking and being noisy in general. Tell them to stop because *you've had enough*. Review the contraction *I've* if needed.

enrage ◆ Draw angry, *enraged*, and *pleased* faces on the board. Pantomime and contrast all three emotions. Have students pantomime as they say "I am *pleased*," "Now I am angry," and "Now I am *enraged*."

ensure ◆ Sew something together and make extra stitches. Say "I want to *ensure* it doesn't come apart."

enter ◆ Show students *entering* the classroom and *exiting* the classroom. Have students *enter* and *exit* the classroom.

entertain, entertainer, entertainment ◆ **1.** *Entertain* the students with a song or joke. Explain that when you *entertain* someone, you are an *entertainer*. **2.** List some of the various types of *entertainment* that your students enjoy; explain that they are all forms of *entertainment*.

enthusiasts ◆ Ask students to say what they love doing on the weekend. Say "Are you [reading, biking, swimming] *enthusiasts?*"

entire ◆ Take a paper and crumple the *entire* piece. Then take another and crumple just a *part*. Empty an *entire* container of paper clips and then put them back and empty only a *part*.

entrails ◆ Show a drawing from an anatomy book that depicts *entrails*. Lead students in sentences.

environment ◆ Show pictures of fish in water and explain that this is their *environment*. They get what they need to live. Show pictures of people on land and in homes and explain this as their *environment*. Ask what people need to survive. Explain that people get this from their *environment*.

envy, enviously ◆ Look at a student as though you very much want something he or she has. Say *enviously*, for example, "[Teresa], I really love your blouse. I wish I had one just like it." Have students imitate. Have a puppet *envy* another's clothes or toys. Say "[Bear] feels *envy* when he sees [Fox's] [toys]."

epidemic ◆ Have one student stick red, round stickers on his or her face. Say "Oh, dear! [Valarie] is sick with a rash!" Have the first student tag the next, and stick red dots on him or her. Say "Uh-oh! [Carlos] caught [Valerie]'s disease!" Have students continue tagging and sticking red dots on one another until the whole class is covered. Say "Look how quickly the virus spread from one student to the other; now we're all sick! It's an *epidemic!*"

equal, equality ➧ **1.** Divide the board in half. Put four stars on one side and three on the other. Ask a student to make both sides *equal*. Continue with other *inequalities*. **2.** Demonstrate that 2 + 2 = 4; both sides have *equality*.

equation ➧ Write a math *equation* on the board.

erosion, erode, eroded ➧ **1.** Show pictures of a hillside and contrast with pictures of a hillside that has been *eroded*. Explain that wind, fire, and rain will *erode* a hillside or mountain. **2.** Have students build a mound of dirt in a plastic container and slowly pour water from a cup on top of the mound of dirt. Point out how it is washing away. Say "This is *erosion* caused by the water."

errands run ➧ (Poetic use that means to *run errands*.) Select various students to *run errands* for you (get your pencil, get a book off the shelf, etc.).

erratic ➧ Pretend that a puppet is flying on an airplane. After a smooth flight, make the flight *erratic*.

erupt, erupts, erupting, erupted ➧ **1.** Show a picture of a volcano *erupting*. Have students dramatize a volcano *erupting*. Compare to a tree *erupting* in flames. **2.** If you have a radio, turn the volume up loud before turning on the power. Turn the radio on and tell the class that the sound *erupts* from the radio. **3.** Have students *erupt* into laughter.

escape, escaped ➧ Have a puppet *escape* from a desk drawer. Lead students in past tense sentences.

escorted ➧ Have a student volunteer walk you to the door. Say "Thank you for walking with me to the door. It was nice to be *escorted*."

etch, etchings, etched ➧ If possible take students outside and let them *etch* their names in the dirt with a stick, or let them make crayon *etchings*. Otherwise, show illustrations of *etchings* and explain how they were *etched*.

ethics ➧ Have a puppet drop a piece of chalk and break it while you aren't looking. Act surprised and say "Who broke my chalk?" When the puppet confesses, say "Thank you for telling me the truth, [Muffin]. Your *ethics* helped you do the right thing."

Europeans ➧ Show the continent of *Europe* on a globe or map of the world. Say "People who live in these countries are called *Europeans*."

eve ➧ With a calendar, point to the day before a holiday. Say "The 24th of December is Christmas *Eve*," and so on with other holidays.

even ➧ — *e'en*, write the word *even* on the board. Then write *e'en*, and explain that the apostrophe replaces the *v*. Show small objects and make up example sentences, such as, "This paper clip is not *even* as big as my thumb," "This sticker does not *even* weigh a pound," or "I saw a baby that is not *even* a day old."

evening ➧ Explain that *evening* is the time when people have dinner, when school is out, and before it is really dark.

eventually ◆ Have a puppet ask you when it will get to have ice cream. Answer the puppet with "*Eventually*." Explain to the class that this means "not now, but at some later time." If needed, use a calendar to show a few days in the future as you say the word.

ever ◆ Draw a time line of a person's life on the board. Label one end of the time line "1 day old" and the other end "100 years old." Say that you are going to mark things that this person has *ever* done. Ask "Has he or she *ever* gone to school?" Depending on students' ideas, mark when he or she went to school. Ask, "Has he or she *ever* gone to the moon?" If students think not, say that he or she has *never* gone to the moon and don't mark the time line. Continue asking questions about what this person has *ever* done.

every ◆ **1.** Have all the students stand up. Say "*Every* child is standing up." Have one sit down and say "Not *every* child is standing up." **2.** Give examples, such as, "*Every* student has a name." "*Every* student has shoes on." "Some students have brown shoes and some students have white shoes." Have all students stand up. Say "*Every* child is standing up." Have one sit down and say "Not *every* child is standing up."

everybody ◆ **1.** Give *everybody* a book. Have *everybody* pass their books back. Have *everybody* stand; then *everybody* sit. **2.** Point to the group and say "You are *everybody*." Contrast with *individual*: "You are not *everybody*."

everyday ◆ Show students clothes that you wear for special occasions. Point to the clothes you are wearing and say "These are my *everyday* clothes." Show a picture of people dressed up for a fancy affair and say "These are *special* clothes."

everyone ◆ Ask *everyone* to raise their hands, to put one foot up, and so on. Then have only some students raise their hands.

everything ◆ Have students move *everything* off their desks. Show *everything* on your desk or in a box.

everywhere ◆ Select an object with limited space, such as a checkerboard or box. Place small items on it *everywhere*. Hide an item. Lead students in looking *everywhere*. Make sentences such as, "We will look everywhere for the button." "Have we looked *everywhere?*"

evidence ◆ Find cookie crumbs on a napkin on your desk. Show students the *evidence* that a cookie was once there.

evolved ◆ Involve students in jointly planning a party. Start with one student's idea and have each student add to it. Say "Our party plan *evolved* as we talked."

exact, exactly ◆ Draw a circle on the board and close it at the *exact* spot where it began. Have students do the same with pencil and paper. Ask for a student volunteer to recite a familiar passage. Then say "That was great, [Claudia]! You said that *exactly* right!"

examine, examination ◆ **1.** Perform an *examination* on a puppet. Ask students if they have ever had an *examination*. **2.** Lead students in *examining* a pencil, a book, etc. Say "Please *examine* this book."

example ❯ Say to the class, "Please draw a hexagon." Wait a moment, and then ask, "Would you like an *example?*" Draw a hexagon on the board and say "Here is your *example* of a hexagon."

exasperated ❯ Set up a scene where you and students are drivers stuck in a traffic jam. Pantomime irritation and say "I am getting angry about being stuck in this traffic. The longer I'm stuck here, the more *exasperated* I get!"

exceed, exceeding ❯ Push a toy truck along a tabletop. Then push another one alongside the first, having it *exceed* the speed of the first. Explain to the class that the second truck is *exceeding* the speed of the first truck.

excel, excellent ❯ **1.** Show students pictures of well-known people who *excel* in something, such as sports. **2.** Write a word three times on the board, using fair, good, and exceptional handwriting. Have students vote for the best one. Say "This handwriting is okay, this is good, this is the best; it is *excellent.*"

except, exception ❯ **1.** Tell everyone *except* one child to raise their hands. Show several paper clips that are good and one bent one. Explain that they are good *except* the one that is bent. Do similar demonstrations with paper that is white *except* for one ink spot, or several sheets of white paper *except* for one colored piece. **2.** Call the role for class, leaving off one student's name. Say "Did I call everyone's name?" When students tell you you've forgotten someone, say "You are right! I called everyone's name with the *exception* of [Jaime]."

exchange, exchanging ❯ **1.** Tell a student, "I will give you my eraser, if you will give me your pencil." Then tell him or her, "I will *exchange* my eraser for your pencil." Repeat with other students. Have students *exchange* places. **2.** Show two puppets *exchanging* items.

excite, exciting, excited, excitement ❯ **1.** *Excite* students about an upcoming holiday or other special event. **2.** Pantomime *excitement* about recess or some other activity that students enjoy. Tell them you are *excited*. Tell them that it will be *exciting*. Lead in sentences.

exclaiming, exclaimed ❯ Dramatize *exclaiming* something and then saying the same thing. Lead in past tense sentences.

excuse, excusing ❯ **1.** Have a puppet forget its homework. Have it act out what happened to it, like "The dog ate it." Say "[Fluffy] is giving an *excuse* for not having his homework." **2.** Bump into a student's desk and *excuse* yourself. Say that you are *excusing* yourself.

executive ❯ Name familiar businesses in your area, such as the local bank. Say for example, "[Mr. Ortega] is the president of the bank. He is an *executive.*"

exercising, exercises ❯ Demonstrate some *exercises* and lead students in *exercising*.

exhausted ❯ Pantomime running and becoming *exhausted* and hardly able to stand.

exist ❯ Pointing to things in the classroom, say "The desks *exist*" or "The students *exist*." Build a tower or building with books or blocks and point out that it *exists*.

Knock it down and say "The tower does not *exist*." —*no longer exist*, contrast with *exist*.

exit ◆ Lead students to an *exit*. Show them the sign over the door and ask them to *exit* through it.

expand ◆ *Expand* a balloon by blowing it up.

expect, expected, expectancy ◆ **1.** Give examples of times when children *expect* things, such as birthdays, or perhaps when students *expect* to have recess or *expect* to go to lunch soon. Say "These are the things you *expect* to happen" or "The *expectancy* is that you will do these things. **2.** Have a puppet toss a toy at another puppet that does not flinch. Have the first puppet say "I *expected* you to jump."

expedition, expeditions ◆ **1.** Show pictures of various *expeditions*. Explain that an *expedition* is a journey taken for a certain purpose. It is also the name of the group of people taking the journey. Have students pantomime forming an *expedition* to climb a mountain. **2.** Lead students in pantomiming the preparations for an *expedition* to the Arctic region. Ask, "What do we need to take on our *expedition*?"

expenses ◆ Write a list on the board of the things that you would need to set up a lemonade stand. Write prices next to each item and compute the total. Say "My *expenses* to start my lemonade stand will be $5.75."

expensive, expensively ◆ Ask the students to name items that cost a lot of money. Say "It would take a lot of money to buy those things. Those things are *expensive!*" Show pictures of beautiful mansions, yachts, diamonds, etc. Then say "Some people like to live *expensively*."

experiences ◆ Ask students to tell you about some pleasant memories. Say "Thank you for sharing your *experiences*."

experiment, experiments, experimenting, experimented ◆ **1.** Ask students to imagine mixing yellow and red paint. Say "What happens?" Then ask them to imagine putting water in the freezer. Say "What happens?" and tell them, "Those are *experiments*." **2.** Fill a container with water and have students test various items to find out whether they float. Say "You are *experimenting* to see which things float" and "You *experimented* with all these things."

expert, experts ◆ Give students an example of someone who is accomplished. Say, for example, "[Mr. Li] knows more than anyone in this school about [computers]; he is the *expert* on [computers]."

explain, explanation ◆ **1.** *Explain* something to the class. **2.** Have a puppet come to class late. Tell the puppet that it is late, and have the puppet give you an *explanation*, perhaps "My *explanation* for being late is that I went to the doctor."

exploding, exploded ◆ **1.** Blow air into a small paper bag, then burst the bag between your hands. Say "An *exploding* bag makes a big noise!" **2.** Blow up a balloon until it *explodes*. Say "Oh! It *exploded!*" Ask students if they would like you to *explode* another one.

explore, explores, explored, exploration, explorer ◆ **1.** Ask students to *explore* the room and try to find an object you have hidden. Open a container of supplies and *explore* the box. Lead students in *exploring* the contents of their desks. Say, "You are doing an *exploration* of the [classroom]." **2.** Explain that when one *explores*, he or she is an *explorer*. Talk about places that *explorers* have *explored*.

express, expressions ◆ **1.** Look at the students thoughtfully and then *express* a thought. Ask students to *express* a thought. **2.** Have students imitate different *expressions*.

external ◆ Show the *outside* of a box, then the *inside*. Lead students in finding other things that are *external* and *internal*.

external bleeding ◆ Draw a figure on a sheet of paper with a scratch on his leg. Draw a few drops of red blood falling from the scratch. Say "When we cut ourselves, we can see blood coming out of our bodies. This is called *external bleeding*."

extinct, extinction ◆ Show pictures of dinosaurs. Explain that all the dinosaurs died long ago; they are *extinct*. Draw a dinosaur on the board, and then erase it. Give example sentences using *extinction*.

extra ◆ Pile high some blocks or books. Then pile them *extra* high.

extraordinary ◆ Show students pictures of *extraordinary* events or people, such as the wedding of a monarch or a model who has *extraordinary* beauty.

extremely ◆ Pantomime being really hungry. Say "I am *extremely* hungry."

eye ◆ —*eyed*, widen your eyes while you look at a student's work. Say "I *eyed* your work." —*giant's eye*, draw a huge face on the board with enormous *eyes*. Reference the giant in "Jack and the Beanstalk," if familiar to students. —*eyes peeled*, ask students to keep their *eyes peeled* on your desk. Demonstrate. Then have someone or something pop up suddenly. —*keep an eye on*, make sure that students understand the individual words in this phrase. Then explain that *keep an eye on* means "watch." Lead students in pantomiming *keeping an eye on* the clock or on another student. —*wide-eyed*, have a puppet tell you something amazing. Respond *wide-eyed*.

eyewitness ◆ Have students observe something you are doing. Ask them to describe it. Say "You are an *eyewitness* to what I did."

fabulous ◆ Use *fabulous* to praise student work.

face, faces ◆ **1.** Have two puppets *face* each other. Ask students to turn and *face* another student in the class. **2.** Point out the many *faces* in the classroom. —*face down*, have students identify the *face* and the *back* of various objects, such as cards, a watch, and especially objects mentioned in the directions for the sand-casting project, such as feathers and seashells. Have students place the objects *face down*. —*face-to-face*, ask students to stand *facing* each other and explain that they are *face-to-face*.

fact ◆ Say *facts* about a book, such as its title and color. Then say *opinions*, such as good or bad. Repeat for other books. Have students state *facts* and *opinions*.

factions ◆ Divide students into different *factions*, each with an opposing non-inflammatory purpose, such as a *faction* that wants the whole world to be colored red and another that wants it colored blue.

fade, faded ◆ Demonstrate how colors can *fade* by drawing with colored chalk on the board and then partially erasing them. Explain that the colors have *faded*. Ask students to find something that has *faded* in the classroom.

fail, failing, failed, failure ◆ **1.** Try to throw a crumpled paper into a wastebasket but miss the basket. Say "I will not *fail* this time." Repeat and succeed. **2.** Contrast *failing* with *succeeding*. Lead students in past tense sentences. **3.** Pantomime trying and *failing* to do something, such as reaching for something. Lead students in similar pantomimes and sentences.

faint, fainted ◆ **1.** Draw several circles on the board and color them. Then make a few tiny, light marks on the board. Explain that the light marks are *faint*. **2.** Have a puppet be doing something and say "I feel *faint*," and then slump into your chair in a *faint*. Ask if students have ever *fainted* or seen someone *faint*.

fair, fairgoers ◆ **1.** Give examples of *fair* and *unfair* classroom rules. A *fair* rule might be, "No pushing in line." An *unfair* rule might be, "Only [Maria] may eat candy in class." Give more examples and have students tell you if each example is *fair* or *unfair*. **2.** Show pictures of a bazaar or *fair* where items are being sold. **3.** Draw several signs, spread across the length of the board, of various pavilions found at a *fair*. Have students pantomime attending the various events. Say "The *fairgoers* had a wonderful time at the *fair*." **4.** See *beautiful*.

fairy ◆ —*Fairy Godmother*, a *Fairy Godmother* is a *fairy* that is like a *mother* to someone. A *Fairy Godmother* takes care of a person. Show pictures of *fairies* and of Cinderella's *Fairy Godmother*.

faith, faithful ◆ **1.** Ask everyone to be quiet. Say "I have *faith* in you to stay quiet while I leave the room for a moment. I believe you can stay quiet even if I'm not here." Leave the room for a few seconds. **2.** Use examples of animals from stories, movies, or television that were *faithful*. **3.** Show pictures of churches and synagogues. Say "People who attend churches and synagogues have *faith*."

fall, falling, fell ◆ **1.** Have something *fall* off a table. Ask students to make their pencils *fall* off their desks. **2.** Draw a leaf *falling* from a tree. Name the *fall* months. **3.** Pantomime a *fall*. Say "I *fell*." Drop an object on the floor and say "The pencil *fell*." —*fall asleep, fell asleep*, have a puppet *fall asleep*, then wake up and say "I am sorry, I *fell asleep*." Lead students in pantomimes of *falling asleep*, waking up, and saying, "I *fell asleep*." —*fall into place*, **1.** Choose a few students to come to the room, and assign each a place to stand. Then tell them to wander around and when you say "*Fall into place*," they are to come back to that spot. **2.** Explain that *fall into place* means that things are working out the way they were planned. —*fell over*, demonstrate with a book or other object. Lead students in past tense sentences. —*free fall*, draw an airplane on the board with two people jumping out of it. Show one with an open parachute and the other without.

false ◆ Write several statements on the board, some of which are *true*, others that are *false*; for example, "Today is Wednesday," "My name is Mrs. Smith," "Today is a school day," etc. Review the list with students and mark each statement "T" for *True* or "F" for *False*.

falsehood ◆ Tell something really outrageous about yourself, such as "I'm eight feet tall." Give example sentences using *falsehood*.

familiar ◆ Show *familiar* things and *unfamiliar* things, such as a staple remover or various unconventional kitchen objects.

family ◆ Show pictures of a *family*. —*family tree*, draw your *family tree* on the board.

famous ◆ Ask students: "Who knows Leonardo DeCaprio? He is *famous*; many people have heard of him." "Who knows Drew Barrymore? She is *famous*; many people have heard of her." "Who has heard of Santa Claus? He is *famous*; everyone has heard of him." Then ask, "Who knows Fred Jones? Nobody has heard of him; he is not *famous*."

fan ◆ —*fanned out*, have students form a tight circle; then have them *fan out*.

fanatics ◆ Show pictures of a soccer game or some other sport in which fans act as *fanatics*.

fancy, fancies, fancied, fancier, fanciest ◆ **1.** Show something that you like and say "I like this; I *fancy* it." Then ask a student to show you something he or she likes and say "He or she likes the book; he or she *fancies* the book." Lead students in past tense sentences, such as "Yesterday, I *fancied* the story we read." **2.** Point to *fancy* things in the classroom. Have students make *fancy* pictures. Then have students make them *fancier* and *fanciest*.

far ◆ Show distances that are *far* and *near*. —*far away*, have one student stand *far away* from you and another student stand close to you. —*far off*, using the globe, show places that are *close* to where students live and *far off*. Have students touch these places. —*thus far*, on the board, draw a time line. On the line, put several math problems. Draw a line for present time. Say "*Thus far* we have finished [three] problems."

fare, fares ◆ Stage a scene on a bus and have one student collect the *fares*. Have the bus conductor say "Your *fare* is fifty cents."

farewell ◆ Wave and walk toward the door. Say "Good-bye! *Farewell!*"

farmer's ◆ See *animal's*.

fascinating, fascinated, fascination ◆ **1.** Show pictures of *fascinating* designs, such as the black and white ones that show a different shape depending on how you look at it. **2.** Walk up to a student and point to something he or she has. Say "I am *fascinated* by this. Tell me about it." **3.** Tell students about something that interests you greatly. Say, for example, "I love mystery stories. I have a *fascination* for them; I can't put a book down until I finish it."

fast, faster, fastest ◆ **1.** Ask three students to walk across the room. Have the first one walk *fast*, the second one walk *faster*, and the third one walk *fastest*. Demonstrate for them if needed. Repeat with other students. Give example sentences using *fast*.

fasten, fastened ◆ Ask students to *fasten* zippers and buttons. Help with past tense sentences.

fat ◆ Draw a line that is *thin* and a line that is *fat* on the board.

fatal ◆ **1.** Use a toy truck and a toy animal. Have the truck hit the animal. Have students try to help save the animal, but the animal does not pull through. Tell students, "The animal died; his injuries were *fatal*." **2.** Use a puppet to demonstrate a *fatal* accident. Say "Oh no! The puppet has been *fatally* injured. The puppet is dead."

fault ◆ **1.** Have a puppet drop a piece of paper because another puppet bumped him. Have them argue: "It's your *fault*" back and forth. Explain that *fault* means "being the one who made a bad thing happen." **2.** Have one puppet show its *faults*, perhaps bad hair, while another one shows how *faultless* it is.

favor, favorite, favorites ◆ **1.** Pantomime doing a *favor* for a puppet. Ask each student to do a *favor* for someone else in the class. **2.** Ask children which flavors of ice cream they like best. Then say "That is your *favorite*." Lead students in plural sentences. **3.** Have students make party *favors*.

faze ◆ Have a puppet concentrate on reading a book. Have a second puppet make a loud noise. The first puppet can act undisturbed by the sound and say "That did not *faze* me." Repeat, this time having the first puppet react to the sound saying, "Wow! That did *faze* me."

feared, fearful ◆ **1.** Have a toy cat chase a toy mouse. Tell students, "The mouse was afraid of the cat. She *feared* the cat." Lead them in sentences. **2.** Pantomime a scene where a dog is chasing you. Act *fearful*. Have students pantomime being chased by a dog and acting *fearful*.

feathers ◆ Show pictures of birds with *feathers*, or show real *feathers*.

feature, features ◆ **1.** On the board, draw a picture of a movie marquee with the names of the *features*. Ask students what *feature* they will watch. **2.** Point to your eyes, mouth, nose, and ears. Explain that these are your *features*.

fed ◆ —*I'm fed up!*, have students make a lot of noise and act exasperated. Tell them to stop; then say "*I'm fed up!*"

fee fi fo fum ◆ Explain that these are silly words that have no meaning. See if students know other nonsense words and phrases in English, or in their first languages. If students have difficulty, make up some new nonsense sounds as an example.

feed, feeding, fed ◆ **1.** Dramatize *feeding* a puppet or doll. Explain that you *fed* it. Ask a student to *feed* it. Lead students in past tense sentences. **2.** Bring in some rabbit, bird, or chicken *feed*. **3.** Show pictures of people *feeding* animals and say "These people are *feeding* the animals."

86

feel, feels, feeling, feelings, felt ◆ **1.** Explain that this means the same as *think*. **2.** Lead students in *feeling* different textures. Have them make sentences, such as "The floor *feels* cold" and "The jacket *feels* rough." **3.** *Feel* your breath and then say that you *felt* it. Have students *feel* their breath. Ask if they *felt* it. **4.** Have students touch things and then tell them that they *felt* it. Include getting close to things that are warm or cold, perhaps water, so they understand how you can *feel* something without touching it. **5.** Pantomime an emotion, such as happiness. Tell students that you *feel* happy. Then pantomime a new emotion, such as sadness, and say "First I *felt* happy; now I *feel* sad." Explain that these are called *feelings*.

feistiest ◆ Show pictures of dogs or puppies. Have a stuffed dog act *feisty*, *feistier*, and *feistiest*.

Felicity's ◆ Make examples of possessives using student names, such as *Maria's* jacket, *Min's* lunch box, and so on. It may clarify to point to *Maria* and say "*Maria*." Then hold up her jacket and say "*Maria's* jacket." Emphasize the difference between *Maria* and *Maria's* as you say the two words.

fellow ◆ Explain that a *fellow* is a boy person or a boy animal. Show pictures of boys, men, dogs, and horses, and make up sentences about them using the word *fellow*.

feminist ◆ Have students list careers they want when they grow up. Put the student's name next to each career. When they have finished, point to those that have been traditionally male. Say "It is all right for [Claudia] to be a [doctor]." Give example sentences using *feminist*.

fetch, fetched ◆ Have a puppet say *fetch* to a stuffed toy dog. Have the toy dog *fetch* the ball and bring it back to the puppet. Say that the dog *fetched* the ball.

fever ◆ Dramatize having a *fever*. Try to loosen your shirt as if you are hot. Feel your forehead and be shocked by the heat. Put a craft stick or straw in your mouth as if it were a thermometer. When you take it out, gasp, "I have a *fever!*" Have students tell you if they have ever had a *fever*.

few, fewer, fewest ◆ Put *many* paper clips on a desk. Contrast that with putting a *few* paper clips on a desk. Remove *some* paper clips so that there are *fewer* clips. Remove more to show the *fewest* paper clips.

fib ◆ Have a puppet say "I live in a castle." Tell the puppet, "That's a *fib*. You live in my desk!"

fickle ◆ Draw several ice-cream cones of different colors. Have a puppet say "My favorite flavor is vanilla. No, strawberry. No, it's chocolate." Then say "[Rabbit] is so *fickle*; she keeps changing her mind!"

fictitious ◆ Have students help you make two lists of people in stories you have read together: one of *real* people; the other of *fictitious* people. Say "These are the *real* people we've read about; these are the *fictitious* characters."

field, fields ◆ **1.** Show or draw pictures of *fields*. **2.** See *area*. **3.** On the board, draw a large circle. Have students tell you one thing they would like to study, such as science. Inside the circle make a list of everything they can study in the *field* of science.

fierce ➧ Make a *fierce* face. Show pictures of *fierce* animals.

fifty ➧ **1.** Lead students in counting *fifty* pennies or other small items. **2.** Lead the class in counting by tens and write the numbers on the board. Underline *fifty*.

fight, fighting, fought ➧ **1.** Pantomime two dolls or puppets *fighting*. Explain that they *fought*. **2.** Have two puppets *fight* (argue) over something noninflammatory—perhaps who will eat the last sandwich or what television program to watch. **3.** Show a picture of boxers *fighting*. —*fight back*, have one puppet pick on another, then have that puppet *fight back*. Repeat the demonstration, this time having the puppet not *fight back*.

figure, figures ➧ **1.** Draw familiar shapes on the board and review their names. Then tell students that they are all called *figures*. Then show animals and point out their *figures*. Ask students to point out *figures* to you. **2.** Have students give you names of well-known sports *figures*. Give example sentences using *figure*, such as "Michael Jordan is a sports *figure*."

figure out ➧ Write an arithmetic problem on the board. Say "I'm having trouble solving this. Who can help me *figure out* the answer?"

file, filed ➧ *File* some papers and say "The teacher *filed* [her] papers."

fill, filled ➧ **1.** *Fill* a container and then empty it. **2.** Explain that you *filled* the container. *Fill* a box with toys. Tell students, "The box is *filled* with toys." Ask them, "What are your desks *filled* with?" —*fill you up*, draw a picture on the board of a large meal. Tell students if they eat it all, they will not be hungry—it will *fill them up*.

final ➧ Have students line up. Indicate that the last student is the *final* one.

finally ➧ **1.** Lead students in walking in place, walking and walking, and *finally* stopping. **2.** Line students up in a row. With each new person that you add to the row, say "Then [Patricio], then [Xavier], then [Bonita]." When you get to the last student, say "And *finally*, [Anita]."

find, finding, found ➧ **1.** Ask a puppet to *find* you a toy. Then have him do so. Repeat with students. Make sure you ask them to *find* things they already know the names of. **2.** Say that you are looking for a student to answer a question or be your helper. Then *find* a helper. Place a group of objects on your desk. Name one of the objects, and invite a student to *find* that object. **3.** Lead students in *finding* things and explain that you *found* them.

findings ➧ See *eyewitness*. Have students give you their *findings* based upon their observations.

fine, fined ➧ **1.** Show *fine* hair contrasted with *thick* string. Show *fine* sand or flour contrasted with *coarse* gravel. **2.** Draw *fine* lines and *thick* lines on the board. **3.** Explain that *fine* means "very good." Lead students in making sentences about things that they consider to be *fine*, perhaps favorite toys, drawings, or clothes. **4.** Play "Simon Says" and establish a *fine* of two steps backwards when they make a mistake. Lead students in past tense sentences.

fine, finer, finest ➧ Show pictures of fancy dresses. Say "This one is *fine*, but this one is *finer*. This is the *finest* of all."

fingering ◆ Demonstrate on a keyboard or guitar or a drawing of a keyboard or guitar.

finish, finished ◆ Draw a triangle on the board, describing as you do the start and the *finish*. Do this with other shapes. Pantomime reading to the end of a book. Close the book and say that you are *finished*. —*finish line*, on the board draw a starting line and a *finish line* for a race.

finite ◆ Draw a line on the board with a beginning and end. Explain that it is *finite*. Draw a second line on the board, starting from the middle and going to the ends of the board in each direction. Tell the class that this line goes on and on and never stops; it is *infinite*.

fire, firing, fired ◆ 1. Show a picture of a rifle and explain that when a person is shooting it, he or she is *firing* it. 2. Have toy soldiers *fire* upon each other. Help students with past tense sentences. —*firing line*, on the board, draw a line of people *firing* at a target. Lead students in sentences using *firing line*.

fireside ◆ Show the area around the *fireplace*.

first ◆ 1. Line up three students. Count off, using their names; for example, "Sharon is *first*, Ed is *second*, and Marie is *third*." Repeat with different students or a sequence of actions. 2. Discuss and demonstrate a project that needs to be done, perhaps cleaning the board. Say "*First*, we will clean the eraser. *Next*, we will throw away the small pieces of chalk. *Later*, we will get new chalk. *Finally*, we will clean the board." Repeat with other examples. —*first-class*, on the board, draw an airplane showing *first-class* and *coach*.

firsthand ◆ Have a student describe to you what chocolate tastes like. Say "This sounds good, but I still don't really know what chocolate tastes like." Then draw a chocolate bar and pantomime taking a bite of it. Say "Mmmm. Now I know what chocolate tastes like because I've had it *firsthand*."

fish ◆ —*fish's*, see *animal's*.

fists ◆ Show a hand and then turn it into a *fist*. Ask everyone to show their *fists*.

fit ◆ 1. Use nesting containers or other things that *fit* perfectly to demonstrate *fit*. Show how the wrong containers don't *fit*. 2. Have students jog in place for at least 3 minutes. Say "We are working to become physically *fit*." —*fit just right*, try on various students' shoes. Explain that they don't *fit*. Then put yours on and say expressively that they *fit just right*.

fix, fixes ◆ 1. *Fix* something that is broken. Perhaps mend a torn paper with tape. Take apart a toy and *fix* it again. 2. Have a puppet break a pencil, then repair it with tape. While you are repairing it, have the puppet tell the class, "The teacher *fixes* the pencil." —*fix up*, have students *fix up* the room for a party.

flapping, flapped ◆ Show pictures of birds and then pantomime the *flapping* action of their wings. Lead students in *flapping*. Lead students in past tense sentences.

flash, flashes, flashed ◆ Show a picture of a lightning bolt and ask if students have ever seen it *flash* in the sky. Explain that it *flashes*. If you have a *flashlight*, turn it on and off. Lead students in past tense sentences.

flat, flatten, flatter, flattest ◆ 1. Have students touch several *flat* surfaces. 2. Show students a picture of a bicycle with a *flat* tire and say "I have a *flat* tire on my bicycle." 3. *Flatten* some modeling clay. 4. Compare *flat* and *unflat* lands. Then compare lands that are *flat, flatter,* and *flattest.*

flatterer ◆ Have a puppet *flatter* you: "You are so beautiful, wonderful," etc. Say "You are a *flatterer.*"

flaunt, flaunting ◆ If you have a flagpole outside, show students the flag, and if it is waving in the breeze, explain that it is *flaunting.* Otherwise show a picture of a flag and explain that when the wind blows it, it is *flaunting.*

flaw, flaws, flawless ◆ Point out a *flaw* and then some *flaws* on a desktop. Compare to a surface that is *flawless.* Have students find things with *flaws* and then find things that are *flawless.*

flee, flees ◆ Have a puppet *flee* a stuffed dog. Give examples of sentences.

flesh ◆ Pinch your *flesh.* Have students copy your action and words.

flick ◆ *Flick* your hand. *Flick* the pages of a book.

flickers ◆ Light a match or candle and show students how the flame *flickers.* Say "The light *flickers.* This match makes *flickers* of light."

flight ◆ 1. Draw a *flight* of stairs on the board. Explain that a *flight* is a set of stairs. If there are *flights* of stairs in the school building, point them out. 2. Draw *flights* of stairs on the board with landings in between each *flight.* 3. Show pictures of flocks of birds in *flight* and say "These birds are *flying*; they are in *flight.*"

fling ◆ *Fling* a wadded piece of paper into the trash.

flip ◆ *Flip* a coin. Let students *flip* coins. —*flip-flop,* lead students in making their hands *flip-flop.* —*flipped up,* demonstrate to students *flipping up* the lid of a pencil box.

float, floating ◆ *Float* a small piece of paper in some water. Tell students that the paper is *floating.*

flop, flops, flopping, flopped ◆ 1. Have a puppet *flop* into a chair. Explain that you *flopped.* Lead students in *flopping* into chairs. 2. Show how a puppet *flops* forward and backward.

floppy ◆ Contrast a hardcover book with a paperback. Explain that one is *floppy* and the other is *stiff.*

flourish, flourishing, flourished ◆ Draw two potted flowers on the board—one *flourishing* and the other not. Lead students in sentences with *flourish, flourishing,* and *flourished.*

flow, flows ◆ Show a picture of a river and lead students in gesturing with their hands to show how the water *flows.* Or, pour a little water onto a desktop and have students observe its *flow.*

flower-fed ◆ Draw a picture of a *flower* and say "Who wants to eat this *flower?*" Pretend to feed the *flower* to someone and then say "You are *flower-fed.*"

flu ◆ Pantomime fever, chills, etc. with a puppet. Explain that it is sick. It has the *flu*.

flue ◆ Show students a picture of a chimney with a *flue*.

flung ◆ *Fling* something into the trash can. *Fling* something over your shoulder. Lead students in past tense sentences.

flunk ◆ Pantomime taking a test, give it to a puppet to correct, and have the puppet tell you that you missed too many and that you *flunked*. Contrast by taking a test again and *passing*.

flurry ◆ Pantomime being in a *flurry* (everyone and everything moving around quickly and somewhat confusedly).

fly, flying, flew, flown ◆ **1.** *Fly* a toy plane or kite by carrying it around. Explain that if you make it *fly*, you are *flying* it. **2.** Have students pretend to *fly* and then explain that they *flew*. **3.** Show pictures of birds in *flight* and explain that they have *flown* very far. Ask students if they can think of other animals or things that have *flown* very far. **4.** Pantomime catching a *fly* ball. Draw a baseball diamond on the board and show the path taken by the ball before you caught it.

focus ◆ Hold your hand up. With your other hand, point from your eyes to your hand and ask students to *focus* on it.

foe ◆ Have two puppets fight and call each other *foe*. (See *enemy.*)

fold, folding, folded ◆ *Fold* a piece of paper; tell students it is *folded*. Lead students in *folding* paper. Help them to make sentences.

fold up ◆ *Fold up* a piece of paper.

folk ◆ Explain that this is another word for *people*. Say "We are good *folk*."

follow, follows, following, followed, followers ◆ **1.** Have students line up single file and march around the room behind you. Say "*Follow* me." Note that children are *following* each other in a line. Say "I am the line leader; the rest of you are *followers*." **2.** On the board, write a list of simple instructions such as, "stand up, turn around, sit down." Have students follow the instructions in the order given. —*follow in his father's footsteps*, check that students understand the individual words in the phrase. Ask students what their *fathers* do. Ask who wants to do what his or her *father* does. Say "You want to *follow in your father's footsteps*."

folly ◆ Contrast examples of good sense and stupidity. Say, for example, "Staying in school is a smart thing to do. Dropping out of school is not smart; it is *folly*."

fool ◆ A silly person. Give and get examples of *foolish* behavior.

foolish, foolishly, foolishness ◆ **1.** Have a puppet put on a paper cup or bag for a hat. Have it stand on its head or do other *foolish* things. **2.** Have a puppet act *foolishly*. Tell students that it is acting *foolishly*, and lead them in acting *foolishly*. Then, have puppets make *foolish* choices, such as trying to write with an eraser, eat lunch with their toes, etc. Tell the class the puppets are choosing *foolishly*. Have them tell you what they should have done.

3. Invite students to act *foolish*. After a minute, say "Okay, enough of this *foolishness*. Let's get back to work."

foot ➤ —*ninety-foot*, show students a twelve-inch ruler and explain that it is the length of one *foot*. Have all students count to *ninety* in tens and write the numbers on the board as they are spoken. Have students name things that could measure *ninety feet*, such as a nine-story building, a jet plane, etc. Draw a nine-story building on the board. Say "This is a *ninety-foot* building." —*peg foot*, draw a *peg* leg on the board. Bend one knee and try to demonstrate how the device fits under the knee, allowing a person with a partially amputated leg to walk. Ask students to draw the *footprints* that would be made by someone with a *peg foot*. —*web feet*, show a duck's *webbed feet*. You can also draw on the board duck's feet without *webbing*, and then add in the *webbing*.

foothills ➤ Draw mountains on the board, then draw shorter hills in front of them. Say "These are the *foothills* of the tall mountains."

footprints ➤ Show illustrations of *footprints* in their recent reading selections.

footsteps ➤ Draw little *footsteps* on the board and say that the puppet walked there. Ask students to listen for your *footsteps* as you walk.

for ➤ **1.** Present a book to a student and say "This book is *for* you." **2.** Explain that *for* means "goes with." "Hot is a rhyme *for* cot," "This lace is *for* this shoe, this belt is *for* these pants, this ribbon is *for* your hair," and so on. **3.** Go after something such as a book. Explain that you are going *for* the book. —*for good*, have two puppets play marbles and each win a game. Then play another game in which one puppet loses all his marbles. Have the loser say "I have no more marbles. I have lost *for good.*" —*for instance*, ask students to give examples of different ways to say "Hello" without words (i.e., hug, handshake, high five, salute, etc.). Instruct them to precede each example with the words, "*For instance,*" such as, "*For instance,* you could give the person a high five," etc. —*for sale*, set up a few toys on your desk, and give students a few pennies. Then have students buy things from you that are *for sale*.

forbidden ➤ Draw a "No Smoking" sign on the board (a cigarette in a circle with a diagonal line through it). Ask students to name things that are *forbidden* at school.

force, forcing, forces, forced, forceful ➤ **1.** Have a student *force* a puppet to sit down. Tell the class, "[Juanita] is *forcing* the puppet to sit down," "[Jaunita] *forces* the puppet to sit down," and "She *forced* the puppet to sit down. **2.** Have students push down hard on their desks. Explain that as *force*. Ask students how *force* can help them. **3.** Pantomime a scene of one puppet *forcing* another into doing something. Tell students, "He is *forceful.*" Contrast with a puppet being *pleasant* or *persuasive*. Tell students, it is not "*forceful.*" **4.** Say "Do not talk to [Fluffy] in a *forcible* way; it is scaring her." **5.** Pantomime *forcibly* sharpening a pencil or erasing the board.

forefathers ➤ **1.** Ask students to name their grandparents and great-grandparents. Say "Those people are your *forefathers.*" **2.** Show pictures of the constitution and some of the men who signed it. Explain that they are called the *forefathers* of our country.

forefeet ❧ Show a picture of an animal and point out the *forefeet*. Lead students in sentences.

foreign ❧ Point out various countries on a globe. Give example sentences using *foreign*, perhaps "England is a *foreign* country."

foreign-born ❧ Ask students where they were born. For any born outside the country, say "You are *foreign-born*. That means you were born outside this country." Ask all *foreign-born* students to raise their hands.

foretold ❧ Say "I predict that we will have a visit from [Fluffy] today." Make the puppet pop out from behind your back. Say "The teacher *foretold* that [Fluffy] would visit the class today."

forget, forgot, forgotten ❧ **1.** Have a puppet leave home without its lunch box and make sure students see that the lunch box was left behind. Hand the puppet its lunch box and tell it, "Don't *forget* your lunch box." Lead students in similar pantomimes, such as coming to your desk without a pencil. Ask students, "What did you *forget?*" **2.** Ask students to remind you of how to play a childhood game. Say "I learned how to play [Tarzan] when I was your age, but I've *forgotten* how to do it."

fork, forks ❧ **1.** Show a picture of a *fork* or draw one on the board. **2.** Show a picture of *forks* in a road.

forlorn ❧ Make a puppet seem *forlorn:* by itself and pitiful. Dramatize feeling sorry for the *forlorn* puppet.

form, forming ❧ **1.** Lead students in sentences, such as, "My favorite *form* of entertainment is a good book" or "What *form* of entertainment do you like?" **2.** Make an animal out of modeling clay. Say "I am making an animal. I am *forming* his head; I am *forming* his body; I am *forming* his legs; and so forth."

formula, formulas ❧ Write a *formula* on the board, such as 1 + 1 = 2 or 3 - 1 = 2. You can also draw a picture *formula*, such as a bag of flour + 2 eggs + milk + a bag of sugar = a cake. Explain that a *formula* tells the way to make something. A math *formula* can tell how to make a number like 2 (1 + 1 = 2 or 3 - 1 = 2).

forth ❧ Model with a puppet by saying, "Come *forth*," and then have the puppet come toward you. Repeat with students.

fortified ❧ Have students build a castle out of blocks. Then have them make it stronger by placing books around the outside of it. Give example sentences using *fortified*.

fortunate, fortunately ❧ **1.** Make strips of paper and write "You Win!" on one of them. Fold them and have each student select one at random. Ask who drew the winning strip. Say "[Rosa] is the lucky winner. She is *fortunate* to have chosen the winning strip." **2.** *Luckily.* Have students help you make a list of things that are *lucky*, and another of things that are *unlucky*. Say "We can feel good about the things on our '*Lucky*' list and bad about our '*Unlucky*' list. *Fortunately*, I found a quarter on the sidewalk; *unfortunately*, I lost it again."

forward ❧ Have students step *forward*; contrast by having them step *back*.

fossil, fossils ⇔ Show pictures of *fossils*, and explain that a *fossil* is something left by the bodies of plants and animals from long ago. *Fossils* can be bones, imprints of bodies, tracks, or a whole body, like that of a frozen mammoth. See *imprints*.

foul ⇔ Show a picture of rotten food and pretend to sniff it. Make a wry face and tell students that it smells *foul*.

founded, founder ⇔ **1.** Ask or tell students who *founded* the school. **2.** Have students build a little town with blocks or modeling clay and tell them that they *founded* it. Explain that the person who *founded* it is called the *founder*.

fourscore ⇔ Write the equation "$4 \times 20 = 80$" on the board. Lead in using *fourscore*.

fourth ⇔ Have students line up; show them the first, second, third, and *fourth* people in the line. —*Fourth of July*, show the *Fourth of July* on the calendar. Ask students if they know what people do on the *Fourth of July* (watch fireworks and parades).

Fran ⇔ Explain that *Fran* is a girl's name. Include it in a list of girls' names that you write on the board. Ask for corresponding first-language girls' names.

France, French ⇔ Help students find *France* on a map or globe and touch it. Explain to students that people and things from *France* are called *French*. Give examples, such as *French* cars, *French* food, and "The girl is *French*."

frantic, frantically ⇔ **1.** Tell students you have lost something. Pantomime being *frantic*. **2.** Pantomime searching for something in your desk *frantically*.

fraud ⇔ Have a puppet say it is a well-known basketball or football star. Lead students in sentences using *fraud*.

fray, frayed ⇔ Show students the *frayed* edge of a piece of cloth or a book.

freak ⇔ Ask students to tell you unexpected things that have happened to them. Lead them in sentences using *freak*.

free ⇔ **1.** Close several students inside a ring of chairs. Say "You are locked in; you are my prisoners." Then pull the chairs away and have students walk out. Say "Now you are not prisoners; you are *free*." **2.** Give examples of living in a *free* country where the laws help the people, and contrast with living in a country where people do not feel *free* because the laws do not help them.

freedom ⇔ Have a puppet be an oppressive king, and lead students in asking the puppet if they can do things, perhaps stand up or sharpen their pencil. Each time, have the puppet say "No." Tell students that the puppet king will not give them *freedom*. Then have students move around the classroom, doing as they wish for a short while, and explain that they have *freedom*.

free-spirited ⇔ Skip around the room and say lightheartedly, "I do whatever I feel like doing. I am *free-spirited*."

freestyle ⇔ Show illustrations of different swimming strokes, such as breaststroke, *freestyle*, butterfly, and backstroke.

freight ➻ Show pictures of trucks hauling *freight*. Explain that the load they carry is called *freight*. Ask for suggestions from students of different types of *freight* that trucks can haul.

frequent, frequently, frequency ➻ **1.** Have a puppet make *frequent* trips to the pencil sharpener or eat *frequent* meals. Contrast by having the puppet make *rare* trips. Ask students about things that they may do *frequently*. **2.** Have two puppets clap—the one clapping four times as fast as the other.

fresh ➻ **1.** Show a picture of *fresh* fruit or vegetables. Contrast with *rotten* ones. **2.** On the board, have a large number of math problems. Start working on them, tire, and stop. Wait for awhile. Appear revived and say "I think I'll get a *fresh* start on those math problems now."

Friday ➻ Show the days on the calendar. Have students say which day it is today and which day *Friday* is or was.

friend, friends, friendly, friendship ➻ **1.** Show two puppets playing together, talking nicely, etc. Tell the students that the puppets are *friends*. **2.** Ask who has a *friend*. Point to some students who are good *friends*. Say "They are *friends*." **3.** Have two puppets be *friendly*. Then have them be *unfriendly*. Have students pantomime being *friendly* and then *unfriendly*. Lead them in sentences, such as "The puppets are *friendly*" and "The puppets are *unfriendly*." **4.** Explain that friendship is about having *friends*. —*best friend*, point out *best friends* in the classroom. Contrast with *friends*. —*fast friends*, have two puppets demonstrate a deep and loyal *friendship* by helping each other, playing with each other, etc. You may want to ask students if they have ever had a *best friend*. Ask them to name some *fast friends* from stories they have read.

fright, frighten, frightened ➻ **1.** *Frighten* a puppet and then say "I gave that puppet a *fright*!" **2.** Have one puppet say "Boo!" to another, who then squeals and runs away. Pantomime being *frightened* and *brave*. Ask students to tell about times they were *frightened*. **3.** Show pictures of scary snakes and spiders. With each picture, tell students, "This is a *frightful* creature." Demonstrate your *fright* and lead students in doing so. Contrast with pictures of things that are not *frightful*.

frigid ➻ On the board, draw a refrigerator with the freezer section open. Point to it and say "This part is *frigid*." Pantomime being very cold.

frog ➻ A *frog* has smooth, moist skin, while a toad has rough, warty skin. Show illustrations of each.

from ➻ **1.** Take some paper out of a desk drawer. Say that you took it *from* the drawer. Lead students in removing paper and other items *from* their desks. **2.** Walk *to* a student and then away *from* him or her. Go *to* your desk and then away *from* it. Ask students to *walk* from their desks *to* your desk. —*from now on*, explain that this means "after now." Give an example: perhaps, "*From now on*, I will put my pencils in this drawer." —*from scratch*, make something, such as cookies or papier-mâché paste, *from scratch*. Say "We're making this *from scratch*."

front ◆ Show students the *fronts* and *backs* of books, posters, and pictures. Have them find the *fronts* and *backs* of things.

front man ◆ Set up a scene where you run a restaurant, and some students are cooks and the others are patrons. Pantomime servicing the customers; have the student cooks pantomime cooking. Then say "Those who are cooking the food do not deal directly with the customers. It is my job to talk with the customers and make sure they are happy. I am the *front man.*"

frost, frosty ◆ Show pictures of windows that have *frost* on them. Explain that they are *frosty*.

froth, frothy ◆ Show a picture of a *frothy* drink, perhaps a root beer *float*. Point out the *froth* on the drink.

frown, frowning, frowned ◆ Lead students in *frowning* and then *smiling*. Lead students in past tense sentences.

froze ◆ Draw a puddle of water and an ice cube on the board. Say "The water *froze* and became ice."

frugal ◆ Draw a piggy bank on the board. Pretend to put some coins in it. Say "I never spend my money; I put it all in my bank. I am very *frugal.*"

fruits ◆ Show examples or pictures of different *fruits* and name each one. Explain that they are all called *fruits*.

frustrating, frustrated, frustration ◆ **1.** Show a picture of a flat tire on a bicycle and pantomime changing it. Portray *frustration* and say "Changing this flat tire is very *frustrating.*" **2.** Attempt to toss a crumpled ball of paper into the wastebasket. After several unsuccessful attempts, say "I can't get the ball into the basket. I am getting so *frustrated!*"

fry, frying ◆ Show a picture of a *frying* pan and model *frying* two eggs.

fuel ◆ Have students pretend to be cars, some with *fuel* and some without *fuel*. Tell the cars with *fuel* to drive and the cars without *fuel* not to drive. Explain that gas is *fuel* for cars. Ask what the *fuel* for human bodies would be.

fugitives ◆ Show pictures of a police officer. Have a puppet steal something off your desk and run from the "police officer." Give example sentences using *fugitives*.

fulfill, fulfilling, fulfillment ◆ **1.** Give students a two-step assignment, such as copying a word from the board and using it in a sentence. Say "In order to *fulfill* this assignment, you must do both parts," "Good work! You are *fulfilling* your responsibility to complete the assignment," and "*Fulfillment* of the task means finishing every item on this list." **2.** On the board, draw a picture of a child dreaming about something like flying an airplane. Draw another picture of an adult doing the same thing. Lead students in sentences using *fulfillment*. **3.** Pantomime a sense of *fulfillment* over completing something that you found difficult to do.

full ◆ —*full of*, fill a cup *full of* pencils. Show a locker or desk *full of* items. Fill a cup with water. Tell students, "The cup is *full of* water." —*full of life*, draw an empty fish tank and a fish tank with many fish on the board. Point to the first tank and say "This is empty. No life in here." Point to the second tank and say "This has many fish in it. It is *full of life.*"

full-scale ➡ Have the students work together to build a castle out of blocks with exaggerated effort and energy. Say "The students made a *full-scale* effort to build the best castle ever!"

fumbling ➡ Gather up a few items from your desk and carry them across the classroom. Pretend to lose your grip and nearly drop the items. Say "I am *fumbling* with them."

fume, fuming, fumed, fumes ➡ **1.** Draw an angry face on the board. Say "This person is angry. This person is so angry he or she is *fuming.*" Draw smoke coming out of the nose and ears. **2.** Have the puppet make a mess of your desk, perhaps by knocking over a container of pencils. *Fume* at the puppet. Tell students that you were *fuming* mad and you *fumed* at the puppet. **3.** Show a picture of a factory or automobile putting out *fumes*. Or draw these on the board. Open a bottle of perfume and let the *fumes* reach the students.

fun ➡ Ask students to dramatize having a happy time. Tell them, "You are having *fun.*" —*making fun of*, have a puppet *make fun of* another puppet, calling it names.

functions ➡ Show students the *functions* of a pencil sharpener, eraser, pencil, etc.

funds ➡ Point to objects in the classroom bought by the school. Say "The school had the *funds* to buy [desks, paper, pencils]."

funny, funnies ➡ **1.** Say or do something *funny*. Tell students "That was *funny.*" Ask for jokes that students know. Laugh at them and tell the students the joke was *funny*. Lead them in sentences. **2.** Show pictures of *funny* hats and contrast with pictures of more serious things. **3.** Show students the *funnies* section of a newspaper.

fur, furry ➡ Show the *fur* of an animal and tell students, "This animal is *furry.*" Ask students to name *furry* animals.

furniture ➡ Show students pictures of *furniture*. First, lay them out on a table and identify each piece. Then, tell them, "All of these are also called *furniture.*"

furrow ➡ Show a picture of a *furrow*.

further ➡ Stand at one side of the classroom. Have one student stand in the middle of the room and another at the opposite side from you. Say "[Fia] is *closer* to me than [Franco]. [Franco] is *further* away than [Fia]."

fury, furious, furiously ➡ Have one puppet express *fury* toward another who took something from it. Have it respond *furiously*.

fuss, fussing, fussed ➡ **1.** *Fuss* over a puppet who has fallen down and hurt himself. Tell the class that you *fussed* over the puppet. **2.** Have a puppet *fuss* and complain. Have another puppet tell it to stop *fussing*.

future ❧ Show today on the calendar and explain that today is the *present*. Show earlier days of the week and explain that these were the *past*. Show *future* days and explain these as the *future*. Ask what students would like to do in the upcoming days or *future*.

fuzz, fuzzy ❧ **1.** Show students the *fuzz* on a peach, a sweater, a stuffed animal, or a bit of *fuzz* from a pocket. Lead them in sentences. **2.** Show a *fuzzy* stuffed animal or a *fuzzy* sweater.

gab, gabbed ❧ Have a puppet *gab* at you. Tell the class that the puppet just *gabbed* and *gabbed*.

gained ❧ Have two puppets run a race. Let one trail behind and then *gain* rapidly. Give a running commentary.

gallop, galloping ❧ Show pictures of *galloping* animals; explain that this is how an animal with four legs runs.

game, games ❧ Show students various *games* in the classroom. Ask students which *games* they have at home.

gap ❧ Point out a *gap* between teeth in a comb, a *gap* in a fence where boards are missing, or show a *gap* between your fingers.

garden ❧ Show pictures of *gardens*, both flower and vegetable. Identify a few of the plants in the *garden*.

gargle, gargling ❧ Demonstrate *gargling* with water.

gas ❧ Show a picture of a *gas* station or pump.

gasp ❧ Lead students in *gasping*.

gateway ❧ Show a picture of a fence with a *gate*. Explain that the opening is called a *gateway*.

gather, gathered ❧ **1.** *Gather* students into a cluster. Tell them that they are clouds and you will be a strong wind. Explain that when you blow at them, they will move apart or disperse. **2.** *Gather* up things from your desk and put them in a container. **3.** Ask a student to *gather* up everyone's book. Say "Thanks, you *gathered* the books very quickly."

gaudy ❧ Show pictures of things or people who look *gaudy*.

gaze, gazes, gazed ❧ **1.** *Gaze* at a student. Have students *gaze* at each other. Lead students in sentences. **2.** *Gaze* at a picture. Contrast with a *glance*. Have students *gaze* and *glance* at things.

gear ❧ Pantomime driving. Draw a *gear* stick on the board and make the sound effects for changing *gears*. Say "I am shifting into second *gear*."

gene ❧ Explain it as a part of your body that is so small that you cannot see it. Explain that it helps your body look and grow the way that it is growing. Give examples of *genes* determining hair, skin color, height, and weight; for example, "You have a *gene* to tell your body to be tall" and "You have a *gene* that says you will have brown eyes."

generally ❧ Have students make lists of things they do most of the time and lists of things they only do sometimes. Give example sentences using *generally*.

generation, generations ► **1.** A group of people in one age group. Talk about your parents' *generation*, your grandparents' *generation*, and your grandchildren's *generation*. **2.** About twenty-five years. Have students name people from previous *generations*.

generous ► Pretend to give money to everyone. Say "I am *generous*; I share my money." Repeat with items that you own. Have students mimic and repeat likewise.

gentle, gently ► **1.** Have a puppet be *gentle* with another puppet and then *rough*. **2.** Have a puppet touch another puppet in a *gentle* manner. Contrast *gentle* with *hard*. **3.** Pet a toy animal *gently* and then *roughly*. Lead students in sentences.

German ► Show *Germany* on a map or globe and explain that people or things that come from that country are called *German*. Give examples, such as *German* cars or movies.

gesture, gestures ► Use *gestures* to indicate "stop," "come here," "look there," and other examples with which students would be familiar. Have students take turns giving *gestures* such as these.

get, getting, got ► **1.** Go to a table and *get* something. Have students go to the supply area and *get* some paper. **2.** Lead students in *getting* things from the art cupboard. **3.** Lead students in sentences, such as "I *get* tired at night" or "I *get* hungry before lunch." **4.** Draw a short stick figure on the board and then draw figures to its right that are taller and taller. Explain that it *got* taller. Do the same with other shapes that *get* bigger or smaller. **5.** Have a puppet try to catch an imaginary fly and then claim to have *got* it. —*get along*, lead students in making example sentences such as, "I can *get along* without toys" and "I can't *get along* without water." —*get by*, crowd two puppets into a small space; then have one puppet *get by* the other. —*get even with*, have one puppet take a pencil from the other and run away. Have the remaining puppet steal something from the first puppet. Give example sentences using *get even with*. —*get off*, have a toy plane or kite *get off* the ground. —*get out*, **1.** Have students form a circle with one student in the middle. Instruct students forming the circle to join hands. Have the student in the middle try to *get out*. **2.** Put a puppet or doll into a drawer and tell it to *get out*. Ask students to tell the puppet to *get out*. **3.** Shoo away some toy animals, telling them, "*Get out! Get out!*" —*get rid of*, **1.** Explain, "I must *get rid of* the bug," and shoo away an imaginary fly. **2.** Throw away a pen saying, "This pen doesn't work anymore. I am going to *get rid of* it." —*get up*. **1.** Have students *get up* and then sit down. **2.** Have a puppet lie sleeping and tell him to *get up! —get you*, dramatize this idiom with two puppets. Have one say "I'll *get you!*" just before it catches the other. —*got hooked on*, became committed to. Check that students understand each word in the phrase. Tell students about a cause that means a lot to you. Say "Once I had worked with this group for a while, I wanted to do everything I could. I *got hooked on* helping these people." —*got over*, pantomime being upset about a bad grade on a spelling test. Have a puppet give you a flower. Say "I *got over* it." —*got sick of*, have a puppet sing one line of a song over and over. Then it frowns and stops. Have another puppet say "Why did you stop singing?" The first puppet says it *got sick of* it. Ask students if they ever *got sick of* doing the same thing over and over, such as a chore or singing a song or reading the same book. Explain that *sick* in *got sick of* doesn't really mean "*sick*," it means "bored." See *sick* and *get.* —*got stuck*, write a word on the board you know students can read. Sound out the letters and then *get stuck*. Say "I *got stuck*. Please help me!" —*got the point*, check that students understand these words individually. Say the phrase *Got the point*. Explain that it means you understand something. Give an example, such as "A dog was barking and nobody could make him stop. Then a boy yelled 'Stop!' The dog *got the point* and quit barking."

giant ♦ **1.** Show a picture of a *giant*. **2.** Compare *small* and *giant* waves by drawing them on the board. **3.** See *colossal*.

gibber ♦ Have a puppet *gibber* at students.

giddy ♦ Pantomime by spinning around and laughing. Say "I am so happy, I feel *giddy!*" Have students imitate.

gift, gifts ♦ Give a puppet a party. Have another puppet give it a *gift* that you have wrapped. Ask students what *gifts* they received for their birthdays.

gigantic ♦ **1.** Draw or show a picture of a *dwarf* rabbit, a common white rabbit, and a *gigantic* rabbit. **2.** See *colossal*. **3.** Show or draw pictures of things that are *gigantic* in size relative to people, such as a huge dinosaur, tree, or building.

giggle, giggled, giggling ♦ Tickle a puppet and make it *giggle*. Lead students in *giggling* and laughing to help them see the difference. Help students with past tense sentences.

Gilberto ♦ Point to a boy in the classroom and say his name. Point to the boy in the story "*Gilberto* and the Wind" and say his name.

girl ♦ —*girl's*, see *Felicity's*.

give, giving, gave ♦ Have one puppet *give* another puppet a small object. Provide example sentences using *give, giving, gave*. —*give me time*, have one puppet ask a question. Have the other think, needing more time to answer, and feeling pressured by the first. Explain that *give me time* is short for "*give me time* to think." —*give someone a hand*, tidy a closet or bookcase and say "I need help. Please *give me a hand*, [name]." —*give up*, **1.** Challenge a student to an arm wrestling match. After a moment, throw up your hands and say "I *give up*." **2.** Have a puppet try to reach something and then move away and *give up*. Or, have it try to find something and *give up*. —*gave up*, look like you are having a hard time reading a book and then put it down and *give up*. Or, look like you are having a hard time writing something and then put down the chalk and *give up*.

glad ♦ Pantomime a little scene of a student coming to you and being *glad*. Explain that *glad* means "happy."

glamorous ♦ Show pictures of *glamorous* people and contrast with people of a more average appearance.

100

glance, glancing ❯ Lead students in *glancing* at things around the classroom, and contrast each *glance* by having the students look at the same object closely. Help with sentences, like "I am *glancing* toward the clock."

glare, glaring, glared ❯ Frown and *glare* at a puppet. Lead students in frowning and *glaring* at a puppet. Say "I *glared* at the puppet." Ask them to *glare* at each other, saying "I am *glaring* at you."

gleam ❯ Show the overhead lights in their classroom and then shut them off and show them the *gleam* of light from a flashlight. Lead students in sentences, such as "The flashlight makes a *gleam* of light."

glib ❯ Act out with a puppet making a political campaign speech. Say "This guy wants to be the next mayor of [San Antonio]. He says he'll give us better schools and lower taxes. He doesn't sound honest. I don't believe his *glib* words."

glides ❯ Pantomime skating across the room. Say "The teacher *glides* across the room on his or her skates."

glimpses ❯ Show a student a picture in a book and invite him or her to take a *long* look. Then flash the picture quickly in front of other students. Say "[Tiong] got a *long* look at the picture; the rest of you got only *glimpses*."

glisten, glistens, glistened ❯ Explain that *glisten* means "to shine under light." Place a shiny object under a light and show students how the object *glistens*. Lead students in past tense sentences.

glitter, glitters, glittery ❯ Show students some *glitter* under a light. Explain that it *glitters* or is *glittery*.

gloat ❯ Tell students that you entered a contest. Say "When I win first place, I am going to *gloat*." Use body language for emphasis.

globes ❯ On the board, draw pictures of balloons and other *globes*, such as the *globe* on a lamp, or show them a *globe* of Earth.

gloomy ❯ Show pictures of *gloomy* and *sunny* days.

glorious ❯ Listen to your favorite music and exclaim, "*Glorious!*"

glossy ❯ Contrast a *glossy* sheet of paper with an uncoated sheet, and a *glossy* magazine cover with a *dull* one.

glow, glowed, glowing ❯ Turn off the lights and shine a flashlight through a piece of paper. Give example sentences using *glow* and *glowed*. Point to a light source. Explain that it is *glowing*.

gnaw, gnawing ❯ Pretend to *gnaw* on a pencil. Demonstrate with a dog puppet chewing a bone. Alternatively, chew through a rope of licorice, using tiny, mouse-like bites. Say "I am *gnawing* through the licorice."

go, going, goes, gone, went ❯ **1.** Have students stand up and *go* somewhere or make a toy car *go*. **2.** Tell a puppet "*Go*," and have it walk away. **3.** Show a doll or puppet *going* to a specific location and say "[Fluffy] wants to *go* to the zoo," "[Fluffy] is *going* to the zoo," and "[Fluffy] has *gone* to the zoo." **4.** Move your hand in a circle and explain that it *goes* in a circle. Do this with other movements. **5.** Take things off a table and explain that they are *gone*.

Have students do the same. **6.** To explain the idiomatic sense of *gone* (as used in the phrase "now I've *gone* and hurt my thumb"), drop a pencil, and say "I've *gone* and dropped my pencil." Have students practice such sentences and actions. **7.** *Went* is used in two senses: (1) Pantomime *went* by walking to your desk and saying, "I *went* to my desk." (2) Explain that *went* also means colloquially "said." Have students use sentences and pantomimes for both definitions. Move a doll from one place to another in the room and explain that the doll *went* to these places. Tell a doll to *go* to your desk. Once done, explain that the doll *went* to your desk. Repeat by telling students to *go* different places and then telling them that they *went*. —*go in the hole*, set up a scene where you are a business entrepreneur and the students run a bank. Give students some play money in various denominations. Say "I want to start a lemonade stand and my start-up expenses total $5.75." Show students you have only $2.00. Borrow the rest from the student bankers. Say "I had to borrow $3.75 from the bank. I had to *go in the hole* for $3.75." — *go on the warpath*, tell a puppet that it is going to have an extra homework assignment. Have it become very angry. Say "Wow! Did [Fluffy] ever *go on the warpath!*" —*goin'*, walk to the door and say "I'm *going* to the door." Then write *goin'* on the board and say "I'm *goin'* to the door." Identify the apostrophe and explain that it shows that a letter or letters are missing from the word. Lead students in similar examples and sentences. —*going to*, **1.** Dramatize sentence pairs, such as "The pencil falls" and "The pencil is *going to* fall." **2.** Make up example sentences, modified to reflect your actual schedule, such as: "We are *going to* do math before lunch" or "We are *going to* have lunch at noon." —*on the go*, explain that *on the go* means "to be *going* places and to be busy." Lead students in pantomimes of being *on the go*. —*went off*, show two puppets talking and one walks off. Explain that it *went off*. —*went on*, **1.** Demonstrate walking, and then stop. Then go on walking. Say "I stopped walking, but then I *went on*." Have one puppet sing and another ask it to stop singing. When the first puppet *goes on* singing, say that it *went on* singing. —*went up*, walk up to a student and explain that you *went up* to her.

goat ◆ —*billy goat*, show pictures and explain that this is a boy *goat*.

goal ◆ Tell students a *goal* that you have, perhaps to have them all speaking English well by June. Have students tell you a *goal* they have.

gobbled ◆ Lead students in pantomiming *gobbling*. Explain that it means "eating fast." Say that hungry dogs *gobble* their food.

god ◆ Show pictures of the Greek *gods*.

gold, golden ◆ Point out *gold* or things of a *golden* color in the room (ring, wristwatch, picture of the sun).

good, goods ◆ **1.** Contrast *good* and *bad* things, people, and foods. **2.** Pantomime tasting something and saying that it's *good*. Contrast this with making a face and saying that it's *bad*. **3.** Circulate through the room and compliment students with phrases, such as "*Good* work" and "You are a *good* worker." **4.** Show different kinds of *goods*, such as canned *goods*, cloth *goods*, etc.

good-bye ◆ Pantomime leaving the room, wave at students, and say "*Good-bye.*" Have students imitate.

goodness ◆ **1.** Show a puppet being very good and say "There is a lot of *goodness* in this puppet." **2.** Explain that *goodness* is also like *Gosh!* which people say if they are a little surprised. Give examples, such as "*Goodness!* You are late," "*Goodness!* I tripped," or "*Goodness!* My shoe is untied."

goodnight ◆ Have a puppet go to sleep, and as you are putting it to bed tell it, "*Goodnight.*"

gore ◆ Show a picture of a longhorn or other similar animal. Show the antlers and demonstrate how they use them to *gore* an attacker.

gorge, gorging ◆ Have a puppet *gorge* itself on paper clips. Tell the class that the puppet is eating much more than it needs. Give example sentences using *gorging.*

govern, governing, governed, government ◆ **1.** Give examples and have students pantomime the ways that a principal, teacher, president, and king *govern.* **2.** Explain that the *government* is a group of people that lead. The *government* of a school is the principal and the principal's helpers. The *government* of a classroom is the teacher, the teacher's aides, and any student leaders. The *government* of the United States is the president and the president's helpers. **3.** Show pictures of the national and state capitols. Show a picture of the mayor, and if possible, videotapes of congressional committees, city council meetings, etc. Give example sentences using *government.* **4.** Create a class council to help make classroom rules. Let the rules *govern* the class. Say "We are *governed* by the council."

gown ◆ Show illustrations of *gowns.*

grab, grabbing, grabbed ◆ **1.** Have one puppet *grab* something from another puppet. Tell the puppet, "Do not *grab; grabbing* is not nice." Tell the class, "The puppet *grabbed* from his friend." —*grab hold,* have students *grab hold* of their desks.

grace ◆ Walk with *grace.* Contrast by walking with an *awkward* gait.

graduated ◆ Pantomime a college *graduation* commencement ceremony. Have students make and wear mortarboards and walk up to your desk single file. Hand each student a rolled up sheet of paper. Say "Congratulations on finishing college. Here is your diploma. You have *graduated* from college."

grand, grander, grandest ◆ **1.** Show pictures of expansive landscapes and *grand* homes. Contrast with pictures of regular houses and small yards. **2.** Show students houses or rooms that are *grand, grander,* and *grandest.*

grandchildren ◆ Draw a family tree on the board that includes three generations, beginning with *grandparents.* Label each row with *grandparents* on top, parents in the middle, and *grandchildren* on the bottom.

grandmother ◆ Draw a picture of a child, a mother, and a *grandmother* on the board. Label them. While pointing to each woman, say "This woman is her mother." Then point to the child and *grandmother* and say "This is her *grandmother*." Ask for first-language names.

grandpa ➡ Show pictures of children with their *grandpas*.

graph ➡ Write *graph* on the board. Explain that it is from the Greek language. (Show Greece on a map and explain that people and things from Greece are called Greek.) Explain that it means "to write."

grasp, grasping, grasped ➡ **1.** Lead students in *grasping* for things around the classroom. **2.** Hold onto a chair or desk and explain that you *grasped* it.

gratefully, gratitude ➡ **1.** Have a student offer to help you with something. Say with exaggerated appreciation, "Thank you! I *gratefully* accept your offer." **2.** Have one puppet give another a pencil. Have the receiving puppet express thanks over and over for the present, showing *gratitude*.

gravity ➡ Pick up something and drop it. Say "The *gravity* made the [book] fall to the floor." See *gravitational attraction*. —*gravity-assist change of direction*, use a globe or draw Earth on the board. Draw a spaceship on a sheet of paper. Launch it from Earth. After it gets to a certain height, turn it and make it orbit Earth. Say "This is a *gravity-assist change of direction*."

gray, grayer ➡ **1.** Show pictures of *gray* or cloudy days. Explain that it looks *gray* out because of the dark clouds. **2.** Lightly color with a *gray* crayon, then color it darker. Explain that first it was *gray* and now it is *grayer*.

graze, grazing ➡ Show pictures of *grazing* animals. Explain that when they eat in this manner, they *graze*.

greasy ➡ Show a picture of margarine and explain that it is *greasy*. Ask if students have ever gotten margarine on their fingers.

great ➡ Look at some recent work that students have done. Say "This is very good; it is *great*." Repeat with many students' work. —*great big*, Contrast *big* and *great big* things for students. Then have them find things that are *big* and *great big*. —*great deal*, Show students a *great deal* of pencils, paper clips, or paper and contrast by showing *small* amounts of the same.

great-grandma ➡ Draw a child, mother, grandmother, and *great grandmother* on the board. Show the relationship of daughter to mother, etc. Ask for first-language names.

great-great-aunt ➡ Draw your family tree on the board, depicting you, your two parents, your four grandparents, and your eight great-grandparents. Then draw a horizontal arrow from one of your great-grandparents to a female figure. Say "The sister of one of my great-grandparents is my *great-great-aunt*."

greedy, greedily ➡ **1.** Dramatize being *greedy* by grabbing things off your desk and loading yourself up with things. **2.** Pantomime keeping things for yourself as you say "I am *greedy*; I won't give things to you." Contrast with *generosity*. **3.** Show pictures of pigs and say "Pigs *greedily* eat their food." **4.** Show students a bowl of candy. Have a puppet grab candy *greedily* without allowing another puppet to have any.

greens ◆ Show pictures of plants and explain that *greens* are the *green* parts of plants.

greeted ◆ *Greet* a puppet and say that you *greeted* it.

grief ◆ Stage the death of a puppet, and then show your sadness. Say "It is so sad that [Fluffy] died. I feel terrible *grief*. Do you feel *grief*?"

grim ◆ Make a *grim* face. Contrast with a *happy* face. Lead students in making *grim* and *happy* faces.

grin, grins, grinning, grinned ◆ Lead students in *grinning*. Help make sentences, such as, "You have a nice *grin*," "She *grins* at her friend," "We are *grinning*," and "We *grinned*."

grip, gripped ◆ **1.** *Grip* the back of a chair. Have students do the same. **2.** Hold a student's hand tightly and have him or her try to pull away. Say "I *gripped* your hand." Have students imitate.

gritting, gritted ◆ Pantomime *gritting* your teeth. Help students with sentences in both tenses.

groan, groaning ◆ Demonstrate a *groan* and lead students in *groaning*.

groom, groomed, grooms ◆ Show a picture of a horse, ideally getting *groomed* by a *groom*. Explain that when a horse is brushed, it is being *groomed*. Explain that the person who *grooms* the horse is called a *groom*.

grooved ◆ Show a *grooved* surface and contrast with a *smooth* one.

grope ◆ Close your eyes and *grope* around your desk for your pen. Ask students to close their eyes and *grope* for something on their desks.

grouch, grouchy, grouchier, grouchiest, grouching ◆ **1.** Act like a *grouch*. **2.** First, explain *grouchy*, which means the same as *crabby*. Have a puppet talk in a slightly *grouchy* way to another puppet. Then, have the second puppet be even *grouchier*, and the first puppet be *grouchiest*. Explain that the puppets are *grouching* at each other.

ground, grounded, grounds ◆ **1.** Take students outside and show them the *ground*. Have them sit on it, walk on it, and jump on it. **2.** Show the *grounds* around the school. Lead students in sentences. **3.** On the board, draw a large cloud with rain. Underneath draw *grounded* planes.

groundwork ◆ **1.** On the board, draw a tall building. Explain that the work must be done on the *ground* before the top can be built. Say "This is called *groundwork*." **2.** Ask students what kind of *groundwork* they need to be able to subtract.

grow, growing, grew, grown, growth ◆ **1.** Show pictures of seeds, seedlings, and plants. Explain that the plants *grow* from seeds. **2.** Show pictures of babies and children. Tell students the babies *grow* into children. **3.** On the board, show plants and children *growing*. Have the children pantomime *growing* tall. **4.** Explain that the seeds and children have *grown*. **5.** Remark how much your students have *grown* since school started. **6.** Explain the *growth* of babies into children and children into adults.

grudge, grudgingly ◆ Have a puppet take a pencil from you. Demand that it return it. Have the puppet give it back *grudgingly*. Tell the class, "This puppet has a *grudge*."

grumble, grumbles, grumbled ◆ Have a puppet *grumble* about something that it doesn't want to do. Assign today's homework. Invite students to *grumble* about it.

grump, grumpy ◆ Lead students in acting like a *grump*. Lead students in looking *grumpy* and in contrast *happy*.

grunt, grunting ◆ Lead students in *grunting* like a pig.

guarantee ◆ Tell students something that is certain, such as, "We will have homework tonight; I *guarantee* it."

guard, guarding, guarded ◆ *Guard* something that you consider special. Lead students in *guarding* something that they own. Show pictures of a dog *guarding* a house; say "The dog *guarded* the house." —*rear guard*, show pictures of soldiers in battle. On the board, draw lines of soldiers with one in the back. Give example sentences using *rear guard*.

guess, guessing, guessed ◆ **1.** Have a puppet hide something in its hand. Have it tell a puppet to *guess* what it is. Repeat with students. **2.** Show students a container of paper clips. Say "Does anybody know for sure how many paper clips there are in this box? No? Well, let's each *guess* how many there might be. My *guess* is 148." Invite students to *guess* a number. **3.** Show students a container of many items, such as paper clips. Ask students to *guess* how many there are. Lead students in past tense sentences.

guest ◆ **1.** Invite students to your house, and say "When you come to my house, you will be my *guest*." **2.** Pretend to have a tea party with students. Say "I'm so pleased you could come to my tea party. It is so nice to have you as my *guests*."

guide ◆ Close your eyes and ask for a *guide* to take you somewhere in the room.

guilt ◆ Have a puppet drop a piece of chalk and break it. Have the puppet act ashamed and come to tell you what it did. Say "[Fluffy] accidentally broke my chalk. The *guilt* he was feeling made him confess."

gullible ◆ Demonstrate with puppets by having one puppet tell another things students know are not true, such as, "The teacher is not here." Then have the second puppet show students that it believes the first and do something wrong. Tell students, "That puppet is *gullible*." Repeat until the children clearly see the concept. Then lead them in pantomimes and sentences.

gulp, gulps ◆ Demonstrate *sipping* water, and say "I am taking little *sips*." Demonstrate *gulping* water and say "I am taking big *gulps*."

gurgling ◆ Pretend you are brushing your teeth. Make *gurgling* sounds with the water and say "I am *gurgling*." Lead students in *gurgling*.

gush ◆ Turn a faucet on full force to show students how the water *gushes* out.

gust ◆ If you have a pen that will stand straight up on your desk, stand it up and blow at it. Tell students, "The *gust* blew the pen down." Have students pretend to be *gusts* of wind and blow papers off their desks.

habit, habits ❧ Dramatize *habits*, such as chewing on your nails, pulling hair, or doodling. For contrast show good *habits* such as brushing teeth and hair, washing hands before eating, etc.

hail, hailing, hailed ❧ 1. Have one puppet *hail* another puppet for winning a race. Repeat by having students *hail* each other for their accomplishments. 2. Call after a puppet. Run over and touch its shoulder. Say "I *hailed* you."

half-hearted ❧ Check that students understand the individual words. Wipe the board *half-heartedly*. Contrast by wiping it *whole-heartedly*.

half-mile ❧ See *mile*.

halfway ❧ Draw a line on the board and show the *halfway* point.

hall, hallways ❧ 1. Show students a *hall* in the building that you are in. 2. Show the *hallways* in the school.

hallow ❧ Explain that a place that is hallow is a special, sacred place that has been blessed. Show pictures of priests, rabbis, and ministers blessing buildings or objects. Give students example sentences using *hallow*.

halting ❧ Walk in a *halting* manner; contrast by walking without hesitation. Read a passage *unhaltingly* and another *haltingly*.

halves ❧ Draw two circles on the board and *halve* them. Show students the *halves*.

hammer ❧ —*hammer out*, have students arrange their desks in a circle. Set up a scene in which you are having a meeting to talk about a special event, such as longer recesses. Say "We are having a meeting to *hammer out* how long recess can be."

hampers ❧ Have a puppet try to move forward while you pull on the bottom of the puppet to *hamper* it.

hand ❧ 1. Ask a student to give you a book, then ask a student to *hand* you a book. 2. *Hand* various items to students and ask students to *hand* them back to you. —*old hand*, give students an example of someone who is experienced at something. Say, for example, "I have been teaching for [15] years; I am an *old hand* at teaching English."

handful ❧ Show students a *handful* of paper clips.

handle ❧ Tell a puppet you have a problem. Ask, "Can you help me *handle* it?" Give the puppet a large package to take to your house. Have the puppet lug it toward the door.

handouts ❧ Give students *handouts*.

handshake ❧ Shake *hands* with students.

handsprings ❧ Demonstrate with a doll or show pictures of people doing *handsprings*.

handy ❧ See *convenient*. Place some markers or crayons on your desk and draw a picture. Have a few out of your reach. Pick up a crayon and say "I'll use [blue] because it's *handy*." Show your hand when you say *handy*.

hang, hanging, hung ◈ **1.** *Hang* up your coat. Tell students that you *hung* it up. Pantomime *hanging* clothes on a hook. Say "I *hung* the clothes." **2.** Show things that are *hanging* on the wall. **3.** Show how a door is *hung* by its hinges.

hangups ◈ Lead a discussion of various things that make different people uncomfortable, such as flying, snakes, heights, small spaces, etc. Say "People are bothered by different kinds of things; people have all different kinds of *hangups*."

happen, happens, happening, happened ◈ **1.** Ask students, "Tell me something that will *happen* today." If no one can answer, answer yourself with expectable events, such as lunch and recess. Each time something is mentioned, say "Yes, that will *happen* today." You can also talk about things that *happened* on earlier days or things that *happened* in school photos or in picture books. **2.** Say "What *happens* when the bell rings?" or "What *happens* when I say it is story time?" **3.** Look out the window and tell students some of the different things that are *happening* outside. Have students do the same.

happy, happier, happiest, happily ◈ **1.** Demonstrate with a puppet being *happy*. **2.** Demonstrate *happy, happier,* and *happiest* through facial expression and appropriate sentences. Lead students in demonstrating as well. **3.** *Happily* clean the board, hum a tune, or other such activities. Repeat the activities *sadly*. **4.** Lead students in smiling *happily.* —*happily ever after,* check that students understand the word *ever*. See *ever*. Draw a time line on the board. Mark the beginning on the left side, and the end of the story on the right side. At the end point of the story, explain that the billy goats lived *happily ever after*. Continue the line out to the right as far as you can draw to explain *ever after*.

harassed ◈ Pretend to work at your desk while a student taps you on the shoulder to get your attention. Say "The student *harassed* the teacher to get him or her to stop what he or she was doing."

harbor, harbors ◈ Show pictures of *harbors* and explain that a *harbor* is a place along the coast where boats can be kept safe. Review *coast* as needed.

hard ◈ Contrast *easy* things with *hard* things. Write on the board the problem 2 + 2 and say it's *easy*. Then write a long division problem and say it's *hard*. Ask students if these words are *easy* or *hard*: write on the board the words *cat* and *antidisestablishmentarianism*.

hard, harder, hardest, harden, hardening ◈ **1.** Have students breathe *hard* as if they have been running. Contrast by having students breathe *softly*. **2.** Have students touch something *hard* and then in contrast something *soft*. **3.** Show *hardened* clay or stale bread. Use an ice cube to illustrate that water *hardens* when it gets cold. Put a dab of glue on paper, and as it dries, show students how it is *hardening*. **4.** Suggest things that students would find *hard* to do, perhaps standing on their heads; and then something *harder* such as a handstand; and finally hardest, perhaps walking on a tightrope. Use pictures as needed. **5.** On the board, draw a few raindrops falling. Say "It is raining a little." Add many more raindrops. Say "It is raining *harder*."

hardly ◈ **1.** Contrast having *many* pencils with having *hardly* any pencils. **2.** Stuff foam peanuts into a cup so they *hardly* fit.

hardships ❱ Ask students what they think it would be *hard* to live without. Respond by saying, "Yes, that would be a *hardship*."

harm, harmed, harmless, ❱ **1.** Have a puppet drop a toy. Then say "The puppet *harmed* the _____." Have a toy animal be frightened of a puppet. Have the puppet say "I won't *harm* you," and then do something kind for the frightened animal. **2.** Show a picture of a sweet-looking rabbit and say it is *harmless*. Contrast with a dangerous-looking animal and say it is not *harmless*.

harmony ❱ Set up the scene where students are to place their desks in a circle. Have them work in *harmony* to get the task completed.

harness, harnessed ❱ Show students pictures of a horse, a *harness*, and a horse being *harnessed* or wearing a *harness*. Identify each and lead students in sentences.

harpoon-shots ❱ On the board, draw a *harpoon* and a trajectory as if it had been shot. Lead students in sentences using *harpoon-shots*.

harsh ❱ Tell the class that the puppet was caught chewing gum in class and must be punished. Ask the class to help you find a fair punishment. Then have the class help you find a *harsh* punishment.

harvest, harvesting, harvested, harvests ❱ **1.** Have puppets *harvest* a crop. Or, show pictures of farmworkers picking fruit from trees or *harvesting* a crop. Have students say when and where we *harvest* things, such as apples, oranges, and potatoes. **2.** Have students help you make a list of things farmers grow, such as corn, broccoli, strawberries, and wheat. Show pictures or draw items on the board. Say "These are the *harvests* from the farmers."
3. Pantomime picking fruits and vegetables from a garden and explain that you are *harvesting* the garden.

has, have, had, hadn't, ❱ **1.** Act out sentences with students: "I *have* a pencil," "I *have* a paper clip," and so on. **2.** Point to things in the classroom and say "We *have* a [pet guinea pig]" or "We *have* [books]." **3.** Pretend to catch a passing bug and say "I *have* it!" **4.** Act out contrasting sentences, such as "I *have* a book," and after putting it down "I *had* a book," or "I *have* a nap" and "I *had* a nap." **5.** Show on the board how *had* and *not* squeeze together to make the word *hadn't*. See *had* and *not*. Lead in sentences such as "I *hadn't* any dinner" or "She *hadn't* any toys." **6.** Give a student a book and say "She *has* a book." Contrast with *have*: "I *have* a book; she *has* a book." **7.** Lead students in making sentences about things in the class, such as, "Paula *has* a hat," "My desk *has* a drawer," or "Juan *has* a pencil." —*have guts*, pantomime being afraid of a toy animal and then pantomime being brave. Explain that you *have guts*. Ask students for examples of times they *had guts*. —*have his way*, have two puppets argue over something several times, with the same one always winning. Explain that the winning puppet gets to *have his way*. —*have the heart*, use a puppet and tell students that it came to you with an idea for a new business. Say "I didn't think it was a very good idea, but I did not want to disappoint it or hurt its feelings. I didn't *have the heart* to tell it what I thought." —*haven't*, explain that this is two words squeezed together: *have* and *not*. See *have* and *not* in the **Visual Glossary** component. —*I've*, explain *I* and *have* individually. On the board, show students how the words *I* and *have* squeeze together to make *I've*. Show them which letters the apostrophe replaces. Lead them in sentences using both *I have* and *I've*. —*I've had enough!*, have students all start speaking and being noisy in general. Tell them to stop because you've *had enough*. Review the contraction *I've* if needed. —*I've had it!*, see *I'm fed up!* under *fed*—*you've*, show on the board how the words *you* and *have* can be squeezed together to make *you've*. See *you* and *have*.

hasten ❧ Have a puppet *hasten* to the door. Repeat with students.

hastily ❧ Do something *hastily*. Say that you did it *hastily*. Lead students in doing things *hastily*.

hatband ❧ —*beading a hatband*, explain that this means "to put *beads* on a *band*, and then place the *band* on a *hat*."

hatch, hatches, hatching, hatched ❧ **1.** Draw a spaceship on the board with a *hatch* open at the side. Pantomime pushing the *hatch* closed. **2.** Show pictures of *hatching* chicks and explain that the chick *hatches* from an egg. **3.** If possible, show a picture of an animal such as a bird, reptile, or dinosaur, which has just *hatched* from an egg. Or, have students dramatize being inside an egg, pecking at the shell, and *hatching*. **4.** Show pictures of chicks and the eggs that they *hatched* from.

hate ❧ **1.** Hold a doll or animal figure and express *love*. Then look at a picture or something else, which can't be easily hurt, and express *hate*. Contrast these, ending with *love*. **2.** Show puppets engaged in a fight, yelling that they *hate* each other. Contrast with *love*.

haul, hauling, hauled ❧ **1.** Have a puppet *haul* a package along. **2.** Lead students in *hauling* books up to your desk and then back to the bookshelf. Contrast with having them *carry* a few pencils to your desk and back. **3.** Show pictures of things being pulled up, either from the sea or possibly from the street to an upper-story window. Explain that these things are being *hauled*. Lead students in pantomimes of *hauling* things.

haunches ❧ Using a toy animal, show its *haunches* and how it sits on them.

haunting ❧ Hum a melody. Say "This song has been stuck in my head for days. It is a *haunting* little tune."

haze ❧ Show pictures with fog or smog and point to the *haze*."

he ❧ Some students may confuse *he*, *she*, and *it*. Have students talk about a specific girl, a boy, and an object, such as "*She* is tall," "*He* is big," and "*It* is blue." Point out boys and girls, contrasting *he* and *she*.

he'd ❧ Explain that this is two words squeezed together: *he* and *would*. See *he* and *would*. Show on the board how *he* and *would* squeeze together to make the word *he'd*.

head ❧ Ask a student to help you with a math problem. Say "You have a good *head* on you." —*head over heels*, draw a picture of someone literally *head over heels*. Lead students in sentences. —*head-on*, pretend that two erasers are buses. Act out a *head-on* crash.

headaches ❧ Pretend to have a *headache*. Lead students in sentences.

headed ● Walk toward the door. Say "I am *headed* toward the door."

headquarters ● Show pictures of Washington, DC. Explain that it is the *headquarters* of the U.S. government.

healer, healing ● **1.** Say "My *healer*, my doctor, is called [name]. What is your *healer* called?" **2.** Make a puppet fall down. Pantomime taking care of its leg. Say "The leg is *healing* nicely." **3.** Show a picture of a nurse *healing* a person who is ill.

health ● Have one puppet be very ill, coughing, lying down, shivering, etc. Tell students that it has poor *health*. Contrast with another puppet doing exercises, such as jogging, and feeling great. Tell students that it has good *health*.

hear, hearing, heard ● **1.** Cover your ears with your hands and explain that you can't *hear*. Uncover them and explain that now you can *hear*. **2.** Dramatize *hearing* by cupping your hand around your ear. **3.** Cup your hands to your ear and drop something that makes a thud. Explain that you *heard* a noise. **4.** Drop a toy on the floor and ask a puppet what it *heard*. Have the puppet tell you that it *heard* a noise. Repeat with students.

heart ● **1.** Draw an outline of a person with a *heart* on the board. Say "This is the *heart* of the person." Have students feel their *hearts*. Cut an apple in half, point to the core, and say "This is the *heart* of the apple." **2.** Pantomime being sad. Say "When I am sad, I feel it in my *heart*." Pantomime being happy. Say "When I am happy, I feel it in my *heart*." Put your hand over your *heart* as you say these. **3.** Have a puppet cry and beg for a cookie. Give it one. Say "I didn't have the *heart* to say no." —*at heart*, show a picture of an older person flying a kite or playing a children's game. Tell students this person is a child *at heart*. Ask students to tell you something their parents or grandparents do that shows how they are *at heart*. —*heart attack*, draw a *heart* on the board. Have a puppet act out having a *heart attack*. Point to the *heart*. Say "The puppet had a *heart attack*. Take the puppet to the hospital."

heartbreaking ● Pantomime a scene, where a puppet gets very sick and another puppet sits by him, crying. Tell students, "The puppet is very sad. His friend is so sick. It is *heartbreaking*." Ask students if they have ever seen a sick animal. Tell them, "It is sad. It is *heartbreaking*."

hearth ● The floor of a fireplace usually extending into the room. Show a picture of a fireplace and the *hearth* or draw one on the board.

heartsick ● Pantomime love and affection for the puppet; then have the puppet abandon you. Pantomime despair. Give example sentences using *heartsick*.

heat, heating ● **1.** Point to a source of *heat* for the room like a furnace or vent. If sunlight comes in, have students reach out their hands to feel the *heat*. **2.** Talk about *heating* food on a stove. Show a picture of a stove. —*heat wave*, draw five boxes on the board, labeled Monday through Friday. Draw a sun in each box. Fan yourself and say "It has been hot for five days. We're having a *heat wave*."

heave ● Take in a deep breath and say "Watch my chest *heave*." Ask students to copy your actions.

heavens ◆ On the board, draw a night sky with stars, planets, and a moon.

heavy, heavier, heaviest, heavily ◆ **1.** Have students feel the weight of objects that are *heavy* and *light*. Have students pick up *light* and *heavy* things, telling you which one is *heavy*. **2.** Compare the weight of three books and say which is *heavy, heavier,* and *heaviest*. Lead students in comparative demonstrations and sentences. **3.** Walk *heavily*. Contrast by walking *lightly*. Lead students in walking *heavily* and *lightly*.

heir ◆ Demonstrate by having one puppet die and leave all of its belongings to another puppet. Explain that the puppet who received all these things is the *heir*.

heirloom ◆ Show *heirlooms* from your family.

hello ◆ Briefly leave the room, then enter and say *"Hello"* to a puppet and have the puppet say *"Hello"* to you. Then repeat with students.

help, helps, helping, helped, helpers, helpful, helpless ◆ **1.** Have a student *help* you in some way, such as carrying or holding something. Once he or she is done, explain that he or she *helped*. **2.** Mention some students who have been your *helpers* recently. Have a puppet pantomime drawing and then ask another puppet to be its *helper*. The *helper helps* the puppet move the chalk. **3.** Ask a student to *help* you put some books away or some other small task. As he or she is doing the task, say "He/she is *helping* me." Repeat with other students as needed. **4.** After it notices that you need it, have a puppet be *helpful* to you, perhaps by giving you chalk, pencils, or erasers. Be *helpful* to a student by assisting him or her with pronouncing a word or finding a book. **5.** Pretend to be in your car and unable to find your keys. Say to a student, "May I get a ride with you? I am *helpless*. I have no keys."

hemisphere ◆ Show a ball and identify it as such. Also identify it as a *sphere*. Compare it to a globe and call the globe a *sphere*. Point to the equator and encircle the top half of the globe and say *"Hemisphere."* Repeat for the bottom half.

her ◆ Some students may confuse *her* and *him*. Have a girl give a book to a boy. Say *"She* gave the book to *him."* Have the boy give the book back to the girl. Say *"He* gave the book to *her."* Talk about the clothes of a boy and a girl in the class. Lead students in making contrasting sentences, such as *"Her* shoes are brown" and *"His* shoes are black."

herd ◆ Show a picture of a person *herding* sheep or cattle.

herd, herds ◆ Show pictures of a *herd* and several *herds* of animals.

here ◆ **1.** Point to where you are on the floor and say *"Here* I am." Point to something across the room and say *"There* is the _____." Repeat with different objects. **2.** Say to a puppet, "Put the pencil *here*" and "Put the pencil *there*."

hermit ◆ Draw a picture on the board of people living together in a little village. Some distance away from this, draw a picture of one person living alone. Tell students that he or she is a *hermit*.

hero ◆ Mention *heroes* that students might be familiar with, such as Superman or Batman. Point out the medal that Hank received because he was a *hero*.

heroism ➨ Act out with two puppets: one large, one small. Draw a burning house on the board. Have students make a siren sound. Draw a ladder to an upper window of the house and have the large puppet climb it and rescue the smaller puppet. Lead students in using *heroism*.

herself ➨ See *himself*.

hesitate, hesitant, hesitations ➨ **1.** Ask a puppet to come to your desk. Have the puppet *hesitate*. Tell the class that it is *hesitant*. **2.** Read aloud and demonstrate *hesitations* as you read.

Hey! ➨ Have one puppet get the attention of another by saying, "*Hey!*"

hickory ➨ Show a picture of a *hickory* tree.

hide, hid, hiding, hidden ➨ **1.** *Hide* a small item. Explain that you *hid* it. **2.** *Hide* behind your desk. Tell students that you *hid*. **3.** Have a student *hide* and say that he or she is *hiding*. Have a student *hide* and explain that [John] *hides* behind the door. **4.** Ask a student to *hide* something. Close your eyes and say "Have you *hidden* it?" As you look for it, say "Where is it *hidden?* Where have you *hidden* it?" **5.** Hide a few things around the classroom and lead students in finding the *hidden* objects. —*hiding place*, **1.** Ask two students to *hide*. When you find one, say "That was a good *hiding place*." **2.** Show students a pencil. Look around the room and say "Where can I put this pencil so no one will find it?" Put it in a few obvious places and get students to say "No!" Then put it out of sight and say "Ah. This is a good *hiding place*."

hideous ➨ Make *hideous* faces. Show *hideous* pictures. Name *hideous* movies. Have students do the same.

higglety ➨ Explain it's just a fun sound. It doesn't mean anything. Have students make up other fun sounds.

high, higher ➨ **1.** Demonstrate by reaching for items in the room that are up *high*. Ask students to find things that are up *high*. Contrast with things that are down *low*. **2.** Hold an object up *high* and then *low*. **3.** Point out things in the classroom that are *high*, *higher*, and then *highest*. **4.** Have students build three towers: one *high*; the next, *higher*; the third, *highest*.

high school ➨ On the board, draw three buildings. Name one *Elementary School*, one *Middle School*, and one *High School*. List the grades under each one.

high-five ➨ Demonstrate a *high-five*.

highlight ➨ Use a *highlight* marker and show students how one can *highlight* text with it. Permit students to *highlight* some text, perhaps from a newspaper, magazine, or a handout.

highly ➨ **1.** Have students list people they respect. Lead them in sentences using *highly*. **2.** See *very*.

high-ranking ➨ Write down names of the positions in the school that make up the hierarchy of the school. Show students what positions would be *high-ranking*, *mid-ranking*, and *low-ranking*.

hike, hiking, hiked ❖ Pantomime walking as if going up a hill. Say that *hiking* is a long walk in the country or in the mountains. Have students pretend that the classroom has a trail and pretend to *hike*.

him ❖ Some students may confuse *him* and *her*. Have students pantomime and speak of actions in regard to a specific girl and boy. For example, they can bring a toy or book to *her* and *him*.

himself ❖ Have a student seat *himself*. Say "He seated *himself*." Give other examples, if familiar to students, such as "He pinched *himself*" or "He bumped *himself*."

hinder ❖ Have a puppet try to leave the room. Grab its arm. Give example sentences using *hinder*.

hint ❖ Explain that the clues that students are given when playing "Clues" could also be called *hints*. As needed, dramatize giving *hints*. Tell students that you hid something in your hand and give them *hints* as to what it is.

hire ❖ See *lay off*. Tell students you have a job that you will pay someone to do. Say "I need to *hire* somebody to [wash these windows] for me. I will pay [$5.00] to the person who will do this job."

his ❖ Point to clothing and shoes worn by boys or girls and lead students in contrasting sentences, such as, "*Her* shoes are brown" and "*His* shirt is black."

hiss, hissing, hissed ❖ **1.** Show a picture of a snake. Demonstrate a *hiss*. Lead students in *hissing*. Say "We *hissed*." **2.** Show a picture of a goose. Imitate the *hissing* sound that geese make.

history ❖ **1.** Ask students to name things they can remember from their past. Say "These are things that happened to you long ago. These things are part of your personal *history*." **2.** Draw a time line on the board, mark a few dates from the past, and mention something that happened on those dates that students should know. Say "These are examples of *history*."

hit, hits ❖ *Hit* a ball with your hand. Show a puppet *hitting* a baseball. Show a toy vehicle *hitting* a bump or a dip in its road.

hitch ❖ **1.** If you don't have a picture of a trailer *hitch* or a *hitch* between two train cars, you can draw one on the board. One type would be a loop of metal that fits over an upright post. **2.** Show or draw a picture of an ox that is harnessed to a large wagon. Say "This is how you *hitch* an ox to a wagon so you can go for a ride."

hoarse ❖ Pantomime having a *hoarse* voice.

hobby, hobbies ❖ Ask students what they like to collect. Say "Collecting [stamps, rocks, or coins] can be a fun *hobby*." Help with sentences in the plural form.

hoist, hoisted ❖ **1.** Show a picture of a crane and how it *hoists* construction materials. Lead students in past tense sentences. **2.** Tie a string around a book. Place the book on a chair seat and run the string up over the back of the chair. *Hoist* the book up and say "I *hoisted* the book up to the top of the chair."

114

hold, holding, held ❧ **1.** Have students *hold* pencils in their hands. Ask a student to *hold* a book for you. After a moment or two, take the book back and explain that he or she *held* it. Repeat with other students. **2.** Lead the students in *holding* various objects. Demonstrate *holding* your breath.

hole, holes ❧ Make a *hole* by curving your fingers together. Point out *holes* in paper or *holes* in shoes for laces. Have students find other *holes*. Make a *hole* by cupping your hand to form a circle. —*black holes*, show pictures of *black holes*, or on the board, draw stars and planets surrounding a *black hole*.

holler, hollering, hollered ❧ Contrast your regular speaking voice with a *holler*. Lead students in *hollering*, and then say that you *hollered*.

hollow ❧ Show a drinking straw. Say that it is empty. It is *hollow*. Compare it with a pencil: "The straw is *hollow*. The pencil is not *hollow*." Lead students in making similar sentences.

home ❧ **1.** Put a toy house on a table (or draw one and put it on the table). Place toy dolls inside or in front of the house. Each time, tell students, "She is *home*." Have students put toy dolls in the *home*. **2.** Show pictures of a *home*. Have students use *home* in sentences.

home run ❧ Draw a baseball diamond on the board. Pantomime hitting a *home run* and "*run*" around the bases with your fingers on the chalk-drawn diagram.

homeland ❧ Explain that the country you were born in is your *homeland*. Show various countries on a globe or world map and ask individuals: "Is India your *homeland?*" "Is Mexico your *homeland?*" and so on. Prompt for correct answers as needed.

homely ❧ Have students each make two signs on sheets of paper. On one sign have them just write words. Have them decorate the other sign with fancy letters, various colors, flowers, stars, etc. Have them hold up their plain signs. Say "These signs are *homely*." Of their decorated signs, say "These signs are not *homely;* they are *beautiful*."

homemade ❧ Bring something *homemade*.

homesick ❧ Explain that *homesick* means "feeling sad because you want to go *home*."

honest, honesty, honestly ❧ **1.** Tell a blatant *lie*, perhaps about your hair color. Then tell students, "I will be *honest* now," and tell the truth. **2.** Have a puppet tell a blatant *lie*. Tell him, "*Honesty* is important to me. Tell me the truth." Have the puppet do so. **3.** Have a puppet turn in a shoddy assignment. Tell the puppet, "I must *honestly* say that this is not good work."

honey ❧ Share special names you reserve for your nearest and dearest. Have students add more names; also translate such words from their first language.

honking, honked ❧ **1.** Show a picture of a goose. Imitate the *honking* sound that geese make. **2.** Show a picture of a car. Tell students that it is the sound a car horn makes. Ask who has *honked* the horn in their parents' cars.

honor ◆ Take students' heroes and have them plan some way to *honor* them.

hood ◆ —*riding hood*, point out the *hood* on Little Green *Riding Hood's* costume. Explain that this is called a *riding hood*, and it means a *hood* for wearing when you *ride* a horse. Show a picture of a horse if needed.

hoofbeats ◆ Draw or show a picture of a horse. Demonstrate clapping your hands together, then slapping them in succession on your thighs to imitate a galloping sound. Say "We heard the *hoofbeats* as the horses ran toward us." Have students imitate.

hoofs ◆ **1.** Draw or show a picture of a horse and its *hoofs*. **2.** Demonstrate the sound of *hoofs* by rapping on your desk with your knuckles.

hooray ◆ Pretend the whole class won a prize. Lead the class in congratulating itself and expressing happiness by shouting, "*Hooray!*"

hoot, hooted ◆ Show a picture of an owl and imitate its *hoot*.

hop, hops, hopping, hopped ◆ Lead students in *hopping*. Tell them that they *hopped*. Start and stop students in *hopping*, alternating *hop* and *hopped*. Help with sentences in the various forms.

hope, hopes, hoped, hopeful ◆ **1.** Pantomime with puppets. Have a puppet say that it is waiting for the basketball game to start. Then have it say "I *hope* that it will start soon." Tell the class, it is *hopeful*. Ask students what they *hoped* to receive for their birthdays. **2.** Ask what *hopes* the children have and share your own. Dramatize example sentences: "I *hope* I get a doll for my birthday!" "I *hope* I get a present!" "Maria *hopes* she will get a bicycle for her birthday!" "I am *hoping* that we have hot dogs for dinner!"

hopscotch ◆ Draw a game of *hopscotch* on the board. Show how to *hop* over the squares. Say "Who plays *hopscotch?*"

horizontally ◆ Hold a pencil parallel to the floor. Say "I am holding my pencil *horizontally.*"

horrendous ◆ Invite students to make a lot of noise. Cover your ears, cower, and say "What a dreadful noise! That is *horrendous*. Please stop!"

horrible ◆ Invite students to make ugly monster faces. Recoil and say with disgust, "Oh! What *horrible* looking faces you're making!"

horrid ◆ Ask students to name foods they hate. Pantomime eating one of these awful tasting things. Screw up your face in disgust and say with great repugnance, "Yuck! That tastes *horrid!*" Have students imitate.

horror, horrified ◆ **1.** Pantomime a scene of two puppets having a big fight. Tell them to stop and say "I am *horrified* by the way you are acting." **2.** Draw a large snake on the board. Walk by the board, and when you notice the snake, recoil and shudder. Say with fear and disgust, "I have a *horror* of snakes." Have students imitate.

hospitality ◆ Act out a tea party with students. Treat them in a friendly, generous way. Say "The teacher treated her guests with *hospitality* at a lovely tea party."

host ❧   See *guest*. Continue tea party pantomime. Say "I am happy to be your *host* at my party."

hostile ❧   Make a puppet act in a *hostile* way toward another puppet. Say "That puppet is acting *hostile*. It is not *friendly*."

hot ❧   **1.** Have puppets touch something *hot*. Contrast with *cold*. **2.** Ask students to name things they really like. Lead them in sentences using *hot*, such as "That car is really *hot*."

hot-tempered ❧   Ask a puppet to help you with a chore and have him fly into a rage. Give example sentences using *hot-tempered*.

hour, hours ❧   Point out one *hour* on the clock and pantomime waiting for an airplane for an *hour*. Then indicate the passage of two or three *hours* and explain that you have waited for the airplane for *hours*. —*half an hour*, draw a clock on the board. Show that to go all the way around the clock is one *hour* or 60 minutes. Show that to go halfway around the clock is *half an hour* or 30 minutes.

household ❧   Explain that *household* has to do with things around a *house*. Have students list things they have in their *house*, things they do to keep it clean, etc.

housework ❧   Explain that *housework* is chores done around the *house*; for example, dusting, vacuuming, making beds, and washing dishes.

hovering ❧   Show students pictures of birds, bees, or helicopters that are *hovering* in flight.

how ❧   **1.** Have one puppet ask the other, "*How* do you count to three?" The other puppet answers, "This is *how*: one, two, three." Have the puppets ask other questions using the word *how*, such as, "*How* do you cut paper?" The answer is, "This is *how*," and pantomime with scissors. Or, "*How* do you eat cookies?" The answer is, "This is *how*," and pantomime by putting a cookie in the puppet's mouth. Make a paper airplane, then ask, "Did everyone see *how* I did that?" **2.** Lead students in making up sentences about the characteristics of objects in the room: "*How* big?" "*How* many pencils are here?" "*How* little this bug is!" —*how about*, lead students in sentences, such as "*How about* lunch?" or "*How about* baseball?" Explain that people say *how about* when they want to do something. —*how come*, give examples, such as "*How come* we study?" And answer with, "To learn." Or, ask, "*How come* we wear jackets?" Answer with, "To be warm." Explain that *how come* means "why." —*How dare you!*, check that students understand the individual words in the expression. Have one puppet bump into the other. The first says very indignantly, "*How dare you* bump into me!" Create other similar scenes with lines: "*How dare you* insult me!" "*How dare you* step on my foot!" "*How dare you* take my food!" —*How I wish!*, have one puppet wish by saying, "*How I wish* I had _____!" Have the other puppet supply the *wish*. —*How soon?*, check that students understand the word *soon*. See *soon*. One puppet says, "We will have recess (lunch, a party) *soon*." The other puppet says, "*How soon?*" The first puppet answers, "In ___ minutes."

Howdy! ➡ Say "Hello" to a student and then say "*Howdy!* " Lead students in saying *Howdy* to each other.

howl, howling ➡ Show pictures of dogs or wolves and imitate their *howl.* Explain that the winds can make a similar noise. Ask if students have ever heard the winds *howl.* Make a *howling* noise and lead students in *howling.*

howled with laughter ➡ After you have checked the individual words in this expression, demonstrate *howling with laughter* and lead students in *howling with laughter.*

hub ➡ On the board, draw a *hub* of a wagon wheel. Take a story you have just read. Put what the story is about in the *hub* of the wheel you just drew.

hubbub ➡ Have students create a *hubbub.* Demonstrate as needed.

huddle, huddling, huddled ➡ Group students into a *huddle.* Lead students in *huddling.* Help them to make past tense sentences.

hue, hues ➡ **1.** Show objects of various colors and describe their *hues.* Explain that *hue* is another word for *color.* **2.** Show students various *hues* of red, brown, and green. Ask them if other colors can have *hues.*

hug, hugging, hugged ➡ Have two puppets give each other a *hug. Hug* a doll. Show two dolls *hugging. Hug* a toy animal and then say that you *hugged* it.

huge ➡ *Huge* means "very, very big." See *big.* Draw a small circle on the board, then a *huge* one. Repeat with various shapes. Contrast *tiny* things with *huge* things.

hum, hums, humming, hummed ➡ **1.** *Hum* a tune. Say "I did not sing the words; I *hummed.*" Have students *hum.* **2.** Ask students if they have ever heard a bee *humming.*

human ➡ Point to several students and include yourself. Say each time, "You are a *human.*" Contrast with pictures of animals, "This is a cat, a dog, a horse, etc." —*human race,* use a globe to make your point. Say "No matter where you live, everyone is part of the *human race.*" —*human technology,* show some of the things that *humans* have made: buildings, cars, etc. Explain that these are *human technology.* Contrast with *nature.* —*Humane Society,* draw or show a picture of an animal shelter. Say "The *Humane Society* is a place where animals with no homes are taken care of until people come along to adopt them as pets."

humble, humblers ➡ **1.** Contrast with two puppets. Have one say how proud it is of something that it made, while another portrays *humbleness.* **2.** Ask students if they feel small when they see an elephant. Say "Elephants are *humblers.*"

humid ➡ Show pictures of *humid* and *dry* climates. Explain the presence and absence of water in these climates.

humility ➡ Have a puppet praise you profusely. Act with *humility.*

humor ➡ Tell students a joke or do something that will make them laugh. Explain that this is *humor.*

hump ➡ Show the *hump* on a camel.

hunch ❯ Predict something and then have it happen. Say "I have a *hunch* that [Fluffy] will pop up from behind the desk."

hundred ❯ **1.** Have students count to *100*. **2.** Have students count to *100* by 10s. **3.** Write *100* and 200 on the board. Have students read these numbers.

hundredth ❯ Help students to count one *hundred* pennies or tokens. With the last penny, tell them, "This is the *hundredth* penny."

hung head ❯ Pantomime this with students.

hung out ❯ Explain that this is a slang expression that can be used to describe teenagers spending free time together. Say, for example, "The kids got together after school and *hung out* at the shopping mall."

hungry, hungrier, hungriest, hungrily ❯ **1.** Lead students in rubbing their stomachs and looking *hungry*. You can also show a picture of baby birds waiting *hungrily* with beaks open for dinner. **2.** Draw one apple on one sheet of paper, two apples on a second sheet of paper, and three apples on a third sheet. Hand the papers to two students. Say "[Maria] is *hungry*; she will eat one apple. [Carlos] is *hungrier*, he will eat two apples." "[Juan] is the *hungriest* of all; he will eat three apples!" **3.** Have a puppet eat something *hungrily*. Contrast by having it eat something in a picky manner.

hunt, hunting, hunted, hunter, hunters ❯ **1.** Have a puppet *hunt* for its book. Have students *hunt* for a pencil. **2.** Show puppets *hunting* for something they lost and then finding it. Lead students in a *hunt* to find something. **3.** Pantomime using puppets or stuffed animals. Say "I am a *hunter*." Show pictures of *hunters*. —*overhunted*, draw some whales on the board. Have students pantomime throwing harpoons at them. Draw "Xs" through the whales they "kill." When there are only two or three whales left, say "Oh, no! We have *hunted* and killed too many whales! They are *overhunted*."

huppa ❯ Show a picture of the canopy under which Jewish weddings are performed.

hurl, hurled ❯ Pantomime *hurling* a basketball into a hoop. Explain that *hurl* means "throw." Lead students in past tense sentences.

hurray ❯ Jump up and down in excitement and yell, "*Hurray!*" Have students do the same.

hurry, hurrying, hurries, hurried ❯ **1.** Lead students in pantomiming being in a *hurry*. **2.** Walk quickly. Say "I *hurried*." Have students imitate. **3.** Ask a student to come to your desk. Ask another to *hurry* to your desk. Tell the class, "He or she *hurries* to my desk." **4.** Walk in a *hurried* manner and lead students in doing the same. **5.** *Hurry* from place to place in the classroom. Lead students in *hurrying* around the classroom.

hurt, hurts ❯ Limp around the room. Say "My foot is *hurt*." Act like an arm *hurts* and say that it *hurts*. Do the same with other body parts. Pretend to bump your arm. Hold your arm and say expressively, "That *hurt*." Repeat with slightly different situations.

hush ❯ Put your finger to your lips and whisper *hush*.

husky ➡ Demonstrate a *husky* voice.

hydrogen ➡ Explain that *hydrogen* is like air, except that it burns and would float on top of air because it is so light.

hypnotic ➡ Ask students to sing a quiet lullaby or other simple and repetitious song. Gradually calm down until you look *hypnotized* by the lilting tune.

hysterical ➡ Have one puppet cry uncontrollably and the other laugh wildly. Say "These puppets are *hysterical!*"

I ➡ Point to yourself and say "*I.*" Point to a student and say "*you.*" Lead students in doing this.

Ida's ➡ See *Brad's.*

idea, ideas ➡ **1.** Ask students to close their eyes and see a picture of a dog. This is the *idea* of a dog. Have them think of what they would like to eat for lunch. Ask them if they have an *idea* of what they will eat. **2.** Sit at your desk and look bored. Say "What shall we do? Any *ideas?*"

identical ➡ Show the students two photocopies of a drawing, or pictures of *identical* twins.

identity ➡ Point to characteristics of two puppets, comparing and contrasting as you go. Explain that these characteristics help make up the puppets' *identity.*

idle ➡ Have a puppet be *idle* when it is supposed to be doing an assignment.

if ➡ Say and demonstrate sentences, such as "*If* you want to talk, raise your hand" or "*If* you like ice cream, stand up." Say silly things, such as "*If* you are a dog, bark."

ignite ➡ Draw a cartoon firecracker on the board with a long fuse. Draw a box of matches on the board and pretend to strike one. Ask, "Who would like to *ignite* the firecracker?" When a student volunteers, draw a flame at the end of the fuse, and make a sizzling sound to indicate the flame moving toward the firecracker. Say "Ka-boom!" when the firecracker explodes.

ignorance ➡ Point to several objects in the room that students know the names of. Ask a puppet to tell you their English names. In each instance have the puppet give you the wrong name in a knowing manner. Tell students, "[Shaggy] is showing us his *ignorance* of the English language." Show him your *knowledge* of the English language and tell him what these things are.

ignoring ➡ Have a puppet *ignore* you. Tap it on the shoulder and have it turn away.

ill, illness ➡ **1.** Pantomime taking care of a student who pretends to be sick. Feel the student's forehead as if to take his or her temperature. Have the student say "I am sick. I am *ill.*" **2.** Have a puppet cook you a messy, ugly meal of paper clips, pencil shavings, and so on. Make a face and tell the class, "The puppet has given me an *ill-made* lunch." **3.** Show pictures of people who are sick and explain that they have an *illness.* Contrast with good health. —*ill at ease,* pantomime acting *ill at ease.* Give example sentences. —*ill-timed,* pantomime giving a test to a puppet or doll. Have the telephone ring next to the puppet, interrupting its test. Give example sentences using *ill-timed.* —*terminal* *illness*, show a picture of someone in a hospital. Then show a picture of a grave. Explain that an *illness* that is *terminal* has no cure.

imagine, imagining, imagination, imaginations ► **1.** Tell students that to *imagine* is to picture something in your head. See *idea*. Lead students in *imagining* things. You might do this by a series of questions, such as "What if the sky were green and the trees were blue?" and "What if squirrels could talk?" As they answer, tell students that they can *imagine*. If they have difficulty, demonstrate with puppets first. **2.** Ask students to think of a new kind of animal. Tell them that they are using their *imagination*. Have students draw cartoon characters, create a play, or something similar. Say "What great *imaginations* you have!"

imitator, imitators ► Have a student make various motions and copy each motion. Say "I am copying Jane. I am an *imitator*." Repeat with students and say "You are good *imitators*."

immaculate ► Divide students into two groups. Invite one group to make a *mess* of their desks and the other to make their desks very *clean*. Say "These desks are very *messy*. These other desks are *immaculate*."

immortality ► Name the fictional characters who have *immortality*, such as Batman and Superman.

immune ► Have students each draw and cut out a germ. Tape a sign with an "A" for Antibody on your chest. Have each student approach you and have their germ attack you but then drop to the ground. Say "These germs can't make me sick. My body has made lots of antibodies, and I am *immune* to this disease." See *antibodies*.

impact ► **1.** Have two puppets collide. Say "Are you all right after that *impact*?" **2.** On the board, draw yourself and then all the things that had an *impact* on you while you were growing up.

impaired ► Have students cover their ears with their hands. Say "People who have trouble hearing are hearing *impaired*." Have students squint. Say "People who have trouble seeing are visually *impaired*."

impatient, impatiently ► Act *patient* while you wait. Then act *impatient*: pace back and forth, look at the clock, and so on. Alternate and repeat as needed. Have a puppet be *impatient* about the upcoming arrival of his or her birthday. Contrast by having him or her be *patient*. Lead students in sentences using *impatiently*.

impenetrable ► Try to stick a pin through a metal container. Lead students in sentences using *impenetrable*.

impolite ► Have one puppet say "May I please have a drink of water?" Have the other say "Gimme some water." Say. "[Scruffy] has bad manners; he is *impolite*."

important ► **1.** Contrast *important* and *unimportant* days in students' lives, perhaps, "Is your birthday special? Why? It is *important*." "Was last Wednesday special? Why? It is *unimportant*." Repeat as needed. **2.** Have a puppet doing routine things, then have another puppet come in and ask the first for help on something *important*, perhaps helping with reading or fixing a broken toy. Have the first puppet say it will help his friend with the *important* task. Follow through with questions to students on things that they consider *important* and *unimportant*. Prompt as needed.

impose ❧ Say: "Just for today, I will *impose* a new rule: you must all take off your left shoe during science class."

impossible ❧ See and explain *possible*. Then have students tell you about things or events that are *impossible*. Evaluate and discuss each item.

impoverished ❧ Show pictures of *impoverished* people.

impracticable ❧ On the board, write a goal for yourself that you are unlikely to obtain, such as becoming a power lifter, ice-skating champion, prima ballerina, etc. List all the reasons why you can't reach your goal. Say "This goal is *impracticable* for me."

impressed ❧ Ask students how many of them can [swim, ice skate, or speak two languages] and tell them you are *impressed* with their skills.

imprint, imprinting, imprinted ❧ Lead students in *imprinting* their hands in sand or modeling clay. Help with past tense sentences.

imprisoned, imprisonment ❧ On the board, draw a picture of someone *imprisoned*. Give students example sentences using *imprisonment*.

improve, improved, improvements ❧ **1.** Ask students to *improve* the appearance of the room by helping you to tidy it. **2.** Write a simple sentence on the board with errors in spelling and punctuation. Have students *improve* it. Lead students in sentences using *improved*. **3.** Draw something on the board, such as a house or garden. Have students take turns making small changes to your drawing. Say "You are making *improvements* on my drawing in an attempt to make it better."

in ❧ **1.** Hold a paper clip *in* your hand with your hand closed. Have students do this and other similar demonstrations of *in*. **2.** Demonstrate *in* meaning "within a space." You can draw a shape on the board and place a dot *in* that shape. Have students make dots *in* the spaces that they create on paper. **3.** Lead students in making phrases, such as "*in* the light," "*in* the dark," "*in* the storm," "*in* the rain," and "*in* the summer."

inability ❧ Ask a puppet to walk. Have the puppet answer that it cannot, because it is a puppet without legs. Explain to the class, "Because the puppet has no legs, it has an *inability* to walk."

inaccurate ❧ Work a math problem incorrectly. Have a student correct it. Say "I was *inaccurate*."

inalienable ❧ Have students tell you things that belong to them that they cannot transfer to another, such as the color of their hair or eyes, or their personality. Give example sentences using *inalienable*.

incisions ❧ Draw the outline of a person on a sheet of paper. Mark where two *incisions* must be made. Ask a student to cut along the lines and make the *incisions*.

include, includes ▸ **1.** Put your arms out to embrace stuffed animals and puppets to *include* them in your love. Draw some shapes on the board. *Include* some in a circle. Have students do this on a piece of paper. **2.** Have a few students form into a group. Then say, "This group *includes* Jose, Maria, Ana, and Carlos."

incoming ▸ Place two boxes on your desk. Write *incoming* on one and *outgoing* on the other. Demonstrate by having puppets put their homework in the *incoming* box. You look at the papers, put them in the *outgoing* box, and then have the puppets pick them up.

incomplete ▸ Have a puppet sing the Alphabet Song and stop partway through. Say "[Fluffy], you didn't finish the Alphabet Song. Your alphabet is *incomplete*." Draw two sides of a triangle; say "This is *incomplete*."

incomprehensible ▸ Have a puppet mutter while you pantomime trying to understand. Give students a puzzled look and say "*Incomprehensible*." Repeat the exercise.

incorporate, incorporated ▸ **1.** Draw a picture on the board. Say "How can I *incorporate* [a tree, a bird, a house] into my picture?" **2.** Set up a scene where you are a business entrepreneur and students are lawyers. Go to the students and say "I want to set up a company to sell lemonade." Pantomime filling out many legal documents and writing a check. Say "We have to do all this paperwork so my company will be *incorporated*."

increased ▸ Have students jointly build a tower out of blocks. Say "Every time somebody added a block to the tower, it *increased* in size."

indeed ▸ Ask a puppet a question that students will know to have an affirmative answer. Have the puppet answer, "Yes *indeed!*" Repeat with students.

independent, independently, independence ▸ **1.** Mention times that students have worked *independently*, such as when doing homework or some special project. Group students together and have one student off on his or her own, being *independent*. **2.** Ask a student volunteer to tie his or her shoe. As he or she does so, offer suggestions and try to help while the student does it alone. Say "[Francesca] has shown [her] *independence* by tying [her] shoe by [herself]."

indifferent ▸ Have a puppet call you over to play. Act *indifferent*.

indignant, indignation ▸ **1.** Act out with a puppet. Have the puppet accuse you of taking its pencil. Act righteously angry and say "I did not take your pencil!" Then say "I became *indignant* when [Spot] accused me of taking his pencil." **2.** Have a puppet accuse you of taking something. Respond with *indignation*.

indispensable ▸ Show tools that are *indispensable* for the students' studies, such as a pencil, ruler, and paper.

indulge ▸ *Indulge* one request by your students. Give example sentences.

ineffectively ▸ *Ineffectively* erase the board.

inexorable ❯ Attempt to persuade a puppet to give you a piece of its candy. Have the puppet refuse, no matter what you do. Tell the class, "[Fluffy] is *inexorable!*" Pair the students up and have them repeat the above with each other.

inexperienced ❯ Say "I am an *experienced* teacher. I am an *inexperienced* skateboarder." Ask students to create similar pairs of sentences.

infect, infected, infection, infections, infectious ❯ **1.** Explain that if you do not want to *infect* a cut, you must keep it clean. Draw a person on a sheet of paper with a scratch on his or her leg. Have each student draw and cut out a germ. Have students place their germs all over the figure's leg. Use a red marker to color the scratch and the skin around the scratch. Say "These germs got into the scratch and made it get *infected.*" **2.** Have one student stick red, round stickers on his or her face. Say "Oh, dear! [Kwan] is sick with a rash! She has an *infection*," and "This is an *infectious* illness. Stay away so you don't get it."

infinite ❯ Talk about time and space having no boundaries and being *infinite.* Draw a line on the board starting from a center point. Have it reach both ends of the board, and tell the class that the line never stops in either direction.

infirm ❯ Pantomime feeling weak and sickly. Say "I feel *infirm* right now. I must sit." Ask students if they have elderly relatives who are *infirm.*

inform, information, informative, informer, informant ❯ **1.** Have a puppet ask you a question. Then say "I will *inform* you," and then answer its question. Have students ask you questions and tell them, "I will *inform* you" before you answer. Lead students in sentences. **2.** Get a telephone book for your area and show students different things that they can find in it such as a pizza parlor, a skating rink, or the local library. Tell students, "The phone book has useful *information.*" **3.** Write some facts that students will understand on the board, such as what time school starts, what time lunch is, and when they will go to recess. Tell them, "This is *information.*" **4.** Show an *informative* picture book, perhaps about birds or animals, then tell them, "That was an *informative* book." **5.** Set up a scene where a puppet steals a pencil. Look for the pencil, announcing that it has been stolen. Have a second puppet come up and *inform* you that the first stole it. Tell the class, "This puppet is my *informant;* it told me who took the pencil" or "This puppet is my *informer;* it told me who took the pencil."

ingenious ❯ Give each student a puzzle to solve. For the more clever solutions, say "That's *ingenious.*"

ingredients ❯ Write a recipe for lemonade on the board. Head the column with *Ingredients;* under it write "lemons, sugar, water, ice." Ask students what *ingredients* they would need to bake a cake.

inherit, inherited ❯ Tell students that when someone dies, they have often named someone to get, or *inherit*, their belongings. When Sam's father died, Sam *inherited* his father's house and land. The house and land now belong to Sam.

initial, initials, initially ❧ **1.** Show students an *initial* in your name. Show them your *initials*. Have students write their *initials*. **2.** Have students line up. Say "[Claudia] is the *initial* person in this line." **3.** Show students the *initial* sentence in a story. Tell them, "In the beginning, we read this sentence." Repeat, saying, "*Initially*, we read this sentence." Repeat the example using other books or series of items where they can easily see a beginning.

inland ❧ Use a map to point out and contrast *inland* areas with *coastal* regions.

inn ❧ Explain that an *inn* is a big house where people sleep when they are traveling. It is another name for a motel.

inning ❧ A part of a baseball game consisting of each team getting three "outs." Say "The last batter struck out. The *inning* was over."

inquire, inquiring ❧ *Inquire* about a puppet's health. Lead students in *inquiring* about each other's health, grades, or weekend plans.

inquisitive ❧ Show students an interesting or mysterious picture and instruct them to ask as many questions as they can about it. Tell them they are *inquisitive*.

inserting ❧ Lead students in *inserting* some sheets of paper into a book.

inside ❧ Have students put a pencil *inside* their desk. Repeat with other objects. Show the *inside* and *outside* of a playhouse or box. Have students point to the *inside* and *outside* of various objects. Indicate the *inside* and *outside* of things in the room. Open the door and have someone go *outside*. Say "Come *inside!*"

insignificant ❧ Contrast *significant* and *insignificant* days in students' lives, perhaps, "Is your birthday special? Why?" Students should answer with something that they remember clearly or that it was very pleasant. Then you can say "Your birthday is *significant*." Contrast with, "Was last Wednesday special? Why?" Students should say that nothing special happened. Then you can say "It is *insignificant*." Repeat as needed.

insincere ❧ Have two puppets exchange a series of compliments that are *insincere*. Ask the class if the puppets are being *honest*. Say "These puppets are *insincere*."

insisted, insistent ❧ Ask a puppet to do something and have it refuse. Persist in demanding that the puppet do as you ask. Say "If necessary, I will become even more *insistent*." Tell students, "You must do your homework. The teacher *insisted* we do our homework."

instantly ❧ Tell the puppet to pick up its pencil *instantly*. Contrast by having it pick up his pencil *momentarily*.

instead ❧ Explain that *instead* means "not this one but that one." Pantomime or illustrate on the board such sentences as: "I will give you this pencil *instead* of that pen," "I wish I had ice cream *instead* of broccoli," and so on. Or, give examples of times when something happened *instead* of the usual; for example, when a substitute teacher taught *instead* of you.

instruct, instructions ❧ **1.** Instruct your students to do something. **2.** Give some *instructions*, such as, "Open your desk," "Stand up," "Sit down," and "Clap your hands."

insult, insults ❧ Explain that an *insult* is something rude, or not nice, that is said about a person or thing.

insurrection ❧ Show pictures of historical *insurrections*.

intellect, intellectually ❧ **1.** Ask students to list everything they know about a particular subject. Say "Thank you for using your *intellect*." **2.** Give two puppets each a jigsaw puzzle to solve. Have one use force to fit the pieces together; have the other think about each move. Say "[Brutus] is trying to force the puzzle pieces together. [Einstein] is thinking about each move [he] makes. He is approaching the task *intellectually*."

intelligent ❧ Write an arithmetic equation on the board and have a puppet solve it. Say "What an *intelligent* [Rabbit] you are!"

intensifying, intensity ❧ **1.** Begin telling students something in a whisper. Begin *intensifying* your communication. **2.** Punch your fist against your open palm. Increase the *intensity*.

intensive ❧ Run students through a drill in pronunciation or grammar. Say "We work hard to learn English. You get *intensive* training in this class."

interactions ❧ Divide students into two groups and invite them to chat among themselves. Say "I like to listen to you talk and to watch the way you act. I like watching your *interactions*."

intercepts ❧ Ask a student to carry a book from one end of the classroom to the other. When the student has walked halfway across the room, walk over and take the book away. Say "The teacher *intercepts* the book from the student."

interest ❧ Set up a scene where you are a business entrepreneur and students run a bank. Explain that for every dollar you keep for a year in a bank account, the bank will pay 5 cents. Give the student bankers single dollars and have them put 5 cents on each dollar. Say "The bank gives *interest* on my savings."

interfering ❧ Have students work together to build a castle out of blocks. Interrupt them from time to time to move a block. Say "I am *interfering* with your progress."

interior ❧ See *internally*. On the board, draw a building. Point to the *interior*. Contrast with *exterior*. Demonstrate with a box.

internal, internally ❧ **1.** See *external*. **2.** On the board, draw a circle. Point to the inside and say "*Internally*." Contrast with *externally*. Lead students in sentences.

interpret, interpreter ❧ Have a student say something in his or her natural language; have another student explain it to the class. Say "I asked Mary to *interpret* what John said; Mary was John's *interpreter*."

intervals ❧ Read a short poem aloud. Read the poem a second time, with exaggerated pauses between lines. Say "Those pauses are called *intervals*."

interview, interviews, interviewed ❧ **1.** Have one puppet *interview* another on a topic of interest to the class. Lead students in past tense sentences. **2.** Run mock job *interviews* with several students. Say "You did very well on your job *interviews*."

into ◆ Have students put their hands *into* their pockets or desks. Drop a piece of chalk *into* a box. Throw paper *into* the trash can.

intrigued ◆ Have a puppet act *intrigued* by something on your desk. Lead students in acting *intrigued* over some interesting object or picture.

intruding ◆ Have several students pantomime playing a board game. Have another student barge in uninvited. Say "[Juanita], you didn't ask if you could join the game, and you weren't invited. You are *intruding*."

inundated ◆ Say "Who wants an ice cream? Oh! I am *inundated* with people who want an ice cream!"

invariably ◆ Ask a puppet whether she would like an ice-cream cone. Have the puppet nod enthusiastically. Say "[Muffin] never says 'No' to the offer of an ice-cream cone; she *invariably* says 'Yes.' "

invasion ◆ Have students gather outside the door, then burst in on you unannounced. Pantomime surprise and say "Oh, it's an *invasion!*"

inventing, invented, invention, inventors ◆ **1.** Show pictures of *inventors*, like Alexander Graham Bell and Thomas Edison, along with what they *invented* (the telephone and the lightbulb). **2.** Ask if students have ever tried to *invent* something. Pretend that you are *inventing* something out of paper clips. **3.** Show pictures of odd *inventions*. Have a puppet hold up objects and claim that they are *inventions*, such as book openers (a pencil could be a book opener), a paintbrush that paints by itself, and other new *inventions*.

investigate, investigated, investigations ◆ **1.** Using available resources, have students *investigate* to find the answer to a question relating to one of the areas in their core curriculum, such as science or social studies. Praise their good *investigations*. **2.** Show an insect or leaf you have found. *Investigate* it by asking everyone in the class what it is. Give example sentences using *investigations*.

investing, investment ◆ **1.** Set up a scene where you are a business entrepreneur and students are *investors*. Say "I am looking for people to lend me money, so I can make my lemonade business grow. If you give me $1.00, I will give you back $1.20 when my business grows." After students hand you their play dollars, say "Thank you for helping my business grow. Thank you for *investing* in my company." **2.** Give students some play money and tell them you are starting a business and need their help. Have them each give you their money. Say "Thank you for giving me this money to help me start my business. You have made a good *investment*."

invisible, invisibly ◆ **1.** Give examples of things that cannot be seen (air, sound, wind). **2.** Hide behind something while you make a puppet talk so that it appears that the puppet is talking. Say "I am *invisibly* making the puppet talk."

invite, invited ◆ **1.** Ask a student to come with you to the back of the class. Tell the class as you are walking, "I *invite* him to come with me." Then *invite* another student to join you, and say "*Invite* a student to come with you." Repeat with other students. **2.** Ask each student to come to a tea party. Say "You are all *invited* to come to my party."

iron, ironing, ironed ◆ Bring an *iron* to class or show a picture of one. Pantomime *ironing* something.

irregular ◆ Have students tap a *regular* rhythm on their desks. Have them continue it as you tap an *irregular* rhythm on your desk.

irrigated ◆ Draw a cornfield on the board that has ditches cut into the soil between the rows of corn. Have students color in the ditches with blue chalk, representing water. Give example sentences using *irrigated*. Show pictures of fields being *irrigated*.

irritable, irritably, irritation ◆ Say "What do you want?" in a patient way, and then say it *irritably*. Say "I am tired. I feel *irritable*. I am feeling some *irritation!*"

is ◆ Lead students in making sentences about themselves, such as "Marcia *is* a girl" or "Thomas *is* on the chair." Limit your sentences to words that students already know. Say a simple sentence using *is*, such as "A clown *is* funny." Then say the sentence omitting *is:* "A clown funny." Tell students this word helps us say sentences correctly. —*isn't*, Show on the board how *is* and *not* squeeze together to make the word *isn't*. See *is* and *not*. —*'tis*, write *it is* on the board and show how the apostrophe replaces the first *i*. Explain that *'tis* means "*it is*." Give examples, such as, "*It is* time to read; *'tis* time to read."

isolated ◆ Have one student stand *isolated* at one end of the classroom; have the others stand grouped together with you at the other end.

issue, issued ◆ **1.** Have two puppets argue over who will win the next [soccer/football] game. Ask them, "What is the *issue?*" **2.** *Issue* reading books to each of the students and lead them in past tense sentences.

it ◆ Some students may confuse he, she, and *it*. Have students talk about a specific girl, a boy, and an object, such as: "She is tall," "He is big," and "*It* is blue." —*'tis*, write *it is* on the board and show how the apostrophe replaces the first *i*. Explain that *'tis* means "*it is*." Give examples, such as, "*It is* time to read; *'tis* time to read." —*it's*, **1.** Write *it* and *is* on the board and show how they are squeezed together to make *it's*. Then lead students in identifying objects in the room using it's: "*It's* a chair," "*It's* a desk," and so on. See *it* and *is*. **2.** Lead students in making sentences in which *it's* is used impersonally as in "*It's* raining," "*It's* snowing," "*It's* me," "*It's* cold."

itch ◆ Pantomime scratching an *itch* and lead students in scratching an *itch*.

items ◆ Point out various things and say "That blue *item* is a book; that small *item* is a pencil." Have students imitate.

its ◆ Explain his, hers and *its* by making sentences, such as "Give Jose his book." "Pass Carla her pencil." "Put the book on *its* shelf."

itself ◆ Show a picture of a cat; ask the class if *it* is a boy or a girl. Then explain that when we do not know, we use *it*. "*It* is a cat." Then say the cat scratched *itself*." Lead students in sentences using her and *herself* and him and *himself* as well.

Jack ◆ Explain that *Jack* is a boy's name; it is the nickname for boys named *John*. Find out if there is a corresponding name in the first language of your students.

jackpot ❧ Play a word game with students. For each word that they correctly identify, add a token or prize to a cup on your desk. If they misidentify a word, have them take their seat. The winner takes the *jackpot*.

jackrabbit ❧ Draw or show pictures of *jackrabbits*.

jammed ❧ Ask everyone to stand in the aisles between the desks. Try to walk down the aisle. Say "You have *jammed* the aisles!"

jangling ❧ With a metal object, make a *jangling* sound.

jealous, jealously ❧ 1. Portray *jealousy* and say "I'm *jealous* of [Lupe] because she has that beautiful bike." 2. Have a puppet *jealously* guard or hold something that would be special. Have students do the same.

Jennifer ❧ Explain that *Jennifer* is a girl's name, but that it is also the name of the juniper in the story, "*Jennifer* Juniper." You can point to a girl, say her name, and then point to a female doll and say *Jennifer* (if students need more explanation).

jerk ❧ Pretend that a drawer is stuck shut and *jerk* it open.

Jesse's ❧ See *Brad's*.

jest ❧ Demonstrate by having two puppets *jest* with each other. Let students *jest* with the puppets as well.

Jewish ❧ A person with a *Jewish* mother and/or someone who practices the *Jewish* faith. Draw the *Jewish* Star of David on the board. Say "Some *Jewish* people wear necklaces with the Star of David. Christian people often wear a cross."

jiggety jog ❧ This has no meaning but just sounds nice. Make up repetitive nonsense words that sound fun. Ask students to repeat them after you and make up their own as well. Relate these to *jiggety jog* by alternating this phrase with the others.

job ❧ If your students have different assigned *jobs* to do, you can say "Sarah's *job* is _____." Or, say "My *job* is teaching you" and "Your *job* is studying."

Joe's ❧ See *Ida's*.

jogging ❧ Lead students in *jogging*. Contrast with *running* and *walking*.

Johnny ❧ Explain that *Johnny* is a boy's name. Point to a boy in the room and say his name. Alternate a boy's name with "*Johnny*" several times.

join, joined ❧ 1. Have students stand in a circle and *join* hands. 2. Invite students in groups of two or three to *join* you at your desk. 3. Lead students in singing a chorus of a song that they know. Then have another student *join* in. Help students make past tense sentences.

joint ❧ Point out *joints* in the human body, such as the elbow, knee, wrist, and shoulder. Explain that a *joint* is where two parts join.

joke, joking, joked ❧ 1. Explain a *joke* as something funny that makes you laugh. Pantomime laughing as needed. 2. Make silly faces and say you were *joking*. 3. Make a funny face and explain that you *joked*. —*a joke*, have a puppet say the alphabet and make mistakes. Say "What *a joke!*" Or, have a puppet count to ten and make mistakes. Say "What *a joke!*" —*practical jokes*, If available, have a buzzer in your hand and shake hands with a student, causing the buzzer to activate. —*the joke was on me*, ensure that students understand the words in the expression. Drop a pencil in plain sight of you and students. Walk all over looking for it, exclaiming that somebody took it. Ask students if they have seen it; pretend not to hear them telling you where it is and keep looking. Finally, look down and find it. Act a little embarrassed and say "*The joke was on me!* It was right there all that time."

joke book ➧ Show students a *joke book* and compare it to a *story book*. Read something that students would understand from each.

jolly ➧ Make a happy face. Say "A clown is a *jolly* person."

jolting ➧ Ask if students have ever ridden a pony that went very fast. Tell them that the pony was *jolting* them. Or, have students bounce in their seats rapidly, and tell them that is *jolting*.

journey, journeyed ➧ **1.** Ask students about trips they have taken with friends or family. Explain that these are *journeys*. **2.** Draw a suitcase on a sheet of paper and have a puppet hold it. Indicate two points on a map of the United States. Have the puppet "walk" from one point to the other. Say "It *journeyed* across the country."

joy, joyful, joyless ➧ **1.** Express *joy*. Lead students in showing *joy* and then looking unhappy. **2.** Contrast *joyful* and *joyless* expressions. Lead students in *joyful* and *joyless* expressions and statements.

jubilant ➧ Have students dance for joy. Say "This is a *jubilant* celebration."

judge, judged ➧ **1.** Have one puppet draw a tulip. Have another puppet draw a daisy. Ask students to *judge* which flower they like best. **2.** Use three paintings or pictures. Ask students to vote for the one they like the best. Lead students in sentences using *judged*.

juggle, juggling ➧ **1.** Crumple three sheets of paper into balls and attempt to *juggle* them. Show pictures of people who are *juggling*. **2.** Write a list on the board of all the roles you play in life, such as teacher, wife, mother, sister, aunt, friend, etc. Say "I do many things and I have to *juggle* my time to do them all."

juicy ➧ Show a *juicy* fruit such as an orange. Draw *juicy* fruits like oranges on the board or show pictures.

July 4, 1776 ➧ Explain that this is an important date—the day when the new country that is now America decided to be free from England.

jump, jumping, jumped, jumpy ➧ **1.** Lead students in *jumping*. Help with past tense sentences. **2.** Have a puppet dramatize being *jumpy* (anxious and on edge). Have another puppet mention that the first is *jumpy*. —*high jump*, draw a stand with a bar across it on the board. Pretend puppets *jump* over the bar. Erase the bar and raise it. Say "The puppets are good at *high jump*." — *jump to conclusions*, draw a door on the board with a plume of smoke curling up from under it. Pantomime feeling the door to feel if it is hot. Lead students in sentences using *jump to conclusions*. —*long jump*, draw a straight path leading to a rectangular sandpit. Pretend the puppets are competing at *long jump*. Say "These puppets are good at *long jump*." Measure how far they *jump* with a ruler.

June ➧ Show the month of *June* on a calendar. Explain that *June* is the sixth month of the year. Lead students in reciting the months of the year up to *June*.

junior high ➧ See *high school*. Explain that *middle school* used to be called *junior high*.

junk ➧ Show examples of *junk*.

just ➧ **1.** Lead students in expressive sentences, such as, "That is *just* great!" or "*Just* look at that picture!" **2.** Hold various pencils up and say "This one is too big, this one is too small, and this one is *just* right." Give examples of things being *just* the same or *just* right. If it will help, explain that *just* means "exactly." **3.** If students understand the word *really*, explain that *just* means "really." Give example sentences said expressively, such as, "It's *just* a beautiful day!" or "It's *just* wonderful!" **4.** Place a pile of paper clips on a table. Pick up *just* about all the paper clips. Explain that *just* about means "almost." **5.** Talk about something that will be happening soon. Say "There is only one more week until spring vacation. Spring vacation is *just* around the corner. **6.** Demonstrate by placing items in a container until it is full. Tell students there are *just* enough items to fill the container. **7.** Ask a student to stand and turn. Change the student's position slightly, and say "*Just* so!" **8.** Put down a book and *just* then open the door. Close a window, and *just* then, turn around. Explain that *just* means "at that same time."

justice ➧ Give an even number of objects to two puppets and say "Here is some candy. Make two equal amounts." Make the puppets divide the "candy" into unequal amounts. Then say "No. This is not fair. *Justice* must be done. Make it fair, please." Finally, have the puppets make two equal piles.

keen ➧ Have students look closely at a picture in their textbook and describe every detail they see. Give example sentences using *keen*.

keep, keeps, kept ➧ **1.** Tell students that a refrigerator *keeps* food cold, an oven *keeps* food hot, and an umbrella *keeps* you dry. **2.** Give a book to a student and *keep* two. Give two books to a student and *keep* one. Have students *keep* specific numbers of books and give away specific numbers. **3.** Let one child play baby-sitter, and the other can play a baby. Tell the baby-sitter to take care of the baby, then say "I want you to *keep* the baby while I am gone." **4.** Stand on one foot for awhile. Say "I *keep* my balance well." Or, say the opposite if you can't. **5.** Tell students where you *keep* various items in the classroom, for example, "I *keep* the books on this shelf" and "I *keep* the erasers in this drawer." Then lead them in sentences, such as, "I lost the book that I kept on that shelf" and "The erasers are in the drawer, where I have always *kept* them." —*keep out*, have a puppet make a playhouse with a sign that says to *keep out*. Have another puppet come along, read the sign, and then leave.

keepsake ➧ Show one of your *keepsakes* and explain why it is special or what it reminds you of. Ask students to tell about one of their *keepsakes*.

kick, kicking ◈ *Kick* the air. Lead students in *kicking* a ball. —*kicked off*, set up a scene where you, a puppet, and the students are playing a game. Have the puppet keep doing things against the rules and *kick* him *off* the team.

kid ◈ Show a picture of a child or point to one of the children in the class. Explain that *kid* is another word for *child*.

kidnapped ◈ Have a larger puppet snatch a smaller one and run off. Say "Oh, no! That big guy just stole our little [Pumpkin]! Someone call the police! [Pumpkin] has been *kidnapped!*"

kill, killing ◈ Use a fly swatter or a rolled up piece of paper and swat at an imaginary fly to *kill* it. Show that you are *killing* the fly. —*killing two birds with one stone*, explain individual words as needed. Then, explain that this is an expression meaning getting two things done at the same time. Give an example, such as, "By reading aloud, you will be practicing your pronunciation and preparing for [Mrs. Rivera]'s class. You will be *killing* two birds with one stone."

kind, kindly, kinds ◈ **1.** Hold a doll *kindly*. Remind students of some incident of someone being *kind* that they may be familiar with, or a person who treats them *kindly*. Contrast this with treating a person *meanly*. **2.** Show pictures of different *kinds* of animals and ask or tell what *kind* each is. —*kindness*, hold a doll with *kindness*.

kindergarten, kindergartner ◈ Take students to a *kindergarten* class. Point out the *kindgartners*.

King ◈ A boy's name.

King Solomon ◈ Show a picture of *King Solomon*. Show Israel and say "*King Solomon* ruled from 972-932 B.C." See *B.C.*

kiss, kisses ◈ Demonstrate with a puppet. Shower a puppet with *kisses*.

knack ◈ **1.** Admire students' artwork and say "You have a *knack* for coloring." **2.** Ask for a volunteer to show the class something he or she is particularly good at. Say "That's great, [Joselito]! You have a real *knack* for [whistling]!"

knapsack ◈ Show a backpack and review *backpack* as needed. Lead students in pantomimes of packing or wearing a *knapsack*.

knead ◈ Show a picture of bread dough and pantomime *kneading* it. *Knead* a piece of soft clay. Explain that *kneading* is like squeezing.

knee, knees, kneed, kneel, kneeling ◈ **1.** Show your *knee*. Have students show their right *knees*, their left *knees*, and both knees. **2.** Push a chair with your *knee* and say that you *kneed* it (to its new location). **3.** *Kneel* as if before a king. Have students *kneel* in the same fashion. Lead students in *kneeling*.

knit, knitting, knitted ◈ If possible, demonstrate *knitting*. Otherwise, show pictures of *knitting* needles and yarn and something that has been *knitted*.

knives ◈ Show a picture of a *knife*, or draw two on the board to illustrate *knives*.

knob ❧ Show a door or drawer *knob.*

knock, knocking, knocked ❧ **1.** Lead students in *knocking* on a door or desktop. **2.** Say "*Knock, knock!*" and *knock* on your desk twice. Ask a student to *knock* twice on the door and say "*Knock, knock!*" **3.** Have a puppet *knock* something off your desk and say "The puppet *knocked* that [pencil] off my desk."

knot, knotted ❧ **1.** Show students how to tie a *knot* with a shoelace or piece of string. **2.** Tie a *knot* in a shoelace or piece of string. Show the *knot* and explain that the string is *knotted.*

know, knows, knowing, known, knew ❧ **1.** Have a student hold something in his or her hand, keeping secret what it is. Tell another student what you *know* about the student and what you believe is in his or her hand: "I *know* that he or she is wearing shoes," or "I *know* that he or she has two legs," "I believe that he or she has a pencil in his or her hand," or "I believe that he or she has a paper clip in his or her hand." Or, write a math problem on the board, look puzzled, then say "I *know!*" and quickly solve it. Give other examples, such as, "I *know* your name," and then say the name. **2.** Lead students in past tense sentences, such as, "She *knew* I was wearing shoes." Hold a paper clip in your hand without showing what it is. Say "I think it's a paper clip." Open up your hand and say "I *knew* it was a paper clip." You can do this with various pieces of colored paper and pretend to guess the color correctly. **3.** Ask if everybody in the school *knows* the gym teacher. Then say "[She] is *known* by everyone." Ask, "Who *knows* my name?" Then say "My name is *known.*" Lead students in sentences, such as, "How many teachers have you *known?*" or "I should have *known* that 2 + 2 = 4."

labor ❧ Show pictures of people working and explain that work is also called *labor.*

labyrinth ❧ Show a *labyrinth.* Have students design a *labyrinth* on the board collaboratively.

lambent ❧ Light a match or candle and show students how the flame flickers. Explain that it gives soft light. Say "We call this *lambent* light." Contrast with the *bright* lights of the classroom.

lamentations ❧ Have a puppet sob piteously. Say "I wondered what happened to [Shaggy] to cause her *lamentations.*"

lands, landed ❧ Toss something into the air. When it *lands*, tell students that it *landed.* Lead students in tossing things and saying that they *landed.*

language ❧ Ask each student to say "My first *language* is _____; now I am learning the English *language.*"

lap, lapping ❧ **1.** Sit down and point out your lap. Using a doll, pantomime a child sitting in your *lap.* **2.** Show pictures of cats and dogs *lapping* milk from a bowl or saucer.

large, larger, largest ❧ **1.** Draw a *large* circle and a *small* one on the board. Lead students in sentences with *large* and *small.* **2.** Point out things in the classroom that are *large* and *small.* **3.** Show students things that are *large, larger,* and *largest.*

large-brained ❯ Show animals with *large* and *small brains*.

lass ❯ Show pictures of girls, women, and female animals. Explain that some people call a girl a *lass*.

lasso ❯ Make a large loop in the end of a long piece of string. Lead students in sentences using *lasso*.

last, lasting ❯ **1.** Line students up and point out the *last* student. Contrast with the *first*. **2.** Ask, "Can spring *last* forever? No, a *lasting* spring is a poetic idea. What is *lasting*? Love, death, good deeds—these things *last* a long time. They are *lasting*." —*last but not least*, explain that being *last* does not mean being worst or smallest. Line students up with a tall student at the end of the line. Point out that he or she is *last but not least*. —*to the very last*, drop some paper clips and pick them up to the very *last* one. Clean the board to *the very last* mark. Put things on your chair and take them off *to the very last* thing.

late, later, latest, lately ❯ **1.** Tell students that they must be in their seats at an exact time and point to that time on the clock. Have one student take his or her seat at the correct time and have another student take his or her seat after the indicated time. Say that he or she is *late*. **2.** Look at your watch very worriedly. Rush around and say with expression, "I'm *late!*" Explain that if a student came to school at 9:05 in the morning, the student would be *late*. You can show the time on a play clock. If a student came to school at 9:30, that student would be *later*. If a student came at lunchtime, that student would be the *latest*. **3.** Describe some significant events that have happened in the classroom *lately*: perhaps a classroom party, a book that you've read aloud, or an open house. Then describe some significant events that happened long ago. Explain that *lately* means "not long ago."

Latin ❯ Show Rome, Italy, on the globe or map of the world. Say "Many, many years ago, people in Rome spoke *Latin*. Give students an example of a *Latin* word, such as *luna* (moon).

laugh, laughing, laughed, laughter ❯ **1.** Demonstrate. Ask others to join you. Say "You have a great *laugh!*" **2.** Lead students in *laughing*. Have them make past tense sentences. **3.** Do something that will make students *laugh*. Then say "I liked your *laughter*." —*laughed at*, have a puppet wear a silly sign while another points and *laughs at* him.

launch ❯ Show pictures of a boat that is *launching*. Explain that when you *launch* a boat, it means that it is leaving land and going into the water.

laundry ❯ Draw a clothesline on the board with socks and shirts and other *laundry* hanging from it.

law ❯ Compare to rules for the classroom. Explain that cities and countries call their rules *laws*. Ask if students have heard about any *laws*. If not, offer some that they may be familiar with, such as the seat belt *law* or the car seat *law*.

lay, lays, laying, laid ❯ **1.** Have a puppet *lie* down. Say "It *lay* down." **2.** Have a puppet *lay* a pencil on your desk. Say "It lays the pencil on my desk" and "The puppet *laid* it on my desk." **3.** Pantomime *laying* bricks. You can use toy bricks or blocks. **4.** Explain that *laying* means "making." Have students help you plan the rest of the day. Say "We are *laying* our plans." Show pictures of wars where villages and fields have been *laid* to waste. —*lay off*, set up a scene in which you are a boss and students are your employees. Tell students, "I'm sorry, but you can't work for me anymore. I have to *lay off* each and every one of you."

lazy, lazier, laziest, lazily ◆▸ Have one puppet be industrious about cleaning off a table while another is *lazy* and refusing to clean off a table. Clean the board in a *lazy* way. Lead students in getting something out of their desks in a *lazy* manner. Explain that *lazy* people don't want to work. Make yourself look *lazy*. Then say "I will clean my desk *lazily*," and begin *lazily* cleaning it. Have students clean their desks *lazily*.

lazybones ◆▸ Ask a puppet to do something; have it lounge on your desk, yawn, and refuse. Say "Don't just lie there, [Shaggy]. Come on and help me. Don't be such a *lazybones!*" Have students act like a *lazybones*.

lead, led, leader, leaders, leadership ◆▸ **1.** *Lead* students around the classroom. Explain that you *led* them. **2.** Play "Simon Says" and say "Simon is the *leader*." **3.** Give examples of national and local *leaders*. **4.** Have a puppet direct students in the building of a castle from blocks. Say "[Bear] is very skilled in guiding you in your task; [Bear] shows great *leadership*."

leafless ◆▸ Draw two trees on the board, one with *leaves*, the other without. Say "This tree has no *leaves*; it is *leafless*."

league champs ◆▸ Ask students to name teams from a specific *league* and then ask who won the season last year. Say "The *league* champs for [year] were [team name]."

leak, leaked ◆▸ If you have a plastic sandwich bag, prick a tiny hole in it, fill it with water, and show students the *leak*. "The bag *leaked*."

lean, leaning, leaned ◆▸ Demonstrate *leaning* against the wall. Ask students to *lean* against a wall. Lead students in sentences using *lean*, *leaning*, and *leaned*.

leap, leaping, leaped ◆▸ **1.** Show a picture of a cat or leopard, and tell the students that when these animals jump, they *leap*. Have students pretend to be a cat and *leap*. **2.** Demonstrate with a game of *leapfrog*, or pictures of people or frogs *leaping*. Lead students in sentences using *leap*, *leaping*, and *leaped*.

learn ◆▸ Explain that teachers *teach* and students *learn*. Mention something that students have *learned* recently.

least ◆▸ Contrast with *most*. Give two students different amounts of paper clips and show who has the *most* and who has the *least*.

leather ◆▸ Show *leather* shoes or belts.

leave, leaves, leaving, left ◆▸ **1.** Show some *leaves*. Tell students that *leaves* is plural for *leaf*. **2.** *Leave* and enter the room. Have students *leave* and *enter* the classroom. Ask a student to *leave* the room. Explain that he or she *left*. **3.** *Leave* some things on your desk where they are and pick up other things. Open a door or drawer and walk away. Say "I *left* the [door] open." Put some small objects on a table. Take all away except one, which is *left*. **4.** Give examples of decisions, such as, "I don't know where to put your lunch; I'll *leave* that decision to you." Then ask the relevant student where the lunch should go. —*left behind*, have students carry something to a location in the room and *leave* it *behind*.

left ◆ Lead students in moving their *left* hands and feet.

leftover ◆ Take eleven paper clips and divide them into three sets. There will be two *leftover*.

legal ◆ Explain that rules people follow are called laws. Following the laws is *legal*, and not following laws is *illegal*. Use examples that students may have familiarity with, such as seat belt or car seat laws, stopping at stop signs, or stealing.

legend ◆ Use examples of *legends* they have read or know, such as La Llorona, from Mexico.

legibility ◆ Write a phrase on the board twice: once with *legible* writing, once with *illegible* writing. Ask students which one they can read. Say "The *legibility* of my handwriting makes it easier for you to read."

lemonade ◆ Tell students that *lemonade* is a drink made with *lemon* juice, water, and sugar. Ask students if they have ever had *lemonade*. If possible, have them taste actual *lemonade*.

lend, loan ◆ **1.** Lead students in making sentences in which *lend* means "give a desirable quality to." For example, "This [decoration] *lends* beauty." Have the students smile and say "Your smiles *lend* happiness to the room." **2.** Explain that the more usual sense of *lend* is "to give temporarily," perhaps by *lending* a pencil. Then, explain that *lend* also means "to give." Demonstrate giving something to someone as needed. **3.** Ask to borrow a student's pencil. Use it and return it. Say "*Loan* me your pencil." **4.** On the board, draw a bank. Pantomime a scene with a puppet where you are a *loan* officer and the puppet is applying for a *loan*. When you are finished, give the puppet some play money.

lenses ◆ Show students the glass portions of a pair of eyeglasses. Lead them in naming other items that have *lenses*, such as contact *lenses*, magnifying glasses, telescopes, cameras, and microscopes. Draw those items on the board.

let, let's ◆ **1.** Have puppets dramatize little scenes in which they are saying, "*Let* me go too," "*Let* me have some candy," "*Let* me stay up later." **2.** Explain that *let's* is a word people say when they want to start doing something. Pantomime: "*Let's* eat," "*Let's* play," "*Let's* go home." Explain that *let's* is short for *let us*. —*let down*, act disappointed. Say "I feel *let down* because [I didn't win first prize.]" —*let go*, pantomime holding onto the back of your chair as if it were a flying trapeze. Invite students to copy your position. Then say "*Let go!*" —*let off*, explain that this is an expression used in Great Britain and it means "to stop." Say "We will *let off* math at [10 A.M.]." —*let things take their course*, check individual words in the phrase. Have one puppet hurt its knee, panic about losing blood, and want to call an ambulance. *Let* the other puppet say "It's not bleeding so much now. *Let's* wait a minute. See, it's stopped bleeding.

Sometimes you must *let things take their course.*" —*let up*, play a loud piece of music. Put your hands over your ears and say "Will that music never *let up?*" Explain that *let up* means "stop." —*never let up*, check that students understand the individual words in the expression. Say "One day it never stopped raining." Draw a rain cloud and raindrops on the board. Look at your watch and say "At 9 o'clock it rained. At 10 o'clock it rained, etc." Finally say "The rain *never let up.*"

letters ❖ **1.** Write *letters* from the English alphabet on the board. **2.** Show examples of *letters* written in different languages.

level ❖ Point out *level* and *slanted* surfaces. —*level off, levels off*, pretend to fly a paper airplane. Show it climbing and then flying horizontally. Say "The plane needed to *level off.*"

levers ❖ Draw a bulldozer on the board. Sit at your desk and hold a pen in each fist. Rest the ends of the pens on your desktop and move them back and forth and sideways, as if pretending to operate the bulldozer. Say "I am operating the bulldozer with these *levers.*"

liar ❖ Have the puppet tell each student something untrue. Then say "[Fluffy] is a *liar!*"

liberty ❖ **1.** Tell students that for the next two minutes, they have free time. Say "You are at *liberty* to do whatever you want for two minutes." **2.** Draw a bird on the board. Then draw bars in front of it and place it in a cage. Say "This bird is in captivity." Draw an open door on the cage and let the bird out. Erase the bird in the cage and draw it flying away. Say "The bird has its *liberty!*"

library, librarian, libraries ❖ **1.** Point to the classroom *library* or show students the school *library*. Ask students on which day they visit the school *library*. Say "What other *libraries* do you go to?" **2.** Ask the class to name the school *librarian*.

lick, licked, licking ❖ **1.** Show a picture of an ice-cream cone. Pantomime *licking* it. Demonstrate *licking* your lips. Explain that you *licked* them. **2.** Show pictures of a fire, and point out how parts of the fire appear to reach up. Say that the fire *licks* the air. If you can show a picture of flames actually *licking* a piece of wood, this would be ideal.

lid ❖ Point out various *lids*.

lie, lied, lies, lying ❖ **1.** Have a puppet *lie* down and then get up. **2.** Have a puppet *lie* on a table. Tell students, "The puppet *lies* on the table," "The puppet is *lying* on the table." **3.** See *fib* and *fraud*. Write out several arithmetic equations on a sheet of paper for a puppet to solve. Have a puppet fail to solve them. Say "[Shaggy], did you finish your work?" Have the puppet say "Yes." Show the paper to the class. Say "[Shaggy], you are *lying* to me; [Shaggy], you *lied* to me." —*lie low*, demonstrate the position and ask individual students to imitate you. Say "I want [David] to *lie low.*"

life, lifeless, lives ❖ **1.** Explain that *life* means "the way that a person *lives*." Give examples, such as, "If you are sad, you have a sad *life*," "If you are happy, you have a happy *life*." **2.** Show pictures of animal or human *life* cycles. Explain that *life* begins when one is born and ends when one dies. Help students with plural sentences. **3.** Ask students to show that they are *alive*. Say "Yes, you are all full of *life!*" **4.** Point to inanimate objects in the room and say "These are *lifeless*." Then point to *living* things and ask, "Are these *lifeless?*" —*life span*, see *lifetime*. —*lifetime*, on the board, draw a time line and put your birth date and also today's date. Say "This is my *lifetime* up until today."

lift, lifting, lifts ❖ **1.** Lead students in *lifting* things. **2.** Have a student pick up a chair. Say "This is how Joe *lifts* the chair." Have students pick things up and repeat the phrase. —*lift off!*, explain *lift* and *off* as needed. Explain that when a rocket goes up in the air, it *lifts* up *off* the ground and people say "*Lift off!*" Show a picture if possible. —*offer us a lift*, check individual words in the phrase. Draw a car on the board, then draw a line through it. Say "My car is broken." Pretend to call a friend. Say "My car has broken down. I must take my son and daughter to school. Can you *offer us a lift?*"

light, lighting, lightly, lit ❖ **1.** Demonstrate how a *light* or lamp produces *light*. Have each student turn the *light* on and off. Point to the *light* it makes each time, and have them repeat the word *light* with you. **2.** *Light* a match and say that you *lit* it. **3.** Flash a flashlight onto something and show the *lighting* that it makes for that object. **4.** Contrast *light* and *heavy* objects. Demonstrate *light* and *heavy* breathing. **5.** Ask students to step *lightly*. Contrast by having them *stomp*. —*lights out*, on the board, draw barracks or a dormitory with many people sleeping inside. Turn off the *lights* and have students pantomime sleeping. Say "After *lights out*, no more talking; it is time to go to sleep."

lightning ❖ Show pictures of *lightning*. Ask students if they have ever seen it. Ask for first-language names. Lead students in sentences.

like, liking, likes, liked ❖ **1.** Contrast things you enjoy with those you don't. For example, smile, and say "I *like* music, reading, cats, and chocolate." Then frown and say "I *dislike* noise and broccoli." Pantomime tasting a food and *liking* it. Lead students in past tense sentences. Have a puppet sing a tune. Tell the class, "[Fluffy] *likes* to sing." **2.** Lead students in pointing out things that are *like* each other and things that are different. Lead students in saying *like* to compare things; for example: "This red crayon is *like* this red crayon," "This blue crayon is not *like* this green crayon" and "The color of these flowers is *like* the color of these crayons." —*This is more like it!*, hand out pennies to students and set up a pretend lemonade stand. Have students buy cups of lemonade. Count your pennies. Say "Yesterday I lost 25 cents at my lemonade stand; today I earned $1.55. Now, *this is more like it!*"

limb, limbs ❖ Draw a tree and a person on the board. Point to the tree branches. Say "These are the tree's *limbs*." Point to the person's arms and legs. Say "These are the person's *limbs*." Show the *limbs* of various trees. Take students outside and have them find the *limbs* on trees. Compare with *branches*. (*Limbs* are large *branches*.)

limitations ❖ Have students take turns stacking books in a pile in your hands. When the pile gets heavy, drop it on your desk. Say "I can't hold any more books. There are *limitations* to my strength."

limited, limitless, limits, ❧   **1.** Have students tell you the *limits* to their space. **2.** Place a mark on the floor and tell students they cannot cross it. Say "You are *limited* to only this small space." **3.** On a clear day, have students look outside at the sky. Point out that the blue sky has no edges or boundaries. Lead students in sentences using *limitless.* —*off limits*, put a sign on a closet door that says, "Do Not Enter." Say "You are not allowed to open that door; that closet is *off limits.*"

line, lines ❧   **1.** Have students draw *lines.* **2.** *Line* students up.

lined ❧   Show the *lining* of a jacket. On the board, draw a nest and show how it might be *lined* with fur.

listen, listening, listened ❧   Say "*Listen* and copy me." Then make a clapping pattern. Cup your hand to your ear to *listen.* Then have the students copy your pattern. Say "You *listened* well." Cup your hand to your ear as if *listening.*

listless ❧   Have a puppet be *listless.* Say that it is tired and sick; it is *listless.* Lead students in sentences.

literally ❧   Drink a cup of water; show students that the cup is empty. Say "I *literally* drank the whole thing!"

little, littler, littlest ❧   **1.** Point out *big* and *little* things in the classroom and have students do the same. **2.** Show things that are *little, littler,* and *littlest.*

live, living, lived ❧   **1.** Tell students, "I *live* in a house, and you *live* in a house." Demonstrate with puppets *living* in a house. Find out where students used to *live.* Give examples, such as, "When you were a baby, you *lived* in [city name]," or "When you were a baby, you *lived* in a house." **2.** Point out persons, plants, and animals in the classroom that are *living.* In contrast, point out things that are not *living.* Have students name things that are *living* and not *living.* **3.** On the board, make a typical budget for a month for a family of four as an example of *living* expenses. Ask students to figure out how they will make a *living* when they grow up.

load, loaded ❧   **1.** If you have a cart, toy truck, or other vehicle, *load* it with books or other objects. You an also draw this on the board. **2.** Pretend you and the students are sailors. Draw a ship on the board and have students pretend to stock the ship with food and supplies. Say "Now that you have *loaded* the ship with food, we are ready to go."

location, locations ❧   Point out different *locations* on the map. Point to different *locations* in the room. Send a student to a specified *location.*

lock, locks ❧   If possible, show students a *lock* and a key and point out other *locks* in the room. Or, draw a *lock* and key on the board.

lodging ❧   Draw or show a picture of a motel, house, or other *lodgings.*

lofty ❧   Contrast important subjects with humble ones. Say, for example, "Things like world peace and human rights are *lofty* matters. Things like what to have for breakfast and what to wear today are not *lofty.*"

lonely, lonesome ❧   **1.** Pantomime by showing a doll or stuffed animal by itself, contrasted with a group of toys that are having fun playing together.

Show a puppet sitting by itself. Have it say that it wishes it could be with its friend. Then have it say "I am *lonely*." Lead students in sentences. Contrast with puppets being *together*. **2.** Have some students spread out in the room so each one is standing *alone*. Have each say "I feel *lonesome*."

long, longer, longest, longs, longed ◆ **1.** Show a book or pencil that is *long* and one that is *short*. Draw *long* and *short* lines on the board. **2.** Draw lines on the board that are *long, longer,* and *longest.* Contrast with lines that are *short, shorter,* and *shortest*. **3.** "When I first moved to California, I *longed* to go back home." Have students describe things they *long* for. —*long-term*, compare *long-term* and *short-term* projects that are ongoing in your classroom—perhaps learning English as a *long-term* project, and learning five new words as a *short-term* project.

look, looks, looking, looked ◆ **1.** Lead students in *looking* at things. Each time say "*Look* at the _____." **2.** Dramatize *looking* by shading your eyes with your hand and *looking*. Lead students in past tense sentences. **3.** Lead students in sentences about things in the room, such as, "This stuffed animal *looks* cute," "This apple *looks* delicious," and "You *look* nice today." —*look away*, make a puppet stand near the edge of your desk and nearly take a bad fall. Turn your eyes away and say "I must *look away!* I can't watch!"

loose, loosed, loosen, loosened ◆ **1.** Contrast small objects that are *loose*, such as paper clips or thumbtacks, with tightly packed modeling clay. **2.** Have students *loosen* their shoelaces and explain that now they are *loose*. Say "Your belts have been *loosened*." **3.** Pretend to have a dog on a leash. Walk the dog to the park, then set the dog free. Say "I *loosed* the dog." Explain that *loosed* is an old-fashioned word no longer in use.

lopsided ◆ Write two words on the board. Write one word very straight and the other with an exaggerated slant. Point to the straight word and say "This word is standing up straight." Point to the slanted word and say "This word is *lopsided*."

lose, loser, losers, lost ◆ **1.** Arm wrestle a student and *lose* every match. From the sports section of a newspaper, find out some well-known team that recently *lost* a game. Give example sentences using *loser* and *losers*. **2.** Dramatize having *lost* your glasses or jacket. Mention a time when a student *lost* something. **3.** Have a puppet wander around as if *lost*. Ask another puppet, "Where am I? How do I get home?" Explain that the puppet is *lost*.

loss, losses ◆ **1.** Hand out pennies to students and set up a pretend lemonade stand. Have students buy cups of lemonade. Count your pennies. Write the arithmetic on the board and say "I spent $5.75 to set up my lemonade business. I have taken in 25 cents selling lemonade today. My *loss* for the day is $5.50 cents." **2.** Have a puppet tell you about its *losses* in life, perhaps toys, friends, or a house that it liked living in.

lot ◆ Tell students you are going to choose by *lot* one student to erase the board. Dramatize with slips of paper of varying lengths. Show the shortest slip and explain that you are going to choose the student who gets it. At the end say "I have chosen you by *lot*."—*a lot*, show *a lot* of paper clips and a few paper clips.

Have *a lot* of students stand up, then have a few stand up. —*lots and lots*, show students *lots and lots* of paper clips. Then show students a *few* paper clips.

loud ❖ **1.** Have students speak in *loud* and *quiet* voices. Lead students in making *loud* and *soft* noises. **2.** Lead students in speaking *loudly* and *softly*.

love, loving, loved, lovely ❖ **1.** Draw hearts on the board. Say "I *love* my mother. I *love* my sister. I *love* my cat. I *love* books." Use body language for emphasis. Ask students to tell who and what they *love*. Pantomime holding and *loving* a doll. Lead students in past tense sentences. **2.** Give a few compliments by saying, "What a *lovely* [bag, coat, sweater] you have." —*best-loved*, show students a copy of one of your favorite books. Hug it to your chest and with exaggerated adoration, say "This is one of my *best-loved* books." —*loving long*, check that students understand the definitions of *loving* and *long*. Have one puppet give another a *long* hug; contrast with a *short* hug.

low, lower, lowered, lowest ❖ **1.** Place things up *high* and then place them down *low*. Point out something hanging *low* on the wall and then, in contrast, *high* on the wall. See *high*. Show the shelves of the bookcase, indicating *low*, *lower*, and *lowest*. Lead students in locating various things that are the *lowest*. **2.** Point to the *lower* part of the board. Contrast with *upper*. **3.** *Lower* your voice or an object.

lowercase ❖ Show *lowercase* letters.

loyal ❖ Show two puppets helping each other and being true friends. Explain that they are *loyal*. Then show two puppets that are being friends, but one will not help the other when it asks. Explain that the puppet was not *loyal*. Mention a *loyal* action that students are familiar with. Or, make up examples of being *loyal*: helping a friend who is hurt or sick, not speaking badly of friends or family, and defending friends and family when in difficulty.

lubricant ❖ Bring in some machine oil or show pictures.

luck, lucky, luckier ❖ **1.** Toss a coin in the air and yell "*Heads!*" Have a puppet yell, "*Tails!*" Say, "_____ wins again, you have good *luck*." Repeat with other examples and sentences. Contrast with bad *luck*. **2.** Have several puppets take turns rolling a die. To whomever gets the highest number, say "You have the best *luck*." Lead students in *lucky*, *luckier*, and *luckiest*. —*good luck*, see *spelling bee* and *team*. Wish "*Good luck*" before they start. Solicit equivalents from students' first languages.

lugged ❖ *Lug* a load of books to your desk. Lead students in *lugging* things. Lead them in past tense sentences.

lull ❖ Tell everyone to relax for a moment. Say "We are enjoying a *lull* in our work."

lullaby ❖ Pantomime rocking a baby in your arms. Sing it a *lullaby*.

lumber, lumbering, lumbered ❖ **1.** Show pictures of trees and a sawmill making *lumber*. Tell students that we use *lumber* to make houses. Have students find things in the room made of *lumber*. **2.** *Lumber* about the classroom and lead students in *lumbering*. Lead students in past tense sentences. Ask students what kinds of animals might *lumber* and what kind might hop or run. Prompt as needed.

luminous ❖ Point out things in the class that are *luminous*. Show pictures of the sun. Explain that it is *luminous*. Ask if the moon is *luminous*.

lump, lumpy ❖ **1.** Put a book on the table and cover it completely with a piece of cloth. Say that now there is a *lump* on the table. **2.** Put some objects on the table under a handkerchief. Run your hand over it and say that it is *lumpy*. Contrast it with the *smooth* surface of the table.

lunar ❖ Show pictures of the moon and explain that it is also called *Luna*. Then explain that things to do with the moon are *lunar*.

lurk ❖ Have a predator (toy lion, tiger, or cat) hide behind a stack of books, peeking out now and then. Have the prey approach. Say "Watch the predator *lurk*, waiting for its prey."

machines ❖ Point out *machines*, such as pencil sharpeners, scissors, staplers, overhead projectors, computers, toy cars, or a cart. Explain that a *machine* is a thing that helps one move things or do other work.

mad ❖ Have a puppet act *mad* at another.

made, make, makes, making ❖ **1.** *Make* a doll out of modeling clay. Say "I can *make* a doll." *Make* a ball out of modeling clay. Say "I *made* a ball." Lead students in *making* things. In illustrations, point out a cook *making* food, someone making a snowman, and so on. Ask students to help you *make* a rhyme. Pantomime preparing a meal and describe each step: "*Make* the corn" or "*Make* the ham." **2.** Lead students in sentences like "My shoes *make* me look taller." Once students understand this usage, switch to past tense sentences. "The shoes that I wore yesterday *made* me look taller." Have students rub their hands together. Explain that rubbing *made* their hands warm. Ask students if running *made* them tired or if eating *made* them full. **3.** Lead students in familiar examples that get across the idea of being forced to do something: for example, "The teacher *made* me sit on the bench." —*made up*, show two puppets having an argument and then *making up*. Tell students that they *made up*. Lead them in sentences. —*make up*, have students *make up* silly rhymes or some similar creative assignment. Have a puppet *make up* a story. Tell the students that the puppet can *make up* stories. *Make up* a story or ask a student to *make up* a story.

madness ❖ Have a puppet do a series of seemingly insane acts, such as trying to touch the ceiling, jumping off a bookshelf, and standing upside down. Say "It is *madness* that makes [Fluffy] do these things. There is no good reason for such behavior."

magic, magical, magically, magician ❖ **1.** Do a *magic* trick, such as producing a quarter from behind a child's ear. Or, show a picture of a *magician* doing a trick, such as pulling a rabbit from a hat. Explain that it is *magical*. **2.** Talk about the fairy godmothers or elves from various folktales. Explain that in these stories they are *magical* and they do things *magically*.

magnificent ◆ Ask students for examples of things that are grand or beautiful. Say, for example, "Yes, the Grand Canyon and our view of the mountains are all *magnificent*."

magnify, magnified, magnifications ◆ Have a *magnifying* glass available and allow students to view objects through it. If this is not possible, draw a pair of objects on the board, one in actual size, and one enlarged, or *magnified*. Use appropiate forms of *magnify*.

mail ◆ Show students an envelope or a package and tell them you are going to the post office to send it to your friend. Then say "I am going to *mail* the letter" or "He is going to get the package in the *mail*."

main square ◆ Use the *main square* of the town as an example.

mainland ◆ On a map, show the *mainland* of the United States. Contrast with islands, such as Hawaii and Puerto Rico.

mainstay ◆ Show a picture of a sailing ship. Point out the *main* mast and the *main* cable that steadies and supports that mast. Explain that this cable is called a *mainstay*.

majority ◆ Ask students which flavor of ice cream they like better: chocolate or vanilla. After you determine their favorite, explain that the *majority* likes (_____). (See *minority*.)

mama's ◆ See *Brad's* or *animal's*.

mammals ◆ Show pictures of fish or birds and explain that they lay eggs that hatch. Then explain that *mammals* do not lay eggs, and they nurse their babies when they are born. If available, show a picture of an animal nursing its young. Contrast with explanations or illustrations of fish and bird feeding habits.

man ◆ Lead students in sentences. First say a person's name, then substitute with the slang term: "Hi, Joe" and then "Hi, *man*."

manacles, manacled ◆ Show a picture of a prisoner in *manacles*. Point out the *manacles* and explain that he or she is *manacled*.

managed, manager ◆ **1.** Ask students to do something they would consider difficult but you are confident that they can do. Once they have completed the task, tell them, "You did that well; you *managed* it." Use other sentences, such as, "The puppet *managed* to cross the street" and "They *managed* to finish that job." **2.** Appoint a student to be in charge of a class activity, such as passing out materials or books. Designate this student as the *manager* of that activity. —*General Manager*, explain that this is the boss of the baseball team. Have one student be the General *Manager* of a team and tell the team what to do.

maneuver ◆ *Maneuver* your chair between two students.

manicurists ◆ Bring in several bottles of nail polish. Pantomime painting the fingernails of a doll. Give example sentences using *manicurists*.

manned ◆ Draw two spaceships on the board. Draw astronauts inside one of them. Say "This spaceship is run by a computer. This one is *manned*."

manners, mannered ❖ **1.** Demonstrate nice table *manners* with puppets. Pantomime drinking tea with very good *manners*. Have a puppet greet you with good *manners*. Lead students in sentences. **2.** Have a puppet demonstrate different ways to behave. Say "[Fluffy] is being ill *mannered;* [Fluffy] is acting well *mannered;* etc."

mano ❖ A Spanish word meaning "hand." It also means "grinding stone."

manufacture, manufacturing ❖ Show illustrations of a *manufacturing* plant and tell what the plant *manufactures*.

many ❖ **1.** Hold up three fingers and ask the class, "How *many* fingers am I holding up?" Point to a pencil on a desk and ask, "How *many* pencils does [Xavier] have?" Repeat as needed. **2.** Put *many* paper clips on a desk. Contrast that with putting a *few* paper clips on a desk.

map ❖ Show the school *map*. Help students find the classroom, lunchroom, music room, and so on. Have students trace with their fingers the paths from the classroom to other parts of the school. Lead them over those same paths through the school. You can also find points of interest on other *maps* like that of the city.

march, marches, marching, marched ❖ If available, play a *march* for the students and lead them in *marching* around the room. Guide them in using sentences with the appropiate forms of *march*.

margins ❖ Show the *margins* on paper or in a book.

Mark ❖ Explain that this is a boy's name. Find out if there is a corresponding name in the first language of the students.

market, marketing ❖ Have students help to suggest ways they could raise money for a party at the end of the year. Ask them how they could *market* some items, such as arts and crafts, candy, etc. Say "When we have our sale, we will be *marketing* our goods." *—on the market,* draw a house and a "For Sale" sign on the board. Say "This family is moving away. They need to sell their house. They have put up this 'For Sale' sign so people driving by will know their house is *on the market.*"

marks ❖ Draw random short lines on the board. Say "Can anybody read these *marks?*" Show students the *mark* your ring or watch makes on your skin.

marry, married ❖ Show a picture of a wedding. Explain that when a man and woman want to live together and have children, they promise to stay together all their lives, so they *marry*. Sometimes they have a party when they *marry*. Explain that after the wedding, they are *married*.

marvelous ❖ Pantomime the ecstatic expression that goes with saying something is *marvelous*.

Mary Mack ❖ Explain that *Mary* is her first name and *Mack* is her last name.

masculine ❖ Point to the boys in the class. Give example sentences using *masculine*.

mass ❖ Show clay in various neat shapes and then show a *mass* of clay.

massive ◆ Draw a *tiny* mouse and an enormous elephant on the board. Say "The mouse is *tiny*; the elephant is *massive*."

master ◆ A person who has control of objects or other people.

match, matches ◆ See what you can find in the classroom that *matches*. *Match* items in the classroom, such as shoes, colors, or paper. —*no match*, have a student hop once, as far as he or she can, within a safe area. Then pretend you are trying to hop farther than the student, but only hop half as far. Say "You win! I am *no match* for you."

mate ◆ Show illustrations of male and female birds and other animals. Explain that they are *mates*.

Matt ◆ Explain that *Matt* is a boy's name. Find out if there is a corresponding boy's name in the first language of the students.

matter ◆ —*no matter what*, pretend to be working on a written assignment. Look up at the clock anxiously and then return to writing. Say sentences expressively, such as "I will finish, *no matter what!*" or "We will win, *no matter what!*"

maul ◆ Have one puppet pretend to *maul* another puppet.

may ◆ **1.** Lead students in making polite sentences asking for things by using *may:* for example, "*May* I talk?" or "*May* I leave?" **2.** Give examples, such as, "There are many black clouds; it may rain" or "There are many gifts; we *may* receive one." —*may as well*, explain that this means "it's an OK idea." Have a puppet say "I want to go to the park." You can respond, "You *may as well.*"

maybe ◆ Explain that people use the word *maybe* when they don't know for sure. Pantomime looking at the sky and saying, "*Maybe* it will rain and *maybe* it won't rain." Other examples are: "*Maybe* I'll get a new bike for my birthday" or "*Maybe* I'll have fun tomorrow."

mayor ◆ Show a picture of the *mayor* of your city or of the nearest city large enough to have a *mayor*.

maze ◆ Show a *maze* or draw one on the board. Have students design a *maze*.

me ◆ Point to a student and say "*You.*" Point to yourself and say "*Me.*" Repeat and then have students point to others and then themselves, saying *you* and *me*. Have students pantomime such sentences as, "Give *me* the book" or "Tell *me* your name."

meal ◆ Use breakfast, lunch, and dinner as examples. Say that each one is a *meal*. Contrast with a *snack*.

mean, meanly, meant ◆ **1.** Ask a puppet a question, which it incorrectly answers. Then say "You *mean* ____." Then have students ask the puppet questions that it incorrectly answers and have them say "You *mean* ____." **2.** Explain that *meant* means "wanted." Examples: "I *meant* to do my homework," "He *meant* to tell me," and so on. Lead students in sentences using *mean*. **3.** Hold a doll kindly. Remind students of some incident of someone being kind that they may be familiar with or a person who treats them kindly. Contrast this with treating a person *meanly*.

meandered ❖   Wandered and drifted. Show the puppet *meandering* around the room. Say "The puppet *meandered* around the room."

measure ❖   Show how to *measure* things.

medal ❖   —*gold medal*, bring in pictures or a book of the Olympics. On the board, draw the different kinds of *medals* given in each category. List *gold medal* winners from past Olympics.

meet, meeting, met ❖   **1.** Have a puppet *meet* and greet another puppet. Explain that they *met*. Or, draw lines on the board that *meet*. Explain that they *met*. **2.** Have two students come to the front of the classroom. Introduce them to each other as if they are just *meeting*. Explain that the two students have *met*.

melancholy ❖   Pantomime *melancholy*.

mellow ❖   Show things that are *bright* and contrast with things of a *mellow* color. Then say each word, *bright* and *mellow*, and have students point to a correct object.

melody ❖   Ask the students to sing a song and then you add some harmony. Say "You were singing the *melody*. I sang the *harmony*." Or, play a song with a *melody* and *harmony*.

melt, melted ❖   Draw an ice-cream cone on the board. Then draw sunshine above the ice cream. Draw drips of ice cream falling down. Explain that frozen things *melt* when they get warm, Say "It *melted*."

memories, memorable ❖   **1.** Tell students some things that you remember from your childhood. Explain that these are called *memories*. Ask who has *memories* of such things as first learning to ride a bike or the first day of school. **2.** Ask students to share *memories* about their native land or a special event in their life. **3.** Tell students about a *memorable* day in your life and have students do the same.

memorizing, memorized ❖   Write a sentence on the board and ask students to recite it several times. Say "You are *memorizing* this sentence. Later, I will ask you to say it again. Because you *memorized* it, you will be able to say it." Remind students of things that they have *memorized*, such as multiplication or addition tables.

mend, mending, mended ❖   Explain that *mend* means "fix." Tear some paper and *mend* it with tape. *Mend* a torn piece of paper with tape. Show where some cloth or a book is *mended*. Demonstrate by *mending* a piece of cloth. Pretend that you are *mending* a hole in the cloth. As you finish, say: "The cloth is *mended*."

mention ❖   *Mention* something to a puppet, perhaps that you like its shoes.

meow, mewed ❖   **1.** Show a picture of a cat. Make the sound of *meow*. **2.** *Mew* like a cat. Lead students in *mewing* and making past tense sentences.

merchandise ❖   Have students tell you things they have purchased recently. Have them list *merchandise* from their favorite stores.

merchants ❖   Have students pantomime being various kinds of shopkeepers hawking their goods. Have them call out:"Buy my fresh strawberries," "Hats for sale," and "Get the best burritos here!" Say "I love to shop here. Look at all these *merchants!*"

merge ◆ Divide the class into two lines. Let each line "feed" into the other so that they *merge* into one line.

merry, merriment ◆ **1.** Have two puppets be *merry* together and then, in contrast, *sad*. Show pictures of people being *merry*. If not available, act *merry* and *sad*. Help students list things that would be considered *merry*, such as holidays, birthdays, school parties, etc. **2.** Pantomime *merriment*. Contrast with *ill humor*.

mesa ◆ Draw a mountain with a flat top on the board. Explain that a *mesa* is a flat area on top of a mountain.

mess ◆ Make a *mess* on your desk with some paper clips, pencils, etc. Tell students that you made a *mess*. Contrast with clean areas of the classroom or the tops of their desks. *Mess* up some things on your desk. Then make them neat again.

message ◆ **1.** Pretend to listen to an answering-machine *message*. **2.** Write a short *message* and give it to one student to give to another.

methods ◆ Show two *methods* for working the same math problem.

Mexican ◆ Explain that people or things from *Mexico* are called *Mexican*.

mid-afternoon ◆ Write 3:00 P.M. on the board and draw the sun in a *mid-afternoon* position.

middle, middle-sized ◆ **1.** Draw three lines on the board and point out the *middle* one. Show three books and point out the *middle* one. Draw various shapes on the board. Draw a line through the *middle* of them. **2.** Line up three books of different sizes: *small*, *large*, and *medium*. Point to each book in turn and say "This is a *small* book. This is a *big* book. This is a *middle-sized* book." Illustrate with illustrations from "Goldilocks and the Three Bears," if the story is familiar to students.

midnight ◆ Contrast with *noon*. Use a clock to demonstrate the passage of time. First have puppets say "It is *noon*. Time to eat lunch." Then have them proceed through the afternoon and evening, pantomiming work or play, dinner, and then bed. Finally, while they sleep, it is *midnight*.

might ◆ Explain that *might* is a word used when one is not sure. Help students make sentences, such as, "I *might* find $100 today" or "It *might* snow today." —*might as well*, explain that this means "it would be OK."

mighty ◆ **1.** Show pictures of lions, tigers, or bears. Explain that they are big and strong. They are *mighty*. **2.** Show a *mighty* warrior, king, or animal that is clearly powerful.

migrating, migrated ◆ **1.** Show pictures of winter, spring, and if possible, pictures of flocks *migrating*. Tell students, "It is winter and the birds fly south. Now it is spring, so they fly north. They *migrate*." **2.** Ask students what countries they are from. Tell them they *migrated* to the United States.

mild ❯ Show a picture of a nice day and say that the weather is *mild*. Show pictures of stormy weather and say that it is not *mild*. Compare spicy foods such as hot salsa to *mild* foods, such as plain tomato sauce.

mile, miles ❯ Relate the distance of a *mile* to something that students are familiar with. For example, if there is a track, tell them they would have to walk or run around it [four] times. Otherwise, estimate the number of trips around the playground. Then have them double the number of trips. —*quarter of a mile*, help students understand *quarter of mile* and find distances that would equate to it. —*square miles*, on the board, draw a large square. Label each side two *miles*. Remind them of the formula for figuring the area and show them that the area equals four *square miles*.

military ❯ Show pictures of soldiers and a *military* post or base.

milking, milked ❯ Show pictures of cows being *milked*. Lead students in dramatizing *milking* a cow. Lead them in past tense sentences.

millennium ❯ Draw a time line on the board. Mark centuries and *millenniums* on it. Explain that each *millennium* is one thousand years or ten centuries. Review thousand if needed.

millionaire ❯ Write "$1,000,000" on the board. Say "A person who has a million dollars or more is called a *millionaire*."

Min ❯ Explain that *Min* is a girl's name. List girls' names and include *Min*.

mind ❯ Have one puppet approach another and ask to use its pencil. Then have the puppet say "You don't *mind*?" Have the second puppet answer, "No, I don't *mind*." Contrast with the second puppet saying, "Yes I do *mind*; please do not borrow my pencil." Lead students in similar pantomimes. —*razor-sharp mind*, ask each student what "2 + 2" is. Tell the ones who give the correct answer with certainty that they have *razor-sharp minds*.

mine ❯ Have everyone point to a possession and say "This is *mine*." Contrast with *yours*.

mingle ❯ Separate the boys and girls into two groups. Have them *mingle*.

miniature ❯ Bring in a *miniature* car, painting, etc.

minimum ❯ Ask students to write between three and six words on a sheet of paper. Point to the three and say "Three is the *minimum* amount." Contrast with *maximum*.

minority ❯ Count the number of boys and girls in the class. Say "[Boys] are the *minority* in this class." (Also see *majority*.)

miracles ❯ Explain that these are things that cannot be explained by science, such as a person recovering from an incurable disease, a dog finding its way home after being lost on a trip, etc. Ask students to give you additional examples of *miracles*.

miser ❯ Draw a piggy bank on the board. Pretend to put some coins in it. Say "I never spend my money. I put it all in my bank. I am a *miser*."

misery ❯ **1.** Hold your jaw like you have a toothache. Give example sentences using *misery*. **2.** Show pictures of sick or starving children from poverty-stricken countries and explain that the children are unhappy, hungry, poor, etc. Explain that they live in *misery*.

misplace ❯ Tell students that you have *misplaced* your pencil and ask them to help you find it. Compare to *lost*.

miss, misses ❯ **1.** Have one puppet leave another. The abandoned puppet cries and says it *misses* the other. Explain that the puppet *missed* its friend. **2.** Throw a piece of paper toward the wastebasket, but *miss*. Then throw the paper and succeed. —*missing in action*, give each student a puppet and have them stage a mock battle. While the fight is going on, remove one puppet from the scene and hide it. Say "[Rabbit] is *missing in action*."

mission ❯ Tell the class that today you have decided to clean all the shelves or something else that needs to be done. Say "My *mission* is to clean the shelves." Have students assist.

mist ❯ Show pictures of landscapes covered in a *mist*. Or use a spray bottle and produce a *mist*.

mistake, mistakes, mistaken, mistook ❯ **1.** Write the word *cat* on the board, but spell it *cta*. Have students correct your *mistake*. Explain that a *mistake* is when you do something wrong but you don't mean to. Pantomime making a *mistake* in writing and crossing it out, backing into someone, and other common *mistakes*. **2.** Write a sentence on the board and make a *mistake*. Repeat a few times and each time, call upon a volunteer to correct the *mistake*. Each time say "I was *mistaken* when I wrote that answer." **3.** Address a student by the name of another in the class. Then apologize and say "I made a *mistake*; I *mistook* you for _____."

misunderstand, misunderstanding, misunderstood ❯ **1.** Have two puppets meet and introduce themselves. One *misunderstands* what the other is called, and it mistakes Jack for Mack. **2.** Have one puppet say to another that it likes his hat. Then have the second puppet get angry and walk away, telling the class, "I don't want to talk to him; it said that it did not like my hat." Tell students the puppets had a *misunderstanding*. Ask if students have ever had a *misunderstanding*. Lead in sentences. **3.** Have a student say something in his or her native language. Act confused and give the student your chalk. When the student says that is not what he or she said, say that you are sorry, you *misunderstood*. Have the student say something in English. Say "Yes! I understand."

misuse ❯ Show the proper way to handle a stapler. Then *misuse* it.

mix, mixes, mixing, mixer ❯ **1.** *Mix* pens and pencils together or *mix* other types of little objects. Explain that your hand is a *mixer*. **2.** Pour and stir two liquids together in a container, such as two colors of paint, or coffee and milk. **3.** Pour two colors of paint into a dish and stir them together. Say "I am *mixing* the [blue] and [yellow] paint together to make [green]." **4.** Show students a *mixture*.

moan, moaning ❯ **1.** Pretend you have hurt your leg and *moan* from the pain. Ask the whole class to *moan*. **2.** Lead students in making *moaning* noises.

mobbed ❯ Use toys or puppets and ask students to assist you. Have each student control a toy or puppet and all converge on one specified location or toy. Explain that the group *mobbed* the [table].

mock ❯ Have students *mock* [imitate] laughing, crying, etc.

modern ❯ Show *ancient* things, perhaps pictures from an archaeological dig. Contrast with *modern* things. Tell them, "These are ancient, and these are *modern.*"

moist, moisture ❯ **1.** Have students feel a damp sponge. Explain that *moist* means "a little wet." Contrast with *soaking* it. Squeeze a few drops of water out of a *moist* sponge. Ask students to feel the *moisture.*

molts ❯ Show a picture of a snake leaving behind a wrinkled, *molted* skin. Say "The snake *molts.*"

moment ❯ **1.** Pause for a *moment* of silence. Let students experience that *moment*. Explain that a *moment* is a short time. Have students come to your desk for a *moment*, look at a book for a *moment*, etc.

mom's ❯ See *animal's.*

monopoly ❯ **1.** Have a puppet maintain a *monopoly* of all your pencils. **2.** Have a *Monopoly* board. Put hotels on one side. Say "I have a *monopoly* of hotels on these streets."

monotonous ❯ Read a passage aloud with no expression in your voice. Say "When I read like that it sounds *monotonous.*" Have students imitate.

monster ❯ Show pictures of *monsters*. Explain that sometimes very large animals like dinosaurs are called *monsters.*

months, month ❯ Show a calendar and ensure that students understand one *month*. Then ask them how many *months* they are in school. Help students to determine this as needed. —*six-month*, on a calendar, show *six* consecutive *months* and have everyone pantomime raindrops falling. Say "In Vietnam there is a *six-month* rainy season."

monumental ❯ See *colossal.*

mood, moods, moody ❯ Have a puppet display a variety of *moods* and say that the puppet is *moody* today. You can also describe the *mood* of the puppet, for example, "[Shaggy] is in a good *mood.*"

mope, moped ❯ Pantomime a *moping* expression. Explain that *mope* means "not feel happy." Have students *mope* and then act *lively*. Ask students if they have ever *moped.*

mops ❯ Show students how to *mop*, ideally with an actual *mop*. Invite a few to try *mopping* as well.

moral ❯ Show pictures of people helping other people. Lead students in sentences using *moral.*

morale ◆ Pantomime good *morale* and poor *morale*.

more, most ◆ **1.** Have the student give you some paper clips. Ask for *more* and have the student give them to you. Repeat with other objects. **2.** Pile up paper clips or other small objects into several piles. Point out the pile with the *most*. Have students find the desk with the *most* things on it or the student with the *most* hair, and so on. Dump out *most* of a container of paper clips. Hold up *most* of your pens or pencils. Place a pile of paper clips on your desk; separate *most* of them from the group. Contrast with some of the paper clips. —*more than*, make two unequal piles of books. Point to the larger pile and say "This is *more than* that." Lead students in similar demonstrations and sentences. —*no more*, pantomime eating a meal. Say "*No more*, thank you!" to an imaginary hostess. Ask students if they have enough homework. Say "Do you want some *more* homework?" Encourage them to reply, "*No more*, thank you!"

morning ◆ Show a picture of the sun coming up. Explain that *morning* is the time before lunch.

mortals ◆ On the board, draw a picture of a person followed by a picture of a grave. Say "People are *mortals* because they can die."

motel ◆ Show pictures of *motels* and explain that this is where you stay for one or more nights. It is not where you live. If needed pantomime with puppets traveling and stopping at a *motel* for the night.

mother ◆ Draw a picture of a family on the board. Point out the *mother*, father, brother, and sister. Ask for first-language equivalents.

motion ◆ Have students make a *motion*.

motivates ◆ Ask one student to volunteer to hop across the room on one foot. Ask the others to cheer him or her on. Say "Your cheering *motivates* [Ana]."

mountainous ◆ Show a picture of *mountains*. Say "Mexico is very *mountainous*."

mouth, mouths ◆ Lead students in pointing to their *mouths*. *Mouth* is used in this lesson in the sense of the *mouth* of a jar. Point out the *mouth* of a jar and explain that it's like a person's *mouth* because it lets things in.

mouthful ◆ Pretend you have a *mouthful* of chocolate and talk. After pantomiming a swallow, say "Could you understand me? I had a *mouthful* of chocolate. Now I'll repeat that with an empty *mouth!*" Take a small sip of water. Say "That was a little water." Take a big gulp, puffing out your cheeks before swallowing. Say "Wow! That was a *mouthful!*"

move, moves, moving, moved ◆ **1.** *Move* various items on your desk and explain that you are *moving* them. Lead students in *moving* their arms or legs. Lead students in past tense sentences. **2.** Explain that when you change houses and take everything from one house to the other, you are *moving*. Ask children if they have ever *moved*. **3.** Place your hand on your heart as you talk about events you have found *moving*. Say "I have strong feelings when I think about young people helping old people. That is *moving*."

Mr., Mister, Mrs., Ms. ◆ **1.** Explain that students' fathers are called *Mister* _____. Use specific last names. Show how "iste" is removed and a period is added to make *Mr.* on the board. **2.** Write the last names of students in the classroom and precede them with *Mrs.* Explain that these are the names of their mothers. *Mrs.* means "a married woman, a woman with a husband." **3.** Write the last names of girls in the classroom and precede them with *Ms.* Explain that *Ms.* can be put in front of the last name of any girl or woman. It is like the word *Mr.*

Mrs. Goose's ➧ Have students practice forming the possessive of their own names. If students understand the words, explain that *Mrs. Goose's* means "belonging to *Mrs. Goose.*"

much ➧ Show *much* paper and contrast it with *a little* paper. Contrast *much* food with *a little* food.

mud, muddy, muddier ➧ If possible, take students outside and make some *mud.* Otherwise, show pictures of *mud* or people with *mud* on them to explain *muddy.* Ask if students have ever gotten *muddier.*

muff ➧ —*muffs a grounder,* demonstrate missing a low ball. In an announcer's voice, say "[Your name] *muffs a grounder* and the team is not happy."

muffled ➧ Have students cover their mouths with their hands and then try to speak.

multiplication ➧ Demonstrate a *multiplication* problem on the board. Have students recite simple *multiplication* facts.

munch, munching ➧ Pantomime *munch* by chewing. Lead students in pantomiming *munching.*

mushy, mushier ➧ Write, "I love you" on the board. Make a disdainful face and say "Sometimes kids think it sounds weird or *mushy* to say 'I love you.' How could we make that phrase even *mushier?*"

music, musical ➧ Play a *music* cassette. Tell students that it is *music.* Then lead students in a *nonmusical* pantomime, followed by a *musical* pantomime. Lead them in sentences.

musk ➧ If you have a perfume with *musk,* let students smell it. Otherwise, show pictures of muskrats, minks, or the Asian *musk* deer and explain that these animals make a smell called *musk.*

must ➧ **1.** Tell students, "You *must* do your homework" and "You *must* come to school on time." Contrast with things they have choices on: "You do not have to go to recess" or "You do not have to watch television." **2.** Draw the numeral 2 on the board but draw it only partially so that it's a little hard to make out. Then say "That *must* be a 2." Repeat with other letters and numbers.

mute ➧ **1.** Have students tell you the noises that various animals make. Ask them if a snake makes noises. Explain that snakes are *mute.* **2.** Play a radio and show how you can *mute* the sound by putting a towel or a coat over it.

mutilate, mutilating, mutilated ➧ Lead students in *mutilating* a piece of paper. Help with sentences.

muttered ➧ Lead students in *muttering.*

my ➧ Point and give examples that contrast *my* and *your:* "*My* nose," "*Your* nose," "*My* shirt," "*Your* shirt," and so on. Have students repeat these with you.

Hold up an item that belongs to *you* and say "This is *my* pencil." Point to something that belongs to a student and say to that student, "This is *your* pencil." Repeat as needed.

myriad ◆ Have students draw dots on the board and keep going until they have drawn a lot. Say "There is a *myriad* of dots."

myself ◆ Bump into something and say, "I bumped *myself*," or talk to *yourself* and say "I am talking to *myself*."

mystery, mysteries ◆ Show *mystery* stories and read the cover introduction to them. "I love books about *mysteries*." Ask a student to move something from one side of your desk to the other while your back is turned. Look at your desk and say "My mug was sitting on this side of my desk, and now it's over here. It's a *mystery* to me!"

myth, mythical ◆ Show some of the *mythical* gods such as Hercules, Zeus, etc. Say "In ancient Greece, people made up stories about gods with super-powers to explain things they didn't understand." Draw a lightning bolt on the board. Say "For example, they explained thunderstorms by saying that when Zeus was angry, he threw lightning bolts to Earth. A story like this is called a *myth*."

nab, nabs, nabbing ◆ Dramatize *nabbing* an object from a student's desk.

naked ◆ Show a fully clothed puppet. Then explain that if the puppet did not have clothes on, it would be *naked*.

name, names ◆ Tell the class your *name* and ask students to say their *names*. —*given name*, write a student's first and last *names* on the board. Underline the first, or *given name*. Ask for other students' *given names*. —*name tags*, make *name tags* for the students. —*pen name*, give historical examples of authors who have used a *pen name*, such as Samuel Clemens who used Mark Twain, or Theodor Geisel who used Dr. Seuss. —*you name it*, check that students understand each word in the expression. Set up a scene where you run a restaurant and students are the patrons. Ask them to find out whether you have various items on your menu by asking, "Do you have [cheeseburgers], etc.?" Answer each question affirmatively. Once each student has had at least one turn, say "We have everything you like to eat at this restaurant. *You name it*, we have it."

Nan ◆ Explain that *Nan* is a girl's name. List girls' names and include *Nan*. Ask students about girls' names that they know.

nap, naps, napping ◆ Show a puppet *napping*. Lead students in pantomiming *napping*.

narrow ◆ **1.** Draw *wide* and *narrow* lines on the board. Ask students to do the same on a piece of paper. **2.** Pantomime creeping quietly past without their seeing you. Move your hand across your brow as if wiping sweat off. Say "Whew, that was a *narrow* escape."

Nat ◆ Explain that *Nat* is the name of the crab in the story, "*Nat's* Nap."

nation, nations, national, nationally ◆ **1.** Point out various familiar *nations* on the globe, including the United States. Explain that they are called *nations* or countries. Have students list the names of *nations* they already know. **2.** Explain that *national* means "belonging to a *nation*." Play the *National* Anthem. **3.** Explain that *nationally* means "within the borders." Give examples, such as, "This car is sold *nationally*." If needed point to the border of the country and show all the places the car would be sold.

natural ◈ Show *natural* things and contrast with things that are *manmade*: perhaps a flower, a wooden pencil and a *mechanical* one, a wooden shelf and a laminate one, etc.

naughty ◈ Have a puppet act *naughty*. Wag your finger at it and tell it it is *naughty*, or not nice. Have students repeat that it is *naughty*.

nauseated ◈ Hold your stomach and pretend you are ill. Say "I feel like I need to throw up. I am *nauseated*."

near, nearer, nearly ◈ **1.** Place a paper clip *near* a book and then *far* away. **2.** Place a stapler *near* a paper. Move it nearer to and then *farther* away from the paper. **3.** Sit at your desk. Have a student stand *nearby*. Contrast with asking the student to move *farther* away. Place a book *nearby*. Place another book *farther* away. Point to objects that are *nearby* others. Contrast with ones that are *far* away. **4.** Place items for sale on your desk. Have a price tag for each one. Pantomime counting your money. Say "I *nearly* have enough to buy this," pointing to one of the items. Show students that you are just a penny short. **5.** Demonstrate *nearly* falling over. Show a bookmark in a book that you've *nearly* finished.

neat, neatly ◈ **1.** Contrast *neat* areas, such as desks, with examples of untidy areas, such as an art room or a bulletin board. Make your desk *neat*. Ask students to make their desks *neat*. **2.** *Neat* can also be used in its slang sense. Admire clothing or possessions and exclaim that they are *neat*. Compare to cool. If students are not familiar with *neat*, explain it with another similar word that they are familiar with, perhaps *cool* or *good*.

necessary, necessity, necessities ◈ **1.** Show pictures of starving children. Then show pictures of well-fed children. Say "These children do not get food and these children do. Food is *necessary*." **2.** Basic requirements. Say "If you are going swimming, what are the *necessities*?" The answer might be a swimsuit, a towel, sunscreen, and water. Ask other similar questions.

necklace ◈ Point out any *necklaces* that the children are wearing or draw one on the board.

need ◈ Give examples: people *need* water, food, and air; children *need* time to play; cats *need* a lot of sleep; fish *need* water to swim in. Contrast with things that people don't *need*.

negative ◈ See *detract*.

neglected ◈ Pass out papers to all but one student. Say "I *neglected* to give you a paper."

neighbor, neighbors, neighboring, neighborhood ◈ **1.** Draw several houses on the board. Have each student stand in front of one of the houses.

Say "You live in houses that are close to each other. You are *neighbors*." Ask students who their *neighbors* are. Show pictures of *neighborhoods* and *neighbors*. **2.** Use pictures of house or apartment doors that are next to one another or pictures of people in *neighboring* doorways. Explain that these people are *neighbors*. **3.** Draw a picture of a little town on the board. Circle a section of it. Explain that this is a *neighborhood*. Circle another section of it and explain that it is a *neighborhood* too. Have students make sentences about their *neighborhood*. —*'hood*, use a map to show a city that is large enough to have an inner city. Say "If each of you lived in buildings next to each other, you would be *neighbors* and live in the same *neighborhood*." Write the word "neighborhood" on the board; draw a vertical line between "*neighbor*" and "*hood*." Explain that *'hood* is a shortened name for *neighborhood*.

neither ❖ Offer a puppet the choice of two books. Say "You may have either the [green] one or the [blue] one." Have the puppet refuse and say "I want *neither*."

nephew ❖ Draw your family tree on the board. Point to yourself and the son of one of your siblings. Say "This is [Skye]. He is my [sister]'s son, which makes him my *nephew*."

nerve, nervous ❖ **1.** Draw a roller coaster on the board. Pantomime approaching the roller coaster as if you are going for a ride. At the last minute change your mind and act scared. Say "I lost my *nerve*." Talk about skydiving, skiing, and mountain climbing taking courage and *nerve*. Draw or show pictures if required. **2.** Have one puppet be a child going to school for the first day. (The other puppet can be the parent.) Have the child puppet act *nervous*.

nest, nesting, nesters ❖ **1.** Explain that a bird builds a *nest* and it lives in it. Lead students in sentences. **2.** Show pictures of birds in their *nests* and explain that the birds are *nesting*. **3.** Show pictures of birds in or building their *nests* and explain that the birds are *nesters*.

net, netted ❖ **1.** On the board, draw a picture of a tennis or volleyball *net*. **2.** Show a picture of a *net* and pantomime catching something in it. —*fishing net*, show a picture of a *fishing net* spread out so its use is clear.

never ❖ Ask students if they have ever ridden a cow, seen a pink elephant, or some other unlikely activity. If they haven't done these things, explain that they have *never* done them. Lead them into making sentences along this line.

new, news ❖ **1.** Contrast *new* and *old* pencils and chalk. In the classroom, find something *new* and something *old*, perhaps a student's *new* clothes or *new* books contrasted with *older* ones. —*brand new*, show something brand *new*. Tell students you just bought it and are using it for the first time. Explain that this means "really, really *new*; never used." Contrast with *used*. **2.** Tell the class *news* about the school, perhaps upcoming events or field trips.

newspaper ❖ —*newspaper editor*, show students a copy of a *newspaper* and point out the name of one of the *editors*. Say "It is the job of a *newspaper editor* to decide which articles are printed and to make any changes that are needed."

next ❖ Show a series of objects and point to the *next* one. Have students line up and name the *next* student in line. —*next door*, draw two houses on the board.

Hold up a puppet in front of each house. Say "[Rabbit] and [Owl] live close to each other. Their houses are right *next door.*"

nibble, nibbling ➠ Lead students in pantomiming *nibbling* a cookie.

nice, nicely, nicer, nicest ➠ **1.** Be *nice* to a puppet by speaking in an appropiate tone. **2.** Show a piece of student artwork and exclaim, "*Nice!*" **3.** Tell the student how *nicely* he or she did on the last lesson. **4.** Exhibit three pictures. Point out which ones you think are *nicer* and *nicest.*

night ➠ —*at night,* create sentences, such as "*At night* it's dark" or "*At night* we go to sleep."

nimble, nimbly ➠ Lead students in pantomiming being *nimble* and contrast it with being *clumsy.* Hop *nimbly;* then contrast by hopping *clumsily.* Have students do the same.

nine ➠ Lead students in counting *nine* objects.

nip ➠ *Nip* off a piece of modeling clay. Let students do the same.

no ➠ Have students put some books on top of their desks. Take them off and say "*No* books." Repeat with other objects.

noble ➠ Give examples of royalty and say they are *noble.*

nobody ➠ Show a puppet sitting at a desk. Beside it show an empty desk. Say, "*Nobody* is sitting at that desk."

nod, nods, nodding, nodded ➠ *Nod* your head, and lead students in nodding their heads. Lead students in past tense sentences.

noise, noises, noisy, noisily ➠ **1.** Have students make various noises such as animals sounds, the tapping of pencils on their desks, and coughs. Use *noise,* *noises,* and *noisy* appropriately. Contrast with *quiet.* **2.** Walk across the room *noisily.*

nomination ➠ Have the class give the names of someone they would like to see as president. After each one, say "Thank you for that *nomination.*"

noncombatants ➠ Show a picture of soldiers. Then draw a chaplain and a medic. Give example sentences using *noncombatants.*

noncommittal ➠ Ask a puppet to accompany you to the movies. Have the puppet act *noncommital.* Lead students in sentences.

none ➠ Put some paper clips, among other objects, on a desk. Take all the paper clips off so that there are *none* on the desk, but the other objects remain. Repeat with other examples.

nonliving ➠ Have students help you make two lists of things they can see—one of things that are *alive* (such as plants, trees, children, goldfish, etc.), the other of things that are not (such as chairs, desks, windows, books, etc.). Say "Our first list is a list of things that are *alive;* our other list is a list of *nonliving* things."

nonsense ➠ **1.** Give examples, such as "Hey, diddle diddle" or "Slinkety-sly" or other made-up words. Have students make up *nonsense* words. **2.** Once students understand this, give and get examples of *nonsense* ideas or ways of operation. Ideas might include, "Would it be *nonsense* to make all people wear the same shoes?" or "Would it be *nonsense* to insist that every country have a king again?"

nonsmoking ◆ Show students the symbol for *no smoking* and explain that rooms or buildings that display this symbol will not let people smoke inside of them. "They are *nonsmoking* rooms or buildings." Ask who has seen the sign and in what locations.

nonstop ◆ **1.** Have puppets talk *nonstop*. Say "They are talking *nonstop*." **2.** Have a puppet pound on a table repeatedly. Have the puppet continue the pounding even though you have asked it to stop repeatedly. Finally, tell the class, as the puppet continues to pound on the table, "Can anyone help me to get this puppet's *nonstop* pounding to go away?"

nontoxic ◆ Show pictures of things that are *toxic* and explain that these are poisons and they can hurt you. Show pictures of things that are *nontoxic* and explain that they will not hurt you.

nonverbal ◆ Use your hand or finger to beckon a student to your desk. Say "I am using *nonverbal* communication." Have students give you other examples.

nonviolent ◆ Have one puppet hit a puppet that remains passive. Say "[Rabbit] is *nonviolent*. His friend is not."

noon ◆ Make the hands point to twelve *noon* on a toy clock. Or, draw this on the board. Explain that *noon* is lunchtime.

north ◆ Show *northern* regions on a map or globe. Contrast with *southern* regions. Tell students, "It is cold in the *north* and warm in the *south*."

not ◆ Show white and colored paper while saying, "This paper is white; this paper is *not* white." Hold up pencils and say "This pencil is big; this pencil is *not* big." Have students make similar sentences. Explain that we use the word *not* to change a sentence to its opposite.

note ◆ **1.** Write a short *note* that students can read and put it on one of the desks. **2.** To a puppet say "Make a *note*. We're having a test tomorrow." Have the puppet write it down.

nothing ◆ Take things off a desk so that there is *nothing* on it. Show a cup with *nothing* in it. Have a student ask you a question and say *nothing* in reply.

notice ◆ **1.** Ask students to take a few minutes to *notice* things in the room. Say "I *notice* there are [five] windows." Have students make similar sentences. **2.** Have students write a *notice* for a yard sale. **3.** Lead the students in *noticing* things in the classroom. —*public notices*, show students the section of the daily local newspaper that posts information about real estate transactions. Say "This is information for everyone to know. These are *public notices*."

novel, novelty ◆ **1.** Ask students to tell you new and *novel* things the class could do. **2.** Do something new and exciting for the day. Say "[Making kites] is a *novelty*.

now ◆ **1.** Show illustrations of long-ago times and scenes of the present time. Alternate these illustrations to make clear the concept of long ago and *now*.

2. Explain that *now* (as used here) has little meaning. Make example sentences, such as, "*Now,* what time is lunch?" "*Now,* count to three."

nuisance ❖ Have one puppet pantomime reading while another continues to interrupt it with questions. Say that the second puppet is a *nuisance.* On the board, draw people sleeping and then draw a barking dog. Lead students in sentences using *nuisance.*

numb ❖ Unable to feel anything. Pantomime being chilled and rubbing your fingers. Smack your fingers against the other palm. Say "My fingers are *numb.*" Limp across the room. Say "My leg went to sleep. It is *numb.* I can't feel my leg." Continue to walk and say "Now I can feel it again."

numeral ❖ Write a *numeral* on the board.

numerous ❖ Show *numerous* books. Say "I have read *numerous* books." Repeat with *numerous* pencils, paper clips, and other objects. Contrast with *few.*

oath ❖ Pantomime a scene of correcting a puppet's bad manners. Then ask the puppet for its *oath* that it will not do that again.

obey, obedient, obedience ❖ **1.** Demonstrate giving commands to a stuffed animal or doll and having it *obey.* **2.** Tell two puppets to do the same task. Have one puppet be *obedient* and do it, while the other puppet is *disobedient* and refuses to do it. **3.** Dramatize *obedience* with puppets. Have a parent instructing a puppet to do a number of chores. The puppet diligently performs them. Tell the students, "Its *obedience* makes its mother happy."

object, objections ❖ Tell a puppet there will be a test today. Have the puppet say "no." Ask the puppet, "Why do you *object* to a test?" Ask students, "Do you have any *objections* to a test?"

object, objects ❖ Point out various *objects* and say "That blue *object* is a book; that small *object* is a pencil." Have students imitate.

oblivion ❖ Show pictures of cities that have been destroyed. Lead students in sentences using *oblivion.*

obnoxious ❖ Have one puppet do something *obnoxious,* such as pester another puppet. Tell the class, "This puppet is *obnoxious!* It keeps pestering [Sweet Pea]!"

observatories ❖ Bring in pictures of *observatories* or show pictures in a science book or encyclopedia.

observe, observing, observation ❖ **1.** Have students do some seat work. Exaggerate watching them at work. Say "I can watch you work; I can *observe* you working." **2.** Pantomime *observing* closely how a plant grows. Write down something. Say "I have made one *observation*…." Lead students in *observing* and writing down their *observations.* Draw a clear night sky on the board, with stars, planets, and a moon. Say "It is a clear night. You can see the stars; it's a good night for *observation* of the stars."

obsessed ❖ Move about the classroom in a driven, frenetic manner, straightening everything in sight. Say "I am *obsessed* with putting everything just right."

obstacles ❖ Put a series of *obstacles* on the floor and have students take turns getting around the *obstacles.*

occupied, occupation ❯ **1.** Pantomime reading a book intently. Have students try to distract you to no avail. Lead students in sentences using *occupied*. **2.** Have students list their parents' *occupations*. Lead them in sentences. **3.** Have a few toy animals march into the puppet's "town," and explain to the class that there is a war happening and the puppet's town is under *occupation*. The soldiers have *occupied* the town.

occur, occurs ❯ Show students a calendar and point out a special date, such as a school event or holiday. Say "Our spring vacation will *occur* on Monday, April 24, this year."

odd ❯ Show two things that are similar; then show one that is different. Explain that the different object is *odd*. Repeat with other objects as necessary.

odds ❯ —*the odds*, ask for a student volunteer to hop across the room on one foot. Ask the other students to decide whether they think the volunteer will be successful. Say, for example, "[Juanita], most of your classmates believe you can hop across the room on one foot. The *odds* are you will be successful."

of ❯ Hold up a cup *of* water as you say "A cup *of* water." Show students other examples such as a box *of* toys or a box *of* chalk, etc.

off ❯ **1.** Knock a paper clip *off* your hand. Take a name *off* the board. Have students get *off* their chairs. **2.** Draw a line on the board and then trace over it and be slightly *off*.

offense ❯ Have students help you list some school rules. Have a puppet break two of the rules. Say "When you break a rule, that is an *offense*."

offer ❯ Have students practice polite ways to *offer* help, such as, "May I help you?"

official, officially ❯ **1.** Show a picture of Congress. On the board, draw a proposed law going to Congress. Use some current legislation or pending legislation. Show the proposed law going through Congress and coming out marked "*official*." Lead students in sentences. **2.** Show documents that have been signed by someone in charge like the principal. Give example sentences using *official*.

offshore ❯ Show pictures of a beach and sea. Show students the *shore* and *offshore* areas.

often ❯ Give examples of things you do *often*, such as eat, sleep, breathe, and hug your dog. Ask students to tell some things they do *often*.

Oh ❯ **1.** Explain that *Oh* is a way of getting attention. Have students practice saying, "*Oh*, _____," and fill in with the name of the person they are addressing. **2.** *Oh* can be a way of telling the other person that you heard what he or she said.

oil ❯ Open and close the classroom door, while making squeaking sounds. Act out *oiling* the hinge. Open and close the door without the sound effects. Say "The *oil* made the door be quiet."

old, older, oldest, olden ❯ **1.** In the classroom, find something *new* and something *old*, perhaps a student's *new* clothes or *new* books contrasted with *older* ones. **2.** Draw a picture of a family on the board, *youngest* to *oldest*. Tell students their ages. Point to the child first and say "He is *young*, she is *old*, he is *older*, and she is *oldest*." Have students give their birthdays and discover who is the *oldest*. **3.** Write a column of centuries on the board: 1600, 1700, 1800, etc. Give example sentences using *olden*. —*old hand*, give students an example of someone who is experienced at something. Say, for example, "I have been teaching for [15] years; I am an *old hand* at teaching English."

old-fashioned ❯ Computers are modern; typewriters are *old-fashioned*.

omen, omens ❯ Use examples of *omens* you know about; for example, finding a four-leaf clover is a good *omen*, but walking under a ladder is a bad *omen*. —*good omen*, draw a horseshoe and say "A horseshoe is a *good omen* for some people. What objects bring you good luck?"

on ❯ **1.** Show a book *on* your desk, then take the book *off* your desk. Do other similar demonstrations. **2.** Set up a scene where some of your students are members of a track or baseball team. Have them select other members to be *on* the team. Make sentences, such as "We are *on* the team." **3.** Turn a light *on* and *off*. —*on and on*, have students walk around the room *on and on*. Have a puppet chatter *on and on*.

once ❯ **1.** Clap one time and explain that you clapped *once*. Then clap two or three times. Nod *once*. Contrast that with nodding two or three times. **2.** Help students make sentences, such as, "*Once* I was a baby" or "*Once* I couldn't talk." Explain that *once* means "not now, but before." —*once upon a time*, explain that this is a way of saying "long ago."

one ❯ **1.** Show students *one* book. **2.** Make example sentences referring to a student. Say "This *one* is named _____," or referring to a stuffed animal, say "This *one* is brown." You can also make sentences using *one* to refer to objects. **3.** Explain that *one* means "a person." It can also mean an animal or a thing. Give examples, such as "*One* has a birthday once a year" or "*One* gets presents on *one's* birthday." —*no one*, have a few students stand in two different spots in the classroom. Count the number of students in each spot. Have students move from *one* spot so that there is *no one* there. —*one another's*, make up examples, such as "Touch *one another's* shoes" or "Smile at *one another*." It might be best to explain *one* and *another* before tackling *one another's*. See *one* and *another*. —*one-one*, organize two teams. Throw a ball to *one* team for *one* person to catch. Write 1 on the board. Repeat this with the other team. Say "So far, the score is *one-one*."

one-fourth ❯ Show a whole circle and then show them *one-fourth* of the circle.

onlookers ❯ Show pictures of sports events with *onlookers*. Have students pantomime being *onlookers*.

only ❯ Have a group of students stand up and have all but one sit down. Now there is *only* one student standing. Or, show students *only* one of something that it would be desirable to have more of, such as *only* one earring, one shoe, one chip in a bag, or one candy.

ooze ❯ Open a bottle of glue and lay it on its side, perhaps on a paper towel. Apply enough pressure to cause some to *ooze* out.

open ❯ **1.** *Open* a door, a drawer, and a book. Lead students in sentences. **2.** Put your hands together so they are closed. Slowly *open* them.

opinion ▸ Ask each student to express an *opinion* about some current event or a recent story the class has read.

opponent ▸ Name a sports team that most of the students would know about and ask who their *opponent* was in their most recent game.

opportunity ▸ Have each student offer you a job. Say "Each of these jobs sounds like a great *opportunity* to learn and try new things."

oppose, opposing ▸ **1.** Have one puppet *oppose* another. **2.** Have one puppet express an opinion and the other state the opposite. For example, "I like vanilla ice cream / I like chocolate; I like classical music / I like rock 'n roll," etc. Say "These puppets are opposite on everything! They have *opposing* viewpoints."

oppressed ▸ Explain that people are *oppressed* when they are forced to do many things against their will.

oral, orally ▸ **1.** Show a book. Tell them the words are written. Then tell students a short story. Tell them, "This time I talked. My words were *oral*. Lead them in simple dramatizations, such as asking them to read written words, then asking them to listen to *oral* words. **2.** Give directions *orally*. Contrast with *written* directions.

orbits ▸ Make a sign that says, "Saturn." Have each student make a sign that says "Moon." Holding their signs, have students walk around you in a circle. Say "This is how a moon *orbits* a planet."

ordeal ▸ Pantomime taking a test and really agonize about doing it. Say "Taking this test is an *ordeal*."

order, orders, ordered ▸ **1.** Put books in *order* according to their sizes or colors. Line up pencils on a table in the *order* of their sizes. **2.** See *chronological*. **3.** Have a puppet *order* another puppet to "come here," then, in contrast, *request* it. **4.** In an authoritative tone, give *orders* to each student to pantomime a chore, such as erasing the board, scrubbing the floor, etc. —*in order to*, explain it by giving comparative sentences such as, "I sat in my chair so I could tie my shoe." "I sat in my chair *in order to* tie my shoe." Repeat with other examples, such as "*in order to* write we need a pencil and paper." —*out of order*, have students give their names in a certain *order* such as down each row or around the circle. Have a puppet interrupt one of the students.

ordinary ▸ Draw a dish of vanilla ice cream on the board. Invite students to draw things on it to make it into a special ice-cream sundae. Say "There is nothing special about a dish of vanilla ice cream. It's an *ordinary* dessert, but this ice-cream sundae is very special."

organize, organizing, organized ▸ Ask students to *organize* their desks. Model the behavior by *organizing* your own desk first. Have students help you *organize* the books on a shelf. Lead them in past tense sentences.

original ▸ **1.** Ask students to draw an invention for something that would be useful around the house. Say "Your inventions show me you have wonderful imaginations. You are very *original*." **2.** Show an *original* of something and then the *copies* you made from it.

ornamenting ❖ Give students an exaggerated account of a familiar school event. Say "I am adding to this story to make it more interesting. I am *ornamenting* the story."

ornery ❖ Ask a puppet to read with you and have it act grouchy and irritable. Say "[Pumpkin] is acting very *ornery.*"

orphan, orphaned ❖ Draw a family on the board. Then erase the mother and father. Say "This child's parents died. This child is an *orphan*" and "The children have been *orphaned.*"

other ❖ Show one puppet of two that you are holding. Then pull out the *other* puppet. Have students show you one hand and then the *other* hand; one foot and then the *other* foot.

other way ❖ Once students understand the words *other* and *way*, demonstrate calling a stuffed animal or doll and having it go the *other way*.

ought ❖ Make example sentences, such as, "You *ought* to brush your teeth after eating" or "I *ought* to exercise each day." —*ought to*, see *should*.

our, ourselves ❖ **1.** Divide students into two groups. Stand with one group and then the other. Lead students in sentences that contrast actual differences between *theirs* and *ours*. Examples: "*Our* hands are empty; *their* hands are full" or "*Our* mouths are open; *their* mouths are closed." **2.** Say to the class, "Let's take *ourselves* for a walk down the hall. Then take them down the hall and back.

out ❖ — *out of __ way*, using little objects, show a car driving on *its way* from its house to school. Check that students understand the idea of *its way*. Show people and animals getting *out of its way*. Have students block the aisle and ask them to move *out of your way*.

outdistanced ❖ Run a race across the room with the students and stop halfway across. Say "I had to stop halfway across the room. You ran all the way across. You *outdistanced* me."

outdoor ❖ Show *outdoor* play equipment, *outdoor* clothes like jackets, or *outdoor* furniture. Talk about *outdoor* games like baseball. Contrast these with *indoor* play equipment, clothes, furniture, and games.

outer ❖ Draw two circles on the board, one inside the other. Point to the *inner* circle and say "This is the *inner* circle." Point to the *outer* circle and say "This is the *outer* circle."

outlast ❖ Have three students balance on one foot. To whomever holds it the longest, say "You *outlasted* everyone. You lasted the longest."

outline, outlined ❖ **1.** Draw an *outline* of a house and say "This is an *outline* of a house." **2.** Draw a picture on the board. Then draw a square around the picture. Say "I *outlined* the picture."

outlive ❖ Show a picture of a tree and a flower. Explain that the tree has *lived* longer than the flower. The tree *outlived* the flower.

outrun ❖ Line up two puppets. Say "Ready, get set, go!" Make the puppets *run* a race. Say to the winner, "You can *outrun* [Fluffy]."

outside ❖ Take students *outside*. Bring them back *inside*.

outskirts ◆ Show a map of a familiar community. Draw a circle with your finger around its circumference. Say "People who live on the edges of this community are said to live on the *outskirts* of town."

outsmart ◆ Act out by playing tic-tac-toe on the board with a puppet. Have the puppet win every time. Tell the class, "The puppet can *outsmart* me at tic-tac-toe."

outspoken ◆ Pantomime a scene where you are talking to two puppets, asking their opinion on things in the classroom, such as artwork or books that they like. Have one puppet be quiet and withdrawn, not wanting to answer, and the other quite *outspoken* in expressing its opinions. Tell the class that one puppet is *outspoken* and one is *withdrawn*.

over ◆ **1.** Point out things that are *over* the students' heads, such as the light fixtures or the ceiling. **2.** Lead students in holding their hands *over* their heads and then *under* their heads, *over* their desks, then *under* their desks. **3.** Move a paper clip across a distance and explain that it is going *over* there. —*all over*, place objects *all over* your desk. Have students toss objects *all over* their desks.

overcome, overcoming ◆ **1.** On the board, write a math problem. Have difficulty solving it; pantomime realizing how to work it. Say "I have *overcome* my problem." **2.** Have a puppet act shy and then less shy. Say "He is *overcoming* his bashfulness." **3.** Draw a picture on the board of a burning building with billowing smoke. Cough and sputter, then keel over in your chair and pantomime unconsciousness. Say "I was *overcome* by all that smoke!"

overcrowded ◆ Put two chairs side by side. Pretend it is a bench. Ask five students to sit on the "bench." Say "That bench is *overcrowded*."

overjoyed ◆ Tell something you were delighted about. With extremely happy vocal and facial expression, say "I was *overjoyed* to hear about my sister's new baby!" Ask students for examples.

overload ◆ *Overload* a toy animal with many objects. Point to a shelf that is *overloaded*. *Overload* a student's desk with so many books the student cannot see over them.

overnight ◆ Ask students if they have ever slept at a friend's house all night. Explain that this is called staying or sleeping *overnight*.

overseer ◆ Pantomime a scene where some of the students are workers and you are the *overseer*. Tell them to work faster and harder, etc.

overwrought ◆ Pantomime being *overwrought* about lost car keys or some other such necessity. Have students be *overwrought* over a missing homework assignment.

owed ◆ Sell two puppets a pencil, and have one pay now. Have the other puppet tell you that it doesn't have the money now. Take the pencil back. Then tell the class, "The puppet *owed* me money, so I took the pencil back." Repeat the pantomime with students.

own, owns, owned, owner ◆ **1.** Find out or point out who *owns* various personal belongings such as jackets and lunch boxes. Give sentences using *own, owns,* and *owned.* **2.** Have students touch their *own* book, then a neighbor's book, their *own* desk, then a neighbor's desk. Show something that belongs to you and have them show you things that belong to them. While displaying the different objects, lead them in sentences: "I have my *own* purse," "You have your *own* shoes," "I have my *own* pencil," "You have your *own* eraser," and "They have their *own* desks." **3.** Identify the *owners* of personal belongings, such as sweaters, jackets, lunch boxes, and toys.

pace, paced ❖ Pantomime *pacing* to and fro like a tiger. Walk at a fast *pace,* and then at a slow *pace.* Move your arm at a fast *pace* and then at a slow *pace.* Lead students in past tense sentences.

pack, packed ❖ **1.** *Pack* various items in a backpack. Ask a few students to *pack* the backpack. Lead students in making sentences about the items placed in the backpack, such as "Carlos *packed* the ball and the pencil." **2.** Show a jar *packed* with pickles. Show a *packed* suitcase.

pack rat ❖ *S*how students all the things you've collected in your classroom. Say "I never throw anything away. I am quite a *pack rat.*"

paddle, paddling, paddled ❖ Show a picture of people *paddling* in a canoe. Point out the *paddle* and pantomime the action. Lead students in sentences.

page ❖ Hand a note to one student and send him or her to deliver it to another student. Point out that the first student is acting as a *page.*

pain ❖ **1.** Pantomime experiencing *pain* after being hit. Say "It hit me hard; I feel *pain.*" **2.** Demonstrate writing with a pencil that has a tip that keeps breaking. Say, "This pencil is a *pain!*" —*pain in the neck,* have one puppet be a nuisance by needing a drink, needing to use the bathroom, wanting candy, and feeling tired and hot. Say "What a *pain in the neck.*"

painting, painted, painters ❖ **1.** Draw a *paintbrush* on the board. Pretend to pick it up and *paint* your chair. Say "I *painted* my chair." **2.** Show students pictures that have been *painted* by *painters* and tell them that if the artist *paints* the *picture,* he or she is called a *painter.* You may need to show *paints* and *paintbrushes* as well. **3.** Lead students in a pantomime of *painting.* Or, allow students to actually *paint.*

pal, pals ❖ Point out friends in the class and explain that they are *pals.* —*pen pal,* set a puppet or doll on a map of the United States in another state. Pantomime putting a letter in an envelope. Send the letter to the puppet or doll. Give example sentences using *pen pal.*

pale, pales ❖ Show pictures of different colors, some *dark* and some *pale.* Explain the difference.

Pam ❖ Explain that *Pam* is a girl's name. Find out if there is a corresponding girl's name in the first language of students.

panic, panicked ❖ **1.** Pretend that the classroom is on fire and you cannot open the door. As you keep trying, display higher levels of *panic.* **2.** Have a puppet fall off the table onto the floor. Act *panicked* and race over to see that the puppet is OK.

pants, panting ◆ **1.** Show pictures of various animals that *pant*. Demonstrate *panting* and lead students in *panting*. **2.** Show a student wearing *pants*.

papers ◆ Bring newspapers to class. —*paper route*, bring a newspaper to class. On a map, show a *route* where someone delivers *papers*.

parade ◆ Show pictures of a *parade*. Ask students if they have ever been to one or marched in one. Organize a *parade* in the classroom.

paradise ◆ Make a list of things that students want if they could have exactly what they wanted. Lead students in sentences using *paradise*.

parched ◆ Show pictures of *parched* earth.

pardon, pardon me ◆ **1.** Have a puppet bump into another and say "*Pardon me*." Have the second one respond, "I *pardon* you." **2.** Also explain that when a person wants to speak to another person, he or she will often use this expression to show that he or she does not want to bother the other person. Demonstrate. —*I beg your pardon!* Walk across the room and pantomime bumping into one student. Say "Oh, *I beg your pardon!*" Explain that *pardon* means "forgive" and that this is very a polite phrase.

parents ◆ Draw a picture on the board of a mother, father, and children. Point out the mother and father as the *parents*.

park ◆ Mention *parks* the children know. Show pictures of *parks*.

parlor ◆ Show pictures of a typical *parlor*. Then show pictures of a milking *parlor* in a barn. Have students use both in sentences.

part, parted ◆ **1.** Cut a fruit into *parts*. Point out the *parts* of the body: nose, mouth, arm, and so on. Have students touch the *parts* of toys or classroom equipment. **2.** *Part* two students. Lead students in past tense sentences.

partner, partners ◆ **1.** Group students by twos, telling each one "*Partner*" as you point to his or her *partner*. Pair students off and have them be *partners* in walking around the classroom. **2.** Divide money between two students. Say "We each have one dollar. We need a total of six dollars to start our lemonade business. Together we will be equal *partners*."

part-time ◆ Show students what 9:00 A.M. to 5:00 P.M. looks like on a clock. Say "*Full-time* work is usually eight hours a day. *Part-time* is less than that." Ask students if they know anyone who works *part-time*.

pass, passing, passed ◆ **1.** Make a *pass* with the name of the class on it and sign it. Give it to a student and say "Carry a *pass* to prove you have permission to leave my class." **2.** *Pass* a ball to another student and have him or her *pass* it to another. **3.** *Pass* students' desks by walking by. Have students *pass* each other. Walk by your desk. Say "I *passed* my desk." **4.** Write *passed* on the board. Point to a calendar and show students how many days have *passed* in the week. Explain to them that as each day is done and a new one begins, one day has *passed*. **5.** Draw a mountain road on the board and use an eraser as a bus and a pencil as a car. Show the bus *passing* the car. —*pass on*, have students *pass* the stick *on* to their teammates in a pantomimed relay race. Or, as they sit, have them *pass* an object *on* among themselves. Have them repeat "*pass it on*" each time they do so. —*passed away*, tell students *passed away* is another way to say someone died. —*passing by*, show a little figure or puppet *passing by* students.

passengers ❖ Draw or show a picture of a bus. Have students make a line of their chairs and pretend to be riding on a bus. Say "You are *passengers*."

password ❖ Give each student the *password*. When each student gives you the *password*, give him or her a gold star or some other reward.

past ❖ **1.** Show things from the *past* and things from the *present* such as typewriters and computers. Say "These are from several years ago; they are from the *past*. These are what we use in the *present*." **2.** Write *past* on the board. Toss a ball *past* a student. Tell students that the ball went *past* her. Using two puppets, have one come up to the other and then, in contrast, have one go *past* the other. Draw a finish line on the board. Show going *past* the finish line.

Pat ❖ Explain that *Pat* is both a boy's and a girl's name. Write a list of boys' and girls' names, including *Pat* on both. Ask for first-language corresponding names.

pat, pats, patting ❖ *Pat* your arm; *pat* your hair; *pat* your stomach. Each time you *pat*, repeat the word. Lead students in *patting*.

patch, patches ❖ **1.** On the board, draw a rectangular garden with areas of different vegetables, including a melon *patch*. **2.** Draw or show a picture of a dog or horse with *patches* of color.

path ❖ Draw a *path* through a garden or lawn.

patient, patiently ❖ **1.** Ask a puppet to do something and have her take a long time to do it. Wait *patiently*. Have her apologize for taking so long, and then tell her that you are *patient*. Repeat, this time being *impatient*. Tell two puppets that you will give them some candy. Have one be *patient* and the other *impatient*. **2.** Set up a scene in a hospital where you are a doctor and one student has a broken arm. Pantomime bandaging the student's arm and say "[Carlos] has hurt his arm and has come to me to fix it. I am the doctor and [Carlos] is my *patient*."

patient's ❖ See *Brad's*

patrons, patronage ❖ **1.** Ask what types of stores students like to visit. Make a list of these on the board. Explain that when they go to these places, they are *patrons*. **2.** Ask students to tell you places they shop. Lead students in sentences using *patronage*.

patter ❖ Show an illustration of a mouse and then demonstrate with your fingers how it can pitter and *patter* across a room. Have students pretend to be mice who pitter and *patter* around the room.

patterns ❖ Draw or show pictures of various animals. Point out spots on a leopard, stripes on a zebra, etc. Say "Look at all these different *patterns*."

pause, pausing ❖ Begin to speak and then *pause*. Continue speaking. Explain that the stop is called a *pause*. Lead students in speaking and *pausing*. Demonstrate by playing a tape and hitting the *pause* button periodically.

pay, paid, payment, payments ◆ **1.** Sell a puppet a paper clip. Say "It costs a nickel." Have a student or puppet *pay* a nickel. Say "[Fluffy] *paid* for the paper clip." **2.** Ask a puppet to *pay* attention. Have the puppet do so. Contrast by having a puppet not *pay* attention. **3.** The nickel that is *paid* is a payment. Show a picture of a television, and explain that it costs a thousand dollars. Then say "Every month I make *payments* on my T.V." —*paid and done*, check that students understand the definitions of *paid and done*, then show students schoolwork that they have finished. Explain that it is *paid and done*. Tell students that when school is over for the day, the day is *paid and done*. —*pay off*, make the last *payment*. Set up a scene where students run a bank and you are the customer. Explain that you had to borrow money from the bank to start your business. Pantomime coming into the bank and handing over some money. Say "I have come to *pay back* the money I borrowed from you. I am giving you this money to *pay off* my loan."

paycheck ◆ Set up a scene where you run a restaurant. One student is a server and the other students are patrons. Have the server pantomime waiting on the customers. Then write a pretend *check payable* to the server and hand it to him or her. Say "Thank you for a job well done. Here is the *pay:* you earned $12.50 today. This is your *paycheck*." See *salary*.

payday ◆ Explain this as the *day* that people receive their *pay* from their bosses. Ask if they know when their parents' *paydays* are. Set up a scene where you run a restaurant and students are servers. Point to Friday on a calendar and say "I will *pay* you to work at my restaurant. I will *pay* you every Friday. Friday is *payday*."

peace, peaceful, peacefully ◆ **1.** Contrast pictures of people engaged in *peaceful* activities with pictures of people fighting. **2.** Show pictures of the end of WWII or some other well-publicized *peace*. **3.** Show pictures of *peaceful* places or landscapes. Contrast with pictures of busy cities. Ask students to relay *peaceful* experiences that they have had. **4.** Have students sit quietly and say how *peaceful* the classroom is. Then ask students to be *noisy*. Tell them that the *noise* is not *peaceful*. Demonstrate being *peaceful* and contrast with feeling *worried*. Sit in a chair *peacefully;* and then sit in the chair as if you were ill at ease. Lead students in sitting *peacefully*.

peck, pecking, pecked ◆ **1.** A *peck* is eight quarts. If possible, point to a container that would approximate that size in the classroom. **2.** Using a toy bird, show students its beak. Have the bird *peck* at your desk.

pedicurists ◆ Bring in several bottles of nail polish. Pantomime painting the toenails of a doll. Give example sentences using *pedicurists*.

peek-a-boo ◆ Demonstrate playing this with a puppet who is a baby. Hide behind something, then pop your head out and say "*Peek-a-boo!*"

peeking ◆ *Peek* between your fingers. Lead students in *peeking*.

peeling ◆ *Peel* off a sticker. Say "I'm *peeling* off my favorite sticker."

peep, peeping ◆ *Peep* like a baby chick. Lead students in *peeping*.

peephole ◆ Make a tiny *hole* in a piece of paper and *peep* through it.

peer, peering ◆ **1.** Have students help you make lists of people who are equal in rank, skill, or worth, such as classmates, teachers, U.S. Presidents, etc. Define the members of each group as *peers*. Have students say to one another, "You are my *peer.*" **2.** Lead students in *peering*.

penalty ◆ Play "Simon Says." Set up a *penalty* for making a mistake.

pendulum ◆ Tie a weight, such as a roll of tape, to the end of a string. Move the string so the weight swings back and forth.

pens, penned ◆ Show pictures of domesticated animals, such as sheep, in *pens*. Give example sentences using *penned*.

perceiving ◆ Have students pair up. Have one student [Jose] stand with his back turned to the other, [Arina]. Have [Arina] flap her arms rapidly. Ask [Jose] if he can feel anything behind him. Explain that he is not able to see what [Arina] is doing, but he is *perceiving* something behind him.

percentage ◆ Draw a pizza pie on the chalkboard. Divide it into slices. Give each a *percentage*.

perfect, perfectly ◆ **1.** Make a *perfect* letter *a* and then one incorrectly drawn. Repeat with other letters and numbers. **2.** Ask a student to spell a familiar word. Say "Very good! No mistakes! You spelled it *perfectly.*"

perform ◆ Ask a volunteer to *perform* (sing, recite, dance, tell a joke) for the class. Help the class make past tense sentences.

perhaps ◆ Explain that people use the word *perhaps* when they don't know for sure. Pantomime looking at the sky and saying, "*Perhaps* it will rain and *perhaps* it won't rain." Other examples: "*Perhaps* I'll get a new bike for my birthday" or "*Perhaps* I'll have fun tomorrow." Lay out some crayons on your desk, and tell students that you will try to guess which color they like best, then say: "*Perhaps* you like blue best" or "*Perhaps* you like red?" Repeat with other students. Reverse and have students guess about other things that you might like.

perilous ◆ Pull students' chairs into the middle of the room in a haphazard fashion. Walk across the room, avoiding all the chairs. Say "This is the safe path across the room." Then pantomime climbing through the chairs with difficulty. Say "This is the *perilous* path across the room."

period ◆ Write a sentence on the board and end it with a *period*. Have students copy your sentence and end it with a *period*. Have students point to *periods* in their books.

perish ◆ Draw a wilted plant and a watering can on the board. Pantomime watering the plant. Say "If I don't water this plant, it will die. It will *perish.*"

permit, permission ◆ **1.** Play "Mother, May I" using the phrase, "Yes, I give you *permission.*" **2.** Give a puppet a *permit* to go to lunch early.

persecution ◆ Show pictures of historical events involving the *persecution* of others: African-Americans as slaves, Native Americans, Irish Americans, etc.

ESL Visual Glossary

persisted ❯ Have a puppet move paper clips from the desktop to a cup. Heckle it, but have it *persist*. Lead students in past tense sentences.

person, personal ❯ **1.** Point out *persons* in the room. Contrast with *things*. **2.** Have students describe the contents of their backpacks. Say "The things in your backpacks belong to you; they are your own, *personal* belongings."

perspire ❯ Check that students understand *fever* and *sick* and explain if needed. Use a doll that is water-resistant. Put it under a blanket and explain that it is sick. Place a few drops of water on its forehead and explain that it has a fever. It is hot and *perspiring*.

persuade, persuaded, persuasion ❯ Have each student give a reason why the puppet should go to the movies. After a while, have the puppet say "Okay, I'll go. You *persuaded* me." Give example sentences using *persuade*, *persuaded*, and *persuasion*.

pest, pests ❯ Give a student a book and tell him or her to keep reading no matter what you do. Try to distract him or her. Finally, say "I am a *pest!*" Offer various students very brief opportunities to be pests around the classroom.

pet, pets, petting, petted ❯ **1.** Show pictures of animals that are often *pets* that people have in their homes. Ask children to name their *pets*. **2.** Lead students in *petting* a stuffed animal. When you are done, tell students, "We *petted* the animal."

Peter Piper ❯ Show students the boy in the "*Peter Piper*" illustration and say "*Peter Piper*." Point to a boy in the class and say his first and last name.

petered ❯ Jog around the room, energetically at first, and then more and more slowly. Say "I *petered* out."

phantom ❯ Show pictures of a ghost and explain that it can also be called a *phantom*.

phase, phases ❯ Show students pictures of a baby growing to an adult. Explain the main *phases* of growth. "The first *phase* is the baby; the second *phase* is the child; the third *phase* is the teenager; and the last *phase* is the adult."

phenomenon ❯ Explain that a *phenomenon* is an event or object that cannot be explained by nature as we know it.

philosophy ❯ Ask students to discuss their views on right and wrong. Say "You are each telling us what you believe to be true about the subject of right and wrong. You are each sharing your *philosophy*."

phoney ❯ Have a puppet pretend to be the teacher and try to teach the class something, muffing it up. Tell the puppet that it is a *phoney*, and that you are the real teacher. Teach students the same thing with no errors.

phonics ❯ Show students some *phonics* cards and show how these help to teach the sounds and letter combinations for the English language.

photographer ❯ Show students a camera and a photograph, or draw them if the items are not available. Pantomime taking pictures of each student. Say "I am a *photographer*."

phrase ● Write a *phrase* and sentence on the board. Show that a *phrase* is a part of a sentence.

physical, physician ● **1.** Have the puppet go for a *physical* checkup at the doctor's office. Say "The puppet is being weighed, measured, and getting an eye test. It is getting a *physical.*" **2.** Ask everyone the name of his or her *physician.*

Picasso ● Show pictures of this artist and help students to pronounce his name. Ensure students understand that this is his name.

pick, picking, picked ● **1.** Lay some objects out on a table. *Pick* one of the objects, and then ask various students to come up and *pick* an object. Make sentences with each chosen object. Show students pictures of plants with vegetables on them and pantomime *picking* them off. Let students try to pick them off as well. Then lead them in saying: "I *picked* the peas" or "I *picked* the beans." **2.** Lead students in *picking* up items from the floor. —*pick him up*, walk about with students as a group, pretending to be on a bus. Place a student at an imaginary bus stop. *Pick him up* by having him join you on the "bus."

pickets ● Show a picture of a *picket* fence and point out the *pickets.*

pickled ● Give students a little taste of *pickles* or *pickled* vegetables. Tell them that these things have been *pickled.*

picky ● Have a puppet be *picky* by finding many faults with another puppet. Contrast this with praising and admiring.

picnic, picnics ● Some of students may be unfamiliar with *picnics*, so you may need to show supplementary pictures of families on picnics. Pantomime having a *picnic.*

piece ● Say "Who likes a *piece* of pizza?" Draw a slice on the board. Say that it is a *piece* of the whole pizza. Hold up individual *pieces* of paper one at a time.

pig's ● Explain that *pig's* is two words squeezed together: *pig* and *is.* Show this on the board.

piggle ● Explain that this is just a sound and has no meaning. —*pigglety*, explain that it's just a fun sound. It doesn't mean anything. Have students make up other fun sounds.

piggyback ● Demonstrate with a puppet. Say "[Rusty], would you like a *piggyback* ride?" Put the puppet on your back, holding its hands on your shoulders. Gallop around the room and say "Isn't this fun? Do you like to ride *piggyback?*"

piles ● Make a few *piles* of books. Ask students to make *piles* of other objects.

Pilgrims ● Show students illustrations of *Pilgrims.* Tell students these were some of the first colonists who came from England.

pin, pinning, pinned ● Demonstrate *pinning* a note or name tag to your shirt. Fold and *pin* a piece of fabric with either a straight *pin* or needle.

pinch ● Pantomime taking a *pinch* of spice.

pines ● Have a puppet *pine* for the one it loves. Then, have the one it loves come to it and make the puppet happy. Lead students in similar pantomimes.

pious ❯ Show pictures of ministers or priests and explain that they believe in their religion very strongly. Explain that anyone who believes in his or her religion strongly is *pious*.

pipes ❯ Show students a picture of a *pipe* organ and point out the *pipes*.

pit ❯ On the board draw a *pit* in a road in cross section. Draw a car to clarify that it's a road. —*the pits*, tell a puppet that it has to take a test. Have the puppet walk slowly in a dejected manner and say "This is *the pits*."

pitch, pitching, pitched ❯ *Pitch* a baseball. Say "I *pitched* it." Show pictures of baseball players or a baseball. If you have a baseball, *pitch* it to a student and ask him or her to *pitch* it back to you. —*pitches in*, attempt to gather a large armload of books. Say "These books are heavy. I need some help." When students jump up to help you, say "I love the way everyone *pitches in!*"

pitch-black ❯ Turn off the lights. Say "It is dark in here." Have students cup their hands over their eyes. Say "Now it is so dark, we can't see anything. It is *pitch-black*." Draw a scene on a piece of paper, then blacken it completely with a marker.

pity ❯ Show a picture of a sad person. Pantomime *pity*.

place, places ❯ **1.** Point to different parts of the room and explain that this is the *place* for ___ and this is the *place* for _____. **2.** Mark some spots on the floor with objects. Have students occupy these. Tell students that these are their *places*. Show students different *places* on the map. Have students change *places* when sitting and then when standing. Show students different *places* in the classroom, in the school building, and on a globe.

plain, plains ❯ **1.** Have students draw two dishes of ice cream. Have them decorate one with various toppings. Say "This ice cream has lots of things on top. This ice cream has nothing on it; it is *plain*." Point to *plain* things in the classroom. Draw a *plain* design on the board, and then a fancy one. Show pictures of *plain* clothing. Contrast with pictures of *fancy* clothing. Show a *plain* piece of paper. Decorate it with a quick drawing. **2.** Show pictures of different *plains*, such as the Great *Plains* of Texas, the *plains* of Mongolia, etc. —*plain as beans*, an expression meaning that something is not decorated. Lead students in making sentences with the phrase.

plan, planning ❯ Pantomime *planning* a picnic. Have a sheet of paper and a pen in front of you and appear to be thinking very hard. Suddenly come up with an idea and write it down. Do this a number of times and then show your "list" to students. Have them *plan* an activity.

planet ❯ Show a diagram of the solar system. Point out the *planets*. Show that Earth is a *planet*.

plant, planting, planted ❯ **1.** Bring in potting soil in a small container. *Plant* seeds in it. **2.** Pantomime *planting* a seed. Show pictures of people *planting* bushes. Lead students in past tense sentences.

plantation ❯ Show a picture if possible. Explain that it is like a very large farm.

play, plays, playing, played, player, playful ◆ **1.** Contrast *play* with *work*. Remind students of times that they have *worked* (studied, cleaned up, or did jobs at home) and *played* (recess). **2.** Lead students in *playing*. Show students a game. Invite them to start it and say "Let's *play* it." **3.** Explain that a *player plays*. Give examples such as *ballplayers*. Say "Who *plays* baseball?" **4.** Show pictures of people *playing* musical instruments or pass out musical instruments that students can *play*. **5.** Have students pretend to be actors performing in a *play*. Show pictures of people on stage. **6.** Act out with a kitten toy. Dangle a string and have the kitten try to catch it. Then crumple a sheet of paper into a ball and have the kitten bat it around. Say "[Kitty] just loves to *play* all day; she is so *playful!*"—*play house*, if students are not familiar with *playing house*, demonstrate it with puppets. Have the puppets make a meal or make the beds by simply pantomiming or by using whatever objects are readily available, such as pencils and erasers. If possible, let students *play house* for a short while. —*play tricks*, have a puppet *play tricks* on students, such as tapping the student on one shoulder and popping up from behind the other. With each trick that the puppet *plays*, tell them, "The puppet *played* a *trick* on you." Ask students, "Can you *play tricks* on the puppet?"

playmate, playmates ◆ Explain that a *playmate* is a friend. Review *friend* as needed. You can point out the *playmates* in the various stories that students have been reading.

playwright ◆ Have a puppet be busy writing on paper. Ask it what it is doing and have it answer that it is writing a play. Say to the class, "The puppet is a *playwright.*"

plead, pleaded ◆ *Plead* for silence, then say "I *pleaded* for silence." *Plead* with a puppet to go to the movies with you.

pleasant, pleasantly ◆ **1.** Show *pleasant* scenery and *unpleasant* scenery. Make *pleasant* and *unpleasant* noises or motions. **2.** Have a puppet sing *pleasantly* while another sings *unpleasantly*.

please ◆ Have one puppet demand something in a rude manner. Contrast with having the puppet ask *politely* and saying *please*.

pleasure ◆ Tell students something you do that you particularly enjoy. Say "[Reading novels] gives me great *pleasure*." Have students give their own examples.

pledge, pledged ◆ **1.** Ask students to make you a promise, such as to do their best in class. Say "You have given me your *pledge* to do your best in class." **2.** Say "If you hop from here to there, I *pledge* to give you one cent."

plenty, plentiful ◆ **1.** Show something you have *plenty* of in the classroom, for example, chalk or paper, and say "We have *plenty* of chalk." Contrast with something that you are almost out of, perhaps paint, and say "We do not have *plenty* of paint." **2.** Show students your supply of paper. Say "We have a *plentiful* supply of paper."

plodded ◆ Walk heavily across the room with a slumped posture. Say "I *plodded* across the room." Have students imitate.

plodding along ❧ Demonstrate *plodding along*.

plot ❧ **1.** On a city map, draw lines where an individual *plot* of land might exist. Do this several times. **2.** Have students help in outlining the *plot* from some story they have read.

plow ❧ Show students a *plow* and pantomime how it works to explain the noun and verb.

pluck ❧ Draw a big turkey on the board. Draw feathers on the turkey. Pantomime *plucking* feathers. Draw some feathers in a pile next to the turkey and erase the feathers on the turkey itself. Say "Watch me *pluck* a large turkey."

plugged ❧ Demonstrate by *plugging* an appliance into a wall socket. Say "The [radio] wouldn't work until I *plugged* it in."

plumbing ❧ Show pictures of *plumbing* or actual *plumbing*.

plundered ❧ Stack a pile of things on your desk. Have puppets *plunder* it.

plunge, plunging, plunged ❧ **1.** Fill a sink with water and *plunge* your hand into it. **2.** Pantomime a puppet jumping into the water. Say "The puppet is *plunging* into the water." Help students with sentences.

pneumonia ❧ Explain as a very bad cold in your lungs. Show lungs if needed.

pocket, pocketful ❧ **1.** Reach into your *pocket* and say "I wonder what is in my *pocket*." Have students check the contents of their *pockets*. **2.** Have a student stuff wadded-up bits of paper into his or her *pocket* until it is full. Show the class his or her *pocketful* of paper.

poem, poetry ❧ **1.** Read some very short rhyming *poems* to students. **2.** Show students a book of *poems* and explain that it is called *poetry*.

point, points, pointing, pointed, pointers, pointless, pointy ❧ **1.** *Point* to students and say "I *pointed*." Start and stop students in *pointing*, alternating *point* and *pointed*. **2.** Show the *point* of a pencil. **3.** Show students a pencil that has no *point*. Explain that it is *pointless*. **4.** Show a pencil or pen that is *pointy* and then show the eraser end that is not *pointy*. **5.** Take the main *points* from a reading the class has already done. Write them on the board.

poison, poisoned, poisonous ❧ Show a picture of a bottle of *poison* with skull and crossbones on it. You can also show a picture of a rattlesnake or black widow spider or any animal that students know to be *poisonous*. Dramatize taking *poison* and dying. Help with sentences.

poke, poking, poked ❧ Lead students in pantomiming *poking* things on their desks. *Poke* a doll in the tummy. Say "I *poked* her in the tummy."

policy ❧ With students write two or three rules that the school has. Tell them these rules are school *policy*.

polish ❧ *Polish* a piece of metal with a cloth or paper towel. —*polished off*, have students erase the board as fast as possible. Tell them they *polished off* that job in a hurry!

polite, politely ❧ **1.** Contrast *polite* and *impolite* actions. To sit up straight is *polite*. To put your feet on the table is *impolite*. Ask students to give examples of *polite* and *impolite* actions. **2.** Have one puppet greet another puppet *politely*. The second puppet acts *rude* by not returning the greeting. The puppets can do other *polite* and *rude* things, such as ask for something with and without saying "please" or receive something with and without saying "thank you."

pollute, polluted, pollution ❧ **1.** Show pictures of *polluted* parks or lots. Explain that the garbage *polluted* these places. Tell students, "Always throw your garbage away, so you do not *pollute*." **2.** Give examples of *pollution*, such as garbage on the ground or in rivers. Ask if they have seen *pollution* at the beach. Explain that if you throw garbage on the ground, you *pollute* the ground.

poor ❧ Give one puppet a lot of money. Give another very little money. Have the puppets tell students, "I am *rich*" and "I am *poor*." Lead students in sentences.

poorhouse ❧ Show pictures from the Depression. On the board, draw a house and label it *poorhouse*. Tell students that during the Depression, people could go to the *poorhouse* when they had no money.

Pop ❧ Explain that some children call their father "*Pop*." Find out from students what they call their fathers.

pop, pops ❧ **1.** Draw a can of soda on the board and call it *pop*. **2.** Blow up a balloon and *pop* it. **3.** Lead students in making a *popping* sound with their mouths. It's the sound that popcorn makes or a bottle of soda sometimes makes when you take the top off. —*pop up, popped up*, have a puppet *pop up* from behind a desk or table. Have students hide beneath or behind a table and *pop up*. Help students with past tense sentences.

poppet ❧ —*my poppet*, ask students if their parents have a special name for them. Share names that you give your children or have heard others use. Examples are *sweetheart, sweetcake*, and *honeypie*. Say to a puppet, "Come here *my poppet!*"

popular ❧ Show two different types of dessert. Have different puppets pretend to select the same dessert to eat. Say, "One dessert is much more *popular* than the other."

population ❧ Give various examples, such as "All students in this class make up the *population* of the class. All the people who live in [name of city or town] make up the *population* of [city]." Ask students for other examples.

portion, portions, portion out ❧ **1.** Draw a pizza pie on a sheet of paper. Cut it into slices. Give a slice to each student. Say "Each of you gets a *portion* of the pizza." Lead students in sentences using *portions*. **2.** Ask a student to *portion out* four pencils between two students.

portray ❧ *Portray* various objects or illustrations to students by covering each with a cloth and taking the cloth off with each *portrayal*. Say that you are going to *portray* a picture.

position, positions ❧ **1.** Have students hold different *positions*. **2.** Place students in different locations around the classroom. Each time say "This is your *position*."

positive ◆ Make several *positive* comments about the classroom; perhaps, "We have lovely windows with a beautiful view."

possess, possessions ◆ 1. Show students things that you *possess* and ask them to show what they *possess*. For example, "I *possess* this pencil. I also *possess* the knowledge of how to use it." Demonstrate. 2. Show students your *possessions* and have them show you theirs. Lead students in sentences.

possible, possibility ◆ Pose contrasting scenarios to students of likely and unlikely happenings. Say, for example, "There's no *possibility* that the school will be closed early today, but it is very *possible* the bell will ring at [3:15]." Help students to make sentences for *possibility*, such as, "It is a *possibility* that the bell will ring at [3:15]."

postponed ◆ *Postpone* an assignment you have given students until the next day or some other time. Give sentences using *postponed*.

posture ◆ Ask two students to stand. Have one stand straight and tall, the other slumped over. Say "[Yen] is using very good *posture*; [Jorge] is using poor *posture*."

poultice ◆ Draw oil, herbs, and mustard on the board. Pretend to mix the ingredients together in a pot and heat them on a stove. Pretend that you are applying the warm mixture to a cloth and laying the cloth on your knee. Say "My knee has been hurting. This nice, warm *poultice* will make my knee feel better soon."

pound, pounds, pounding ◆ 1. Have a student feel the weight of an object that weighs a *pound*, perhaps a grapefruit. You could also use several items that total a *pound*. Have students weigh various things to get a feel for what a *pound* is. 2. *Pound* on a desk and say "I am *pounding* the table."

pour, pouring, poured ◆ *Pour* water into a glass. Tell students that you *poured* it. Fill a cup with water. Transfer it to an empty cup and say "I am *pouring* the water into this empty cup."

pout ◆ Demonstrate a *pout*.

power, powerful ◆ 1. Show batteries and outlets that give electrical *power*. 2. Show pictures of *powerful* animals, point to their muscles, and remark upon their size. Then say "This is a *powerful* dog" or "This is a *powerful* tiger." Contrast with pictures of birds, kittens, etc. Tell students these animals are not *powerful*. 3. Pantomime attempting to push or lift your desk without succeeding. Say "I am not strong or *powerful* enough to lift my desk." 4. Show *powerful* people and explain that they are strong. Then give students examples of *powerful* decisions and make expressive sentences; for example, "I will learn English" or "I will clean my room." Contrast as expressively with weak decisions, such as "Well, let me think" or "I am not sure . . . ." —*power is out!*, demonstrate to students by shutting off the lights in the classroom. Explain to them that when the *power is* really *out*, the lights will not turn back on until workers fix it. Have students make sentences.

practical ◆ Lead the class in performing *practical* and *impractical* actions for walking to the doorway. *Practical* actions might include walking quietly, or walking to the door by desk rows. *Impractical* ones might include hopping, running, or crawling to the door.

practice, practicing, practices, practiced ◆ **1.** Ask children to *practice* the alphabet. **2.** *Practice* writing an alphabet letter on the board. Write the letter repeatedly, until you get it right. Lead students in *practicing* a song or rhyme. **3.** Draw a line on the floor. Hop from one side to the other. Hop on the line and then start over until you do it correctly four times in a row. You can also use a puppet. Explain that you are *practicing*. **4.** Say a word and have students repeat it six times. Say "You *practiced* saying the word [*practice*]."

praise ◆ *Praise* a student for something that he or she has done well. Have him or her *praise* another student, and so on.

prance, prancing ◆ Show pictures of a horse. Lead students in *prancing* like horses.

prankster ◆ Have a puppet play a trick on you, such as putting something on your chair that you pretend to sit on. Say "Oh, [Goofy], you tricked me again. You're such a *prankster!*"

pre- ◆ Write *pre-* on the board. Explain that when we put this prefix in front of a word, it means "earlier" or "before." Show this with sample words.

precarious ◆ On the board, draw a picture of a person on a narrow ledge. Explain that the person is in a *precarious* position.

precede ◆ Line students up and call each by name, saying whom they *precede*. "Jenny *precedes* Sky," "Joshua *precedes* Bonita," etc.

precious ◆ Have students list things that are very important to them. Lead them in sentences using *precious*.

precook ◆ Pantomime a scene of cooking meat and then putting it aside. Say "I am going to *precook* the meat." Do some other chopping, etc., and then get the *precooked* meat to cut up and add to your mixture.

predator ◆ Show pictures of one animal hunting another. Explain that the hunter is called a *predator* and the hunted is called the *prey*.

predicament ◆ Show pictures of people in various *predicaments*, such as embarrassment or having some problem. Give example sentences.

predict, prediction, predictions, predictable ◆ **1.** Ask students to *predict* what they will do the next day in class. **2.** Do a simple science experiment, like mixing baking soda and vinegar. Tell the class what will happen before you mix the chemicals. **3.** Ask students to give their *predictions* about what will happen the rest of the day. **4.** Act out with a puppet. Describe her daily routine and say that she does the same thing every day. Say [Mina] does the same things day after day. This is her routine for Monday, Tuesday, Wednesday, and Thursday. What do you think she does on Friday?" When the class answers, say "Yes, [Mina] is very *predictable*."

pregnant ◆ Show pictures of *pregnant* women.

prehistoric ◆ Show students a history book. Show pictures of *prehistoric* people. A simple approach would be to explain that *prehistoric* means "long ago, like when the dinosaurs lived." If you wish to be more exact, you can draw a time line on the board and mark a spot where humans started keeping a history and explain.

prejudice ◈ Give and get examples of *prejudice* with animals or colors (noninflammatory subjects); for example, "Dogs are smarter than horses."

prepared, preparation, preparations ◈ **1.** Divide the class in half. Have one-half play and the other half pantomime studying a spelling list. Then pretend to give a spelling test. Say "These students were playing; they are not ready for this spelling test. These other students studied their words; they are *prepared* for the test." **2.** Ask students to list things they do in *preparation* for coming to school. **3.** Have students act out all the things that would have to be done to get ready for a class picnic. Say "This is great! With all these *preparations* we're going to be ready to have a great picnic!"

present, presence ◈ **1.** Show students a picture of a *present*. Pretend that you have a *present* for a puppet behind your back. **2.** Explain that *present* also means that someone is there. Lead students in sentences, such as "Is Sarah *present?*" and "Your *presence* is welcome."

preserved ◈ Show "jerky" or canned goods. Lead students in sentences using *preserved*.

preside, presides, president, presidential ◈ Have students form two groups and each group decide who will be *president*. Have those people *preside* over one lesson for each group. Set up a scene where your class is going to have an English club. Have the class elect a *president*. Ask students to name the current *president*. Lead students in sentences using *presidential*.

press ◈ Using your hand, *press* the back of a chair until it moves.

pressure ◈ Beg a puppet to let you go to the store with it. Keep up until the puppet finally gives in. Tell the class, "I put a lot of *pressure* on the puppet."

presumed, presumption ◈ **1.** Tell a puppet you are going to give it a test. After it acts surprised, say "I *presumed* you studied." **2.** Show students pictures of different scenes. Ask them what they think is happening. These are their *presumptions*. Lead students in sentences using *presumption*.

pretend, pretending, pretended, pretense ◈ Lead students in *pretending* to fly like a bird. So they don't confuse *pretending* with flying, *pretend* some other things—eating a banana, sleeping, and so on. Ask students to *pretend* to be sick. Tell them, "You each made a *pretense* at being sick."

pretty, prettier, prettiest ◈ **1.** Show *pretty* scenes and flowers and an *ugly* picture of city billboards, litter, and signs. **2.** Show things that are *pretty*, *prettier*, and *prettiest*.

prevailing ◈ Draw a sailboat on a sheet of paper and place it on your empty desk. Have the majority of students stand on one side of your desk, with one or two on the other side. Have all students blow on the paper. Say "The strongest winds are coming from this side of my desk. They are the *prevailing* winds."

prevent, preventing, prevented ❯ Have students stand in a cluster in front of the door. Say "I'd like to leave the room, but you have blocked the door. You are *preventing* me from going out of the room" and "You have *prevented* me from leaving the room."

preview, previews, previewed ❯ Explain *view* as needed. Ask if students have ever *viewed* a movie. Then ask if students have ever seen *previews* for movies not yet released. Talk about other things that can be *previewed*.

previously ❯ Have a puppet tell you something. Say "I did not know that *previously*."

pre-wash ❯ Explain *wash* as needed. Pantomime spilling ketchup on your white shirt. Explain and pantomime *pre-washing* it to help get the stain out. Then pantomime washing it.

prey ❯ Show pictures of cats and mice. Explain that cats eat mice, so mice are called *prey*. Repeat with pictures of birds and caterpillars.

price, priceless ❯ **1.** Explain that if something costs 50 cents, the *price* is 50 cents. Act out selling a small object with a *price* tag. Pantomime a scene with a student of selling a paper clip. Say "The *price* is a nickel." Have the student give you a nickel. Repeat as needed. **2.** Have something you value. Have students offer to buy it. Turn them down. Lead students in sentences using *priceless*.

primary ❯ Show the *primary* colors—red, blue, and yellow. Show how when they are mixed, we get many other colors.

prime ❯ Have students tell you their favorite TV shows; point out those that are in *prime* time.

primitive ❯ Use counting sticks to add. Contrast by using a calculator.

print, printed ❯ **1.** Point out *print* on a page. **2.** Show students *printed* pages from a book. Ask students to find a *printed* page in a book.

prisoner ❯ On the board, draw a picture of a person in jail. Give example sentences using *prisoner*.

privately ❯ Show students two puppets. Have one go off by itself and read a letter, get dressed, or comb its hair *privately*. Contrast this with having the puppet do these things with the other puppet watching. Lead the children in making a wish *privately*.

privileged ❯ Divide the class into two groups. Give one group more toys, crayons, paper, etc. than the other group. Say, "The group with more materials is more *privileged*."

probably ❯ Name things that students would think of as *probabilities*, such as, "It will *probably* be sunny today," "It *probably* won't snow today," or "We'll *probably* have time to do math today." Have students make up similar sentences.

probe ❯ On the board, draw a picture of a tooth. Draw a picture of a dental *probe*. Show how the dentist *probes* our teeth for cavities.

problem, problems ❯ Try to fit a large object into a small container. Explain that you have a *problem*. Other *problematic* tasks might be untangling a string, solving a hard math *problem* on the board, or not coming to school on time. Ask students about *problems* they have had. —*no problem*, have a student ask you to help him or her tie his or her shoe. Say *"No problem,"* and tie the shoe. Reverse and ask students to help you with simple tasks, where they answer with *"No problem."* —*no problem is too big, no problem is too small.* Have a puppet come to you and say "I have broken my leg." Respond with, "No *problem is too big,"* and pantomime putting a cast on the leg. Make it a rather elaborate job so students see how big the *problem* really is. Have a puppet come to you and say "I have scraped my leg." Respond with, *"No problem is too small,"* and pantomime putting a bandage on the leg. Make it a simple and swift action so students see how small it was to fix.

process ❧ On the board, show the step-by-step *process* for solving a math problem.

proclamation ❧ Dramatize making a *proclamation* that recess will be at a certain time or that you are going to read a story. Contrast that with simply telling students the same information.

prodded ❧ *Prod* something with a pencil or your foot.

prodigious ❧ Show pictures of *prodigious* buildings. Name the biggest building in town. Say "That is a *prodigious* building." See *colossal.*

product, products ❧ Show students pictures of various *products* that one can buy from the grocery store.

professional ❧ Show pictures of *professional* athletes. Say "You kids play [baseball] for fun. People on the [name of baseball team] team are paid to play baseball. They are *professional* baseball players."

profit, profits, profitable ❧ **1.** Take an item such as a can of beans. On the board, write what the beans cost and the cost of canning. Then write how much you paid for it. Subtract the cost from the price. Label it *profit.* **2.** Hand out pennies to students and set up a pretend lemonade stand. Have students buy cups of lemonade. Count your pennies. Write the arithmetic equation on the board and say "I spent $5.75 to set up my lemonade business. I have taken in $6.50 selling lemonade today. My *profits* for the day are 75 cents." **3.** Pantomime buying a pencil from a student for a nickel. Then turn to another student and sell the pencil for a quarter. On the board, write "25¢ - 5¢ = 20¢" and say "I earned twenty cents by selling that pencil. That was very *profitable."*

profoundly ❧ Have students sit at their desks with their eyes closed, not fidgeting or talking. Have them do this until there is silence. After some time, say "It is *profoundly* silent in here." Ask students to open their eyes.

programmers ❧ Show students a computer, or draw or show a picture of one. Have them each pretend to type on the keyboard. Say "It is your job to give the computer instructions for doing various tasks. You are computer *programmers."*

progress ❧ Draw a hill on the board. Have a puppet "climb" the hill. Every now and then comment about the *progress* the puppet is making. Ask students to think about how much English they knew when they first came to school and how much they know now. Say "Your English is getting better and better. You are showing great *progress* in learning English."

prohibit ◆ Draw a stick figure of a child running with a circle around it and a line through the circle. The sign *prohibits* us from running. Show other similar signs.

promise, promised ◆ Have a puppet ask you if it can go to the park on Saturday and solicit a *promise* from you. Then have the puppet repeatedly come back to you and ask if it still gets to go. Each time answer, "Yes, I made a *promise.*" Finally, have Saturday come and take the puppet to the park. Lead students in similar pantomimes.

prompt ◆ Tell two puppets to join you for tea at 4 o'clock. Have one puppet be *prompt* and arrive at the correct time. Have the other be *late.*

proof, prove ◆ **1.** Show your driver's license. Say "This is *proof* that I know how to drive a car." Ask students to give you *proof* that they know another language or spelling or something they can demonstrate. Pick up something and drop it. Say "When we drop something and it falls to the ground, it is *proof* there is gravity." **2.** Ask a puppet to *prove* that 2 + 2 = 4. Have the puppet add two paper clips to two paper clips and count the total as four. Say "Do you know how to write the word *no*? *Prove* it." Ask students to *prove* other things such as knowing their own phone numbers.

prop ◆ —*propped up*, *prop* something *up* against the board ledge.

propel, propelled ◆ *Propel* a nerf ball or some similar object.

proper ◆ **1.** Have two puppets greet you, one in a *proper* manner and one in an *improper* manner. **2.** Demonstrate *proper* table manners using a puppet. With each demonstration, tell the class, "The puppet is eating *properly.*" **3.** Divide students into two groups. Have one group count to ten in order; have the other group count randomly. Say "The first group counted to ten *properly*; the second group got their numbers all mixed up."

proposition ◆ Tell students your plan for today's lesson. Say "Here's what I suggest we do today. Here's my *proposition* for today's lesson."

prospering ◆ Show pictures from fairy tales where a person is *prospering*, or doing well.

prostration ◆ Draw a large sun on the board. Pantomime discomfort from the heat of the sun by fanning yourself, tugging at the neck of your clothing, getting dizzy and tired, and finally slumping over on your desk. Say "The heat from the sun made me feel weak and tired; I was suffering from heat *prostration.*"

protect, protects, protection, protective ◆ **1.** Pantomime getting a scratch. Put a Band-Aid on it. Lead students in sentences using *protect.* **2.** Show a book with a cover and explain how the cover *protects* the book. **3.** On the board, draw a picture of the sun. Underneath, draw a person. Then draw a hat on its head. **4.** Show pictures of animals in their dens. The den is their *protection.* **5.** Have one student volunteer to act the part of a hunter while you act as a mother lion, with the other students as your cubs. As the hunter pretends to track you, gather your cubs to you and roar at the hunter. Say "The mother lion doesn't want her babies to get hurt. She is very *protective* of them."

protest, protests ❧ Pantomime a *protest* with puppets. Have one puppet *protest* that puppets do not have the same rights as students. Puppets want to go to recess and lunch. Have the puppet lead students on a peaceful march to *protest*.

proud, pride, proudly ❧ **1.** Write something on the board. Show it to students, dramatizing your *pride*. Tell them you are *proud*. Ask if they have done things that have made them feel *proud*. Walk around in a *proud* fashion, saying how *proud* you are of something familiar to students. **2.** Write something on the board. *Proudly* display it and your pleasure in your work. Have students walk around the room *proudly* displaying their latest artwork. Have puppets *proudly* talking about climbing a hill. Lead students in sentences, such as "The teacher *proudly* showed our artwork" or "The teacher *proudly* showed her writing."

prowling ❧ Show pictures of a cat, lion, or tiger *prowling*. Pantomime *prowling*.

prune ❧ Pantomime *pruning* a plant.

pry ❧ Ask the puppet various personal questions. Have the puppet become upset. Have the puppet say "Please don't *pry*."

psychology ❧ Break the word up into its roots: *pyche* and *ology*. Above *psyche* draw a picture of a spirit or "mind"; draw a picture of someone studying it. Explain that *psychology* means "the study of the mind or spirit." See *spirit* and *study*.

public address system ❧ Point to the loudspeakers. Say "The principal uses our *public address system* to deliver messages to everyone in school."

published ❧ Give students identical *published* books. Show them how they can all read the same thing because there are many copies of it. Contrast this by writing a sentence on a piece of paper. Give it to one student and explain that the books were *published*, but this sentence is not *published*.

puff, puffing ❧ Blow out air against a piece of paper. *Puff* out air. Lead students in *puffing* out air.

pull, pulling, pulled ❧ *Pull* an object across your desk. Have students *pull* objects across their desks. *Pull* your hair. Say "I *pulled* my own hair!"

pulse ❧ Show students how to find their *pulse* on their wrists or their neck.

pun ❧ Say "What is black, white, and red/read all over? The newspaper!" Explain that this type of joke is a *pun*.

punching ❧ **1.** Have two puppets *punching* a pillow. **2.** Tell students that *punching* is sometimes used to mean "herding cattle."

punishable, punished, punishments ❧ **1.** Have a puppet fail to turn in its homework. Say to the puppet, "You will be *punished* by not getting to play after school." **2.** Have students help you list some school rules. Have a puppet break one of the rules. Issue a *punishment*, such as "time out." Say "[Spot] broke one of our school rules and got *punished* for it. Breaking the school rules is *punishable*" or "What are some other *punishments* besides time out, that would be fair for breaking the school rules?"

punt ❖ Drop a ball with your hands and *punt* it with your toe before it hits the ground or pantomime the action.

pupil ❖ Point to yourself and then to a student. Say "I am the *teacher* and you are the *pupil*."

purchased ❖ Pantomime buying a pencil from a student for a nickel. Say "I *purchased* a pencil from [Carla]."

pure ❖ Show a *pure* white paper or a *pure* blue paper. Then make colored marks on the paper so that it is no longer *pure*. Show a *pure* pile of paper clips and then put a few bits of paper in the pile so that it is no longer *pure*. Show a cup of *pure* water. Add some dirt or paint to it so that it is no longer *pure*.

puree ❖ Draw or show students a banana and a jar of banana baby food. Say "Babies can't chew and swallow a whole banana the way you can. We have to mash it up for them first. We *puree* the banana."

purloin ❖ Show a puppet *stealing* something. Explain that *purloin* is an old-fashioned word, and that today we say *steal*.

purposes ❖ Say "Each of you has your own *purposes* for doing something. You play soccer because you like it, and you study hard because you like to learn."

purr ❖ Have students imitate *purring* by making a vibrating sound deep in their throats.

pursue, pursued ❖ **1.** Have one puppet *pursue* another. Have students pair up and take turns *pursuing* each other. **2.** Show a puppet *pursued* by another puppet.

push, pushing ❖ **1.** Have students *push* things across their desks. **2.** Lead students in *pushing* and *pulling* things across their desktops.

put ❖ Have students *put* their pencils in various spots on their desks and in their desks. —*put a stop to*, have two puppets argue. *Put a stop to it.* —*put down*, show pictures of soldiers confronting civilians, such as during the sixties; at Wounded Knee during the seventies; at Tienenman Square in China; in Chiapas, Mexico; etc. Give example sentences using *put down*. —*put off*, check that students understand the individual words. Explain that *put off* means that you will "wait until later." Find things that students can *put off*, such as putting away their books or wiping their desktops. —*put out*, Draw a scene showing a fire. Have a puppet pretend to use a bucket of water to *put out* the fire. —*put to bed*, *put* a puppet *to bed*.

puzzled ❖ Point to a calendar. Say "What day is it today? Is it [Monday or Tuesday]? I am *puzzled*."

quack, quacking, quacked ❖ Show an illustration of a duck. Lead students in *quacking* like a duck. Say "We *quacked* like ducks."

qualified ❖ Show your driver's license. Say that you are *qualified* to drive a car. If you are a student, you are *qualified* to eat in the school cafeteria, or if you are six years old, you are *qualified* to attend first grade.

182

quality ❖ Quickly write some sloppy letters on the board. Carefully write a second group of correctly done letters on the board. Explain that one set is a low *quality* and the other set is of high *quality*. Have students write some high-*quality* and low-*quality* letters on paper.

quantity ❖ Show students your *quantities* of paper clips, rubber bands, pencils, etc. Contrast a small *quantity* of paper clips with a large *quantity*.

quarter, quarters ❖ **1.** Show students four *quarters*. Cut a whole into fourths. **2.** See *dwelling*. —*quarter-acre*, see *acres*.

quench, quenching, quenches ❖ **1.** Show a picture of a fire and pantomime *quenching* it with water. **2.** Say to students, "I am thirsty." Drink some water, then say "Now I am not thirsty; water *quenches* thirst."

quest ❖ Take students on a *quest* to find all the pencils in the classroom or to pick up all the trash on the playground.

question, questions ❖ Ask students a *question*. Have a student ask you a *question*. Have students ask *questions* of other students.

quick, quickly ❖ **1.** Make *quick* movements with your hands. **2.** Speak *slowly* and then *quickly*. Raise your hand *slowly* and then *quickly*. Walk *quickly*, and then walk *slowly*. —*quick as an arrow*, check that students understand the individual words in the phrase. Then explain that an arrow moves through the air very *quickly*. If someone moves very *quickly*, we can say *quick as an arrow*.

quiet, quietly, quieter ❖ **1.** Ask students to be *quiet* for a moment. Contrast by asking them to be *noisy*. Ask students to be *quiet*. Say "I love *quiet* moments like this." **2.** Have students talk and walk *quietly*. **3.** Ask all students to all speak at the same time. Then ask only half of the students to speak at once, and say that it is *quieter* now.

quit ❖ **1.** Start writing your name on the board and then *quit* writing your name and explain that you *quit*. Have a student start writing his or her name on the board and then tell him or her to *quit*. **2.** Frown and then stop. Say "I *quit* frowning." Have a puppet jump up and down and then *quit*.

quite ❖ **1.** Draw on the board figures that are tall and *quite* tall; thin and *quite* thin. Explain that *quite* can mean "very." **2.** Write your name on the board, but stop before you are *quite* done. Then complete it so that you are *quite* done. Lead students in actions that are not *quite* done, then are *quite* done. —*quite a*, once students understand the word *quite*, point to actual things or pictures in the room and lead students in sentences, such as "That's *quite a* nose the elephant has" or "That's *quite a* tail the cheetah has."

quiz ❖ Explain that a *quiz* is a short test and demonstrate if necessary.

quote ❖ Ask a student to say something. Then say "Sarah said, ('_____.') I *quoted* Sarah." Repeat with other students.

quoth ❖ See *quote*. Explain that *quoth* is a very old way of saying *quote*.

Rabbit's ❖ Make up examples: *Rabbit's* shadow, *Rabbit's* ears, or *Rabbit's* tail. Make up examples involving students, such as Maria, *Maria's* sweater; Carlos, *Carlos's* nose.

rabies ❖ See *disease* and add that *rabies* can kill.

race, races, raced ❖ **1.** Engage students in a variety of *races*, such as who can put his or her pencil away the fastest, or who can count to five first. Say "Let's have a *race*. Who can clap three times and stamp his or her feet three times the fastest?" Demonstrate and then oversee a few *races*. **2.** Ask a student to run fast and then explain that he or she *raced*.

racket ❖ Bang things together to make a *racket*. Explain that a *racket* is a lot of noise.

radar ❖ Show pictures of *radar* dishes and explain that these can help ships and planes find their way at night or in bad weather.

radio, radios ❖ **1.** Show students a *radio*. Demonstrate its function. **2.** Explain that a two-way *radio* is a telephone without wires.

rage ❖ Have a puppet go into a *rage*. Contrast this with the puppet being mad, so that students see the degree of anger connected to *rage*.

rain, rains ❖ Show a picture of *rain* and say "When it *rains*, I will get wet." —*heavy rains*, show pictures of *light* and *heavy rain*. If needed, use a faucet running lightly and heavily to help ensure students understand this context. —*rainy day*. Explain this as a time of greater need.

raise, raising, raised ❖ **1.** Show pictures of a family during different phases of the children's growth. Give example sentences using *raise*. Say "I was *raised* to be polite to strangers. What are you being *raised* to do?" **2.** Tell students that to *raise* someone is to help him or her grow up. Have a puppet be a parent and another be the child. Have the parent help the child eat, choose clothes, and go to school. Have the child puppet celebrate several birthdays. **3.** Demonstrate *raising* your hand three times, then say "I have *raised* my hand three times." —*raised dots*, Braille. Show students how to make *raised dots* in paper by making indentations with pencil points. Have them close their eyes and feel the bumps in the paper with their fingertips. Examples of Braille writing might be found at a library.

rake, raking, raked ❖ Show the picture of a *rake* and pantomime *raking*.

ram ❖ Have a toy vehicle *ram* into something. Lead students in making sentences about this. Invite volunteers to repeat your actions with the vehicle and create sentences of their own.

rambunctious ❖ Have puppets be loud and agitated. After a moment say "You are so *rambunctious* today!"

ramp ❖ Make a *ramp* with a book and have a toy car or truck travel up it.

range, ranged ❖ Use a map to show the large areas where buffalo used to *range*. Say "They *ranged* here."

rank ❖ Pretend that you just found an old lunch bag with rotting food. Tell students that it smells very bad. It has a *rank* smell.

ransom ❖ —*king's ransom*, check that students understand *king* and *ransom*. Explain to students that this is an expression meaning "a lot of money," not to be taken literally. Ask students to name very expensive items. Say "It would take a lot of money to buy those things. Those things cost a king's *ransom!*"

rap ◆ *Rap* your knuckles on a desktop and lead students in doing the same.

rapid, rapidly ◆ Make two toy animals run, one faster than the other. Explain, "This one is a *rapid* runner; this one is not." "He ran *rapidly.*"

rash ◆ Ask two puppets where they would like to go for summer vacation. Have one puppet think and answer deliberately; have the other answer quickly and impulsively. Say "[Connie] made a thoughtful choice. [Carlos] rushed into his answer without taking time to think; he made a *rash* choice."

raspy-throated ◆ Say "My throat is dry. I have a *raspy-throated* voice." Take a drink or pantomime having a drink. Say in a normal voice, "That's better. My throat is no longer *raspy.*"

rather ◆ Offer a puppet a choice of two colored papers. Have the puppet say "I'd *rather* have this one." Repeat with choices of imaginary foods and so on.

rations ◆ **1.** Show pictures of soldiers in battle. Have a limited amount of water and let each student have a measured amount only. Give example sentences using *rations.* **2.** Look in someone's lunch box. Say "These are your food *rations* for today!"

raucous ◆ Tell students that their behavior is often *raucous* during recess. They are often loud and energetic.

ravel ◆ Show a hem or seam that has begun to *ravel.*

raw ◆ Show pictures of cooked and *raw* meat.

rawhide ◆ Show students *rawhide.* Lead students in sentences.

reach ◆ **1.** Lead students in *reaching* for things. **2.** Mark a line on the floor where students must stand and then measure how far they can *reach* from that spot. Say "[Jose] has the longest *reach.*" **3.** Set up a scene where you and a few students are traveling to different destinations. Each time you *reach* a new destination, tell the class, "We have *reached* New Mexico" or "We have *reached* Paris." Ask a student to come to your desk. Once he/she arrives, tell the class that he/she *reached* your desk. Repeat with other students. Give other examples: perhaps take students to the playground and say en route, "When we *reach* the playground we will play ball." **4.** Have students ask you questions. Take a long time in answering and look like you are deep in thought. Finally, answer the student's question, prefacing it with, "I have *reached* my decision."

react ◆ Have a student make a loud noise and *react,* perhaps by jumping back.

read, reader ◆ Ask students what they have *read* lately. Begin by telling them what you yourself have *read. Read* and explain that you are a *reader.* —*reads lips,* have students plug their ears and whisper something they won't be able to hear. Have students unplug their ears and ask them what you said. Of the student who comes closest, say "Apparently [Lucia] *reads lips.* She was able to tell what I said without being able to hear me."

ready ◆ **1.** Have a puppet get *ready* to go outside by putting on its coat. **2.** Ask students what might make a crayon *ready* to break, perhaps if the crayon had a crack in it already. **3.** Set up a short walking race in the classroom for two competitors. Ask them if they are *ready*, and then say "Go!" Insist on getting a nod when you ask if they are *ready*. Repeat this several times.

real ❖ Draw a sketch of a pencil on the board. Compare it with a *real* pencil.

really ❖ Make things somewhat neat on your desk and then make things *really* neat. Stand up tall, and then stand up *really* tall. Have students sit up tall, and then sit up *really* tall.

reason, reasons, reasoned ❖ **1.** Have a puppet give you poorly done homework. Ask the puppet why and have it answer, "The *reason* is because I did not understand the questions." Ask the class to give you *reasons* for things that you ask about; write these on the board to show how many *reasons* they can come up with. Examples might include, "Why do we go to school? Why is it important to learn English?" Make sentences, such as "The *reason* I am tired is that I worked hard," or "The *reason* that I'm late is that my watch stopped." Explain that *reason* means "why." **2.** Write an arithmetic problem on the board. Have a puppet struggle to solve it. Help it *reason* its way through the problem. —*within reason*, ask children what they would like for their birthday. Say "That is *within reason*." Then ask if they would like a spaceship or a live monster, and say "No, that is not *within reason*."

reassemble ❖ See *assemble*. Have students *reassemble*.

reassess ❖ See *assess*. *Reassess* the puppet's exercises.

reassure ❖ **1.** Have one puppet tell another it is worried about its spelling test. Have the other puppet *reassure* it. Tell students, "This puppet had to *reassure* its friend." Lead students in similar pantomimes. **2.** Have a puppet cry. *Reassure* it. Say "Students *reassured* it."

rebels, rebellions ❖ **1.** Show pictures of *rebels*, such as the Zapatistas in Mexico or some other country. Lead students in sentences. **2.** Show pictures of historical *rebellions* or give examples. Give example sentences.

rebuild, rebuilt ❖ Stack some erasers and pencils, and then knock them down. Ask a student to *rebuild* what you did. Say "You *rebuilt* it! Thank you!"

receive, receives, receiving, receiver ❖ **1.** Give something to a student. As she *receives* it, say "She *received* it." Contrast with another student who does not *receive* it. Say "I want to *receive* a [pencil] from you." As students give you a pencil, say "I am *receiving* a pencil." Give something to a student. As she *receives* it, say "She *received* it." Contrast with another student who does not *receive* it. **2.** Have a student hand paper to you. Say "I'm the *receiver*."

recent, recently ❖ Show a calendar and refer to something that happened a long time ago. Contrast it with something that happened yesterday. Tell students about something you did just the other day. Say, for example, "*Recently*, when I was out shopping..." Have students tell things that happened to them a short while ago. Contrast with things you did *long ago*.

recipes ❖ Write a favorite *recipe* on the board. Say "This is how I make [apple pie]. This is one of the *recipes* I got from my grandmother."

recite ❖ *Recite* the Pledge of Allegiance with the class. Tell the students you *recited* it. Ask if students can *recite* anything from their native languages.

recognize, recognition ❧ **1.** Hold up various objects belonging to your students and say "Do you *recognize* this?" **2.** Have a student show you photographs of different people. Pantomime *recognizing* some and not *recognizing* others. Contrast recognizing and not *recognizing*. Look at a student and ask the class who the new girl is. When they tell you that she is not new, apologize and say that you did not *recognize* her. Repeat with another student by saying, "Hello Bonita, I *recognize* you." Have students pretend to *recognize* and not *recognize* each other.

recoiled ❧ Draw a fierce snake on the board. Then *recoil* and pretend to be horrified by it. Give sample sentences.

reconsider ❧ Have one puppet ask permission of you to go to recess. Tell the puppet, "No," then stop a moment and say "I will *reconsider*." Dramatize thoughtfulness and then give your permission. Repeat the above with students asking to do things that you can *reconsider*.

reconstructing, reconstructed ❧ Build a tower from blocks and have a puppet knock it down. Rebuild it. Give example sentences using *reconstructing*.

record, recording ❧ Demonstrate the tape *recorder* and how you *record* into it. Encourage students to *record* a simple sentence into it. Play their *recording* back to them.

recover, recovered ❧ **1.** Help a puppet to *recover* a toy that it has lost. **2.** Show a sick puppet, then have it get better. Tell students it *recovered*.

recriminations ❧ Have one student accuse another of stealing something. Have the other say "No, you did it." Have this continue for a time. Give example sentences using *recriminations*.

recruitment ❧ Set up a scene where you are a *recruiter* for a team. *Recruit* as many students as you can by promising how much fun it would be, etc. When you are done, say "I am good at *recruitment*."

recycle, recycling ❧ Have students help you make a list of the disposable items they put in a special bin rather than in the garbage. Say "Yes, cans, boxes, and newspapers are things that can be used again. We *recycle* these items and use them again and again." Say that we are *recycling* when we do this.

redevelop ❧ Show pictures of vacant lots with old buildings on them. Tell students that soon new buildings and stores will be there. Men will tear down the old buildings and build new ones. They will *redevelop* it. Then show pictures of a shopping mall or new apartment complex. Lead students in sentences. If necessary, have students *redevelop* a vacant lot with some building blocks.

reduce ❧ Place a large number of paper clips on your desk and explain that you will *reduce* the number of paper clips on your desk. Then take some away. Call upon volunteers to come up to your desk and *reduce* the number of paper clips or pencils or other objects.

refill ❧ Fill a glass with water, and then *refill* it. Lead students in sentences.

reflect, reflects, reflected ❧ **1.** Show how you can *reflect* light with a mirror. Have students *reflect* light. **2.** Read the class a passage from a story and ask them to think it over. After a minute, say "You thought about what you heard; you *reflected* on the story."

re-form ➧   Give each student a piece of modeling clay. Ask them to make a ball. Then ask them to *re-form* it into a snake.

refreshments ➧   Give examples of foods that are classified as *refreshments*. Ask students about *refreshments* they may have had.

refund ➧   Pantomime returning an item to a store and getting a *refund*.

refurbish ➧   Draw a dilapidated house on the board. Have each student take a turn making alterations to the drawing to fix up the house. Say "Now that poor old house looks like new again. You worked hard to *refurbish* that house."

refuse, refuses, refused ➧   **1.** Have a puppet *refuse* to eat its vegetables, saying "I won't!" or *refuse* to take a bath, saying "I won't!" **2.** Have a puppet offer you a book. Say "No, thank you." Tell the class, "I *refused* to take her book." Have one puppet ask another for a drink of water. Then have the second puppet *refuse* to get it for him. Tell students, "The puppet *refused* to get him water." Lead students in similar pantomimes.

regret, regretting, regretted ➧   Have a puppet invite you to go to the movies. With exaggerated sadness, tell the puppet, "I *regret* I am unable to go out with you," "I am really *regretting* not being able to go out with [Fluffy]," and "I *regretted* not going out with [Fluffy]."

regulations ➧   See *policy*. Lead students in sentences using *regulations*.

reheated ➧   Draw a stove and a pot on the board. Say "I had soup for dinner last night. I *reheated* it and had it again for lunch today."

reign ➧   Show pictures of kings and queens. Explain that they are the bosses of the entire country. Say "Kings and queens *reign* over some countries."

rejoiced ➧   Tell a puppet, "You may play outside." Have the puppet respond with exaggerated happiness. Say "He *rejoiced* at that good news." Have students imitate *rejoicing*.

rejoin ➧   Have students stand in a circle and *join* hands. Have them let go of each other's hands and then ask them to *rejoin* their hands.

relate, relates, relation, relations relative, relatives ➧   **1.** Pick up a pencil and write with it. Then say "Writing *relates* to pencils." Pick up a book and read from it. Ask, "Reading *relates* to what?" Answer for students if needed. Repeat with other examples as needed. **2.** The *relation* of teacher and student shows that the teacher would have nobody to teach if he or she did not have a student. The student would have nobody to learn from if the teacher were not there. Create pantomimes of this and other examples to show *relations* between individuals and groups. **3.** Talk with students about things that they can compare to something else, such as time or emotions. When you are having fun, time passes quickly. When you are not, time passes slowly. Time is *relative*. If there is somebody that you really like, you can easily forgive something he or she has done wrong; if it is someone you don't like, it is harder to forgive. Emotions are *relative*. **4.** Draw a picture of a family, then draw the father's *relatives*, labeling the brother, sister, his parents, etc. Ask students to count how many *relatives* they know well.

relativity ➥   Place a pencil in a glass half-filled with water and view the pencil from various angles. Say "Einstein's ideas predicted that light could be bent by gravity, as it is bent here in this water. This is one part of his theory of *relativity*." —*Theory of Relativity*, you can explain that Einstein developed a *theory* that mass and energy could change shape or size at different speeds. The *theory* also includes the concept that mass and energy are equal. Depending upon your students, you may wish to limit your explanation to the information provided under *relativity* and suggest that as they learn more English skills, more can be explained to them.

relaxed ➥   Ask everyone to stand up as straight as possible. Then say "Now be *relaxed*." Model both postures yourself.

relay ➥   **1.** Set up a team of runners. Have two stand against the back wall and two at the board. Have one runner run across the room and tag another runner. Repeat until all runners have participated. Say "This is a *relay*." **2.** Pantomime a *relay* race. Explain that it's called a *relay* race because the stick is *relayed* from person to person.

relief, relieve, relieved ➥   **1.** Have a puppet carry a heavy load on its back and dramatize how tired it is. Then have the puppet remove its heavy load and rest. Tell the class that it is a *relief* to put down the heavy load and rest. **2.** Have a student stand guard at the door. After a minute, approach the guard and say "I have come to *relieve* you from guard duty." **3.** Pretend to be very thirsty. If needed, review *thirsty*. Drink some water and say "I am *relieved* of my thirst."

religion, religions ➥   **1.** Ask puppets about their *religion* as follows: "What is your *religion*?" Have them answer: "I am Christian," "I am Buddhist," and "I am Jewish," etc. Then have the puppets say "We believe in a higher power, each in a different way." Tell the class, "Many people believe in a higher power. Their way of believing is called *religion*." **2.** List different *religions*, such as Buddhism, Judaism, Christianity, Moslem, etc. on the board.

religious works ➥   Explain that these are books that are used in church; they are *religious works*.

reluctantly ➥   Ask a puppet to write on the board. Have the puppet shake its head "no." Have the puppet finally write on the board. Have a puppet tidy up your desk *reluctantly*. Contrast by having the puppet tidy up *eagerly*.

rely ➥   —*rely on*, tell one student to be in charge while you leave the room. Exit the room very briefly. Upon your return say "Is everything OK? Thank you. I can *rely on* you." Another example might be to say what you *rely on* to get to school in the morning. Answers might include car, bus, feet, or a neighbor.

remain, remains ➥   **1.** Have a group of students walk to your desk while you ask another group of students to *remain* seated. **2.** Gather up all but one of the paper clips on your desk and give them to a student to hold. Tell the class, "This paper clip *remains* on my desk."

remark, remarkable ⟡ *Remark* upon some things that students have done, such as making a great catch to win a game, etc. Contrast by having the puppet do something *unremarkable*, like sitting. Don't *remark* upon it and explain that it is *unremarkable*.

remedy, remedies ⟡ Sneeze and speak as if you had a cold. Say "What *remedies* are there for a cold?" and "That was just the right *remedy* for your cough."

remember, remembrance ⟡ **1.** Say students' names and pretend not to *remember* one of them. Then say "I *remember*, it's _____." Have students *remember* what they wore or ate for lunch yesterday. **2.** Show some souvenirs. Say that these things help us to *remember* places, events, and people. A *remembrance* is like a souvenir.

remind, reminds, reminded ⟡ Hold up a story that was recently read and say "This story *reminds* us of islands. When I think of this story I think of islands." Repeat with objects: "Chalk *reminds* me of teaching," "This announcement on the bulletin board *reminded* me of our field trip," etc. Have students point to objects and say what they are *reminded* of.

remote ⟡ Use an example of the room farthest from your classroom. Say "The gym is in a *remote* corner of the school building. It is very far away."

remove ⟡ Have students *remove* some books from the classroom. *Remove* objects from your desk and have students do the same. Write something on the board. Erase it with exaggerated care. Demonstrate by *removing* a lid or cover.

rename, renamed ⟡ Give a puppet a name, and then tell the class that you would like to *rename* the puppet. Have students help you to *rename* it. Lead students in past tense sentences.

renew, renewing ⟡ **1.** Show students how they can *renew* their borrowing time on a library book. **2.** Have a puppet do some exercises and then have it rest. Tell the class, once it's done resting, that it has *renewed* its energy. Say "Resting is one way of *renewing* your energy." Have it exercise again.

renounce, renounced ⟡ Offer a puppet a crown. Have the puppet refuse to take it. Say "Fluffy *renounced* the crown."

renting ⟡ On the board, draw a picture of a house and an apartment house. Ask students if they are *renting* their apartments or houses. Lead students in sentences.

repair, repairing, repaired, repairman ⟡ **1.** *Repair* a torn piece of paper with some tape. Say "I am *repairing* this tear." When you finish, say "I *repaired* it." **2.** Have a puppet discover that his washing machine is broken and say "My washing machine is broken. I will call the *repairman*." Then have another puppet come and say "I am the *repairman*; I will fix your washer." Have the *repairman* do some repairs and say "It is *repaired*." Ask students for examples of other things a *repairman* could fix.

repeatedly ⟡ Have a puppet say his name *repeatedly*. Have students tap their pencils *repeatedly*.

repentance ❯ Act out by taking something from one of your students. Then say "I took [Gavino's] pencil. What I did was wrong. I'm sorry I did it. I feel *repentance* for my action."

repetitious ❯ Say the same phrase over and over again. Lead students in sentences using *repetitious*.

replace ❯ Demonstrate by removing a book from a shelf and putting a different one in its place. Say "I *replaced* the red book with the blue one."

reply, replies, replying, replied ❯ 1. Have a puppet say "Hello!" Have the other puppet *reply*, "Hello!" One puppet asks, "What is your name?" and the other *replies*. 2. Lead students in *replying* to your questions.

report ❯ Have one puppet be the principal. Have another puppet *report* to the first.

repossess ❯ Pantomime selling a toy car to a puppet. Flip one month on the calendar for each payment the puppet makes. Then flip a couple of months without the puppet making any payment. *Repossess* the toy car.

represent ❯ Write the numeral 2 on the board. Hold up two pencils to show what 2 *represents*.

reprint ❯ Print your name on the board, and then tell students, "I will *reprint* it."

repulsed ❯ Draw a large snake on the board. Pantomime strolling by it, and suddenly noticing it in your path. Recoil and scream in exaggerated horror. Say "I am *repulsed* by snakes!"

reputation ❯ Ask students to tell you what they like about someone they admire. Say, for example, "You have named many good things about our school principal. [Mrs. Nelson] has a *reputation* for being a good principal."

request ❯ *Request* to borrow a pencil or piece of paper. Have students *request* to borrow things from each other.

require ❯ Try to write on the board without chalk. Say to the class, "I *require* chalk to write on the board. What do you *require* to write on paper?" Give and get examples.

rescue, rescues, rescuing, rescued ❯ Demonstrate a scene where a puppet is about to fall and you *rescue* it. Have a puppet *rescue* another from drowning or from getting run over by a toy truck or car. Show a picture of a firefighter *rescuing* a person or an animal. Draw a burning building on the board. Have one puppet save the other from the fire. Say "[Sparky] *rescued* [Fluffy] from the burning building."

research, researcher ❯ Help students *research* an assigned topic. Say "Today we will do some *research*." Show them how. Sit at your desk with several books open around you. Pantomime careful study of the books. Say "I am looking for the information that I need. I am a *researcher* to get all the information we need."

resemble, resembles ❯ Show students pictures of two animals, or two people, that look alike. Say "These two animals look alike; they *resemble* one another." Explain that frogs and toads look alike. One *resembles* the other. Show pictures to demonstrate.

resent, resentful, resentment ◆ **1.** Have a puppet accuse you of lying. Act righteously angry and say "That's not fair! I am not a liar!" Then say "I became *resentful* when [Spot] accused me of lying" and "I *resent* it when somebody calls me a liar!" Ask students if they have ever *resented* something. **2.** See *resentful*. Say "I have *resentment* for people or puppets that call me a liar. Ask students what they have *resentment* for.

reserve ◆ —*protected game reserve*, place animal puppets and toys on your desk. Have students make signs on sheets of paper that say things, such as "Keep Out," "No Hunting," "Safe Area," etc. Place the signs in a circle around the animals. Say "The animals are safe now. We have created a *protected game reserve*."

resist, resisting, resisted, resistance ◆ **1.** Tell the puppet to get off your hand, and have the puppet show *resistance*. Tell the class the puppet is *resisting*. **2.** Try to get a puppet to leave the room. Have it *resist*. Lead students in sentences using *resisted*.

resolve ◆ Have students list things they would like to do in life. On the board, draw a person dreaming about doing something. Then show that person really doing it. Have each student *resolve* to do what he or she listed.

respect ◆ Pantomime showing *respect* to older people, children, animals, etc. Ask students to tell you ways they show *respect* to others.

rest, rested, restless ◆ **1.** Have a puppet do two or three different things— perhaps draw, read, and write. Tell the class that the puppet will now have free time for the *rest* of the day. Have the puppet do a few activities as you announce the passage of time. **2.** Lead students in exercising and then tell them to *rest*. Repeat. **3.** Have a puppet be *restless* and bored. Contrast by having the puppet be *contented* or at peace.

restart ◆ Start to read a story. Then stop and tell students, "Let's *restart* the story."

restoring ◆ Build a city out of blocks and have students knock it down. Rebuild it and say "I am fixing a broken-down city. I am *restoring* the buildings so they can be used again."

restrained, restraints ◆ **1.** Show a puppet trying to run in class. *Restrain* the puppet by holding it back. **2.** Tie the hands of a puppet. Give example sentences using *restraints*.

resumed ◆ Play a simple game the students enjoy. Stop them for a moment, and then *resume*. Do this a number of times.

resurface ◆ Show students the surface area of several objects: desks, boards, etc. Then show scratched or marred *surfaces*. Tell students, "To *resurface* means to put a new *surface* on it." Demonstrate by taking a piece of paper, and scribbling on it so that it is marred. Glue a clean sheet of paper over it. Have students *resurface* a piece of paper with you.

retell, retelling, retold ◆ **1.** *Tell* students a poem, and then *tell* students you will *retell* it and do so. **2.** Read a passage aloud and ask a student to tell the story in his or her own words. Say "[Cecelia] is *retelling* the story I just read, using [her] own words." **3.** Once you have completed *retelling* the poem, tell students, "I am done. I *retold* the poem."

retrain ❖ *Train* a puppet to add two things together. On the board, write the problem 2 + 2. After the puppet cannot do it, *retrain* it. Lead students in sentences.

retreat, retreating ❖ **1.** See *advance*. **2.** Have the line of students walk backwards away from you. Give example sentences using *retreating*.

retrograde ❖ Draw Earth on the board, showing it rotating on its axis. Draw a spaceship moving in an orbit in the opposite direction of Earth's rotation. Say "The spaceship is flying in a *retrograde* orbit." See *orbits*.

return ❖ Ask a student to give you something and then *return* it. Take a book from a bookshelf and *return* it. Have students come to your desk and *return* to their seats. Lead them in sentences, such as, "Sarah *returns* to her seat" and "Sergio *returns* to his seat."

reunion ❖ Have students move to the perimeter of the classroom, facing the walls. Have them count to ten, with each number representing one year. Then have them turn and regroup, pantomiming delight at seeing each other again after such a long time. Say "Isn't it fun having a *reunion* of the class after ten years apart?"

revealed ❖ Hide something under your coat. Ask students to guess what it is. Remove your coat in a dramatic way and say "I have *revealed* the hidden object."

reveille ❖ Play a recording or pantomime playing *reveille*.

revenge ❖ Have one puppet take a pencil from the other and run away. Have the remaining puppet run after the first and take *revenge*.

reverse ❖ Have students move their hands forward and then move them in *reverse*. Have them move their feet forward and then in *reverse*.

review ❖ **1.** Refer students to a previously learned vocabulary list. Say "Let's look at this list again to see how much we remember. Let's *review* this list." **2.** See *critic*.

revolution, revolutionize ❖ **1.** Tell a story of an oppressive king who would not let the people have happy lives. Tell students that the people got tired of this, made their own army, and fought the king and his soldiers. This is called a *revolution*. Let students pantomime a *revolution* against a puppet king who will not let them go to recess anymore. **2.** Divide students into two groups. Have the first group be riding horses, while the second group drives in cars. Have the cars travel to school more quickly than the horses. Explain to the class, "There was a time when everyone traveled by horse or by walking. Now we have cars. Cars *revolutionized* travel. We can go faster and farther."

reward ❖ Remind students of *rewards* they may be familiar with, such as receiving a gold star, a high grade, or a happy face on their papers for good work. Show a puppet finding something that belongs to another puppet. Have him return it and receive a *reward*. Lead students in similar dramatizations.

rewrap ❖ Wrap and *rewrap* a book or other object.

rewrite ❯ *Write*, erase, and then *rewrite* your name on the board.

rhyme, rhymes, rhymed ❯ Make simple sentences that *rhyme*. Lead students in making *rhymes*. Lead students in sentences.

rhythms ❯ Lead students in beating different *rhythms* on their desktops.

rich, richer, riches, richness ❯ **1.** Use play money or draw some money on paper and ask two students to help you. Give one of students some of the money and say that he or she is *rich*. Give the second student more money than the first student and say that he or she is *richer*. Repeat with other students. **2.** Surround one puppet with many items and a second puppet with nothing. Explain that the first puppet has many *riches* and identify the items. Explain that the second puppet is very *poor*.

rid ❯ Place little scraps of paper or other unwanted objects on a table. Say that you must *rid* the table of these things. Remove them.

rides, riding, rode ❯ **1.** Demonstrate a puppet *riding* on another or on a stuffed animal. Show a puppet *riding* in his horse-drawn wagon to some location. Compare to driving a car. "The puppet is *riding* to school." "Now the puppet is driving to school. **2.** Ask if any of your students have bikes. Pantomime *riding* a bike and then say that you *rode* it.

ridiculous ❯ Show some *ridiculous* images like a monkey with clothes on or many clowns in a little car. Laugh at these *ridiculous* things. Or, tell about some *ridiculous* things like a bee that doesn't like honey or money that can't buy anything.

rig, rigged ❯ **1.** *Rig* a tower from blocks. **2.** Set up a scene in which you and a puppet are running for president. Coach students to vote for the puppet. Write your own name on several slips of paper and place them in a ballot box with exaggerated secrecy. Have students cast their votes by writing the puppet's name on slips of paper while you cast one vote for yourself. Count the votes and say "I won because I *rigged* the votes."

right, rights ❯ **1.** Write $2 + 2 = 5$ and $2 + 2 = 4$ on the board. Ask students to say which is *right* and which is *wrong*. **2.** Dramatize trying on different sweaters or jackets that obviously don't fit. Then put yours on so it's just *right*. Do the same with shoes. **3.** Draw some dots on the board in various locations. Point to the first dot and say to the class, "Look *right* here." Repeat for the other dots. **4.** Lead students in moving their *right* hands and feet. **5.** Explain *rights* as the things we are allowed to do. Ask students about *rights* they have, such as using the rest room when they need to, going to recess, eating lunch or snacks, being allowed to talk to the teacher, and so forth. Ask them what it would be like if they did not have these *rights*. With students make two lists: things that students can do and things that teachers can do. Give example sentences using *rights*.

Right! ❯ Have one puppet tell another puppet something that is true, such as "We are puppets." Have the second puppet respond with, "*Right!*" Repeat and lead students in similar dialogue.

rim ❯ Point out the *rim* of a cup or bowl.

ring, rang, rung ❯ *Ring* a bell; say that you *rang* it. Say to students, "The bell has *rung*."

riot, riots ❯ Create a model town out of blocks. Have puppets create a *riot*, knocking down several of the blocks in the town. —*riot-torn*, tell the class that the town is *riot-torn*.

rip, ripping, ripped ❯ Dramatize by *ripping* a piece of paper. Say that you *ripped* it.

ripe ❯ If possible, show actual fruits that are *ripe* and *unripe*. If actual fruit is not available, pantomime eating an apple that is *unripe* and making a sour face, then one that is *ripe*. Do this for various fruits. You can dramatize how hard an *unripe* banana, tomato, or plum is.

rise, rose ❯ Release a balloon outside and watch it *rise*. Lead students in past tense sentences. —*rise and shine*, check for understanding of individual words in the phrase. Explain that this is a phrase used to wake someone up. Pantomime sleeping at your desk and have students shout, "*Rise and shine!*" Wake up and smile at them.

risked, risky ❯ Demonstrate by placing a doll at the edge of your desk. Say "The doll sat in a dangerous place; she *risked* falling off the desk and hurting herself. It is *risky* to sit on the edge of the desk."

ritual ❯ Show pictures of graduations, weddings, etc. Have students tell you what happens at each. Give examples sentences using *ritual*.

rival ❯ Have puppets play a game such as checkers. Lead students in sentences using *rival*.

river ❯ Show pictures or draw one on the board.

riveted ❯ Pantomime *riveting* two objects together. Explain that *riveting* means "to join two pieces of metal with a bolt."

road ❯ —*right down the road*, draw a *road* on the board. Show how *right down the road* means "without turning aside from the *road* at any point." Show how it means "just going *down the road*."

roam, roamers ❯ Move small dinosaurs or other animal figures about so that they *roam* across a desk. Explain that these animals are *roamers*.

roar, roars, roaring, roared ❯ **1.** *Roar* like a lion. Have students *roar* like lions. Say "Which animal *roars*?" **2.** Draw an airplane on the board or use a toy to demonstrate how an airplane *roars*.

roasted ❯ Show a picture of meat *roasting* in a pan.

rob, robbed, robber ❯ **1.** Have a puppet *rob* you of a pencil or piece of chalk. Say that you have been *robbed*. **2.** Have puppets steal items from students. Describe them as *robbers*. —*train robbers*, show a picture of a train. Have puppets *rob* a train. Tell students, "Those puppets are *train robbers*."

rocking ❯ Pantomime *rocking*.

role ❯ Dramatize a story the class has read. Give each student a *role*.

roll, rolling, rolled ❯ *Roll* a ball on the ground. Say that it is *rolling.* Demonstrate with a ball or other suitable object. Lead students in past tense sentences. Ask students to *roll* their pencils across their desks.

romp, romping ❯ Show pictures of puppies *romping.*

Ron ❯ Explain that *Ron* is a boy's name. List boys' names and include *Ron.*

Ron's ❯ See *Brad's.*

rookie ❯ Show pictures of baseball, football, and basketball. Explain that when people start a new sport, they are called a *rookie.* Say "I just joined a softball team. I am a new player. I am a *rookie.*"

room, rooms ❯ **1.** Stuff a container full of pencils so that there appears to be no room for more. Then move the pencils closer and make more *room.* **2.** Show students various *rooms* in the school.

rope ❯ Bring some *rope* to class.

rot ❯ Hold up some food, smell it, make a face, and hold your nose. Explain, "It *rots!*" and drop it in the trash.

rotate, rotating, rotated ❯ *Rotate* a globe. Say "The globe is *rotating.*" Lead students in past tense sentences.

rotten ❯ Have two puppets sitting in a pretend class with you. One puppet is obedient, listens, and follows directions. The other is disobedient, talks out, and doesn't follow directions. Say "This puppet is being naughty; it is *rotten.*"

rough ❯ Have students feel something *rough* and, in contrast, something *smooth.*

roughhouse ❯ Have two puppets *roughhouse.*

round ❯ Draw a circle on the board and explain that it is *round.* Show other examples of *round* things, such as a paper plate, the rim of a glass, or a ball. —*all-round,* have students help you make a list of qualities they like in people. Say "If someone had all these qualities, you would think he or she would be great in every way. You would call this person an *all-round* good guy." —*making his rounds,* check that students understand the individual words. Set up a scene in a hospital where you are a doctor and the students are patients. Walk around the room with a clipboard, checking each patient and making notes. Say "Every morning, the doctor goes from patient to patient *making his rounds* to see how everyone is doing."

route ❯ Draw a *route* on the board, perhaps from home to school.

routine ❯ Give examples of *routines* you use in class.

row ❯ **1.** Draw a *rowboat* with oars and a river on the board. Pantomime *rowing.* Lead students in sentences using *row.* **2.** Arrange students in such a way that you can refer to the front *row* and the back *row.* **3.** Line up some paper clips in a *row,* and then scatter them or place them in a circle for contrast. Point out *rows* of books or *rows* of desks.

rowdy ❯ Invite students to gallop around the room and pantomime whooping noisily. Give example sentences using *rowdy.*

royal ❯ Show pictures of kings, queens, princes, and princesses. Point out their royal clothes, *royal* crowns, *royal* carriage, and so on. Contrast things that are not *royal*. Explain that *royal* means "for a king, queen, prince, or princess." Lead them in naming items that belong to the king and queen, for example, "the *royal* truck," "the *royal* chair," etc.

rubbing, rubbed ❯ *Rub* your hands and lead students in *rubbing* their hands.

rude ❯ **1.** Ask for something politely and contrast by grabbing the same thing in a *rude* way. Have one puppet be *rude* to another by not returning a greeting. Tell students that the puppet is *rude*. Contrast with *polite* actions. Tell students that the puppet is not *rude*. **2.** Pantomime eating a meal with two puppets. Have one of them say "Would you please pass the ketchup?" Have the other say "Gimme the salt." Say to students, "This puppet was very polite and used good manners; this puppet was *rude*."

ruffled my feathers ❯ On the board, draw a bird with *ruffled* feathers. Have a puppet scold you. Pantomime having your feathers *ruffled*. Give example sentences using *ruffled my feathers*.

ruin, ruined ❯ Give students each some money. Set up a scene where you run an ice-cream store. Have students walk by your store and refuse to buy. Say "Oh, no! If nobody buys my ice cream, I won't make any money and I'll have to close my store. My business will be *ruined*."

rule, rules, ruling, ruled ❯ **1.** Mention a class *rule*. Ask students what class *rules* they know. **2.** Pantomime being a leader and *ruling* your class. Give them orders to follow, tell them where they are to stand, etc. **3.** To *rule* means "to make the laws for someone else to follow" and "to make them follow those laws." England *ruled* the colonies. Have students take turns making up *rules* for others in the class to follow. Each time you call upon a volunteer, say "It is now [Javier's] turn to *rule*." Thank each person who *ruled*.

rumbling, rumbled ❯ **1.** Draw clouds, rain, and lightning on the board. Explain that *rumble* is "to make a big noise," like the noise thunder makes. **2.** Make *rumbling* noises.

rumor ❯ Explain to the class that a *rumor* is something one has heard and does not know to be true. Demonstrate with puppets. Have one puppet talk to another about something that it heard and the other puppet answers with, "That is just a *rumor!*"

run, running, ran ❯ **1.** Demonstrate *running* and tell students to *run*. Stop them and say "We *ran*." Start and stop them, alternating *run*, *running*, and *ran*. **2.** Ask students who they want to *run* for president. See *nomination*. —*on the run*, have a puppet be very busy cleaning something up quickly. Explain that he is *on the run*. Lead students in cleaning the classroom *on the run*. —*ran after*, have one puppet *run after* another. —*ran away*, have a puppet *run away* and say that it *ran away*. —*ran into*, show a puppet walking along and *running into* a stuffed animal and greeting it.

run down ❯ Have a toy car *run down* a toy construction site pylon.

runaways ❯ Explain that sometimes slaves escaped. They were *runaways*. Demonstrate *running away* from something.

runny ❯ Pantomime blowing your nose. Say "My nose is *runny*."

runs on ❯ Show a toy vehicle driving away from a puppet.

rushes ❯ Have students *rush* around the classroom. Contrast by having them move *slowly*. Lead in sentences, such as "She *rushes* to her desk."

Russian ❯ Help students find and touch *Russia* on a world map. Explain that people and things from *Russia* are called Russian. Give examples. Ask what people and things from their countries are called.

rustle, rustling ❯ **1.** Have students cut leaves out of sheets of paper. Have them hold up the leaves and blow on them gently. Say "This is how leaves *rustle* in the breeze." **2.** Demonstrate by rubbing two sheets of paper together. Lead students in *rustling* paper.

S.S. ❯ Show pictures of Nazi Germany, the Jewish Holocaust, etc. Tell students that the *S.S.* was Hitler's secret police.

sabotaged ❯ Pantomime writing a composition. Have a puppet ask you to go to the movies. Leave your homework and go off with the puppet. Give example sentences.

sacred ❯ Bring or show pictures of items that are considered *sacred* by different groups. Lead students in sentences.

sad, sadder, saddest, sadly, saddened, sadness ❯ **1.** Pantomime crying. Say "I feel *sad*." Lead students in a pantomime of looking *sad* and then looking happy. **2.** Look *sad* and say "I am *sad*. I am acting *sadly*." **3.** Show a puppet *happily* eating a lollipop or playing with toys. Have another puppet come along and take his toy, which causes him to cry. Explain to the class that it is *saddened*. **4.** Show three puppets crying. One puppet is sniffling, the next is crying, and the third puppet is howling. Describe each puppet as *sad*, *sadder*, and *saddest*. **5.** Have a puppet show its *sadness* over the loss of a special toy. Contrast by having the puppet find this toy and show its *happiness*.

safe, safer, safest, safely, safety ❯ **1.** Show people who are *in danger* and contrast them with people who are *safe* —perhaps students in the room. **2.** Then show somebody in a tree or in some type of danger and ask, "How could he or she be *safer*?" "How could he or she be *safest*?" **3.** Show how to plug and unplug an electric cord *safely*. **4.** Demonstrate passing a pair of scissors *safely*. **5.** Demonstrate a toy mouse scurrying into a tight spot that a cat can not get into. Tell students, "The mouse has found *safety*." Discuss *safety* rules that you have in your school. Show a picture of a forest fire and contrast with a picture of a forest. Then have toy animals run from the forest-fire picture to the forest picture. Explain that the animals ran to *safety*.

sag, sagging, sagged ❯ Stand and then *sag* a little. Stretch a rubber band taut and then let it *sag*. Lead students in past tense sentences.

said ❯ Tell a puppet, "*Say* Hello." Then have students tell the puppet to *say* "Dog." Tell students, "The puppet *said* 'Dog.'"

sail, sails, sailing, sailed, sailor ◆ **1.** Move a picture or model of a *sailboat* as if *sailing*. Show pictures of *sails*. **2.** Pantomime *sailing* in a boat and say that you *sailed*. Show pictures of sailboats as needed. Have students pantomime *sailing*. **3.** Show a picture of a *sailboat* and a *sailor*, and identify each.

sake ◆ Show pictures of Mother Theresa or others who have devoted their lives for the *sake* of others. Tell students that *sake* means "good." —*for the sake of*, have a puppet make lots of noise while students pantomime working at their desks. Say "[Pumpkin]! You're being so noisy, we can't concentrate on our work. You must be quiet *for the sake of* your fellow students."

salary ◆ Set up a pretend lemonade stand. Ask one or two students to work for you, squeezing lemons and pouring lemonade. After a minute of work, hand them each some money and say "Your *salary* is [25 cents]."

sale, sales ◆ Play a little game of selling things to students with play money. Hold up an item and say "This is for *sale*." Take them through the action of exchanging the item for the play money and repeat as necessary. Explain that when stores sell things for less money than they normally cost, they are having *sales*. —*yard sale*, draw a house and *yard* on the board. Have each student choose something to pretend to *sell*. Divide students into two groups. Have one group pantomime *selling* and the other *buying*. Say "We're having a *yard sale*."

salute, salutation ◆ **1.** Model raising your right hand held straight to your forehead, facing the American flag if available. Have students imitate. Say "It is a sign of honor and respect for the country to *salute* the flag." **2.** Ask students for examples of different ways to greet people, such as by saying "Good morning," "Hi, how are you," "Hello," or with a handshake, high five, or hug.

Sam ◆ Explain that *Sam* is a boy's name. Find out if there is a corresponding name in the first language of your students.

same ◆ Show two paper clips that are the *same*. Bend one and show two that are *different*. Repeat with various objects, each time calling them the *same* or *different*. —*all the same*, show or draw a picture of liver and onions. Point at it and frown. Say "I hate liver, but *all the same*, I ate it." With a picture of a cake, pantomime delight. Say "I love cake, but *all the same*, I'll give it to you." Offer the picture to a student.

sample, sampled ◆ Bring in something that students can *sample*, such as different kinds of breads, flavor of jams, etc. Say "We have *sampled* several [kinds of bread]; which do you like best?"

sandwiched ◆ Have two students *sandwich* a third. Lead students in sentences. Compare with a *sandwich* people eat.

satellite ◆ Give one student a picture of a man-made *satellite*, such as *Sputnik*; have another draw a moon. Hold a sign that says "Earth" and have the two students walk around you in a circle.

satisfy, satisfied, satisfactory ◆ **1.** Act very hungry by rubbing your stomach. Pretend to *satisfy* your hunger by eating. Say "The food is *satisfactory*."

2. Give students a seat work assignment. Review their completed work and say with obvious pleasure, "I am very pleased with your work. I am *satisfied.*"

Saturday ❖ See *Friday.*

saucer-shaped ❖ Show students a saucer. Explain that things shaped like the *saucer* are *saucer-shaped.* Help students to find things that are *saucer-shaped.*

sauerkraut ❖ Show students real *sauerkraut* and have them taste it. Or, show them pictures of *sauerkraut* and explain that it is cabbage, cut and soaked in salt water and allowed to ferment in its own juices.

save, saves, saving, savings, saved ❖ **1.** Hand out paper and *save* a special piece for art class. Hand out pencils, but *save* some special ones. **2.** Dramatize being in trouble. Cry, "*Save* me! *Save* me!" **3.** Find illustrations for "The firefighter *saved* the baby from the burning building" or "The firefighter *saved* the kitten from the tree." **4.** Ask each student what he or she is *saving* for. **5.** Have a puppet put some money in a jar or other container. Tell students, "The puppet *saves* his money." Repeat until the puppet has enough money to buy something. Then have the puppet take the money and buy the item. **6.** Draw a piggy bank on the board. Pantomime putting money in the bank. Say "I am not going to spend this money. This money is my *savings.*" Ask students what they want to buy with their *savings.* —*saved the day,* once students understand *saved* and *day,* explain that *saved the day* means "helped." See *day.*

saw, sawing ❖ Draw or show a picture of a *saw* and a long plank of wood. Have each student draw and cut out a *saw* from a sheet of paper. Have students pantomime *sawing* the wood with their *saws.*

say, says, saying ❖ **1.** Tell a puppet, "*Say* Hello." Have students tell the puppet to *say* something. Ask students to *say* easy words, such as *you, me, it,* or *is.* Explain that when we speak, we *say* things. Ask students "What did I *say?*" **2.** Have one puppet tell the second puppet, "*Say* a, b, c." Have the second puppet *say* these letters. Tell the class, "The puppet is *saying,* 'a, b, c.'"

scampered ❖ Pantomime *scampering* quickly like a small animal.

scanning ❖ Hold a book and *scan* it quickly.

scar ❖ Show students a *scar* that you have or draw a person with a scar.

scare, scary, scared ❖ **1.** Have one puppet *scare* another by saying "Boo!" *Scare* a doll or puppet by making *scary* faces. **2.** Pantomime being *scared* of a toy snake. Then pantomime being brave. —*scared stiff,* pantomime fear and don't move.

scat, scats ❖ Have a puppet say "*Scat!*" to a stuffed animal and have the stuffed animal run off. Make sentences such as, "It *scats.*"

scatter ❖ *Scatter* paper clips across your desk. Lead students in *scattering* items on their desks.

scatterbrained ❖ Dramatize being distracted and giddy while listing all the things you have to remember to do today. Say "Oh! I have so much to do today, I'm feeling a bit *scatterbrained!*"

scavenging ◆ Show the puppet *scavenging* for food. Make it say "I forgot my lunch today. Have you got any food?" Then in your own voice say "The puppet is *scavenging* for food."

scholar ◆ Have one puppet read with great interest; have another puppet play outside. Say "[Yuri] likes to read and learn; he is a *scholar*. [Pedro] likes to play, play, play."

scholastic ◆ See *scholar*. Continue the example and say "[Yuri] is serious about his studies; he has a *scholastic* approach to life."

school chant ◆ Lead students in the *school chant*.

school's ◆ See *animal's*.

science, scientist, scientists ◆ Show pictures of *scientists* at work in a lab. Explain that *scientists* are people who look at things and think about how they work. The field is called *science*.

science fair ◆ Display books of *science fair* projects. Show a picture from one of them of students participating in a *science fair*.

scoffed ◆ Make fun of a puppet. Ask the puppet how it feels to be *scoffed*.

scold, scolding, scolded ◆ Make a mess and have a puppet *scold* you.

scoop up ◆ *Scoop* something *up* into your hand.

scope ◆ Show and explain what you can reach and what you cannot reach. Have students touch things within their *scope* and mention things out of their *scope*.

scored ◆ Have a spelling bee. Give each student points for each correct spelling. Tell the class what each student *scored*.

scorned ◆ Tell a puppet what it did wrong. Ask the puppet how it feels to be *scorned*.

scoundrels ◆ Have two puppets hide your chalk while you pretend not to notice what they're doing. Pantomime searching for your chalk and say "Where is my chalk? I can't find it anywhere!" Have the puppets giggle. Say "Did you two hide my chalk? Oh, you *scoundrels*! You played a trick on me!"

scout, scouts ◆ **1.** Pantomime a scene of students playing volleyball with one of the students being the *scout* and watching the game. Have the *scout* approach one of the players and say "You are a very good player and I would like you to come and play on my team." **2.** Show pictures of *scouts*, both modern-day and more historical pictures. Pantomime *scouting*.

scowl, scowled ◆ Lead students in *scowling* and then looking happy.

scramble, scrambled ◆ Have your hand *scramble* across a table. Lead students in past tense sentences.

scrap ◆ Tear paper into *scraps*.

scrape ◆ **1.** Notice something stuck to the floor and *scrape* it off with a ruler. Lead students in *scraping* something off their desk. **2.** Pantomime a scene where you break something belonging to another and lie about it. Say "I don't know what to do to make this situation right. I am in a tough *scrape*." **3.** Point out the *scraped* knee or elbow of a student.

scratch, scratching, scratchy ❯ 1. *Scratch* an imaginary itch. Take care that students know the difference between *scratch* and *itch*. 2. Have students feel rough or *scratchy* fabrics, such as sweaters or heavy jackets. Contrast with the *smoother* fabrics of shirts or dresses.

scrawl ❯ *Scrawl* your name across the board.

scrawny ❯ Show a picture or draw one on the board of a *scrawny* cat. Contrast with a *fat* cat.

scream, screaming ❯ Pantomime *screaming*. Lead students in pantomiming *screaming* by showing the action more than making the concomitant noise.

screech ❯ Use a toy car to demonstrate the *screeching* sound of car brakes. Call upon a volunteer to repeat the sound.

screen ❯ Point out the TV *screen* in a picture. Point out a computer or other *screen* in the room.

screenplay ❯ Ensure that students understand *screen* and *play* (drama). Explain that a *screenplay* is the name of the written story of a movie.

scrimp ❯ Hang sheets of paper on the wall with tiny bits of tape. Say "If I *scrimp* on this tape, I will have plenty left for tomorrow."

script ❯ 1. Write two words on the board, one in printing, one in cursive. Say "This is *printing;* this is *script.*" 2. Show students a *script* for a play.

scritch-scratch ❯ Lead students in *scratching* their fingernails on paper to demonstrate the sound of *scratching.* Explain that *scritch-scratch* is a made-up word that means "a *scratching* noise."

scrolls ❯ Show pictures of *scrolls,* or make a *scroll* by taping together several pieces of paper with a story on it.

scrub ❯ *Scrub* a desktop.

scrunch ❯ Demonstrate by crumpling a sheet of paper into a ball. Have students imitate.

sculpt, sculptor ❯ Show students a picture of a *sculptor* at work. Explain that the student is *sculpting.*

scurry, scurrying, scurried ❯ Ask students if they have seen a mouse run. Demonstrate the *scurrying* motion of a mouse with your fingers. Tell students, "When a mouse runs, it scurries." Lead them in past tense sentences.

sea ❯ —*sea level,* on the board, draw the cross section of a mountainous landscape that leads to the *sea.* Point to *sea level.* —*at sea,* make example sentences or phrases with the expression *at sea,* such as "It rains *at sea,*" "ships *at sea,*" or "They are *at sea.*" Include only those words that you are certain students already know.

search, searching, searched ❯ Lead students in searching for something in the classroom. Lead students in past tense sentences.

season ❯ Show students a calendar and point out the times of year various sports are played. Comment, "This is [baseball] *season.*"

secede, seceded ▪▸ **1.** Set up a scene where students represent some of the northern and southern states. Write the name of the state they are to be representing on a piece of paper and pin it to their shirt. First, have all the "states" get along well and work well together. Then have the "states" begin to fight with each other, and finally the southern "states" *secede.* **2.** On a photocopy of a map of the United States, draw a red outline around eleven Southern states: AL, AR, FL, GA, LA, MS, NC, SC, TN, TX, VA. Cut the map apart along the red line. Give example sentences using *seceded.*

secluded ▪▸ On the board, draw a room with a partition. Behind the partition, show a *secluded* person.

second ▪▸ Line up three students. Count off using their names: for example, "Sharon is first, Ed is *second*, and Marie is third." Relate to one, two, and three. Repeat with different students or a sequence of actions. —*second it*, set up a scene in which students nominate someone for class president. One person nominates someone and another person says, "I *second it.*" Write on the board the name of the student who made the nomination and the name of the student who *seconded it.* Show that the latter comes second. —*second base*, draw a baseball diamond on the board and label *second base.* —*second cousins*, on the board, draw a family tree that shows *cousins* and *second cousins.*

secondhand ▪▸ Have a student volunteer to give you something, such as a book or a sweater. Say "I got it *secondhand.*" Have a puppet tell you something it saw on the playground. Tell students you heard it *secondhand.*

seconds ▪▸ Use a watch with a *second* hand. Count *seconds* in unison with the class.

secret, secrets, secretly ▪▸ Whisper something in a student's ear. Aloud, tell the student not to tell because it's a *secret.* Explain that a *secret* is something that you don't tell. Have students whisper *secretly* to each other.

secret annex ▪▸ Draw a crude map of the school on the board. Say "If there were a hidden building here [point to a place], it would be called a *secret annex.*"

secretary ▪▸ Tell the class who the school *secretary* is. Explain that some of her duties are writing letters, making appointments, and answering telephones.

security ▪▸ Ask students to help you make a list of people they would go to if they felt afraid, such as mother, father, teacher, or police officer. Say "Your [mother] helps you feel safe; [she] is a source of *security* when you are afraid."

see, seeing, saw, seen, sight ▪▸ **1.** Lead students in shading their eyes to look. Tell them what you *see.* Ask them what they *saw.* **2.** Pantomime by shading your eyes and searching. Model sentences that start with, "*I see …*" Pantomime *seeing* a picture by peering at it. Ask students to look at something and then ask them what they *see.* Repeat with other examples. **3.** Shade your eyes and search. Ask students, "Have you *seen* my pencil?" **4.** Have students cover their eyes and explain that now they don't have *sight.* Uncover them. Now they have *sight.* Have a puppet walk by a toy animal and jump away in fright. Tell the class, "[Pumpkin] was surprised by [Kitty]. She jumped at the *sight* of her." Have students pantomime reacting at the *sight* of a bear. One student can play the bear. —*I see*, have two puppets dramatize this expression. Have one puppet *say* something very confusing and the other says, "*I don't see*." Then have the first say something clearly and the other says, "*I see*." Explain that *I see* means "I understand."

seed ❖ Bring some *seeds* to class. —*seed corn*. Show some and explain that it is *corn* that is planted to grow more *corn*.

seek, sought ❖ Organize a game of *hide-and-seek*. Say "I will close my eyes and count to 50 while you hide, and I will try to find you. Stay quiet and hidden while I look for you; you hide and I will *seek*." *Seek* for something in the classroom. Lead students in past tense sentences.

seem, seems ❖ Show a mirror to a puppet. The puppet says, "Another puppet *seems* to be in the mirror." Have a small student hide behind a larger student except for the arms so that the larger student *seems* to have four arms. Show that the student *seems* to have four arms, but he or she really has two.

seeping ❖ Make a slit in a plastic bottle. Float it in a sink or pan. Say "Water is *seeping* through the crack in the bottle." Pour out the water from the bottle to prove the statement.

seize, seized ❖ Have a puppet hold a piece of paper. *Seize* the paper. Have a puppet grab a pencil from you. Say with indignation, "[Spike] *seized* my pencil without asking!"

seldom ❖ Name activities that you often do and those you *seldom* do. These might include cleaning your teeth and cleaning the basement. Say to students, "We do not take a field trip often. We *seldom* take a field trip." Contrast with other activities that are *frequently* and *seldom* done.

self, selflessly ❖ **1.** Point to *yourself* and say "*Self*." Point to individuals in the class and repeat. Expand upon this with *yourself* and *myself*. **2.** Have a puppet ask if it can help students with their school work. Say "Fluffy works *selflessly* to help other students."

self-pity ❖ Say "I'm so bad. Everybody hates me." Have students pantomime. Lead students in sentences using *self-pity*.

self-serve ❖ Draw a gas pump on the board. Pantomime driving up to it and pumping gas into your car. Say "At this gas station, I have to pump the gas myself. This is a *self-serve* station."

sell, sold ❖ *Sell* a paper clip. Say to a puppet, "It costs a nickel." Have the puppet give you a nickel and say "I *sold* the paper clip and the puppet bought it."

send, sent ❖ Hand a note to one student and have him or her *send* it to another student. Tell them you *sent* the note. *Send* a student on an errand in the classroom. Say "I *sent* [her] to water the plant."

senses, sensing ❖ **1.** Have a student sneaking up on you from behind. Act alert: sit up straight, open eyes wide, and listen carefully. Say "The teacher *senses* someone is behind [her]." **2.** Give examples of *sensing* by seeing, hearing, smelling, and feeling.

sensitive ◗ Have a puppet hurt itself and cry. Comfort it with words and gestures. Say, as though experiencing the puppet's pain, "I am so sorry [Pumpkin] hurt [herself]. When [she] is upset, I get upset too. I am very *sensitive.*"

separate ◗ Have students *separate* crayons by colors.

sequel ◗ Show students a set of storybooks with *sequels.* Use examples of movie *sequels.*

serious ◗ Look very *serious* and then look *silly.* Say something *serious* and then do something *silly.*

serve, serves, served, servers ◗ **1.** Pretend that you are a waitress *serving* lunch and say "It is the job of a waitress to *serve* food to the customers in a restaurant. The waitress is the *server.*" Ask, "Has anyone *served* food at home?" **2.** Pantomime *serving* tea to a puppet. Explain that you *served* tea to the puppet. **3.** Bring a badminton or tennis racquet to class and pantomime *serving.*

service ◗ Pantomime being an airline attendant. Serve each student something to drink. Ask "How was the *service*?"

set, sets, setting ◗ **1.** Use toy cars to dramatize racers getting in the right place to start a race. **2.** Show students pictures of the sun going down and explain that it is *setting.* Explain that the sun *sets.* —*set off*, dramatize one puppet *setting* others *off* on a race. Or, *set* students *off* on a race. —*set them straight*, Write a math problem on the board. Have puppets give several wrong answers. Have a puppet *set them straight.*

setback ◗ Have students work together to build a castle out of blocks. After a minute, take some of the blocks away from them so that they have to redo the work. Say "You have suffered a *setback.*"

settle, settled, settlers ◗ **1.** Explain that *settle* means "to live in a place permanently." Ask students the name of the city where their families have *settled.* **2.** Show pictures of early *settlers* and explain that they traveled long distances before choosing a place to build their homes and towns.

seven ◗ Lead students in counting *seven* objects. Repeat in their first languages.

several ◗ Show students *several* items. Contrast with a *few* items. Lead them in sentences.

sewing ◗ **1.** Bring in a needle and thread. Pantomime *sewing.* **2.** Show a picture of a *sewing* machine.

shabbiness ◗ See *richness.*

shade, shady, shadier, shading ◗ **1.** If possible, take students outside to enjoy a *shady* spot under a tree, then find a *shadier* spot. Otherwise, show students pictures of trees with *shade.* **2.** Lead students in *shading* their eyes.

shadow ◗ **1.** Produce a *shadow* against the wall with a flashlight and suitable item. Point to the *shadow* and tell students, "*Shadow.*" **2.** Stand in front of a light source and show your *shadow*. Have students draw a sunny scene with trees and *shadows*.

shake, shaking, shook ● **1.** Lead students in *shaking* their heads, *shaking* glitter out of a bottle, or *shaking* pencil shavings out of a pencil sharpener. **2.** *Shake* a student's hand and say that you *shook* it.

shall ● **1.** Make up example sentences about the future modified to reflect your actual schedule, such as, "We *shall* do math before lunch" or "We *shall* have lunch at noon." **2.** Explain that this is also a way of asking something. Lead students in making sentences, such as "*Shall* we leave?" or "What food *shall* we eat?"

shallow ● **1.** Demonstrate with two containers of water. Fill one to the top and say "The water is *deep*." Fill the other just a little and say "The water is *shallow*." **2.** In a bowl, show students *shallow* water.

shame ● Catch a puppet taking something from your desk. Say "*Shame* on you."

Shane's ● See *Brad's*.

shape ● Show different *shapes* on the board. Have students draw different *shapes*.

share ● —*fair share*, divide something unfairly. Ask a student to correct your mistake and make *fair shares*. —*sharing time*, first check that students understand the words *share* and *time*. Have two children *share* a desk or a book. Explain *time* by moving the hands of a clock to various *times* and pantomiming appropriate activities such as eating lunch, going to recess, or going to sleep. Then, pantomime *sharing time*. If your class has a *sharing time*, remind students of this by pantomiming what was recently *shared*.

sharp, sharpen, sharpened ● **1.** Show some *sharp* scissors. **2.** Ask a student to *sharpen* a pencil. Show the class *sharp* and *dull* pencils and crayons. Lead students in past tense sentences.

shatter, shattered ● Show a picture of a broken window. Ask, "Who *shattered* the glass?"

she ● **1.** See *he*. **2.** (A boat.) Show students pictures of boats and ships. As you point to each one, say "*She* is big," "*She* is beautiful," and "*She* is small." In contrast, refer to other objects with the word *it*. Explain that in English, boats are called *she*. —*she'll*. Show on the board how *she* and *will* squeeze together to make the word *she'll*.

shear ● Show pictures of sheep that are being sheared. Help students to pantomime *shearing* a sheep.

shed ● Demonstrate by putting on your coat and letting it fall to the floor. Have students imitate.

sheer ● Show students *sheer* curtains or pictures of *sheer* fabrics. Explain that you can see through a *sheer* fabric.

shelf ● Show a *shelf* in the classroom.

shelling, shells ● **1.** Demonstrate *shelling* a piece of shrimp or other seafood. **2.** Show or draw pictures of *seashells*. Lead students in sentences.

sheltered ➧ Have one student stand in the middle of the room; have another crouch under the desk. Say "This student is out in the open and unprotected. This one is safe under a desk. [He] is *sheltered*."

shimmering ➧ Show students how glitter can *shimmer* under a light. Explain that the glitter is *shimmering*.

shine, shines, shiny, shining, shined, shone ➧ **1.** Draw a picture on the board of a sun and the rays *shining* out from the sun. **2.** Point out that the sun or a light in the room is *shining*. *Shine* a lamp or flashlight. **3.** Show a piece of metal that *shines* in the light. **4.** Show foil or some other *shiny* material. **5.** Show *dull* and *bright* objects. Make contrasting sentences, such as "This one is *shining*, this one is not." **6.** Say "The light *shone* upon the sea."

ship, shipped, shipping ➧ Pantomime preparing a package for *shipping*. Call a *shipping* company and request a pickup. Have a puppet take the package away. Say "I *shipped* the package to my grandmother." —*ship off*, check that students understand individual words in the expression. Make one puppet annoy another puppet. Have one puppet say "Please send him away! *Ship* him *off!*" Draw a ship on the board. Draw the puppet on the boat and wave good-bye. —*slave ship*, show pictures of *slave ships* and explain that these were the *ships* that brought *slaves* to our country many years ago. Let students know that this is no longer done.

shiver, shivered ➧ **1.** Tell students that you are very cold and *shiver*. Ask students if they have ever been sick and cold. Ask them if they *shivered*. **2.** Say "I *shivered*, because I am cold."

shock ➧ **1.** Pantomime being *shocked* by something you see. **2.** Ask if students have ever felt an earthquake *shock*. **3.** Set up a scene in a hospital where you are a doctor and a puppet has been in a car accident. Pantomime checking the patient's blood pressure and pulse. Say "This patient's blood is not flowing properly through its body; it has low blood pressure and a rapid pulse. These are signs of *shock*."

shook ➧ —*shook hands*, demonstrate with students. Say "We *shook hands*." —*shook head*, lead students in *shaking* their *heads* and explain that they *shook* their *heads*.

shoot, shoots, shooting, shot ➧ Pantomime *shooting* a ball through a basketball hoop. Draw a target with a bull's-eye on the board. *Shoot* a wad of paper at the target. Say "I *shot* at the target."

shore ➧ Point out the *shores* of several countries on a world map or globe.

short, shortage ➧ **1.** Contrast *tall* with *short*. **2.** Draw *tall* and *short* lines on the board. Have students do the same on paper. **3.** Give some of the students a pencil but run out. Say "We have a *shortage* of pencils. I have run out of them."

shortcut ➧ Take a circuitous route to cross the room, weaving between the desks and chairs. Then walk a straight line from one side of the room to the other. Say "The first time, I took the long way. The second time, I took a *shortcut*."

short-lived ◆ Blow up a balloon and let it go so it flies around the room. "Our fun with the balloon was *short-lived*." Have students give examples of other *short-lived* activities.

shortstop ◆ Draw a baseball diamond on the board and mark where the *shortstop* stands. Demonstrate what the *shortstop* does by pantomiming.

should ◆ **1.** Lead students in sentences and pantomimes that show the idea "will probably" for *should*. Suggestions are "This shoe *should* fit you," "This tape *should* mend the paper," and "This candy *should* taste good." **2.** Give unlikely examples, such as, "If you *should* find gold" or "If you *should* find a million dollars." Explain that *should* helps people say things that may not happen.

shoulder ◆ Touch your *shoulder*, touch a student's *shoulder*, and say "*shoulder*." Lead students in touching their *shoulders*.

shouldn't ◆ Show on the board how *should* and *not* squeeze together to make the word *shouldn't*.

shout, shouting, shouted ◆ Have a puppet *shout* at another puppet. Have students tell the puppet not to *shout*. Lead the class in past tense sentences. Contrast *shouting* with talking.

shoved ◆ *Shove* something into a puppet's hand. Contrast with *giving* the puppet something.

shovel, shoveling ◆ Show a picture of a *shovel*. Pantomime using a *shovel*. Tell students that you are *shoveling* snow or dirt.

show, shows, showed ◆ **1.** Smile and *show* your teeth. Explain that you *showed* your teeth. Lead students in *showing* their neighbors their hands and feet. **2.** Have a student *show* someone [her] pencil, and explain to the class, "[Ming] *shows* her pencil to [Ben]."

shred ◆ *Shred* a piece of paper with scissors.

shrewd ◆ Draw several shirts in different places on the board. Draw price tags of varying amounts next to each shirt. Pretend to be shopping and scrutinize the shirts and price tags. Say " I am a very *shrewd* shopper."

shriek, shrieking ◆ Have a puppet *shriek*. Say "I don't like that *shrieking* sound."

shrill ◆ Make a *shrill* noise.

shrink, shrinking, shrank, shrinkage ◆ **1.** Blow up a balloon and let it *shrink*. **2.** Blow up a balloon and let the air out slowly. Say "The balloon is *shrinking*." Then, say that it *shrank*. **3.** Draw two T-shirts on the board. Pantomime washing one and having it become smaller. Give sample sentences using *shrinkage*.

shriveled ◆ Show students examples of things that have *shriveled*, such as a dead plant.

shuffle, shuffling, shuffled ◆ **1.** *Shuffle* playing cards. Say that you *shuffled* them. **2.** Give a demonstration of *shuffling* your feet as you walk across the room.

shut, shutting ◆ Lead students in *shutting* a door, window, or container.
—*shut away*, Place a book into a drawer, cabinet, or closet. Say "I have *shut*

the book *away.*" —*shut down,* review the meanings of each word. If you have a computer or electronic game in the classroom, tell students that you will *shut it down.* Otherwise, draw a computer on the board and explain *shut down.*

shy ❥ Pantomime being *shy* and peeking between the fingers of your hand, looking down at your feet. Pantomime being *bold.* Have students pantomime being *shy* and *bold.*

Siberia ❥ Show *Siberia* on a map of the world.

sick, sickly ❥ **1.** Act *sick* by feeling your forehead and coughing and sneezing. See *ill.* **2.** Show pictures of *sickly* people or animals. Contrast with pictures of *healthy* people or animals. Ask students if they know of anyone who is *sickly.* **3.** Have students repeat a word over and over. Then tell them, "I am *sick* of that word." Look disgusted.

side, sides ❥ Show students the *sides* of paper, the *side* of your desk, and both *sides* of a wall.

sidewalk ❥ Show a *sidewalk* or a picture of one.

siege ❥ Have a puppet get an onslaught of illnesses, one right after the other. Explain to the class that the puppet has been hit with a *siege* of illnesses.

sigh, sighs, sighing, sighed ❥ Demonstrate a *sigh* and lead students in *sighing.* Say that you *sighed.*

sight ❥ —*in plain sight,* place something on your desk where every student can see it. Explain that it is *in plain sight.*

sign, signs, signed, signature ❥ **1.** *Sign* your name on the board. Explain that when you write your name, you *sign.* Say "This is my *signature.*" Have students *sign* their names on a piece of paper. **2.** Pretend to be a doctor and check a student for indications of life (i.e., pulse, breathing, reflexes). Say "I have checked [Eric] for *signs* of life and [he] seems to be okay!"

sign language ❥ Pantomime some *signs* such as a finger over one's lips to signify silence. Say "This is part of a *sign language* that everyone understands."

sign language interpreter ❥ Have a student stand next to you at the front of the classroom and say "I love you," while you show students the *American Sign Language* sign (hold up the thumb and index and pinkie fingers of your right hand). Say "A *sign language interpreter* uses *American Sign Language* so deaf people know what someone is saying." See *American Sign Language.*

signal ❥ Start by waving your hand. Have students show you different *signals* they know.

signifying ❥ Make various sounds and have the class tell you what they mean (i.e., laughing for happiness, crying for sadness, and gasping for fear). Say "When I laugh like this, it is a sound *signifying* happiness."

silent ❥ **1.** Ask for a moment of *silence.* Afterwards, say "I love a *silent* moment." Ask students to be quiet and once the room is completely *silent,* tell them, "We are *silent.*" **2.** Have everyone walk *silently.*

silly ❖ Show pictures of *silly* clowns, animals, and expressions. Show a number of different *silly* things so that students realize that *silly* does not always mean "clown," for example. Make *silly* faces and have students make *silly* faces. Have puppets do *silly* things like stand upside down or wiggle around.

silver ❖ Show coins or jewelry made out of *silver*. Lead students in sentences.

silversmith ❖ Hold up things made of *silver* (earrings, bracelet, wristwatch, spoon) and say for each one, "This is made of *silver*; a *silversmith* made it."

Simon ❖ Explain that this is a man's name. Ask students for other names of men.

simple, simply, simplicity ❖ **1.** Do something that students would find *simple*, like writing their names. Tell them, "This is easy. It is *simple*." **2.** Ask a student volunteer to show off a special talent, such as whistling or juggling. With awe and admiration say "[Carmen], that was wonderful. That was *simply* awesome!" **3.** Show students something *elaborate*, like a picture of a sequined evening dress. Tell them, "This dress was *elaborately* made." Discuss the details of it. Show them a plain dress and tell them this dress has *simplicity*. Compare its *simplicity* to that of the evening dress.

since ❖ **1.** Make comparative sentences and demonstrate using *because* and *since*. For example, "*Because* you are late, you will need to stay after class." "*Since* you are late, you will need to stay after class." **2.** Use a calendar and indicate a day earlier in the week. Say "*Since* Tuesday we have learned twelve new words." Repeat with a variety of examples and lead students in sentences.

sing, singing, sang ❖ *Sing* to students and have them join you in *singing*. Ask others to *sing*. Give example sentences using *sang*.

single ❖ **1.** Have one student stand apart from the rest of the class. Point to the lone student and say "This is a *single* student." Point to the others and say "This is a *group* of students." **2.** Put a *group* of paper clips hooked together on a table. Then, show students a *single* paper clip that is not hooked with others.

sink, sinking, sank ❖ Place an item that will slowly *sink* in a container of water. As it begins to fill with water and *sink*, explain that it is *sinking*. Say that it *sank*. Have volunteers repeat the demonstration. —*half sunk*, put some water in a bowl. Show an object *sinking*. Say "It *sunk*." Show another object partially submerged and say "This is *half sunk*."

sip, sipping, sipped ❖ Demonstrate *sipping*. Have students mimic *sipping*, and lead them in sentences.

sir ❖ Dramatize speaking to the principal, or another male authority with whom students are familiar. Address him as *sir*. Have students address him as *sir*.

sister ❖ —*little sister*, draw on the board three stick figure children: *little sister*, *middle sister*, and *big sister*. Name the middle child and explain that the little figure is "her *little sister* Julia."

sister-in-law ❖ Draw stick figures on the board. Draw two married couples. Say "This man and this woman are married. The wife has a *sister*." Draw a line from the man to the wife's *sister*. Say "This woman is this man's *sister-in-law*."

sit, sits, sitting, sat ▸ From a standing position, *sit* in a chair. Ask a student to *sit* in a chair and tell the class, "[Mia] *sits* in the chair," "[Mia] is *sitting* in a chair," and "[Mia] *sat* in a chair."

sites ▸ Name different *sites* in the classroom. Have students go to a named *site* on command.

sitter ▸ Explain that one kind of *sitter* looks after children when their parents are away.

situation, situations ▸ **1.** Use a story the class has read. Take one scene and have the class give the characters and setting. Call this scene a *situation*. **2.** Demonstrate a variety of *situations* that can come up with puppets: a problem with a friend, being sick, winning a prize and so on.

six ▸ Show the students *six* objects. —*six times eight*, this means the same as 6×8.

size, sizes ▸ Show books of different *sizes*. Lead students in sentences, such as "This book is a smaller *size* than this book." Show students your shoes and explain that yours are a bigger *size* than theirs. Have students compare the *sizes* of different objects. —*twice the size*, once students understand the word *size*, draw objects that are *twice the size* of another. Explain that *twice* is like the word *two*.

sizzled ▸ Show a picture of meat in a frying pan and explain that as it cooks, it *sizzles*. Imitate this noise. Lead students in past tense sentences.

skated ▸ Show a picture of roller *skates*. Pantomime *skating*. Lead students in past tense sentences.

skeleton ▸ Show a picture of a dinosaur or human *skeleton*.

sketch, sketches, sketchy ▸ **1.** *Sketch* a few things on the board, such as a chair, a table, and a house. Explain that they are not full pictures; they are just *sketches* drawn with a few lines. Show artists' *sketches* and contrast with paintings. **2.** Act out with a puppet who gives you brief, incomplete answers to your questions about what it did over the weekend. Say "You're not telling me much. This is *sketchy* information."

skid ▸ Use a toy car and demonstrate how it *skids* to a stop.

skill, skills ▸ **1.** Show pictures of art and explain that the artist had *skill*. Show students' work and remark upon their *skill*. **2.** Demonstrate two forms of writing on the board. One is slow and awkward, the other fast and smooth. Point out which you wrote with *skill*. Ask students what *skills* they have, for example, riding a bike, running, or singing.

skim ▸ Sprinkle glitter or other matter that will float on water in a container. Use a spoon and *skim* it off. Allow students to *skim* some off as well.

skinny, skinnier, skinniest ▸ Draw *skinny* lines on the board and wide ones. Once students understand *skinny*, compare pictures of *skinny* animals or people. Have students show you the *skinny* one, the *skinnier* one, and the *skinniest* one.

skip, skips, skipped ❖ *Skip* for students. Lead students in *skipping*. Have students *skip* around the classroom.

skirmish ❖ Have two puppets argue. Explain that they had a small fight or *skirmish*. Give example sentences using *skirmish*.

skit, skits ❖ Give examples of some of the *skits* that students did to act out stories. Explain that a *skit* is a little play.

sky ❖ Take students outside and show them the *sky*.

slam, slamming, slammed ❖ *Slam* the door shut. Tell students you *slammed* the door.

slanted ❖ Have students find *slanted* surfaces, and in contrast *flat* ones.

slap, slapping, slapped ❖ Tell students that it is not good to *slap* someone. Have one puppet *slap* another on the hand. Lead students in past tense sentences.

slatted ❖ Show pictures of trucks with *slatted* sides.

slave, slaves ❖ **1.** Have a puppet work very hard and refuse to pay him. Call him your *slave*. Explain to students that this was a very bad thing people used to do to other people. Also, explain that it is no longer done in America. **2.** Show pictures of *slaves*. **3.** Close several students inside a ring of chairs. Say "I own you. You must do as I say. You must work for me; I will not pay you. You are not free to come and go. You are my *slaves*." Say to the others, who are walking about, "I do not own you. You may do as you wish. You are *free* to come and go."

sleek, sleekly ❖ Show students *sleek* surfaces, perhaps polished wood or metal.

sleep, sleeping, slept, sleepily ❖ **1.** Show a puppet *sleeping*. Have the puppet *wake up*. Lead students in pantomiming *sleeping* and *waking* by saying, "*Sleep*," and have students lay their heads on their desks and pretend to *sleep*. Say "*Wake up*," and have them raise their heads. **2.** Lead students in pantomiming *sleeping*, *waking up*, *woke up*, and *slept*. **3.** Have a puppet be very tired, talking and walking *sleepily*. Tell students, "It is talking *sleepily*," "It is walking *sleepily*."

sleepyhead ❖ Have a puppet ignore your attempts to wake it. Say "I can't wake up [Jose] no matter what I do. What a *sleepyhead* [he] is!"

slice, sliced, slices ❖ Draw a picture of a pie on a piece of paper and *slice* it into *slices* with your scissors. Explain that you *sliced* it.

slick, slicker, slickest ❖ **1.** Rub your hand along a *slick* surface in the classroom. **2.** Have students rub their hands across *slick*, *slicker*, and *slickest* surfaces or fabrics.

slicker ❖ Show students pictures of a *slicker* and explain that you wear a *slicker* when it rains. Show a picture of rain or draw rain on the board.

slide, sliding, slid ❖ *Slide* a book or other object along your desktop. Have students *slide* a book across their desks. Take them outside and have them go *sliding* down the *slide*. Tell students that they *slid*.

slightly ◈ Make your voice *slightly* louder or *slightly* quieter. Show shapes on the board that are *slightly* bigger or smaller than the last.

slinkety-sly ◈ Explain that *slinkety-sly* is not a word. It is made up. But it sounds like the words *slinky* and *sly*. Demonstrate moving in a *slinky* (sneaky) way. Demonstrate looking *slyly* out of the corners of your eyes.

slinking ◈ Pretend you are a cat *slinking* after a mouse. Have students imitate.

slip, slipping, slippery, slipped ◈ 1. Pretend to *slip* and say that you are *slipping*. Tell students, "I *slipped*." Explain that the floor was *slippery*. 2. *Slip* a note into an envelope or box. Have students *slip* pieces of paper into their desks.

slither, slithers, slithering, slithered ◈ 1. Show pictures of a snake and say that when it moves, it *slithers*. Lead students in past tense sentences. 2. Demonstrate *slithering* movements with a toy snake or with your arm. Have students imitate the motion and say that the snake *slithered*.

slivers ◈ Show a piece of old wood. Tear off some *slivers*. Or, illustrate on the board.

slope ◈ Demonstrate small pebbles rolling down a *slope*.

sloppy ◈ Write a sentence on the board using *sloppy* writing. Contrast by writing the same sentence *neatly*.

slowly ◈ Speak *slowly* and then *quickly*. Raise your hand *slowly* and then *quickly*.

slow-moving ◈ Walk around the classroom *slowly* and say "I am a *slow-moving* teacher."

slowness ◈ Show the *slowness* of a manual pencil sharpener as compared to the speed of an electric sharpener. Show the *slowness* of adding 650 five times as compared to multiplying 650 by five.

slowpoke ◈ Show one puppet doing things *quickly* and the other being a *slowpoke*.

sly ◈ Pantomime a scene between two puppets where one is trusting of the other who is acting *slyly*. Have students pantomime similar scenes with each other.

smacks, smacked ◈ 1. *Smack* your hand. 2. Pantomime tasting food. *Smack* your lips and comment, "It tastes so good I *smacked* my lips."

small, smaller, smallest ◈ 1. Show students *large* and *small* things. 2. Show pencils of various sizes while saying, "This one is *big*; this one is *small*; this one is *smaller*; and this one is *the smallest*."

small feathers ◈ Show students snowflakes and explain that the snowflakes are being called *small feathers*. Also, show students *small feathers* so they can see the differences and similarities.

small-time ◈ Name a major league baseball team and a minor league team. Say "The [New York Yankees] is a famous baseball team. Almost nobody has heard of the [New Haven Ravens]; they're a *small-time* team."

smart, smarter, smartest ◈ 1. Ask a student to count to ten. Say that he or she is *smart*. Have a puppet attempt and fail to count to three. Say that the puppet is not *smart*. (Ensure that you choose something that you know all the students can do). **2.** Write three arithmetic equations on the board: one with two numbers, the next with three, the last with four. Have one puppet solve only the first problem; the other, two; and the third, all three. Say "[Rabbit] figured out the answer to the first problem. What a *smart* [Rabbit] he is. [Bear] was able to solve both problems. [Bear] is *smarter* than [Rabbit]. [Owl] figured out all three problems. [Owl] is the *smartest*."

smell, smells ❖ Pantomime by sniffing. If you have some perfume, you can have students *smell* it. Talk about things with strong *smells* like smoke and different kinds of food cooking.

smile, smiling, smiled ❖ **1.** *Smile* at the children. Lead them in *smiling* and making sentences. **2.** Pass a *smile* along a line of students. No laughing, just *smiling!*

smoldered ❖ Show pictures of a *smoldering* fire. Say "A fire like this could *smolder* for hours."

smooth, smoothly ❖ **1.** Compare two surfaces, a *smooth* and a *rough* one. Have students feel them. **2.** Divide students into two groups. Have each group arrange their chairs as if they are riding in a car. Have one group bounce around in their seats; have the other group sit quietly. Say "This group's car is giving them a *rough* ride. The other group's car is riding *smoothly*."

smudging ❖ Have each student use a soft leaded pencil to draw a line on a sheet of paper, then rub it with his or her fingers. Say "You are *smudging* your lines."

snag ❖ Show students a *snag* in a fabric, perhaps a sweater, jacket, book bag, or a soft-sided lunch box.

snakey smile ❖ Explain that this is an untrustworthy, calculating *smile*. Show pictures of *snakes*.

snap, snapping, snapped ❖ *Snap* a rubber band into the air. Do other fast motions to dramatize *snap*. Lead students in *snapping* their fingers. Make past tense sentences, such as "We *snapped* our fingers."

snare ❖ Make a large noose with a piece of string. Place the loop on your desk and hold up the straight piece. Move a pencil into the loop and then jerk the string up so it catches the pencil. Say "I caught the pencil in my *snare*."

snarl ❖ Tangle some yarn or thread. Say "The yarn is *snarled*."

snatch, snatching ❖ Demonstrate this by *snatching* something from your desk. Lead students in sentences using *snatch*.

sneak, sneaking, sneaky ❖ **1.** Demonstrate by *sneaking* up behind a student. **2.** Have a toy snake move silently around the room. Say "*Snake* is *sneaking* around the room." **3.** Make a puppet sneak something from someone's desk. Say "Where did you get that? You are *sneaky*."

sneer ❖ Lead the class in a *sneer*. Have students try to curl their lips and *sneer*.

sneeze, sneezing, sneezed ❖ Have a puppet *sneeze* and say that it *sneezed*. Lead students in pantomimes of *sneezing*.

sniff, sniffs, sniffing, sniffed ❥ Demonstrate *sniffing*. Have students *sniff* the air. Lead them in past tense sentences. Explain that an animal *sniffs* the air.

snip, snap, snout ❥ Explain that these are just nonsense sounds.

snip, snipping ❥ *Snip* some paper with your scissors. Lead students in *snipping* paper or string. Show pictures of a barber *snipping* off the ends of someone's hair. Pantomime the action.

snob ❥ Have a puppet act like a *snob* toward another puppet. Contrast by having the puppet act *nice*.

snooping ❥ Have a puppet pry its way into your desk drawer and look curiously at all the contents. Say "Why are you *snooping* around in my desk drawer?"

snooze, snoozing ❥ Pantomime *snoozing* with your head on your desk.

snorting ❥ Draw or show a picture of a horse. Demonstrate *snorting*. Lead students in sentences.

snowrock ❥ Show pictures of *snowballs*.

snug ❥ Try on a shoe that is too tight. Say "This is a *snug* fit." Wrap yourself in a coat and explain that you are warm and *snug*.

so ❥ **1.** Help students make sentences, such as "I was tired, *so* I went to sleep" or "I was hungry, *so* I ate." **2.** Make expressive sentences and pantomime: "I'm *so* cold!" "I'm *so* hot!" "I'm *so* tired!" **3.** Explain that *so* means "in that way." *So* he did means "it's the way you said." Have a puppet say "He fell," and the other say "*So* he did." Ask a student to walk to the door and follow him or her. Say "[She] walks to the door, and *so* do I." —*so much that*, check that students can use the words *so*, *much*, and *that* in sentences. Lead students in saying and pantomiming sentences, such as, " I worked *so much that* I'm tired" and "I wrote *so much that* the page is full."

soak, soaks, soaked ❥ *Soak* a paper towel or napkin, and explain that it is *soaked*. Demonstrate how a sponge absorbs the water. Say "The sponge *soaks* up the water."

soar ❥ Demonstrate with your hand something flying up steeply. Say "See it *soar*."

sob, sobbed ❥ Have a puppet *sob*.

social security number ❥ Show students your *social security* card. Tell students, "Every person in the U.S. has his or her own number."

sockets ❥ Show them a lightbulb *socket*.

socks ❥ Have students touch their own *socks* or draw a pair of *socks* on the board.

soft, softly ❥ **1.** Let students feel something *soft*, such as cloth or cotton and, in contrast, something *hard*, such as a book. **2.** Speak *softly*.

software ❥ Show the *software* package and CD-ROM. Explain that the computers have to be told how to do things. The *software* tells the computer what to do. If possible, demonstrate by placing the CD-ROM in the drive, and typing in a command to start the program.

soggy ◆ Wet a paper towel or napkin. Explain that it is *soggy*.

soil ◆ Show students the *soil* that will be used in making a home for earthworms.

solar flares ◆ Draw a picture of the sun with large flames leaping from it and say "These are *solar flares*."

solitaire ◆ **1.** Demonstrate a game of *solitaire*. **2.** Show a ring with a *solitaire* stone. Explain that *solitaire* means "one."

solos ◆ Have the whole class sing a familiar song. Then sing a verse of the song by yourself. Say "When I sing by myself, I sing a *solo*. How many of you have sung *solos?*"

solution ◆ Have students suggest problems, such as forgetting to bring lunch to school. Suggest *solutions*, such as asking friends to share their lunches.

solve ◆ Give students a math problem. Tell them you want them to *solve* it. Take them through the steps of *solving* the problem so that they get the idea. Repeat as needed.

some ◆ Put a group of paper clips on your desk and knock *all* of them off. Contrast that with knocking *some* of them off. Do other similar examples.

somebody ◆ Have a student take a pencil off your desk without your seeing who it is. Say with expression, "*Somebody* took my pencil." Have a student put the pencil back without your seeing who it was. Say "*Somebody* put a pencil on my desk." Have a student knock at the door and say "*Somebody* is at the door."

someday ◆ Ask students about their wishes and dreams. Say "*Someday* that might come true." Make example sentences, such as "*Someday* you will win a prize" or "*Someday* you will read very well." Explain that *someday* means "sometime or day but we don't know when."

something ◆ Explain that you have *something* in your hands behind your back. Have them guess what that something is. Say that you see *something* red on the wall. Have students guess. Tell students to find *something* in their desks that they like. Give students examples, such as "Watching TV is *something* I like to do" or "Dancing is *something* fun." Explain that *something* can mean a thing that you cannot see or touch. —*something for nothing*, check that students understand the individual words. Set up a scene in which you ask each student to give you *something*. Tell them to refuse you because you have neither money nor anything to barter with. Say "You had *something* I wanted, but I had nothing to give you in return. You can't get *something for nothing*."

sometimes ◆ **1.** Make up sentences using the word *sometimes* that reflects your actual schedule. Examples are, "Every day we exercise; *sometimes* we do stretching," "Every day we eat lunch; *sometimes* we eat apples for lunch," "Every day we do math; *sometimes* we play math games." **2.** Contrast *sometimes* with *always*. You might say "We *always* do our lessons but *sometimes* we play a game."

somewhere ◆ Make up sentences with *somewhere*, such as, "I want to go *somewhere* new" or "I went *somewhere* in America." Have students go *somewhere* in the classroom.

song ◆ —*whale song*, make a *whale* noise and have students make similar sounds. Say "Listen to the sad *whale song*."

soon ◆ **1.** Contrast things that will happen *soon*, such as recess or lunch, with things that will happen in a *long time*, such as finishing the third grade or summer vacation. You can also contrast the birthdays of students, ones that will be coming *soon* and ones that are coming in a long time. **2.** See *first*. —*How soon?*, one puppet says, "We will have recess (lunch, a party) *soon*." The other puppet says, "*How soon?*" The first puppet answers, "In ___ minutes."

soot ◆ Bring some *soot* from a fireplace to show students, or show pictures of fires that include *soot*.

soothed, soothing ◆ **1.** Have a puppet cry. Now *soothe* the puppet with kind words and gestures. Say "I have *soothed* the poor puppet." **2.** "The hot water is very *soothing*."

sophomore ◆ Explain that a *sophomore* is in the tenth grade. Have students write first grade through tenth grade. Circle tenth grade. Explain that this is the tenth year in school or the *sophomore* year.

sore ◆ Explain to students that this is another word for *angry*. Review *angry* as needed.

sorrow ◆ Show pictures of people expressing *sorrow*.

sorry ◆ **1.** Have one puppet bump into another puppet and say it's *sorry*. Have one puppet hurt itself and the other say it's *sorry*. Have one puppet drop something, and the other say it's *sorry*. **2.** Show pictures of people expressing *sorrow*. Say "I feel *sorry* for these people."

sound, sounds, sounded, soundless ◆ **1.** Drop a book and say that it *sounds* like a book falling. Lead students in making a variety of *sounds*. **2.** Make various animal noises and say what animals they *sound* like. **3.** Mention ideas for what to eat at lunch and say whether it *sounds* good. **4.** Have students make various *sounds*. These can include words, animal noises, or other noises. Each time say "That *sounded* loud" or "That *sounded* like a dog barking." **5.** Have students make a lot of noise for a few seconds. Say "It is very noisy in here!" Have students be silent. Say "It is very quiet in here. There is no *sound*. It is *soundless*." —*sound sleeper*, act out with puppets. Have them both pantomime *sleeping*. Invite students to shout, "Wake up! Wake up!" Have one puppet awaken quickly. Say "This puppet woke up; it is a *light sleeper*. This other puppet is still sleeping; it is a *sound sleeper*."

sour ◆ Ask who has eaten a lemon or lime. Explain that they are *sour* tasting.

source ◆ Draw a sun on the board. Underneath it draw a plant. Draw rays from the sun to the plant. Say "The sun is the *source* of our light and heat."

south ◆ Show students a globe and point out north, *south*, east, and west.

space, spaces ◆ **1.** Compare with *place*. Have students stand in different *spaces*, saying, "You stand in this *space*, and you stand in that *space*." Show students different *spaces* such as an outside space, the classroom, their desks, and your desk. Lead them in such sentences as "This is the outside *space*," "This is the classroom *space*," and "This is your desk *space*." **2.** Draw our solar system on the board with the sun, planets, and moon. Roll a sheet of paper into a tube. Pantomime using it as a telescope and say "I love looking out into *space* with my telescope."

span ❖ Draw a river with banks on the board. Draw a bridge across the river. Explain that the bridge *spans* the river.

spare, spared ❖ **1.** Have a puppet ask for a pencil. Say "I have a *spare* pencil." **2.** Begin to write on the board and have the chalk break. Tell students, "It is okay; I have a *spare*." **3.** See *infectious* and repeat the activity, but this time have more students get tagged with the infection while others are *spared*.

sparkle ❖ Show students the *sparkle* of glitter under a bright light.

sparks ❖ On the board, draw pictures of a fire with *sparks*.

spatial ❖ See *space*. Explain that when we talk or experiment with *space*, it is *spatial*.

spattering ❖ Dip your fingers in a cup of water and flick the water onto a dark-colored piece of paper as you say "I am *spattering* the water."

spawned ❖ Show pictures of salmon laying their eggs.

speak, speaking, spoke, spoken ❖ *Speak* to students and have students *speak* to you. Tell students that when we talk, we *speak*. Lead students in *speaking*. Say "I *speak* French. I *speak* Spanish. I *speak* English." Have students add other languages to this list. Say something to students followed by, "I *spoke*" and "I have *spoken*." —*to speak of*, demonstrate something you are not very good at. Say "My [drawing} is not much *to speak of*."

special, specialty ❖ **1.** Give examples of *special* things, such as a student's *special* toy or *special* article of clothing. Have students tell about their *special* treasures. Show a picture of a birthday party. Say it is a *special* day. Show students several sheets of lined paper and one sheet of colored paper. Say the colored paper is *special*. **2.** Give examples of *specialty* shops or people with a *specialty*, such as sports stars or performers.

species ❖ Draw or show pictures of various animals in the cat family, such as a domestic cat, a lion, a tiger, and a leopard, etc. Say "These are all different *species* of cats."

speck, specks ❖ Show *specks* on the board.

speech, speeches, speechless ❖ **1.** Ask students to give *speeches*. Have one student give all the good arguments the class used for the pizza party. Or, have a student tell the class about something he or she knows well. **2.** Tell the puppet some very exciting news and have the puppet be *speechless*.

speed, speedy ❖ **1.** Read a sentence aloud slowly. Say "I am reading *slowly*." Gradually read faster and faster. Say "I am reading faster; I am increasing my reading *speed*." **2.** Explain that *speedy* means "fast." Tell students to put the things away on their desk and to be *speedy*. Then have them repeat it *slowly*.

spelling bee ➡ Explain that this is a competition to see who can spell the most words correctly. Hold a short *spelling bee*.

spend, spends, spent ➡ **1.** Pantomime a scene of a student selling a paper clip. Say "You will have to *spend* a nickel." Have the student give you a nickel. **2.** Have the student give you a nickel, and say that the student *spent* a nickel. **3.** Ask two or three students to come to your desk. Have students stay there for one or two minutes. Say "Students *spent* two minutes at my desk." Have a student time one of the lessons. Ask, "How much time have we *spent* on the lesson?"

spendthrift ➡ Have a puppet go on a shopping spree and buy many more things than it truly needs. Tell students the puppet is a *spendthrift*.

spewing ➡ Pantomime eating pizza and spitting it out. Say "Excuse me! I was *spewing* it out because the pizza was too hot." Show pictures of a volcano *spewing* lava.

spike, spiky ➡ **1.** Have a student gently toss wadded paper toward you. Hit it hard with your hand. Tell students you *spiked* the paper. **2.** Show a picture of shoes with cleats on them and explain that they are *spiky* shoes.

spill, spills ➡ **1.** Accidentally *spill* a little water or some paper clips on the desk. **2.** Demonstrate by filling a cup with paper clips. Knock the cup over so some paper clips fall out. Say "This is how the teacher *spills* the paper clips."

spin, spins, spinning, spun ➡ **1.** Show students a cocoon that has been *spun*. **2.** Show students a picture of sheep's wool and a picture of the sheep being sheared. Then show them a skein of yarn and a *spinning* wheel. Tell them, "First we cut the wool from the sheep. Then we *spin* the wool into yarn on the *spinning* wheel. Then we have yarn." **3.** *Spin* a ball on the floor. Have students *spin* a ball. **4.** Lead students in *spinning* around. **5.** *Spin* a coin. Say "Right now I am *spinning* a nickel. Yesterday, I *spun* a quarter."

spirit ➡ Bring a recording of the National Anthem. Pantomime singing with *spirit*.

spit, spat ➡ Have a puppet *spit* and say that it *spat*. Pantomiming *spitting*. Lead students in present and past tense sentences.

splash, splashing ➡ *Splash* some water in a sink. Lead students in *splashing* water.

splendid ➡ Have a student read aloud a familiar passage. Say with enthusiasm, "That was an excellent job of reading, [Manuel]. That was *splendid*."

splinter ➡ Rub your finger across some wood and pretend that you got a *splinter*. Say "Ouch! I got a *splinter* in my finger. I got a little piece of wood here, look!"

split ➡ On the board, draw a picture of an axe *splitting* a log.

spluttered ➡ Demonstrate by *spluttering* to the class. Have students *splutter* to each other. Lead them in past tense sentences.

spoil, spoiling, spoiled ➡ **1.** Have one puppet playing contentedly with toys and be obviously happy. Have another puppet come up to it and pester it, *spoiling* its pleasure. Have students do similar pantomimes. **2.** Draw a series of four yellow bananas on a piece of paper. Have the class watch as you make a black spot on the second banana, several black spots on the third banana, and blacken the entire fourth banana. Point to the fourth banana and say "If a banana sits too long, it will *spoil*." **3.** *Spoil* a piece of paper by making marks on it. *Spoil* a nice sphere of clay by cutting marks into it. **4.** *Spoiled* children try to get what they want by whining, crying, and in other ways intimidating their parents. Dramatize with puppets.

spokesman ❧ Use examples of sports figures who are *spokesmen* for certain products. Lead students in sentences using *spokesman*.

sponsor ❧ List television programs that students know. Ask who *sponsors* each one.

spooky ❧ Show pictures of things you think are *spooky;* such as spiders or bats.

spoonful ❧ Fill your hand with paper clips. Say "This is a handful of paper clips." Fill a spoon with paper clips. Say "This is a *spoonful* of paper clips."

sportsmanship ❧ Arm wrestle a student and show good *sportsmanship* when you lose.

spot, spots, spotting, spotted ❧ **1.** Lead students in touching *spots* that are on the walls or board. **2.** Look around the room and name things you see, using *spot* and *see* interchangeably. For example, say "I *see* a flag. I *spot* a flag. I *see* a computer. I *spot* a computer. I *see* a poster. I *spot* a poster." Hide a small object in the classroom, such as a pencil. Say "Do you *spot* it?" **3.** Make *spots* of chalk on the board. **4.** Ask students to find or suggest a quiet *spot*, a noisy *spot*, a sunny *spot*, and a dry *spot*.

sprain, sprain ❧ Pantomime twisting your ankle and limping. Say "Ouch! I *sprained* my ankle."

sprawl ❧ Show pictures of squid or octopuses with their tentacles *sprawled*.

spray, spraying ❧ Demonstrate by *spraying* water with a *spray* bottle. If you have a sink that will *spray* water, this would also be a good demonstration.

spread, spreading, ❧ **1.** Have students *spread* themselves around the classroom. Then have them move close together. Lead students in *spreading* their arms out wide. **2.** Pantomime *spreading* butter on a slice of bread. Say "I am *spreading* butter on my toast." **3.** Spill a small amount of water on a desk. Say "Look how the water is *spreading* across the desk." —*spread the word*, set up a scene where you are starting an ice-cream company. Say "Would you please tell your friends and family? I need your help to *spread the word* about my new ice-cream store."

spree ❧ Lead students on a cleaning *spree*. Ask if they have ever gone on a shopping *spree*.

sprinkle, sprinkling, sprinkled, sprinkler ❧ **1.** Demonstrate *sprinkling* drops of water. *Sprinkle* bits of paper or paper clips. Demonstrate with a salt shaker or glitter. **2.** Show pictures of *sprinklers*, and point out actual *sprinklers* outside, or, if students understand them, the fire *sprinklers* in the school.

sprint, sprints, sprinting ❖ **1.** Take students outside and lead them in a few *sprints*. **2.** Have a student run quickly across the room. Say "[Juanita] is *sprinting*."

sprout, sprouts ❖ Show students pictures of *sprouting* plants or actual *sprouts*.

spur ❖ —*spur of the moment*, talk to students about the lesson plan for the day. Then say suddenly, "I know what we'll do! I just thought of something fun on the *spur of the moment!*"

spy ❖ Lead students in *spying* things or people in the classroom. Say "We are *spying* on [Jaime] and [Cecilia]."

squad ❖ Have students form into reading *squads*. Have each *squad* make a sentence, such as, "We are a reading *squad*."

square, squarely ❖ **1.** Draw a *square* on the board. **2.** Look a student *squarely* in the eyes.

squash, squashed ❖ *Squash* a piece of modeling clay. Make a loose ball out of crumpled paper. Smash it flat on your desk with your hand. Say "The ball is *squashed.*" *Squash* a marshmallow or a make-believe bug under your shoe.

squawk, squawking, squawked ❖ Demonstrate and lead students in *squawking*. Give example sentences. Show pictures of birds that *squawk*.

squeak, squeaks, squeaking, squeaky ❖ **1.** Show a picture of a mouse. *Squeak* like a mouse and say that you are *squeaking*. Explain that the mouse *squeaks*. Have students *squeak* like a mouse. **2.** Make a *squeaky* noise.

squealed ❖ Lead students in *squealing*. Help with past tense sentences.

squeeze, squeezing, squeezed ❖ *Squeeze* some glue out of a container. Lead students in pantomiming *squeezing* through a small hole.

squiggle, squiggly ❖ **1.** Have students draw *squiggles*. **2.** Show students how to make *squiggly* lines. —*black squiggles*, show cursive handwriting on the board. Ask students what they used to call it before they knew what it was.

squint, squinting, squinted ❖ Lead students in *squinting* at the bright lights in the classroom. Ask if they have ever *squinted* at the sun.

squirm, squirms, squirming, squirmed ❖ **1.** Ask students to act out what it would feel like if they had ants crawling inside their clothes. Say "This feels tickly and crawly. These ants are making us *squirm!*" Ask a student to imitate you *squirming* in your seat. Say "He or she *squirms*." **2.** Hold a puppet and have it *squirm* in your hands. Say that it *squirmed*.

squirt, squirting, squirted ❖ *Squirt* some paint or glue out of its tube. Pantomime squirting a puppet with a *squirt* gun. Lead the class in past tense sentences.

stab, stabbed ❖ Accidentally *stab* yourself with a saftey pin. Lead students in past tense sentences.

stabilize ◗ **1.** Place a pencil in an empty paper cup. Move the cup so the pencil flops around. Then pour something, such as paper clips, into the cup and show that the pencil is less wobbly. Say "I put [paper clips] in the cup to help the pencil stand up. The [paper clips] helped to *stabilize* the pencil in the cup." **2.** Stand on one foot. Begin to lose your balance and grab the back of a chair to *stabilize* yourself.

stack ◗ Build a *stack* of books or papers and show the *stack*.

staff, staffs ◗ **1.** Explain as the people who work for you. Set up various scenes where you are a boss and students are your *staff*; include kitchen, office, medical, and educational scenarios. **2.** Show pictures of people, such as a shepherd or an ancient Egyptian ruler, holding *staffs*.

staggering ◗ Pantomime carrying very heavy bags and *staggering* under the strain. Say "I am *staggering*."

stain ◗ Make a *stain* with paint on a paper towel.

stair ◗ Point out one *stair* in an illustration of *stairs*.

stake ◗ On the board, draw a picture of a *stake*. Demonstrate how it is used to mark the boundaries of a piece of land. Show how it is used in growing tomato plants.

stale ◗ Point to a student's packed lunch. Say "This is *fresh*. This was made today. This is not *stale*."

stalemate ◗ Have a puppet name a game she or he would like to play. You name a different one. Continue to disagree about what you should play. Say "We've reached a *stalemate*."

stalk, stalking, stalked ◗ Show a picture of a lion or other predator *stalking* its prey. Lead students in past tense sentences.

stammer, stammering, stammered ◗ Demonstrate a *stammer* and say that people will sometimes *stammer* when they are frightened. Lead students in sentences using *stammering*.

stamp, stamps, stamping ◗ **1.** Show students a postage *stamp*. **2.** Make a *stamping* noise with your feet. Say "I am *stamping* on the floor."

stampede ◗ Have students pretend to be cattle or buffalo. Have them run noisily across the room in a group. Say "Watch out for the *stampede!*"

stand, stands, stood ◗ **1.** *Stand* and then sit. Then *stand* again. Say that you *stood*. **2.** Ask everyone to make a noise. Then say "Stop! Quiet! I can't *stand* it!" —*can't stand*, have a puppet sing poorly and the second puppet complain expressively, "I *can't stand* your singing!" Have one puppet bump into the second repeatedly and have the second puppet complain, "I *can't stand* your bumping into me!" —*stand on two feet*, act out with puppets. Have one puppet say "My mom ties my shoes for me, brushes my teeth for me, and gets me a drink." Have the other puppet say "I tie my own shoes, I brush my own teeth, and I get my own drinks. I *stand on* my own *two feet*." —*standing by someone*, tell a puppet that you want to learn how to ride a bike. Have the puppet say "I will *stand by you.*" Then pantomime learning, perhaps getting angry and frustrated. Your puppet friend helps you. Finally, master riding the bike and say to the puppet, "Thanks for *standing by me.*"

standard ❯ Ask students to demonstrate the *standard* way to add or subtract.

standstill ❯ Ask everyone to walk around the room and then say "Stop, please! Now we are at a *standstill.* Nothing gets done during a *standstill!* Please go back to work."

staple ❯ Have students help you make a list of foods that are common and used regularly. Say "[Beans and tortillas] are *staples.*"

stare, stared ❯ *Stare* at something; have students *stare* at something. Help students to make past tense sentences.

stargazers ❯ Draw birds on one side of the board with *stars* on the other. Have students roll sheets of paper into tubes to make telescopes. Divide students into two groups. Have one group look through their telescopes at the birds, the other at the stars. Say "You are bird-watchers, and you are *stargazers.*"

stars, starry ❯ Draw *stars* on the board. Say that sometimes there are many *stars* in the sky. "Then we have a *starry* night." —*all-star*, have students help you make a list of famous athletes. Say "If there was one team comprised of all these players, it would be an *all-star* team." —*yellow star*, draw such a star on paper and cut it out. Explain that during World War II Jewish people were forced to wear a *yellow star* on their clothing to identify them as being Jewish.

start, started ❯ *Start* writing something on the board. *Start* walking or *start* drawing. Make past tense sentences. Have students pantomime getting into a vehicle and *starting* it.

startled, startlingly ❯ **1.** Have students shout on the count of three. Jump and act very surprised. Say "Oh! You *startled* me!" **2.** Contrast by saying, first in a calm voice and then in an exaggeratedly excited, loud voice, "We're going to do our reading now." Say "The teacher gave the reading assignment in a *startlingly* different manner."

starve, starving ❯ **1.** Explain that when someone is very hungry and does not get food to eat they might *starve.* **2.** If students miss lunch they are very hungry and may say, "We are *starving.*"

state ❯ **1.** Show students the different *states* of the United States. **2.** Show pictures of people in various conditions. Ask students to describe the *state* they are in.

state, statement ❯ *State* something to the class, such as "Today is [Tuesday]." Lead students in making similar *statements.*

stay, stays, staying, stayed ❯ **1.** Have some students stand up together. Have some go away and have some *stay.* **2.** Ask a student to stretch his or her arms wide. Say "*Stay* there for a minute." Say "She is *staying* there" and "She *stayed* there." —*stay behind*, choose two students to *stay behind* while you lead the rest to the front of the classroom.

steady ▶ Hold a cup *steady*, and then hold it *unsteadily*.

steal, stole, stolen ▶ Have a puppet *steal* a pencil from your desk. Tell the class that the puppet *stole* your pencil. Using puppets, have one puppet take something secretly. Have the puppet who had the item *stolen* look for it, saying, "It was *stolen*."

steel ▶ If there are any *steel* structures in the school, point them out. Show pictures of *steel* structures. Show something made out of *steel*, like a door lock or a car frame.

steep ▶ Draw two hills on the board—one very *steep*, the other rather flat. Say that it is hard to walk up the first hill because it is very *steep*. Have students hold up two books to make a *steep* angle and then a less *steep* angle.

steering ▶ Lead the children in dramatizing *steering* a car.

step, steps, stepping ▶ **1.** Demonstrate various kinds of *steps*. Lead students in *stepping*. **2.** Leave the classroom for a moment. *Step* back into it. Say "I *stepped* into the classroom." Have students *step* into the hallway and then *step* into the classroom. —*step out*, have a puppet be a doctor and say that it has to eat his lunch now. Explain, "When the doctor leaves his office, we say he or she *steps out*." —*step up*, pantomime by *stepping* toward someone or something.

step-by-step ▶ Describe a simple task for students, such as making a sandwich, and list the steps on the board, numbered 1, 2, 3, and so on. Say "This is the *step-by-step* procedure I follow for making a sandwich."

stepfamilies ▶ Explain that when people remarry after a divorce or death, new families are created called *stepfamilies*." People in these new families are called *stepmother*, *stepbrother*, and so on.

stick ▶ *Stick* your hand in a pocket or desk drawer. Have students do the same. *Stick* a straw into a pocket or desk drawer, leaving some portion of it *sticking out*. —*stick out*, point out how the nose and ears *stick out* from the face, but the mouth doesn't. Arms and legs *stick out*. Have students find things around the room that *stick out*. —*stick up for*, have one puppet criticize you. Have the other *stick up for* you. —*stick with*, see *persisted*. Have a student count paper clips and *stick with* the job as another student tries to be distracting.

sticklike ▶ Show a picture of a praying mantis and a *stick*. Tell students, "The praying mantis looks like a stick; it is *sticklike*."

sticky ▶ Show students *sticky* things like glue and tape.

stiff ▶ Contrast a rubber eraser with a pencil. Say that the eraser is not *stiff*, but the pencil is *stiff*.

still ▶ Pantomime sentences, such as, "I dropped a penny, but I *still* have a nickel." Explain that *still* means "even now." Draw a time line on the board. Start the time line at 12 noon, and explain that students start eating lunch at noon. They are *still* eating at 12:10, *still* eating at 12:15, and then by _____, they start playing. Repeat with other examples.

stinky ▶ Have a puppet hold its nose, point into the wastebasket, and claim that it is *stinky*.

stir, stirring, stirs ◆ **1.** Pantomime spooning sugar into a mug and mixing it in. Say "This is how I *stir* my coffee." Have students imitate. Pantomime *stirring* batter in a bowl. **2.** Make a creature out of your hand, or use a small stuffed animal and make it move and then be still. Say "Did you see the creature *stir?*" Pretend to miss seeing it move each time. Ask, "When does it *stir?*" Prompt students to say "It *stirs* when you are not looking." —*stirring up*, poke a puppet until it becomes angry. Give example sentences using *stirring up*.

stitch, stitches ◆ **1.** Show some *stitches* on shoes. **2.** *Stitch* some fabric together or show a picture of someone *stitching* fabric.

stock ◆ Place items, such as paper clips, tape, folders, and scissors, on a shelf. Say "This is our *stock* for the school year."

stoke, stoked ◆ Show a picture of a fire on the board. Draw a woodpile next to it. Then tell students "When I put more wood on the fire, I *stoke* the fire." Erase some of the wood from your woodpile and draw a little more wood in your fire.

stomp, stomping, stomped ◆ *Stomp* your feet. Have students imitate. Lead students in *stomping* off in anger, and then walking pleasantly. Help with past tense sentences.

stoop, stooping, stooped ◆ *Stoop* down for students and lead them in *stooping*.

stop, stops, stopping, stopped, stoppable ◆ **1.** Move a toy truck forward, then hold up your hand to signal *Stop!* Explain that you *stopped* the truck; that the truck is *stopping*; and that the truck *stops*. **2.** Ask for two student volunteers to be wind-up toys. Have one move around the classroom quickly and evasively; the other in a slower, more predictable pattern. Try unsuccessfully to catch the fast student; then succeed in catching the slower student. Say "I couldn't catch [Francesca]; she was too fast for me. I did catch [Mateo]; he was slower and *stoppable*."

storage ◆ Have students help you put books and supplies away in a closet. Say "Let's put these things in *storage*."

store, stores, storing, stored ◆ **1.** Show pictures of *stores*. Find out what is each student's favorite *store*. **2.** Say to a student, "Will you bring me the chalk? I *stored* it over there." Put some supplies away and explain that you are *storing* them. —*chain stores*, have students help you make two lists of shops: some that can be found in multiple locations, others that are unique. Say "There are lots of these *stores*; they are called *chain stores*. There is only one of each of these other *stores*." —*dime store*, on the board, draw a large building. Draw a time line to some previous date, such as 1950. Say "This kind of *store* used to be called a *dime store*."

storm ◆ Show pictures of a *storm*.

story, stories ◆ **1.** Draw a building with five *stories* of windows. Lead students in sentences using *story* and *stories*. **2.** Name different *stories* students have read.

storyteller ‣ Have a puppet tell a short story. Tell students a short story. Tell the students that the puppet is a *storyteller*.

stout ‣ Show pictures of *stout* objects or people; contrast with *thin* objects or people.

straight ‣ 1. Draw a *straight* line. Contrast with a *crooked* one. Demonstrate an eraser or can rolling *straight* toward a puppet. Contrast rolling *straight* toward with rolling at an *angle*. 2. Have students hold out their arms *straight* and then hold them in a *bent* fashion.

straighten ‣ —*straighten up*, pantomime *straightening up* your desk. Have students *straighten up* their desks.

strain, straining, strained ‣ Have a puppet *strain* to reach a book. Have students *strain* to reach something above their heads. Pantomime *straining* while carrying heavy books.

strands, stranded ‣ 1. Show *strands* of your hair. 2. On the board, draw a bus route. Show the school and a house far away. Draw a puppet standing next to the school. Using a toy bus, show the bus leaving the puppet *stranded*.

strange, stranger, strangers ‣ 1. Draw a circle on the board. Then draw a picture of a slightly abnormal circle; tell students that it is different or *strange*. Show other examples of *strange* and normal things. 2. Demonstrate with a puppet. Look at it quizzically and say "I never saw this guy before. He is a *stranger* to me." Show a picture of a child with its family and friends. Point out that people in the classroom are friends. People walking by outside (if they are not known to students) are *strangers*.

straps ‣ Ask a student to show the class his or her backpack. Point out the *straps*.

stray, straying, strayed ‣ 1. Stand with students at one side of the classroom. Have everyone walk across the room while you wander off in another direction. Say "This is how I *stray* from the group." 2. Take students on a walk with the puppet, perhaps down the hall. Have the puppet keep *straying* from them.

streak ‣ On the board, put the puppet's good grades in a line. Put one bad grade at the end of the line. Point out the end of the student's *streak* of good grades.

stream ‣ Draw or show a picture of a *stream*.

strength ‣ 1. Ask a student to volunteer to hold some heavy books for you. As you pile them into the student's arms, say "Boy, are you strong! You must have great *strength* to carry all those heavy books." 2. Have a puppet force itself to stay away from a piece of candy. Tell the class that the puppet has a lot of will power or *strength* to stay away from the candy.

stretch, stretches, stretching, stretched ‣ 1. Demonstrate *stretching* your arms out wide, up high, and down low. With each *stretch*, repeat the word and lead the children in *stretching*. Lead them in past tense sentences. 2. Show students illustrations of land that *stretches*, such as a prairie or a tundra.

strew, strewn ‣ *Strew* items across the top of a table or your desk. Lead students in past tense sentences.

strict ◈ Give example sentences using *strict*. Write a sentence on the board. Sternly ask a puppet to copy the sentence exactly as you have written it. Have the puppet copy it with variations. With a harsh demeanor, demand that the puppet follow your directions precisely. Say "The teacher was very *strict*."

stride, strode ◈ *Stride* across the room with long steps. Have students *stride* around in a circle. Lead in past tense sentences.

strike, striking, struck, stricken ◈ **1.** Have one puppet *strike* his desk. Tell the class that one puppet is *striking* his desk. **2.** Show how the hands of a clock move to the hour. When it gets to the hour, say "Bong." Repeat for several different hours. Each time say "The clock *struck* one," "The clock *struck* two," and so on.—*strike zone*, use a piece of paper to make a home plate. Have one student be the batter, another student be the umpire, and a third student be the pitcher. Show students the *strike zone*. Explain that if the batter does not hit the ball when it crosses the home plate in the area of the *strike zone*, the umpire will call, "*Strike* one," "*Strike* two," and "*Strike* three." Have students demonstrate. —*strikes a pose*, check that students understand the individual words in the phrase. Draw or show a picture of a camera. Pretend that you are a photographer and students are models. Invite them to assume various positions for the camera. Pantomime photographing students and say "This is how a model *strikes a pose*." **3.** Read something funny and pantomime being *stricken* with laughter.

string, strung ◈ *String* pieces of paper with needle and thread. Say how many pieces you have *strung*.

strip, strips, stripped ◈ **1.** *Strip* a bulletin board of all its contents. Tell the class that you have *stripped* it. Take off the jacket of a book. Say that you have *stripped* the cover off the book. **2.** Use scissors to cut a sheet of paper into *strips*.

striped ◈ Show pictures of *striped*, solid, and patterned shirts.

stroke ◈ *Stroke* a stuffed animal.

strong, stronger, strongest ◈ **1.** Act *strong* and able to lift something easily, and then act *weak* and unable to lift it. Have students feel each other's muscles to see how *strong* they are. **2.** Blow hard on a paper to demonstrate a *strong* wind; then, in contrast, blow *softly* to demonstrate a light wind. **3.** Demonstrate *stronger* and *strongest* by being able to lift increasingly heavy things. **4.** Hand one student a heavy book; hand a second student two heavy books. Have both students lift their books in the air. Say "[Ysabel] is *strong*; she can lift one heavy book. [Teresa] is *stronger* than [Ysabel]; she can lift two heavy books." **5.** Pantomime lifting weights. Draw some free weights on the board. After your mini-workout say "I feel *stronger* now. Feel my muscles."

strumming ◈ Draw or show a picture of a guitar. Pantomime *strumming* a guitar.

stubborn ◈ Pantomime by having a puppet try to get you to do something. Stand firmly, cross your arms, assume a hard expression, and refuse to cooperate. Say "I don't want to do it. I am being *stubborn*."

stubby ◈ Show a long piece of chalk and a *stubby* piece.

stubs, stubbing ❖ Pantomime *stubbing* your toe.

stuck ❖ Demonstrate with a toy truck by having it drive into some "mud" and get *stuck*. Be certain students understand *mud* before doing the demonstration. Glue two pieces of paper together and show that they are *stuck*.

student ❖ Point to a *student* and say "I am the teacher and you are a *student*. —*student-run*, make a list of extracurricular activities at your school and of those typical of a high school. Say "At this school, the after-school activities are supervised by teachers and parents. In high school, many after-school activities are *student-run*."

study, studies, studying, studied ❖ **1.** Write three numbers on the board. Ask students to *study* the numbers. Erase the board. Ask what the smallest number was. Say "You *studied* hard." Show pictures of students or other people *studying*. Pantomime *studying* a book. **2.** Show students the different books that they use for math, social studies, and science. Explain that these are their *studies*.

stuff, stuffing, stuffed ❖ **1.** Hold up a *stuffed* bear and say "The material inside the [bear] is called its *stuffing*. The [bear] is *stuffed*." **2.** *Stuff* things into a bag or box. Have students pantomime *stuffing* things into their desks. Lead students in past tense sentences.

stumble, stumbling, stumbled ❖ **1.** Walk along and pretend to *stumble*. **2.** Read a sentence fluently. Say "That was easy; I read the sentence smoothly." Read the sentence but *stumble* over your words. Say "I *stumbled* when I read that sentence."

stun, stunned ❖ Have a puppet run into something. Have it act *stunned*. Say "[Shaggy] was *stunned* by that!"

stung ❖ Show a picture of a bee or some other *stinging* insect. Ask if students have ever gotten *stung* by a bee.

stunt ❖ Have a puppet perform a *stunt*.

stupendous ❖ See *colossal*.

stupid ❖ Ask students if they know of any *stupid* TV shows. Have them explain why they believe they are *stupid*.

sturdy ❖ Compare something soft, such as an eraser, with something *sturdy*, such as a piece of wood.

style ❖ Write consonants in different *styles*. Explain that they are the same letters written in different *styles*. Ask students which *style* they like best.

submit, submissive ❖ **1.** Have each student write a sentence on a sheet of paper. Say "Please *submit* your sentence to me." **2.** Act out with two toy animals; have one be *aggressive* and the other be *submissive*. Let students take turns making one animal be *aggressive* while the other is *submissive*.

substitute ❖ Give each student a picture to color that has the color printed in each section. Have them *substitute* for some of the colors.

subtitles ➤ Ask a student to write a simple sentence in his or her first language. Then ask the student to translate it. Write the translation below. Say "These are *subtitles* in English."

subtle ➤ Have a puppet ask you where something is. Use a *subtle* indication by just nodding your head. Contrast with pointing at it with your finger.

subtraction ➤ Demonstrate a *subtraction* problem on the board. Have students recite simple *subtraction* facts.

succeed, succeeding, success, successful, successfully ➤ **1.** Have a puppet *succeed* in climbing a stack of books. Contrast with the puppet not *succeeding*. Lead students in sentences: "He did *succeed*" and "He did not *succeed*." **2.** Once students understand *succeed*, have a puppet climb a stack of books. When it has *succeeded*, have it tell the class that it is a *success*. Describe different times when students have been *successful* and comment, "You are a *success* at tying your shoes" or "You are a *success* at brushing your hair." Give students something they already know how to do. For each action they do correctly, say "That was a *success*." **3.** Once students understand *succeed* and *success*, have a puppet climb a stack of books. Then have it talk about how it is a *successful* book climber. **4.** Pick up a book *successfully*, then attempt to pick up the book *unsuccessfully*.

successor ➤ Show a puppet or other toy character being a king. Have the king die and his *successor* become the new king.

such ➤ Admire things in the room, perhaps student drawings or writings posted around the room. Say "*Such* beautiful work!" —*such a*, admire student writings or drawings posted on the walls, exclaiming, "*Such a* beautiful drawing!" or "*Such a* lovely piece of handwriting!" You can also say "*Such* a beautiful day!" or "*Such* a rainy day!"

suck, sucking ➤ Show a picture of a baby *sucking* on a bottle.

sudden, suddenly ➤ **1.** Lead students in a *sudden* motion and then a *slow* motion. Alternate. **2.** Do something *suddenly*, such as raise your arm or turn around. Have students do something *suddenly* and then do something *slowly*. *Suddenly* jump or raise your arm. Have students do something *suddenly*, then do something *slowly*.

sue ➤ Have one puppet tell another one to give back its personal belongings. Have the second puppet refuse. Have the first puppet go to a lawyer (explain as needed) and *sue* to get his belongings back.

suffocating ➤ Put a coat or a sweater over your face and make panicked noises. Remove the clothing and say "I was *suffocating* under there. I couldn't breathe."

suggest, suggested, suggestion ➤ **1.** Have one puppet get its hand stuck between two books. In an expressive tone of voice, another puppet *suggests*, "You could pull real hard" or "You could ask someone to help." Explain that the second puppet is *suggesting*. **2.** Ask the class to *suggest* what they would like to do after lunch. Call on a student. After he or she has answered, tell the class, "_____ *suggested* that we [read]. That is a good *suggestion*." Repeat with other students.

suitable ❯ Show students pencils that are *suitable* for writing, chalk *suitable* for the board, or books *suitable* for reading. Lead them in sentences.

sullenly ❯ Have two students play a game of tic-tac-toe at the board. Have the loser pretend to sulk and act bitter and hurt. Say "He is responding *sullenly* to his loss."

sum ❯ Show students the *sum* of 2 + 2.

summit ❯ Show a picture of a mountain and point to the *summit*.

sun ❯ —*The sun is up*, draw the *sun* rising above the horizon on the board.

sunbeam ❯ Draw a *beam* of light coming from the *sun*. Ask students to draw a sun with *sunbeams*.

sunburn ❯ On the board draw a figure wearing a bathing suit. Draw a big *sun* beaming down on the figure. Color the figure's skin with pink chalk. Lead students in sentences using *sunburn*.

sunlight ❯ Take students outside. Show and name the *sun* and *sunlight*. Or, show pictures of *sunlight*.

super ❯ Describe as *super* some recent, wonderful experience that the class has had. Find out if there's some *super* experience that students have had outside of class, perhaps a birthday party, field trip, or holiday celebration.

superhero ❯ Name some superheroes, such as Superman or Batman. Have students name other *superheroes*.

superior, superiority ❯ **1.** Write a *superior* letter on the board, and contrast with a poorly written letter. Have students write a *superior* letter on a piece of paper. **2.** See *staff*. As you perform some of the pantomimes, assume an air of *superiority* and contrast with an air of *humility*.

supernatural ❯ Bring pictures of things from nature. Explain that things outside of nature are *supernatural*. Have students make a list of *supernatural* things, such as ghosts or spirits.

superstition, superstitious ❯ **1.** Say "Some people believe in *superstition* and do *superstitious* things for good luck. It is a *superstition* to believe that a black cat brings you bad luck." Ask for more examples. **2.** Use examples from mythology, such as Zeus throwing lightning bolts. Give example sentences.

supervising, supervision ❯ Set up a scene where you run a restaurant and students are the workers. Assign them various tasks and give them directions as they pantomime doing their work. Say "I am the boss; you work for me. I am telling you what to do and how to do it. I am *supervising* you." Have a puppet *supervise* a child picking out a book from the classroom shelves.

supper ❯ Show puppets having *supper*.

supply, supplier ❯ **1.** Set up an imaginary lemonade stand. Draw or point to a pitcher of lemonade. Say "This is the lemonade we have for sale today. This is our *supply* of lemonade." **2.** Draw a large truck on the board; write "Super Stickers" on the side of the truck. Say "I buy my stickers from a company called 'Super Stickers'; 'Super Stickers' is my sticker *supplier*."

supportive ◆ Ask a student to write a sentence on the board. Be very helpful and encouraging as he or she works. Say "This is how to be *supportive* of somebody's efforts." Ask students ways they can be *supportive* of others.

suppose ◆ Look like you are thinking about something and say with uncertainty, "I *suppose* I can do all this work" or "I *suppose* it will be fun." Ask expressively while looking up, "Do you *suppose* it will rain?" or "Do you *suppose* it will be sunny?"

suppressed ◆ Ask a student to tell a joke, or have a puppet do it. Clap your hand over your mouth and pantomime shaking with silent laughter. Say "I didn't want to laugh out loud. I kept my laugh in; I *suppressed* my laugh."

surface ◆ Have students run their hands over different *surfaces*, such as their desks, books, and chairs.

surge, surging ◆ Show students pictures of an ocean with waves that are *surging* toward the beach.

surly ◆ Have the puppet ask you for some help with something and answer him in a *surly* way.

surprise, surprised, surprises, surprisingly ◆ **1.** Hide something in your hand and say that you have a *surprise*; get students to guess what it might be. After a few guesses, show students what the surprise is, perhaps a sticker. **2.** Suddenly produce an object from behind your back and look *surprised*. **3.** Draw three children on the board, one considerably taller than the other two. Say "Each of these children is five years old, but this one is *surprisingly* tall for [his] age."

surrender, surrendered ◆ Challenge a student to an arm wrestling match. After a moment, throw up your hands and say "I *surrender*."

surround, surrounding, surroundings, surrounded ◆ **1.** Have paper clips *surround* a pencil. Repeat with other small objects. Explain that the paper clips are *surrounding* the pencil. Form a circle with students. Have two stand inside the circle. Explain that they are *surrounded* by the others. Place a toy house inside a wall built of blocks. Say "There is a wall *surrounding* this house." **2.** Give examples of various animals and their habitats. Say "Different animals live in different *surroundings:* fish live in water, birds live in trees, and lizards live in the desert."

survive ◆ Explain that *survive* means "to live." Ask which animals can *survive* in cities. Ask what people need to *survive*. Show a picture of a dead plant or draw one on the board. Explain that the plant died; it did not *survive* because no one watered it.

suspicious ◆ Ask a puppet a question and have the puppet give an obviously wrong answer. Act *suspicious* and tell students that you don't believe the puppet.

swallows, swallowing ◆ **1.** Lead students in *swallowing* a piece of imaginary food. **2.** Explain that this means to stop crying and say "[Clara] is *swallowing* her tears."

swampy ❖ Show a picture of a *swamp* and point out those details that make it *swampy*.

swap, swapping, swapped ❖ Divide students into pairs. Have each pair exchange something, such as pencils. Say "You are *swapping* [pencils] with one another." Have students *swap* one object for another. "You *swapped* [pencils] for [markers]."

swarming ❖ On the board, draw a hive with bees *swarming* out of it. Or, show a picture of bees *swarming*.

swatted ❖ Pantomime *swatting* at a fly. Lead students in past tense sentences.

sway, swaying, sways, swayed ❖ **1.** Lead students in *swaying* their bodies. Demonstrate *swaying* back and forth. Ask the class to *sway* together. Move back and forth in your chair. Have students *sway* in their seats. **2.** Have a puppet *sway* you to buy a new car and say "The facts *swayed* me to buy a new car."

swear ❖ *Swear* with great sincerity to something that you have done or will do. Say "I *swear* I will clean the kitchen."

sweat ❖ Draw a picture of a person with *sweat* on his or her brow or show such a picture. Ask if students have ever run fast and become *sweaty*.

sweep, sweeping, swept ❖ Demonstrate *sweeping*. Say that you *swept*. Start and stop students in pantomimes of *sweeping*, alternating *sweep* and *swept*.

sweet ❖ **1.** Show students pictures of *sweet* fruits, perhaps melons, bing cherries, or strawberries. Contrast with pictures of *sour* fruits like lemons and limes. **2.** Show or draw pictures of things that are *sweet* like cookies, cakes, or honey.

swell ❖ Inflate some balloons. Show that they *swell*.

sweltering ❖ Draw a large sun on the board. Pantomime feeling very hot by fanning yourself and loosening your collar. Say "It is hot in here. I'm *sweltering!*" Have students imitate.

swift, swiftly ❖ **1.** Ask a few simple questions and say "That was a *swift* answer!" to the first person with an answer. **2.** Walk *swiftly*. Contrast with walking *slowly*.

swim, swam, swimming ❖ Show a picture of a duck *swimming* in water. Tell them that the duck is *swimming*. Say that you *swam* last summer. Ask who else *swam* last summer. Show students pictures of children *swimming*. Lead them in a pantomime of *swimming*. Use the word *swam* in past tense sentences about *swimming*. —*swam off*, explain that this means "*swam* away." Lead students in pantomiming *swimming off*.

swindler ❖ Have the puppet offer to hold a dollar for you. When you give the puppet the dollar, make it run away with it. Say with outrage, "Hey! It took my dollar. What a *swindler!*"

swing, swinging ❖ Tie an object to a string and make it *swing*. Say "The pencil is *swinging*."

swirl, swirling, swirled ❖ **1.** Draw a *swirl* on the board. It can be any figure that looks like a coil, curl, or spiral. **2.** *Swirl* water, sand, or small items such as paper clips in a container. **3.** Lead students in turning around and around as if they were being *swirled*.

switch, switched ❖ Have students *switch* seats, *switch* jackets, or *switch* pencils. Draw some train tracks on a board with a train and show students how a train can *switch* tracks. Lead the class in past tense sentences.

swollen ❖ Draw a normal-looking thumb and a *swollen* thumb on the board.

swoony ❖ Hum a slow song and dance in a *swoony* way. Show pictures of young people *swooning* over rock stars at a concert.

swoop, swooping, swooped ❖ Pretend to be a bird and *swoop* down. Have students *swoop*. Lead students in pantomiming their hands *swooping* down out of the sky like a plane.

syllable, syllables ❖ Write one-, two-, three-, and four-*syllable* words on the board. Draw vertical lines between the *syllables*. Say "I am breaking these words into *syllables*." Point at the *syllables* and pronounce them.

symbol, symbols ❖ Show a United States flag. Say that the flag is a *symbol* of the country. Show other types of *symbols* such as a crosswalk *symbol*, a No Smoking *symbol*, or a rest room *symbol*.

sympathy, sympathetic ❖ Give *sympathy* to a puppet that is grieving over a broken toy.

syncopated ❖ Sing a song that everyone knows and have everyone tap their hands to the beat. Sing it again while you stress one or more beats usually not accented. Say "This way the beat is *syncopated*."

tablet ❖ Explain that *tablets* are something to write on, and that they used to be made of wood, clay, or stone. Show a pad of writing paper. Say that it is a *tablet* of paper.

tackle, tackled ❖ **1.** Write a difficult arithmetic problem on the board. Say "Who would like to try and solve this problem? Who is brave enough to *tackle* it?" **2.** Have one puppet *tackle* another. **3.** Show a picture of a football player *tackling* another player.

tag ❖ Play a game of *tag* with students.

take, took ❖ **1.** Have students *take* a trip around the classroom. Have students *take* a trip to the hallway and back. **2.** Have a puppet tease you. Laugh and say "I can *take* it." **3.** Have students *take* toys out of a cupboard by pointing to the toy you want them to *take* out and say "*Take* this toy." **4.** Have two students *take* a different number of pencils from a box. Say "The first student *took* three pencils. The second student *took* two pencils." Have a puppet *take* something from you; tell the class that it *took* it. **5.** Set up a scene where you and students are *taking* a class in photography or some other activity. Lead students in past tense sentences. —*take a stand*, using puppets, put on a skit about a particular issue that is important to your class, perhaps recess or art. Have one puppet *take a stand* for a longer recess and the another be against it. —*take advantage*, have a puppet buy something from you. Charge too much money. Tell the class, "I *took advantage* of the puppet." Give example sentences using *take advantage*.

—*take apart*, use a puzzle. Fit a few pieces together, then *take apart* the pieces. —*take care of*, using a stuffed toy, pantomime feeding, bathing, and petting it. Tell students that you *take care of it*. —*take for granted*, make a list of the things you expect students to do, such as come to class, do their homework, and try their best. Say "I assume you know you should do these things without being asked. I *take for granted* that you will." Ask students what they *take for granted* about you. —*taking place, took place*, divide the class into two groups, each with a separate task. Explain to each group individually, "While you are [putting books on the shelves], something else is *taking place* with [Group 2]." —*taking time*, check that students understand the word *time*. Practice the phrase *taking time* by noting on a watch how long it *takes* to do such things as have everyone stand up, put something away in their desks, and so on. —*took a long time*, see *reached*. Ask students about things that have waited for that have *taken a long time* in coming.

tale, tales ◆ **1.** Explain that a *tale* is another name for a story. See *story*. **2.** Tell students a familiar fairy *tale*, such as "Jack and the Giant Beanstalk." Say "This is a made-up story about a giant. It is an example of a fairy *tale*."

talent ◆ Have students name celebrities. Say for example, "Yes, [John Travolta] is a very good actor. He has a great *talent* as an actor."

talk, talking, talked ◆ Ask individual students to *talk* to each other by pointing to two students and saying, "*Talk* to her" and "*Talk* to him." Demonstrate with a puppet if needed. Lead students in *talking*. Invite students to *talk* to each other and tell them that they are *talking*. —*talk things over*, have two puppets argue. Then have them *talk things over* and resolve their problem. —*talked into*, see *persuasion*. Lead students in sentences using *talked into*.

tall, taller, tallest ◆ **1.** Contrast objects that are *tall* and *short*. Draw a person on the board who is *short* and one who is *tall*. Show students things that are *short* and contrast with things that are *tall*. Have students find *tall* things in the classroom. **2.** Ask two students to stand back-to-back, then ask the class to decide who is *taller*. **3.** Build block towers—one *tall*, the next *taller*, and the third *tallest*.

tally up ◆ Hand out pennies to students and set up an imaginary lemonade stand. Have students buy cups of lemonade. Count your pennies. Say "Let's count how much money we earned today. Let's *tally up* our earnings."

tame ◆ **1.** Pantomime with a toy animal. Have it act wild and dangerous and then *tame* it. Let students *tame* the toy animal as well. **2.** Show pictures of wild horses and "bronco busting." Lead students in sentences using *tame*.

tangent ◆ Touch a pencil to a globe at a single point. Say "The pencil is at a *tangent* to the globe."

tangle, tangling, tangled ◆ Run a comb easily through one doll's hair. Say "That was easy; her hair is smooth." Struggle to get a comb through another doll's hair. Say "That was hard; her hair is *tangled*." *Tangle* several pieces of string.

tap, tapping, tapped ◆ Lead students in *tapping* their desks with their hands and *tapping* the floor with their feet. Lead students in past tense sentences.

tape, tapes, taping, taped ◆ *Tape* a piece of paper to a bulletin board and tell students that you are *taping* it. Explain that you *taped* it.

target, targeted ◆ **1.** Draw a *target* on the board. Then have students make balls out of crumpled sheets of paper and have them throw their balls at it. **2.** Draw two circles on the board. Label one "A" and the other "B." Have certain students throw wadded paper at the *targeted* circle.

task ◆ Assign students various *tasks* to perform in the classroom, such as emptying the pencil sharpener, cleaning the board, and cleaning the erasers. —*no easy task*, check understanding of individual words. Write an arithmetic equation on the board. Pantomime struggling to solve it. When you finally write the answer, say "Whew! That was hard. Solving that equation was *no easy task!*"

taste, tastes, tasty ◆ **1.** Have students *taste* some spices if available. If not, lead students in pantomiming *tasting* various delicious foods. Eat something and tell students it *tastes* good. Have them pantomime *tasting* their lunches. **2.** Pantomime eating something delicious. Say "Fried chicken is very *tasty*." Ask students to name *tasty* foods.

tattered ◆ Show a picture of a *tattered* shirt or blanket. Or, show an actual one if you have it.

tattletale ◆ Have one puppet take a toy away from a second puppet. Have the second puppet run up to you and say in a whiny tone, "Mrs. Jones! [Turtle] took my toy away from me!" Explain that the second puppet is a *tattletale*.

taut ◆ Tie a piece of string to a chair or table leg and pull it *taut*. Have students pull the string *taut*.

tax, taxes, taxation ◆ **1.** Make a one dollar price tag and stick it on an item on your desk. Write an equation on the board to calculate the sales *tax*. Put the *tax* money in a jar labeled *state* or *city government*. **2.** Lead students in sentences using *taxation*.

tea ◆ —*tea for two*, pantomime with a puppet having *tea for two*.

teach, taught ◆ *Teach* students a new word, and then say that you *taught* them. Mention things that you have *taught* students, and that they have learned.

team ◆ Show illustrations of *teams* for sports that students are familiar with. Divide the class into two *teams* for a spelling bee.

teamwork ◆ Ask students to work as a group to build something with blocks while you build something by yourself. Say "I built a tower all by myself. You worked together as a *team*. That was good *teamwork*." Ask three children to move something heavy like a desk. Say "That's great *teamwork*."

tear, tearing, tore, torn ◆ **1.** *Tear* a piece of paper. Say that you are *tearing* it, and that it is *torn*. Also explain that you *tore* it. **2.** Show a puppet *tearing* along (running quickly).

tease ◆ Have one puppet *tease* another. Let the second one say "Stop *teasing* me."

technology ❯ Explain simply as the things made by humans.

tedious ❯ Ask students to help you pick up all the staples stuck in the carpet. After a few moments, express that you are bored and ask if they are also bored. Tell students this is a *tedious* task. Demonstrate a repetitive task, such as collating a handout. Say "I am sorting papers. It is a boring task. It is *tedious*, but it must be done." Have a puppet count paper clips. Say "That is a *tedious* job."

teenagers ❯ Write the numerals 13-19 on the board. Then tell students, "Starting at 13, all the way through 19, you will be a *teenager*. Ask who has a brother or sister who is a *teenager*. Then ask the ages of the *teenagers*.

teeth ❯ Show students your *teeth*. Have students find their *teeth*.

tele- ❯ Write *tele-* on the board. Explain that it is from the Latin language. Review Latin as needed. Explain that it means "at a distance." Review *distance* as needed.

telegraph ❯ See *tele-* and *-graph*. Show a *telegraph* system (*telegraph* key, poles, and wire) from the period. Show the Morse code book and explain that for each letter of the alphabet, there is a different set of beeps. Have two students ready to send and receive messages. Have one student send the beeps for the letter *A* to the other student. He or she should pantomime pushing on the *telegraph* key as he or she makes the sounds verbally. Have the student at the receiving end write the letter *A* when he or she receives it. Have him or her show the *telegram*.

tell, telling, told ❯ Explain that *tell* means "say." Examples are to *tell* a story, riddle, or secret. *Tell* students what you would like for lunch. Then say "I am *telling* you what I would like for lunch." Ask a puppet to *tell* students to stand up. Explain that the puppet *told* them to stand up. Repeat with a variety of examples. —*told out*, explain that *told* is like the word *tell*. Have a puppet *tell* another puppet something. Then explain that the puppet *told* it. Explain that *told out* means "*told* until the end."

tell a fib ❯ *Tell an* obvious *lie* such as, "I was not in school yesterday." Explain that this was *a fib*. Say "I *told a fib*. I was in school yesterday."

temper ❯ Pantomime with puppets. Ask one to do something and have it respond angrily. Say "[Rabbit] has a terrible *temper*." Have the other respond agreeably. Say "[Turtle] has a sweet *temper*."

temperatures ❯ Have students give examples of hot things and cold things. Give example sentences using *temperatures*.

temple ❯ Show pictures of different types of *temples*, such as Greek, Mayan, Aztec, and so on.

tempting ❯ Bring some chocolates or some other luscious sweet. Place them in front of you. Pantomime reaching for them, but not getting any. Go back to work. Do this several times. Say "Those are very *tempting*."

tend, tending, tended ❯ Have a puppet *tend* his garden, cows, and chickens. Lead students in similar pantomimes. Have a puppet *tend* to some flowers or a baby.

tender, tenderly ❯ Touch a doll *tenderly* and lead students in touching a doll *tenderly*.

tense ❯ Contrast by demonstrating a very relaxed posture with a tight, nervous posture. Say "I was feeling very *calm* and relaxed, but now I am *tense*."

tension ❯ Pantomime chewing your nails while holding a math test. Tell students about something that makes you nervous. For example, pantomime anxiety, and say "I am feeling nervous about the speech I have to make tonight. I am feeling a lot of *tension*."

ten-year-old ❯ Show students a calendar and explain that it covers one year. Ask students how old they are. Say of each student, "[Maria] is an eleven-year-old girl; [Carlos] is a *ten-year-old* boy; and [John] is also a *ten-year-old* boy."

terrapins ❯ Show pictures and explain that these are large turtles that live in water.

terrible ❯ **1.** Compare *terrible* things to *wonderful* things. "It is *terrible* if your pet gets sick; it is *wonderful* when you get a new puppy." **2.** Show pictures of *terrible* things that inspire fear, such as a tornado. Lead students in making *terrible* faces.

terrified ❯ Draw a big snake on the board. Walk by it, scream, and pantomime extreme fear when you see it. Say "When I saw that big snake, I was *terrified!*"

territory ❯ On a map, show what a *territory* is. Explain that it is the land owned by an individual, group, or nation. —*enemy territory*, refer students to the two opposing countries in your war scene with the toy soldiers.

testing ❯ Ask students to spell common words. Say "I am *testing* you."

texture, textures ❯ Have students feel various *textures*, such as shoe leather, clothing, paper, and desktops. Have them describe the different *textures* with their eyes closed.

than ❯ Hold up two objects and say "This one is bigger *than* this one" or "This one is whiter *than* this one."

thank ❯ Ask a student to bring you something and then *thank* him or her. Repeat with other students. Have one puppet give something to another puppet and get *thanked*.

thankful ❯ Give something to a puppet. Have the puppet say *thank you* and display his gratitude. Tell the class, "He is *thankful*." Repeat the demonstration with students.

that ❯ Point to a picture in a story and say "*That* is a dog." Show students an object nearby and one further away. Then, contrast meanings by pointing and saying, "This object is here and *that* object is there." Lead students in sentences like "This is a pencil *that* writes," " This is a hand *that* draws," and "These are eyes *that* read." —*That's it*, have two puppets dramatize this expression. Have one puppet say rhymes like *piggle, wiggle, figgle*. The other doesn't understand until he says, "*That's it!* You are making rhymes!"

thaw ❯ Show pictures of snow and the sun. Explain that when spring comes, the sun melts the snow and *thaws* the ground.

the ❖ Explain that when we say *the* name of a thing, we often put *the* in front of it. Help students make sentences such as, "I see *the* board" or "Here is *the* book." Point to various things in *the* room and say "*The* desk" or "*The* chair." Have students repeat after you. Say a sentence, such as "See *the* book." Then say *the* sentence without *the:* "See book." Tell students that *the* helps us say things *the* right way. Lead students in several correct and incorrect examples. Have them tell you which way was right.

their ❖ Divide students into two groups. Give everyone in one group a piece of white paper, and everyone in the other group a piece of colored paper. Say to the first group, "Your paper is white. Point to the second group and say "*Their* paper is colored." Repeat with the second group.

them ❖ Separate students into two groups. Point to the group you are in and say "Us." Point to the group farther away and say "*Them.*" Have something in your hands and give it to the other group, saying "I am giving this to *them.*" Have students repeat this, and make similar sentences.

theme ❖ Show a short piece of writing on a subject and explain that it is a *theme.*

themselves ❖ Divide the class into two groups. Hold up an object for one group to see. Then say to the other group, "They saw it for *themselves.*" Alternate and repeat. —*all by themselves*, show a group of paper clips in a pile followed by two *all by themselves*. Repeat with other objects.

then ❖ Explain that *then* means "next" or "after." Line students up, one after the other, and each time you add someone to the line, say "*Then* Sonya, *then* Anita, *then* Xavier," and so on. Give examples of doing a series of activities, for example, "We learn and *then* we have recess" or "We go to school and *then* we go home." Give examples, such as "If I can't eat, *then* I'll drink" or "If I can't watch TV, *then* I'll read a book."

theories ❖ Pretend to be a scientist and invent a *theory*. Say "Scientists have many *theories.*" Ask students to tell you *theories* for various phenomena.

theorizing ❖ Engage students in a discussion of how the solar system came about. Say "You are doing a good job *theorizing* about the origin of the solar system."

therapy ❖ Show pictures of a physical *therapist* working on a person's body. Explain that the physical *therapist* is giving *therapy* to the injured person and that the *therapy* will help the injury to heal.

there ❖ **1.** Help students make sentences, such as "*There* is dirt in my shoe" or "*There* are clothes in my drawer." Explain that *there* helps make sentences; it has little meaning. **2.** Lead students in making sentences to describe *there*, such as "*There* is the door." Contrast with *here*. Point to where you are on the floor and say "*Here* I am." Point to something across the room and say "*There* is the _____." Repeat with different objects. Show a map and say "*Here* is [our city], *there* is [our state]." While pointing to a map, lead students in sentences, such as "I would like to go *there*" or "I will go *there* one day." —*there's*, see *didn't*.

therefore ❖ Draw a school bus on the board. Have students pretend to drive away in it as you run to catch it. Say "I missed the bus and will have to walk to school; *therefore*, I will be late."

these •▸ Contrast *these* and *those*. Point to things on your desk and say "*These* are my things." Point to things on students' desks and say "*Those* are your things."

they •▸ Divide students into girls and boys standing separately. Describe the two groups: "*They* are girls" and *they* are boys" or "*They* are wearing dresses" and so on. Point to a group of students, use *their* names in a sentence, and say *they* in the following sentence; for example, "[Sandy], [Xavier], and [Ling] are sitting. *They* are sitting."

they're •▸ Write *they're* on the board. Show how *they* and *are* squeeze together to make *they're*. See *they* and *are*.

thick, thickness •▸ **1.** Contrast a *thick* stack of paper with a *thin* piece of paper. Have students draw *thick* lines and *thin* lines on the board. **2.** Using a ruler, measure the *thickness* of several books.

thief, thieves, thieving •▸ Pretend that a puppet has robbed you of a pencil. Say "My pencil is gone! He took my pencil! *Thief ! Thief !*" Have two puppets take something from your desk and try to leave the room with it. Call them "*Thieves*." Show a puppet stealing something. Say "That puppet is a *thief*." Then say "It is a *thieving* puppet." Lead students in sentences with *thief* and *thieving*.

thin, thinned •▸ **1.** Contrast a *thick* stack of paper with a *thin* piece of paper. Have students draw *thick* lines and *thin* lines on the board. **2.** Pantomime *thinning* [Fluffy's] hair. Say you *thinned* it.

thing, things •▸ Point to *things* in the room. Name them and then say "It is a *thing*." Repeat with several *things*. Contrast this with pointing to people and saying, "A person." —*no such thing*, tell students, "There are people, but there are no monsters." Then say "There is *no such thing* as a monster." Repeat with other contrasting examples and sentences.

think, thinking, thought, thoughts •▸ **1.** Write a simple math problem on the board like 2 + 2. Dramatize *thinking* about it by scratching your head. Explain that you *thought* about it, and then write your answer. Ask students to say their names, and then ask them to *think* their names. Lead them in past tense sentences. Lead students in sentences, such as "I *think* I'll move my chair," and then move a chair, or "I *think* I'll read a book," and then pick up a book. Have a student ask you a question. Pause before answering, with a look of exaggerated concentration on your face. Say "I'm *thinking*." Demonstrate *thinking* about something. Then say what you *thought*: "I *thought* about my cat." **2.** Ask the class for their *thoughts*. **3.** Ask a student to either walk, hop, or jog, but not to tell you what he or she will do. Before the student does it, say to the class, I *think* he/she will hop." Once the student does one of the choices, say "I was wrong, I *thought* [he] would hop, but [he] [walked]" or "I was right, I *thought* [he] would hop, and [he] did."

third •▸ Line up three students. Count off, using their names. For example, say "[Sharon] is first, [Ed] is second, and [Marie] is *third*." Repeat with different students or a sequence of actions.

thirst, thirsty ❯ **1.** Fill a cup with water. Explain to students, "When I need food, I feel hunger. When I need water, I feel *thirst*." Hold your throat and pant as if *thirsty*. Take a drink and explain that you were *thirsty*. **2.** Have students read poetry or some other artistic works. Act as if you cannot get enough. Say "I have a great *thirst* for poetry."

this ❯ Lead students in making sentences, such as, "*This* is my nose" or "*This* is yellow." Make sentences about nearby objects, such as, "*This* book is little and *this* book is big" or "*This* shoe is black, and *this* shoe is brown." Contrast with objects further away, saying "*That* is a bookshelf" and "*That* is a lunch box."

thorn, thorny ❯ Draw a plant with *thorns*. Say "Some plants have many *thorns*; they are *thorny*. If possible, show students an actual *thorny* plant.

thorough, thoroughly ❯ *Thoroughly* clean the top of your desk. Contrast by *barely* cleaning the top of a student's desk.

those ❯ Make two piles of markers. Point to the pile closer to you and say "I will use *these* markers." Point to the pile farther away; tell students, "You may use *those* markers."

though ❯ Set up a scene where the puppets are outside playing and it begins to rain. Ask them to come inside. Have the puppets decide to stay out in the rain. Say to students, "*Though* it was raining, the puppets stayed outside." Repeat with other examples.

thousand, thousands ❯ Explain that there are about one *thousand* days in three years—from the time students were in kindergarten until the end of second grade. Write *1000* on the board many times. Ask, "How many *thousand* is that?"

thrash ❯ Have two puppets *thrash* about your desk.

threading, threaded ❯ Demonstrate *threading* a needle. Once done, say that you *threaded* the needle.

three hundred ❯ Write 100, 200, and 300 on the board. Have everyone read the numbers in unison. Write 100 three times. Explain that it equals 300.

threshing ❯ Show a picture of a *threshing* machine and wheat field to explain.

through ❯ If you have a telescope, have students look *through* it. Otherwise, have students close their hands in a circular shape and look *through* them. Place chairs or desks near each other and have students walk *through* them. Have students walk *through* a doorway. Line some up in two columns and have others walk *through* the columns. Say with each demonstration, "Go *through* the _____."

throw, throwing, thrown, threw ❯ *Throw* something into the trash and say that you *threw* it away. Lead students in *throwing* something in the trash and saying that they *threw* it away. Tell students that you will *throw* a ball. Once done, tell students that you *threw* it. Have students do the same, making sentences for both *throw* and *threw*. Lead students in sentences, such as, "I have *thrown* a ball many times." —*throwing caution to the wind*, show pictures of Evil Knevil or some other stuntperson or bungee jumper. Lead students in sentences using *throwing caution to the wind.*

thrust ❖   On the board, draw a rocket leaving Earth with flames coming out to show the *thrust.*

thud ❖   Drop a book on a table with a *thud.* Say "That book made a *thud.*"

thump, thumping, thumps ❖   *Thump* a table with your hand. *Thump* on a desk. Ask another student to *thump* on his or her desk. Tell the class, "[She] *thumps* on the desk."

thunder, thundering, thundered, thunderous ❖   **1.** Show pictures of lightning. Ask students if they have ever seen it. Ask if they have heard a loud noise after the lightning. Tell them that the noise is called *thunder.* **2.** Shout in a deep and *thundering* voice. **3.** Lead the class in making *thunderous* roars.

thus ❖   Lead students in sentences, such as "I am hungry, *thus* I will eat." Show that one action logically follows the other.

tick ❖   Listen to a clock *tick.*

tickle ❖   *Tickle* a puppet and make him laugh.

tide, tides ❖   Draw a beach, waves, and a moon. Explain that the moon pulls the water up and down the beach, creating high *tide* and low *tide.* On the board, draw a shoreline at high *tide.* Then draw one at low *tide.* Lead students in sentences.

tidy ❖   Make a mess on your desk and then *tidy* it up. Tell students that your desk is now *tidy.*

tie, ties, tying, tied ❖   **1.** *Tie* a knot in string. Lead students in *tying* a knot. **2.** *Tie* a knot in a shoestring or string and explain that it is *tied.* **3.** Use sentences, such as, "She *ties* her shoe" and "He *ties* his shoe." Draw an ice-cream cone on the board; write the word *vanilla* over one and *chocolate* over the other. Ask students to write the name of the flavor they prefer on a sheet of paper. Take the folded papers from students and say "I have [3] votes for vanilla and [3] votes for chocolate. We have a *tie!*" **4.** Contrast people with whom you are connected and those with whom you are not. For example, say "I do not have a relationship with the people at [name of another school]. I am *tied* to the teachers I work with here."

tight, tighten, tightening, tightly, tightness ❖   **1.** Pretend you are opening a jar. You can't because it is closed too *tight.* Tie a knot in a shoelace or piece of string. Explain that it is *tight.* **2.** Have students shut their mouths loosely and then *tightly.* **3.** Screw a lid on a jar, then *tighten* the lid to keep the jar closed. **4.** Put a belt on and *tighten* it. Say "I'm *tightening* my belt." **5.** *Tie* a knot in a shoelace or piece of string. Explain that the *tightness* of the knot prevents you from untying it.

tightly knit ❖   Show a *tightly knitted* object.

Tillie ❖   Show students the mouse in the story "*Tillie* and the Wall." Explain that *Tillie* is her name.

Tim ❯ Explain that *Tim* is a boy's name. Write a list of boys' names and include *Tim*.

time, times, timed ❯ **1.** Lead students in clapping three *times*, jumping three *times*, nodding three *times*, and so on. Do the same with two *times* and one *time*. **2.** Pointing to a clock or watch, read the *time* with sentences, such as "The *time* is 10:00 o'clock." **3.** While watching the clock with students, wait for a minute to go by. Explain that that was a minute of *time*. **4.** Give students an assignment to do in a certain *time*. —*it's time for*, look at the clock and make up sentences, such as "*It's* 10; it's *time for* reading" or "It's 12; *it's time for* lunch." Explain each word in the phrase as needed. See *it, is, time, for*. —*nineteen times*, write the numbers 1 through 19 on the board. Clap once. Have everyone repeat "Once." Then clap twice. Have everyone say "Twice." Continue this until you have clapped *nineteen times*. —*time capsules*, on the board, draw a large *capsule*. Pantomime putting things into it. Draw it being buried. Draw a *time* line into the future. Draw someone digging it up in a future *time*. Give example sentences using *time capsules*. —*time line*, on the board, draw a *time line* for the school year. —*time machines*, put a chair in the middle of a space. Say "This is a *time machine*. It can take you back to the year you were born. When were you born [Felipe]?" Write the year on the board. Show a picture of a baby and comment, "This is [Felipe] in [year]."

timid ❯ Have a puppet be *timid* about speaking in front of the class and then be brave.

tingling ❯ On the board, draw an ant crawling up an arm. Describe the sensation as *tingling*.

tinkering ❯ Explain to the class that the pencil sharpener is broken. *Tinker* with it in an attempt to fix it. Explain that your *tinkering* did not fix it. Invite students to *tinker* with it.

tiny ❯ Give and get examples of things that are *tiny*. Compare and contrast with *little* and *big*.

tip, tips, tipping, tipped ❯ **1.** Lead students in touching the *tip* of a pencil, a pen, or their noses. Have them touch the *tips* of their fingers. **2.** Lead students in *tipping* to one side. **3.** Set up a scene in which a student is a waiter and serves you some food. Give the waiter some money and say "This is your *tip*." **4.** Have students work together to build a castle out of blocks. As they are working, give them little suggestions for improving their work or making it easier. Say "The teacher gave students *tips* for building a better castle."

tiptoe, tiptoeing ❯ Lead students in *tiptoeing*. Walk quietly through the classroom on the balls of your feet. Say "I am *tiptoeing*, so I won't make too much noise." Have students imitate.

tired ❯ **1.** Lead students in yawning and looking *tired*. **2.** Tell students that you are *tired* of your shoes and you want to buy new ones. Ask them about things that they are *tired* of.

'tis ❯ Write *it is* on the board and show how the apostrophe replaces the first *i*. Explain that *'tis* means "it is." Give examples like "*It is* time to read; *'tis* time to read."

titanic ❯ See *colossal*.

title, titles ❯ Show students a book and its *title*. Ask them to find the *titles* on three books.

to ❯ **1.** Draw a signpost with several signs marked *to* the beach; *to* the snack bar; and *to* the bathroom. **2.** Walk *to* a student and away from him or her. Go *to* your desk and away *from* it. Ask students to walk *from* their desks *to* your desk.

to be done ❯ Make example sentences, such as "There is cleaning *to be done* here" or "There is learning *to be done* in math class."

toad ❯ See *frog*.

today ❯ **1.** Explain *today* as the time since they woke up to the time that it gets dark. Using pantomimes and pictures on the board, show the sun coming up, a puppet arising, and so on. Note the passage of events such as lunch and recess. Compare to *yesterday*. **2.** Compare *today* to times in the past: "*Today*, we use computers" or "Hundreds of years ago, there were no computers."

together, togetherness ❯ **1.** Pair students and tell them, "You are *together*." Divide the pairs and tell them, "You are alone." Alternate the words and have students pair up or separate. **2.** Place two small objects *together*. Then move them away from each other so that they are apart. **3.** Show pictures of people with their arms around each other or working *together*. Give sentences using *togetherness*.

toll ❯ Give statistics from hurricanes, wars, and so on. Say "[WWII] took a heavy *toll* in lives."

tomorrow ❯ Use the calendar or the days of the week to explain. "Today is Monday so tomorrow is Tuesday." —*tomorrow is another day*, pantomime a scene where everything is going wrong: you can't find your keys, your head hurts, you've lost your lunch, you hurt your knee, and so on. Finally, tell the class, "Today is an awful day. Oh well, *tomorrow is another day*, perhaps things will be better."

tone ❯ Lead the class in speaking with different *tones* of voice, such as a soft *tone*, a loud *tone*, an angry *tone*, a happy *tone*, and so on.

tongue ❯ —*tongues*, ask each child to speak his or her first language and count how many *tongues* are spoken in your classroom. —*golden tongue*, act out with a puppet. Have the puppet say something eloquently and articulately. Say "You said that beautifully. You have a *golden tongue*." Have students speak as clearly as they can, with *golden tongues*.

tonight ❯ Show a picture depicting night. Explain that *tonight* means "this night." You can also use a calendar. Ask students to tell you what they will be doing *tonight*.

too ❯ **1.** Have a student tell you something he or she likes. Then say "I like _____ *too*." Ask a student to approach you, then say to another, "You can come *too*." Repeat with other examples. **2.** Carry something and act as if it's *too* heavy, try to reach something and act as if it's *too* high, or try to find something and act as if it's *too* hard to find.

toothless ◈ Draw two faces on the board, one with teeth and one that is *toothless*.

tooting ◈ Lead students in imitating the horn of a ship. Say that the ship is *tooting*.

top, tops ◈ **1.** Have students touch the *tops* of their heads. Have them touch the *tops* of boxes and the *bottoms* of boxes or other containers. **2.** Mention some superstars, cartoons, or TV shows that students might think are *tops*. Use your hand to show the *top*.

topic ◈ Give students a list of *topics* to write about. Ask each one to choose a *topic*.

toppled ◈ Knock over a stack of books. Say "The books *toppled* over!"

tortured ◈ Have a toy cat *torture* a toy mouse. Make the mouse squeak and try to get away. Tell students, "The cat *tortured* the mouse."

toss, tossing, tossed ◈ **1.** *Toss* a ball or other object to a student. Have the student *toss* it back to you. Demonstrate tossing something in the trash. **2.** Ask a long-haired girl to *toss* her hair. Say "She is *tossing* her hair around."

total agreement ◈ Explain as an expression meaning "everyone agrees." Ask students if they want recess to last longer. Say "I'm glad we are in *total agreement*."

toting ◈ Carry your briefcase and say "I am *toting* my briefcase."

tottery ◈ Pantomime walking a tightrope or balance beam with your arms held out at shoulder height, wobbling to maintain your balance. Say "It isn't easy to walk on this narrow path; I'm feeling rather *tottery*."

touch, touching, touchy ◈ **1.** Have students *touch* things in the classroom. Lead students in touching things. **2.** Greet a puppet. Have the puppet respond grouchily. Say "[Fluffy] is *touchy* today." —*golden touch*, lead students in *touching* things gently, quickly, roughly, etc. Each time, say: "You have a gentle *touch*" and "You have a quick *touch*." Then take a black marker and *touch* it to paper. Tell students, "The marker has a black *touch*." Repeat with a golden crayon, saying the crayon has a "*golden touch*," and then "King Midas has a *golden touch*."

tough ◈ Have a puppet act *tough*, and then have him act timid or scared.

tourist ◈ Bring photos from one of your vacations. Say "I was a *tourist* in [the location]."

tow, towing, towed ◈ Pull a toy car or boat as if *towing*. Draw a car and a trailer.

toward ◈ Walk *toward* a student, and then walk *away* from the student.

tower ◈ Demonstrate *towering* over a student. Show students things that *tower* over them—perhaps bookshelves or file cabinets.

trace, traces ◈ **1.** Have students *trace* something. **2.** Write something on a piece of paper in pencil. Erase it and show students the *traces* of the original message.

track ◈ —*tracking down*, make marks like footprints with chalk on the floor and *track down* the stuffed animal that "made them."

tracks ❯ **1.** Draw a set of railroad *tracks* on the board or show a picture. **2.** Show students pictures of *tracks* in various recent articles. Explain that *tracks* are another word for *footprints*.

trade, trading, trades, trader ❯ Exchange something with a student. Say that you are *trading*. Have students pretend to exchange things. Explain that to *trade* is the same as "to exchange." Have students *trade* books or seats. Lead students in *trading* pencils and erasers for pennies or play money. Explain that *trading* can be selling or buying. —*slave traders*, show pictures of *slave traders*.

tradition ❯ Tell students about a holiday *tradition*. Say, for example, "There are many *traditions* around holidays. In America, it is a *tradition* to eat turkey on Thanksgiving." Ask students to share their family *traditions*.

tragedy ❯ Have students help you make a list of *tragedies* that can happen to people, such as fire, death of loved ones, sickness, car accidents, and so on. For each correct suggestion tell the class, "That would be a *tragedy*."

tragic ❯ Ask students to imagine very sad stories. Give the example of a person's pet dying. After each sad example, say "Yes, that is a *tragic* story."

trail, trailing ❯ **1.** Draw a *trail* on the board, and include some trees and bushes. Show a picture of a trail in a forest or a *trail* on the playground. **2.** Draw an airplane on the board *trailing* a banner.

train, trained ❯ Lead students in saying their addition tables. Say "This helps *train* you in math." Show pictures of animals being *trained*.

trample, trampling, trampled ❯ Show a picture of grass. Have students draw grass on sheets of paper. Place the drawings on the floor and have students stomp on them. Say "This grass is not standing up; you walked on it and it is lying down. This is *trampled* grass."

transcribe ❯ Have students read a passage aloud while you write it on the board. Say "I will *transcribe* it on the board."

transferred ❯ Demonstrate *transferring* a pencil from one container to another.

transform, transforming ❯ **1.** Draw a large circle on the board. Ask a student to *transform* it into a pizza. **2.** Show pictures of a caterpillar *transforming* into a butterfly.

translate ❯ Ask a bilingual student to *translate* a simple sentence for you.

transmitter ❯ On the board, draw a person with a microphone and a radio with an antenna and sound waves. Draw a person receiving the sound waves. Say "This is a *transmitter*" while pointing to the radio.

trapped ❯ Have students pretend that a little piece of paper is a bug. Throw it in the air and have students *trap* it in their hands.

travel, traveled, traveler, travelers ❯ **1.** Explain that *travel* means "to go places." Ask students about places where they might *travel*; for example, "Do you *travel* to school?" or "Do you *travel* to the store?" Show pictures of people in cars, trains, or airplanes *traveling*. Show a little figure, puppet, or stuffed animal *traveling* from place to place over a globe or map. **2.** Have each student choose a destination on the globe and say "I am going to *travel* to [destination]." Then say "Okay, *travelers*. Time to go to the airport."

treacherous ◆ Show pictures of canoers traveling down river rapids, or skiers skiing down mountains. Explain that the people do not know what could happen to them as they go down the river or mountain. These places are very *treacherous*. Pantomime with a puppet going down the mountain and hitting a rock hidden by the snow.

treason ◆ Pantomime a scene of a puppet betraying another puppet who is a general or leader of a country. Have the puppet promise to work for its leader and then go over to its leader's enemies, perhaps a group of stuffed animals, and work for them instead.

treasure, treasury ◆ **1.** Show students pictures of *treasure*. Explain to them that it is called *treasure* because if you sell it, you can get a lot of money. **2.** Show a picture of a palace. On the board, draw a side section showing the *treasury* full of jewels, money, and so on. Give example sentences using *treasury*.

treat, treats ◆ Say "I have a *treat* for everyone." Give students a piece of candy or other *treat*. Mention some things that students might consider to be *treats*: sweets, a trip to the movies, a hug, or a sticker.

treatment ◆ See *remedies*.

tree's ◆ See *animal's*.

tremble, trembling ◆ **1.** Have a puppet *tremble* when a stuffed animal acts mean to it. Have students *tremble* like the puppet did. **2.** Make your voice or hand *tremble*. Have students copy you.

tremendous ◆ **1.** See *colossal*. **2.** Show or draw pictures of things that are *tremendous* in size relative to people, like a huge dinosaur, tree, or building.

trend, trends ◆ Tell students that new things that everybody likes and wants to have are often called *trends*. Use examples of clothing or toys that your students may be familiar with. "My sister and her friends are all wearing bell bottom jeans. It is a *trend*."

trespassing ◆ Have each student make and hold up a sign that says, "No *Trespassing*." Have them pretend their desks are their homes. Walk up to the first student and say "May I come in?" Approach the next student and barge in to his or her "home." Say "I came in without asking. [Fernando] did not give me permission to enter. I am *trespassing*."

trial ◆ Have a practice spelling bee. Tell students, "This is our *trial* spelling bee." See *spelling bee*.

tribe, tribes, tribal ◆ Draw a picture of several families living together in a community. Tell the class that these are families living together, and they are called a *tribe*. Show pictures of *tribal* groups from Asia [the Hmong and the Montanaird] and Africa [Pygmies].

tribute ◆ Explain that a *tribute* is a demonstration of respect and appreciation for someone. Say "I know [student's name] has [an action] recently. Let's pay [him or her] a *tribute* and give [her] a round of applause." Clap.

trick, tricks ◆ **1.** Use a picture of a dog doing *tricks* or pantomime a *trick* like producing a quarter from behind a child's ear. **2.** Have students guess which hand holds a coin. Dispose of the coin discreetly. Show empty hands and say "That's a good *trick!*"

trickling ◆ *Trickle* some water through your fingers over a cup or dish. Show water *trickling* from a faucet.

trifling ◆ Have students make lists of important things and unimportant things. Label the unimportant things *trifling*.

triggered ◆ On the board, draw a picture of a dog barking at a porcupine. Then draw the porcupine "throwing" its spines. Give example sentences using *triggered*.

trim ◆ Show pictures of animals that are *trim* and in contrast those that are *fat*.

trip, trips, tripping, tripped ◆ **1.** Show pictures of families taking trips by plane, car, or train. Pantomime packing, getting in a car, driving, arriving, getting out of a car, and greeting someone. **2.** Walk across the room and pantomime stumbling over something. Say "I *tripped!*"

trip trap ◆ Explain that this is just a sound.

tripod ◆ Draw a *tripod* on the board.

triumph ◆ Talk about sports events. Ask who won a recent match or game. Say "It was a *triumph* for [name of team]."

trivial ◆ Make two lists: one for *important* things and one for *trivial* things.

trot, trotting, trotted ◆ Show pictures of horses or ponies. Explain that when they walk very fast, they *trot*. Ask if anyone has experienced this. Lead students in pretending to ride a *trotting* pony. Ask if anyone has ever *trotted* on a pony.

trouble, troubles, troublesome ◆ **1.** Show pictures of people with various kinds of *trouble*, such as a flat tire, termites in the house, and so on. Have a puppet tell all the bad things that have happened to it: "I slipped on a banana peel." Make the *troubles* as funny as possible. **2.** Have one puppet do something wrong and tell it it is in *trouble*. Give some form of punishment. **3.** Tell a story about a child who liked to do annoying things. Say "This was not a pleasant child. He was always doing naughty things; he was *troublesome*."

trudged ◆ Pantomime walking in a tired way across the room. Say "The teacher *trudged* across the room."

true, truly, truth, ◆ **1.** Say something that is obviously *true*, such as "The lights are on in the classroom." Compare to a *lie* that would be just as obvious, such as "It is nighttime right now." Tell students that you are going to say something *true*, such as "I have brown hair." Then, tell students that you are going to say something that is not true, such as "I have blue hair." Have students tell you things that are *true* and not *true*. **2.** Express with meaning things that you *truly* like. Contrast by repeating the same sentences without conveying genuineness or sincerity. **3.** Say "There are [two] boys in the class. Is that the *truth?*" Then say "There are [100] girls in the class. Is that the *truth?*"

trumpeted ◆ Show a *trumpet* or a picture of one. Make a tube from a sheet of paper. Hold it to your mouth and make the loud, blaring sound of a *trumpet*. Say "The teacher *trumpeted.*" Have students imitate.

trundle ◆ Show a picture of a wheelbarrow. Pantomime how you push it around. Lead students in sentences using *trundle*.

try, tries, tried ◆ *Try* to reach something and fail. Explain that you tried. *Try* again and again and finally reach it. Have a puppet *try* to reach something and fail. Say as the puppet is *trying*, "The puppet *tries* to get the book." —*a try*, check that students understand the verb *try*. Explain that *trying* something is called *a try*. Ask to give *a try* at pronouncing a new word.

tuck, tucked ◆ **1.** Have students *tuck* a doll into a doll bed, a flap into an envelope, or a note into a pocket. **2.** *Tuck* something under your belt. Lead students in sentences using *tucked*. —*tuckered out*, have a puppet do some work and then say "I am *tuckered out!*" Let the puppet have a nap.

tuffet ◆ Show students a low stool or chair. Explain that it is a *tuffet*.

tug-of-war ◆ Have two puppets play *tug-of-war*.

tumble, tumbling, tumbled ◆ Have a puppet *tumble* off your desk. Explain that it *tumbled*. Show a puppet *tumbling* off your desk.

tummy ◆ Have students touch their *tummies*. —*tummy ache*, pantomime having an upset stomach. Say "I must have eaten something that made me sick. I have a *tummy ache.*" Have students imitate.

tune ◆ Have students hum a *tune*. Ask them, "What is that song? I like that *tune.*" Sing a *tune* and have students join you.

turbulent ◆ Ask students to act out what they think it would be like to be inside a washing machine.

turn, turns, turning ◆ **1.** Have students take *turns* at writing their names on the board. Use the word *turn* frequently while describing whose *turn* it is. **2.** Lead students in *turning* the pages of a book. **3.** Pantomime buying something from a student for $1. Sell the same item for $2 to a puppet. Say "That's how you *turn* a profit!" —*turned up*, look around the room and say "Where's [Fluffy]?" Have the puppet *turn up* a little while later. Say "I'm glad you *turned up*. We would have missed you."

tutor ◆ Have one puppet *tutor* another on its addition facts. Contrast by having the puppet teach the same addition facts to the entire class. *Tutor* a puppet on some addition tables, and contrast by working with the entire class on the same tables.

twentieth ◆ If you have *twenty* students, line them up and show the *twentieth* student. Otherwise, have students count *twenty* books and show them the *twentieth* book.

248

twice ▸ Have a puppet jump *twice*. Have students jump *twice*.

twin ▸ Show pictures of *twins*. Ask students if any of them have *twin* sisters or brothers.

twinkle ▸ Demonstrate *twinkling* by turning a flashlight on and off. Say "The stars *twinkle* at night."

twirl, twirled ▸ Demonstrate *twirling* a pencil. Have students *twirl* a pencil and say "I *twirled* and *twirled*."

twist, twisted, twisty ▸ **1.** Lead students in *twisting* at the waist, or *twisting* a piece of rolled up paper. Take a towel and *twist* it. Lead students in past tense sentences. **2.** Draw two roads on the board, one straight and the other with many turns and curves. Say "This road is straight, but this road is *twisty*."

twitching ▸ Blink and wink your eye. Tell students you can't stop your eye from *twitching*.

two ▸ Point out *two* of something. Examples might include *two* girls, *two* braids, *two* shoes, *two* eyes, or *two* bags. Write *two* on the board. Have students count two objects.

ugly, uglier, ugliest ▸ **1.** Contrast pretty and *ugly* things and pictures. **2.** Show pictures of things or scenes that are *ugly* and ones that are beautiful. Ask students which are more *ugly* than others. Have a student arrange the pictures in a sequence of *ugly, uglier,* and *ugliest*.

umbrella-shaped ▸ Show or draw a picture of an *umbrella*. Show or draw a picture of a mushroom. Say "The mushroom looks like an *umbrella*; it is *umbrella-shaped*."

umpire ▸ Show a picture of an *umpire*. Say "[She] knows how to *umpire* the game."

unable ▸ Ask students if they are able to be in school at 10 o'clock at night. Say "Of course, you are *unable* to do that!"

unacceptable ▸ Write your name on the board in a sloppy fashion. Tell the class that it is too messy; it is *unacceptable*.

unanimously ▸ Draw two ice-cream cones on the board, one vanilla and one chocolate. Have all students pretend they prefer vanilla. Have them vote for their favorite flavor. Say "Vanilla was chosen *unanimously*."

unaware ▸ Ask students to tell you something about themselves they think you don't know. Say "I didn't know that! I was *unaware* that [whatever students say]."

unbearable ▸ Set up a scene where a puppet gets hurt and is in a lot of pain. Have the puppet say to the class, "The pain is *unbearable*. It is too much pain."

unbending ▸ Show students things that are *unbending*. Contrast with *bending*.

unbraiding ▸ Demonstrate *braiding* and *unbraiding* with string. Lead students in *braiding* and *unbraiding*.

unbutton ▸ Demonstrate with a jacket or other suitable item.

uncertain ▸ Ask a puppet to write its name on the board. Have it attempt to do it, but ask you many questions about the formation of the letters. Tell the class,

"It is *uncertain.*" Contrast with *certain* by having the puppet write its name without assistance.

unchartered ➧ Draw a map, an ocean, and a ship on the board. Say "Ship captains use maps so they know where they are sailing." Draw an "X" through the map. Say "When ships sail in waters that do not have a map, they are sailing in *uchartered* seas."

uncle ➧ First explain *brother* using pictures of families. Once this is clear, ask if their mother or father has a *brother.* Explain that he is their *uncle.*

unclenched ➧ *Clench* and *unclench* your fists. Ask students to do the same.

uncommitted ➧ Have a puppet ask you to go to the movies. Shrug your shoulders and say "I'm not sure." Give other examples using *uncommitted.*

unconscious ➧ Show two puppets roughhousing. Have one puppet be knocked out. Tell the class, "This puppet is *unconscious* and this puppet is *conscious.*" Ask who is *conscious* in the class.

uncontrollably ➧ Have a puppet sob *uncontrollably.* Try to comfort it to no avail. Give example sentences.

uncooked ➧ Show a picture of raw meat. Explain that the meat needs to be *cooked.* Show *uncooked* vegetables. Say "The vegetables are *uncooked.*"

uncover ➧ *Cover* and *uncover* things in the classroom.

under ➧ Lead students in placing a book *under* their desks, and contrast with *over.* Show pictures with the sun high in the sky and the things *under* it. Put your hand *under* a book and over a book. Have students do the same. —*under your thumb,* have a puppet assign you chore after chore. Say "You are my boss and I have to do what you tell me to do, but you are working me very hard today. I really feel like I am *under your thumb.*"

underground ➧ Explain that this a place under the surface of the earth. Show pictures of animals that live *underground.*

Underground Railroad ➧ Show pictures of a station of the *Underground Railroad.* On a map trace its route. Give example sentences.

undermine ➧ Make a rectangle out of blocks. Remove blocks from the bottom until the whole structure falls. Give example sentences using *undermine.*

underneath ➧ Have students put a hand *underneath* a paper or book.

understand, understanding, understood ➧ Have a student say something in his or her native language. Act confused and say "I don't *understand.* Have a student say something in English. Act enlightened and say "Yes! I *understand.*" Lead in past tense sentences.

undertow ➧ Show students pictures of the ocean waves coming up on the beach. Explain that when the waves go back out to sea, they can pull you with them. Ask if students have ever experienced this. Explain that this is called an *undertow.* Pantomime playing in the waves and getting caught in the *undertow.*

underwater ➧ On the board, draw a line representing the surface of the water. Draw in *underwater* rocks, plants, and fish.

undo ❖ Show students how to *undo* a knot, zipper, button, and so on.

unearthed ❖ On the board, draw the top of Earth's surface with human-made things underneath. Draw someone digging one of the objects up. Give example sentences using *unearthed*.

uneasy ❖ Pantomime looking around the room in an *uneasy* manner. Lead students in sentences.

unemployed ❖ Contrast *employed* and *unemployed*.

unequal ❖ Show students *equal* and *unequal* amounts of various things found in the class, such as paper clips, pencils, paper, and so on.

uneven ❖ Line up two edges of paper, making them *even*. Then make them *uneven*.

unexplored ❖ Have students tell you things they would like to learn but know nothing about. Say "Those are still *unexplored* studies."

unfair ❖ Contrast *fair* and *unfair* by first giving two puppets fair and equal amounts of paper clips. Then give one puppet more than the other. Have the puppet that was shorted complain about how *unfair* it is.

unfinished ❖ Begin to write math problems on the board. Then start writing something else. Leave it *unfinished* also. Do this with one more activity. Give example sentences.

unfolded ❖ Lead students in *folding* and *unfolding* paper. Help them to make past tense sentences.

unforgettable ❖ Pantomime *remembering* and *forgetting* something like phone numbers. Explain that *unforgettable* is something you always *remember* like your own name.

unfriendly ❖ Show a puppet acting in an *unfriendly* way to a student. Say "The puppet is not *friendly*. It is *unfriendly*."

unhappy, unhappily ❖ As needed, review *happy*. Then have a puppet be *happy* and *unhappy*. Have the puppet *happily* and *unhappily* do things. Lead students in sentences. Lead students in looking *unhappy* and then *happy*. Draw *happy* and *unhappy* faces on the board. Say something in a *happy* manner and contrast by saying the same thing in an *unhappy* manner. Have students do the same.

unheard ❖ Have a puppet say something and pretend not to hear. On the board, write "*un* = not." Lead students in sentences using *unheard*.

unhook ❖ If you have a *hook*, you can hook and *unhook* it. Otherwise, show a picture of a *hook* used for clothing and explain *hook* and *unhook*.

unify ❖ Divide the class into two groups. *Unify* them.

uninvited ❖ Explain that *invited* means that you were asked by someone to go somewhere or do something with him or her. *Uninvited* means the opposite of *invited*.

Union ❖ Show students a map of the United States. Say "This is the United States of America, also known as the *Union*." Point out the Northern states and say "During the Civil War, the Northern states were referred to as the *Union*."

unique ❯ Acknowledge something special about each student. Say "You are *unique*."

unison ❯ Ask students to speak or read in *unison*.

unit ❯ Show different types of things that break down into *units*, such as *units* of a book or *units* of measurement.

unite, united ❯ Have students stand in a row and join hands. Explain that they have *united*. Repeat and ask them to *unite*. Have students join hands in a circle. They are *united*. Have them drop each others' hands so that they are no longer *united*. Have students separate into two or three groups. Bring the groups together. Tell students they have *united*.

unjustly ❯ Have one puppet steal something, but accuse another *unjustly*. Give example sentences.

unknown ❯ Hide something from students in a box. Explain that it is *unknown*. Have an *unknown* student hide behind a door.

unless ❯ Give students realistic and familiar examples, such as "Students can't get a gold star *unless* they do their work" or "People can't live *unless* they have food."

unlock ❯ *Lock* and *unlock* a door. Explain that *un* means "the opposite."

unmarried ❯ Give examples of people who are *married* and those who are *unmarried*, such as students being *unmarried* and some of their parents as *married*.

unmistakable ❯ Cover your eyes and say "One of you say something and I'll try to guess who it is without looking." When you guess correctly, say "[Mona], I would know your voice anywhere. Your voice is *unmistakable*."

unpack ❯ *Pack* and *unpack* a backpack.

unpleasant ❯ Contrast *pleasurable* and disagreeable alternatives for ways to spend the weekend. For example, say "There are so many things I could do this weekend. Swimming at the pool would be fun. Cleaning the house would be *unpleasant*."

unprepared ❯ Ask each puppet to recite a short passage. Have the first puppet recite it flawlessly. Say "[Muffin] studied a lot; it was *prepared*." Have the other puppet falter and say "I didn't practice. I am *unprepared*."

unprotected ❯ See *sheltered*.

unscientific ❯ Pantomime a scene with puppets where one is a scientist researching butterflies, and the other is just making guesses about butterflies. Of the first, say "He is very *scientific*." Of the second, say "He is very *unscientific*."

unseeing ❯ Have students put their hands over their eyes. Say "You are now *unseeing*."

unselfish ❯ See *selflessly*. Give each puppet some markers. Have one puppet hoard them protectively; have the other share them with students. Say "[Spike] is keeping all its markers to itself, but [Pumpkin] is very *unselfish*."

unsolved ❯ On the board, write two math problems: one *solved* and one *unsolved*. Lead students in sentences.

unstick ◆ *Stick* a paper to a bulletin board, and then *unstick* it.

unsuccessful ◆ Have a student try to solve a math problem but fail. Say "[Rabbit] was *unsuccessful*."

unsuitable ◆ Draw clouds and rain on the board. Show two pictures—one of a person dressed in a raincoat, rain hat, boots, and umbrella, and the other wearing shorts, a T-shirt, and sandals. Give example sentences using *unsuitable*.

unsupervised ◆ Divide students into two groups and give them a seat work assignment. Watch over one group closely, giving them assistance as needed. Leave the other group alone. Say "I am watching this group and helping them with their assignment. I have left the other group alone; the other group is *unsupervised*."

untangling ◆ Demonstrate with some string. Have students *tangle* some string and then *untangle* it. As they proceed, tell them they are *untangling* it.

untended ◆ Show a picture of a *well-tended* garden and contrast with an *untended* garden.

untidy ◆ Have one student make his or her desktop very neat; have another make his or hers messy. Say "[Mirabel]'s desk looks very *tidy*. [Gabriel]'s desk looks very *untidy*."

untie, untied ◆ *Tie* and then *untie* a shoelace. Lead students in *tying* and *untying* their shoelaces.

until ◆ Lead students in making sentences, such as, "We study *until* recess" or "We play *until* the bell rings." Explain that *until* means "for a time." —*'til*, explain that *'til* means "*until*." Lead in sentences with both.

untrue ◆ Give examples of things that are *true* and *untrue*: fish swim and birds fly; bugs are very big; cats bark. Ask students to say things that are *untrue*.

unusual ◆ Contrast illustrations of *usual* animals with *unusual* versions such a hairless or tailless cat. Show freaks of nature such as a two-headed calf. Or, you can lead students in *unusual* actions, such as hopping to the board in contrast with the more *usual* walking. Do something *unusual* in class. Contrast with something *usual*.

unveiled ◆ Cover your face with a piece of cloth. The cloth is a *veil*. Demonstrate how you *unveil* your face. Show a picture of a bride or a traditional Bedouin woman wearing her *veil*.

unwilling ◆ Demonstrate by having one puppet *willing* to clean his room, while another is *unwilling* to clean his room.

unwrap ◆ *Wrap* something up and then ask a student to *unwrap* it. Model as needed. *Wrap* and *unwrap* a pencil. Explain that *un* means "the opposite."

unzip ◆ *Zip* and *unzip* a zipper.

up ◆ **1.** Contrast *up* with *down* by pointing or reaching *up* and *down*. **2.** Lead students in pointing to items that are *up* above them. Contrast with *below*. **3.** Explain that the word *up*, in hopped *up* to, ran *up* to, came *up* to, and crawled *up* to, means "came to someone or someplace and stopped." Use your fingers to crawl *up* to an object on your desk. See *down.* —*up and down,* have a puppet walk *up and down* and describe it as *up* and *down.*

upheavals ◆ Engage students in a discussion of things that can happen to families that would cause upset and major changes, such as divorce and loss of a job. Say "These things are called *upheavals.*"

upon ◆ Have students place a pencil upon their paper or put a book *upon* their desk. Put things *upon* your desk. Lead students in placing objects *upon* their desks.

upper ◆ Show students the *upper* part of the board. Point out *upper* and *lower* shelves on bookshelves. Point to the bottom edge of the board. Say "This is the *lower* edge of the board." Point to the top edge of the board. Say "This is the *upper* edge of the board."

uppercase ◆ Show examples of *uppercase* letters.

uprisings ◆ Have students stand up one at a time. Give example sentences using *uprisings.* Show pictures of historical *uprisings,* such as the Whiskey rebellion, the Boston Tea Party, and so on. See *rebellions.*

uproar ◆ Have students make a lot of noise. Lead them in sentences using *uproar.*

upset ◆ Have the puppet tell you some bad news. Respond with worry and agitation in your facial expression and tone of voice. Say "I was *upset* by [Jenna]'s bad news." —*upset stomach,* pantomime having an *upset stomach.* Say "My *stomach* is *upset.* I have an *upset stomach.*"

upside down ◆ Hold up a book so students can read the title. Say "I am holding the book *right side up.*" Then turn the book bottom side up and say "I am holding the book *upside down.*"

upstairs ◆ See *downstairs.*

urban ◆ Show pictures of a city and say "This is a city; it is an *urban* place. These buildings are in the city; they are *urban* buildings." Compare with things in the country, saying that these are not *urban.*

urge, urging ◆ See *relay. Urge* students to run as fast as they can or to get their assignment done rapidly. Dramatize *urging* students to do their homework, to eat a good breakfast, and so on.

urgent ◆ Imitate the sound of the school's fire alarm. Pantomime hurrying students out the door. Lead students in sentences using *urgent.*

us ◆ Have students stand in two separate groups. Stand with one of the groups. Hand things to the other group. Each time say such things as, "I'm giving *them* the book" and "Give *us* the book."

usable ◆ Show students two pencils: one that is broken and one that is not. Of the first pencil, say and demonstrate, "This is not *usable.*" Of the second, say and demonstrate, "This is *usable.*"

use, used ◆ Show students that you *use* a pen to write, a stapler to staple, and a pencil sharpener to sharpen pencils. Lead students in past tense sentences. —*used to,* give an example, such as "Children *used to* be babies," or mention something that you know students *used to* do or where they *used to* live.

Describe something you did in the past but no longer do. For example, say "When I was in kindergarten, I *used to* take naps."

useful, usefulness ◆ **1.** Draw a candle on the board. Say "It would be *useful* to have a match to light the candle." Try to open a bottle unsuccessfully. Then, use a bottle opener. Show the opener to students and say "This is *useful.*" **2.** Demonstrate the *usefulness* of a sharpened pencil and contrast with the *uselessness* of an unsharpened pencil.

useless, uselessness ◆ **1.** Show students a battery-operated item such as a tape recorder. Say "This [tape recorder] needs batteries to run. Without batteries it won't work; it's useless." **2.** Demonstrate the *usefulness* of a sharpened pencil and contrast with the *uselessness* of an unsharpened pencil.

user ◆ Demonstrate by using different things. Say each time, "I'm the *user.*"

ushering ◆ *Usher* someone to the board. On your way say "I am *ushering* you to the board." Give more examples.

usual, usually ◆ **1.** Contrast illustrations of *usual* animals with unusual animals. Lead students in walking in *unusual* ways, such as hopping to the board in contrast with the more *usual* walking. **2.** Check that students understand *usual.* Then make sentences, such as "*Usually,* we have lunch at ___ o'clock" or "*Usually,* we leave school at ___ o'clock."

vacant ◆ Explain that if no one lives in a house, the house is empty or it is *vacant.* Ask students to describe a *vacant* lot (or space) they walk by on their way to school. Show students *vacant* seats and *vacant* desks.

vacation ◆ Show pictures of families on vacation. On the calendar show times when students might go on *vacation.* Ask students about *vacations* they have taken.

vain ◆ Lead students in acting *vain.* —*in vain,* crumple three sheets of paper into balls and attempt to juggle them without succeeding. Say "I am trying *in vain* to juggle these balls."

valiant ◆ Show a picture of a burning building. Have students pretend to be firefighters. Have them imagine what it would feel like to get past their fear in order to do their job. Say "Firefighters have to be very brave to save people from burning buildings. Firefighters are *valiant.*"

validate ◆ Have a puppet tell about some incident that occurred, such as a fight on the playground. Ask if the other puppet can *validate* his story. Then have the second puppet reiterate the story and provide a few more facts to *validate* it.

value, valuable ◆ **1.** Have a puppet ask another what the values of various objects are. Have the second puppet put *values* on them, like "5 cents," "a dollar," and so on. **2.** Show some *valuables,* such as watches and rings. Say "These are *valuable.*"

valve ◆ —*pressure-release valve,* show an actual *valve* or a picture of one. On the board, show how it works. Give example sentences using *pressure-release valve.*

vandalizing ● Show a toy car with the tires removed and the windows smashed. Say "The car has been *vandalized.*"

vanishes, vanished ● 1. Write something on the board. Erase it and say "When I erase the board, the word *vanishes.*" 2. Make some things disappear and say that they *vanished* or disappeared.

varied ● Write your name on the board in *varied* styles: block letters, small letters, and cursive. Say "I wrote my name in lots of different ways. I *varied* the way I wrote my name." Have students *vary* their writing.

various ● Show students the *various* pencils that you have at your desk. Contrast by showing them something that you have only one of, such as an eraser or stapler.

vast ● Use a map to point out *vast* areas.

vaulting ● 1. Show pictures of *vaults* from famous buildings. 2. Show pictures of athletes *vaulting* or *pole-vaulting.* Give example sentences using *vaulting.*

vegetables ● Draw or show pictures of various *vegetables.* Name each one and point out that they are all *vegetables.*

vein ● Show the *veins* on your hands and arms.

velocity ● Have students line up behind you. Pretend you are a train engine and they are the cars of the train. Have them make choo-choo sounds as they move around the room behind you. Gradually move faster and faster. Say "This train is moving with increasing *velocity.*"

verge ● Show a picture of a person with a diploma. Say "This person is on the *verge* of becoming a college graduate."

verifying ● Write several simple arithmetic equations on the board. Have other students *verify* the answers using a calculator.

versatile ● Take a pencil. Say "A pencil is *versatile.* It can scratch my back, it can write a note, and it can be used as a ruler."

vertical, vertically ● 1. Write three columns of numbers on the board with lines running straight up between them. Say "This is how to make *vertical* columns of numbers." 2. Hold a pencil straight up and down. Say "I am holding my pencil *vertically.*"

very ● Show a dot on the board that is small and one that is *very* small. Then show a dot on the board that is big and one that is *very* big. Draw a row of circles on the board. Point out some last ones and then the *very* last one.

veto ● Explain that a person who is the boss of others can say "no" to something that others wish to do. Demonstrate by having students vote to go to recess early, and you *veto* the idea.

vibration ● Ask students to sing a song while holding their hands to their throats. Ask if they can feel the *vibration.*

vicious ● Use a toy dog and have it become *vicious* with a puppet.

victim, victims ● Have one student place red dot stickers on his or her face. Say "[Margarita] is sick with a rash. [She] is the latest *victim* of the illness that is going around the school." Show pictures of *victims* such as a *victim* of a crime.

victory ❖ Use the sports page. Lead students in sentences using *victory* with teams and athletes.

view, views ❖ **1.** Show a panoramic picture. Explain that when you look out from a tall building, you have a good *view* of the city. **2.** Ask students to stand in different parts of the room to *view* a picture. Say "[Joaquin] *views* this picture from over there."

vigorously ❖ Demonstrate by washing the board *vigorously*. Have students imitate on their desks.

village ❖ —*village compound*, have students build a town with houses and stores out of blocks. Then have them build a wall in a circle around the town. Say "You have built a town with a strong wall around it. You have built a *village compound*."

vindicate, vindictive ❖ **1.** Show a picture of a judge in a courtroom. Say "The judge found the accused not guilty. The accused was *vindicated*." **2.** Accidentally knock something of a puppet's to the floor and apologize. Have the puppet do something destructive, such as dump your pencils on the floor. Say "That was not nice. It was *vindictive*."

VIPs ❖ Ask students to list important people. Call it the *VIP* list. Tell students "These are *Very Important People*."

visible ❖ Have students help you make two lists—one containing examples of things that cannot be seen, such as air, sound, and gravity and others that can be seen, such as people, chairs, and trees. Say "We can't see air, sound, or gravity; these things are *invisible*. We can see people, chairs, and trees; these things are *visible*."

visit, visited, visitor ❖ Ask one student to *visit* another. If students have gone on a recent field trip, describe this as a *visit*. Or, students may have had relatives or friends *visit* or may have *visited* relatives or friends. Explain that *visiting* is going to a place for a short time. Dramatize by having students or puppets go to see and talk to someone. Say "You are *visitors*."

visually ❖ Ask students to look around the room. Ask them what they have *visually* recorded.

vital ❖ Ask students what their most *vital* and important possessions are. Give them some examples, such as photographs, pets, and trophies.

voice ❖ Have a puppet speak in a soft *voice*, a loud *voice*, a kind *voice*, and a crabby *voice*. Each time, mention to students what kind of *voice* it is. Get students to speak in different *voices*.

void ❖ Show empty containers and explain that the containers are *void* of any contents. Fill the containers and explain that they are not *void* of anything.

volume ❖ If you have a radio or a T.V., show students the *volume* knob and demonstrate how you can raise and lower *volume* with it. Otherwise, have students speak in loud and soft *volumes* as a group.

volunteers ◆ Ask students for help with something. Say "I have a little job. Who will help me? Do I have any *volunteers?*"

vote, voting, voted ◆ Have students *vote* on their favorite color, their favorite food, or their favorite amusement park. Take *votes* on some of the following: colors, T.V. shows, and food. After talking for a minute, say "We are *voting* on this now." Have each student write the name of his or her favorite television show on a slip of paper and place it in a box. Say "You named your favorite television show; you *voted* for your television show."

vouch ◆ Have a puppet do a flip off your desk while your head is turned away. Have the puppet tell you excitedly what it did. Ask students who saw it. Say "Can you *vouch* that this puppet did a flip?"

voyage, voyaging, voyaged, voyager ◆ **1.** Explain that when you take a long trip on a boat, you take a *voyage.* Show pictures of ships sailing on the open ocean. Say "The people on the ships are making a *voyage* across the ocean." **2.** Say "I love voyaging. Last summer I voyaged to [France, Spain, and Portugal]." Ask students to say what they like or dislike about traveling and *voyaging.* **3.** Show pictures of people *voyaging* at sea. Explain that they are called *voyagers.*

W.C. ◆ Tell students that *W.C.* stands for *water closet,* and it is British for "bathroom."

waddled ◆ Demonstrate *waddling* like a duck or goose. Or, show a picture of a duck and say "It *waddles* instead of walking."

wade ◆ Show pictures of people *wading* in water.

wag, wagged ◆ Draw or show a picture of a dog. Mimic and say that dogs *wag* their tails. Say "Yesterday when I got home, my dog *wagged* its tail."

wait, waiting, waited ◆ **1.** Have one puppet ask for an ice cream from another. Have the second puppet bring it slowly to the impatiently *waiting* puppet. Contrast with bringing it quickly so that there is no *wait.* Seat students in a circle and tell them you will play a game, but they must *wait* for the puppet to come join them. Have them *wait* and then have the puppet arrive. Ask a student to bring you something while you *wait,* checking your watch. As the student brings it to you, say that you are *waiting.* Lead students in similar dramatizations. **2.** Pantomime *waiting* by tapping your foot and looking at your watch. Explain that you've *waited* a long time.

wake up, wakes, woke, woke up ◆ Have one puppet *wake* another puppet *up,* saying "*Wake up.*" Show how a puppet *wakes* from a nap. Explain to students that you *woke* the puppet up or you *woke* it *up.*

wakeful ◆ Explain to students that, when they are not sleeping, they are *wakeful.* Explain that often light can keep one *wakeful.* Ask students to name other things that could keep one *wakeful,* such as loud noises, traffic, and so forth.

walk, walking, walked ◆ Demonstrate *walking* and tell students to *walk.* Stop them and say "We *walked.*" Start and stop them, alternating *walk* and *walked.*

wallowed ◆ Have a puppet demonstrate.

wander-thirst ❯ "Walk" two fingers all over a map and keep saying, "I'm thirsty!" Have a puppet say "What do you want to drink?" Say "I don't have a real *thirst*, I have a *wander-thirst*. I want to *wander* some more." Then continue *wandering* all over the map.

want, wants, wanted ❯ Hold your hands open as if waiting for something and say "I *want* ice cream" or "I *want* to play." Show a puppet looking at something. Explain that it *wants* it. Pantomime looking at a piece of candy longingly, saying "I *want* the candy."

wariest ❯ Draw a kitten, a large dog, and a lion on the board. Pantomime reactions to these animals and say "I am comfortable with a kitten. I am *wary* of a large dog. I am *wariest* of a lion."

warm, warms, warmer, warmly ❯ **1.** Have students feel their *warm* foreheads and contrast this with a *cold* metal surface. Have students *warm* their hands by rubbing them together. Show pictures of the sun and explain that it *warms* things. Show pictures of snow or rain and explain that these *cool* things. **2.** Ask students to put their jackets on. Tell them, "The jackets make you *warm*." Then ask them to take off their jackets. Tell them they were *warmer* with their jackets on. Use other examples, such as "The sun makes you *warmer* than the rain."

warn, warning, warned ❯ Bring pictures of *warning* signs. Draw a traffic sign that shows a curve ahead. Explain that the sign is a *warning* to drive carefully. Lead students in sentences using *warn*. Give example *warnings*, such as "Be careful when you cross the street" or "Be careful not to touch hot stoves."

was ❯ Contrast and pantomime sentences, such as "My hand is up" and "My hand *was* up." Lead students in making sentences about objects, such as "The book is here." Then remove the object and have students say "The book *was* here." —*wasn't*, show on the board how *was* and *not* squeeze together to make the word *wasn't*. See *was* and *not*.

wash, washing, washed ❯ Demonstrate *washing* your hands. Lead students in *washing* their hands. Ask students, "Who *washed* their hands today?" Demonstrate or pantomime *washing* dishes. Once done, lead students in past tense sentences.

waste, wastes, wasted, wasteful ❯ **1.** Tell students that to *waste* something means "to not use it." Demonstrate by tossing a usable pencil in the trash. **2.** Ask students to list anything that *wastes* their time. **3.** Draw a pizza on a sheet of paper. Cut it in half, then cut one half into slices and distribute them to students. Throw away the leftover half. Say "I'm not going to save the leftover pizza; I am being *wasteful*." Have more paper clips than you need. Throw the extra away. Give example sentences using *wasteful*.

watch, watching, watched ❯ Ask students to *watch* your hands as you move them around or up and down. Pantomime *watching* by shading your eyes with your hand. Have a puppet *watch* you say hello to the class. Ask students to *watch* you sharpen a pencil. Ask one student to *watch* another walk to the door. Repeat with other examples. Model as needed. —*watch out*, explain that the usage here is "to be careful." Ask a student to bring you a drink and to *watch out* for spills. —*watch out for*, check that students understand *watch*. Then dramatize *watching out for* danger by walking stealthily, shading your eyes, and looking about warily for danger.

water, watered ❖   *Water* a plant or show pictures of a plant being *watered*.

wave, waves, waving, waved ❖   **1.** Pantomime saying good-bye and *waving* with your hand. *Wave* a ruler in the air in a slightly menacing manner. **2.** Show or draw pictures of ocean *waves*.

wavering ❖   Demonstrate by giving a puppet two things to choose from. Have the puppet go back and forth between the two choices having obvious difficulty deciding. Explain to the class that it is *wavering*. Ask if students have ever *wavered* over a decision.

wavy ❖   Show pictures of straight and *wavy* hair.

way, ways ❖   **1.** Draw a figure on the board and a house at some distance. Draw a path from the figure to the house. Explain that this is the *way* to the house. Repeat with other similar drawings. **2.** Give examples, such as "The *way* that we take turns is to raise our hands," "Another *way* we take turns is to make a line," and "The *way* we clean our hands is to wash them." Walk over to the pencil sharpener and explain that this is the *way* to the sharpener. Repeat with other destinations in the classroom. Have students follow your lead. Have students show you different *ways* to do things, such as walking or sitting. —*out of its way*, using little objects, show a car driving on *its way* from its house to school. Check that students understand the idea of *its way*. Show people and animals getting *out of its way*. —*Way to go!*, ask a student to perform a familiar task. When he or she has completed it, respond enthusiastically and say "That was great, [Ysabel]! Good for you! *Way to go!*"

we ❖   Divide students into two groups. Stand with one group and then the other. Lead students in sentences that contrast actual differences between *you* and *we*. Examples are: "*We* are standing and *you* are sitting" or "*We* are talking and *you* are quiet."

weak, weakest, weakness ❖   **1.** Arm wrestle with a student. Lose and then say "I am *weak*. You are *strong*." Attempt to pick up something heavy. Tell students that you cannot because you are too *weak*. **2.** Have one puppet lift one book, a second puppet lift two books, and a third puppet lift three books. Ask, "Which puppet do you think is the *weakest*?" **3.** Have a puppet force himself and fail to stay away from a piece of candy. Tell the class, "The puppet gave in to his *weakness*."

wealthy, wealthier ❖   Give one puppet a lot of money. Give another very little money. Have the puppets tell students, "I am *wealthy*" and "I am *poor*." Lead students in sentences. Give two students some money, giving more to one than the other. Say "Both of you have a lot of money, but [Bernardo] has more money than [Linda]. [Bernardo] is *wealthier* than [Linda]."

wear, wears, wearing, wore, worn ❖   **1.** Put on a coat or sweater and say "I *wear* my coat when it is cold." Tell students, "We *wear* pants," "We wear shirts," "We *wear* socks," and "We *wear* clothes." Show students a puppet and explain that it *wears* clothes. Lead students in sentences, such as, "What do you *wear* on your head?" or "Tomorrow I will *wear* my new shoes." Describe what you and some of the students are *wearing*. Put on a jacket or sweater and say that now you are *wearing* it. Lead students in sentences, such as "Today I *wore* brown shoes" or "Today Blanca *wore* a dress." **2.** Show students a pair of shoes with *wear* on them. Give example sentences using *wearing*. **3.** Show students the *worn* edges or the *worn* cover of a book. Show them *worn* backpacks, purses, or other objects.

weary ❖ Sit at your desk and work on something. Pantomime growing *weary*. Pantomime being *weary* at the end of a long, hard day. Contrast by being energetic.

weather ❖ Show pictures of various types of *weather*. Ask students what kind of *weather* they like best.

weave, weaves, weaving, weaver ❖ **1.** Demonstrate by passing strips of paper over and under one another. Say "This is how a spider *weaves* her web." **2.** Show a picture of a *weaver*. Demonstrate *weaving* by cutting some paper into strips and *weaving* them.

wed, wedding ❖ Show pictures of *weddings* and explain that the couple *wed*.

wedge ❖ Show a *wedge*, perhaps a triangular block or a door stopper. Draw a pie on the board. Pantomime cutting it and draw a single slice. Say "Who would like a *wedge* of pie?"

weed ❖ —*weed-infested*, draw two rectangles on the board—one with grass and flowers, the other with *weeds*. Say "This patch of land has a lovely yard and garden. The other patch is full of *weeds*; it is *weed-infested*."

weeding ❖ Draw some cornstalks on the board. Draw some grass and *weeds* in between the rows of corn. Pantomime *weeding* out the grass and *weeds*. Have students imitate.

week ❖ Show students a calendar. Have them recite the days of the *week*. Tell them these days make one *week*.

weekend ❖ Explain that the *weekend* is Saturday and Sunday. Use a calendar to show Saturday and Sunday. Show students those days of the week that make up the *weekend* and the work week.

weigh, weighs, weight ❖ **1.** See *pounds*. **2.** *Weigh* some things using scales. Have the student feel the *weight* of an object that *weighs* a pound, perhaps a grapefruit. Have students *weigh* various things. **3.** Ask students to guess the *weight* of some objects. Demonstrate *weight* differences by comparing a small book with a big one. Say "The big book is heavier; it has more *weight*."

welcome, welcoming ❖ Have students *welcome* each other to the class. Have a puppet dramatize *welcoming* a visitor. Have a student walk into the classroom and have the rest of the class *welcome* him or her.

well ❖ **1.** See *better*. **2.** Write a word on the board *well* and *poorly*. Walk *well* and *poorly*. —*Very well*, explain that this means "Okay." —*well-aimed*, have students make balls out of crumpled sheets of paper and invite them to throw them into the trash can. Every time a ball lands in the trash can, say "That ball was *well-aimed.*"

well-being ❖ Dramatize having good health by walking quickly and energetically. Contrast by dramatizing having bad health by coughing, sneezing, and holding your forehead as if with a headache. Say "Good health is the same as *well-being.* For my *well-being,* I eat right and exercise."

well-to-do ❖ Divide students into two groups. Have one group draw lots of money on sheets of paper. Have the other group draw one coin. Say "The people in this group don't have much money; they are poor folks. The people in this group have lots of money. They are *well-to-do* folk."

went up in flames ❖ Check that students understand each word in the expression. Show pictures of burning buildings on the board. Say "The buildings *went up in flames.*"

were ❖ Have students make sentences using *were* about actual things that happened the day before. Write a sentence such as "We *were* tired" on the board and draw a chain to show how *were* connects the two other words. Explain that the word *were* has little meaning but helps make sentences: "We *were* dancing" or "We *were* singing."

west ❖ Show north, south, east, and *west* in the classroom. Have students walk *west.*

wet ❖ Make something *wet* with water.

what ❖ Explain that *what* asks a question. Lead students in making sentences. Ask questions with *what,* such as "*What* is your name?" Point to something and ask, "*What* is that?" Call on volunteers to ask questions with *what.* —*What a…!,* note something special in the classroom, such as student artwork. Lead students in practicing this idiom. You can say "*What a* pretty picture!" "*What a* big bug!" and so on. —*what if,* engage students in a discussion of *what* it would be like to have the features of various animals, such as wings, claws, sensitive ears, fur, feathers, and huge teeth. Get them started in their imaginings with sentence starters, such as "Suppose," "Imagine," "*What* would happen *if,*" and "*What if.*" Have students imitate the "*What if*" sentence starter. —*what the heck,* have students play a game and invite you to join them. Protest initially and then agree to play by saying, "Oh, well, *what the heck.* I might as well give it a try." —*what's the use,* write a complex arithmetic equation on the board. Puzzle over it for a while, and then put down the chalk in frustration. Sigh deeply and say with exaggerated discouragement, "Oh, *what's the use?*"

whatever ❖ **1.** Lead students in making sentences, such as "What thing is that?" and "*Whatever* is that?", "What thing do you want?" and "*Whatever* do you want?" Use your voice to communicate the greater intensity of *whatever.* You can explain that *whatever* means "what thing." See *what.* **2.** Offer students pencils and erasers and say "You may have *whatever* you want."

wheel ❖ Show a picture of a car, bicycle, or wagon and point to a *wheel.*

when ◆ Make sentences that students may know, such as "What do we do *when* the bell rings?" "Where do you sit *when* you come into the classroom?" or "What do you do *when* I say raise your hand?"

whenever ◆ Make a sentence with *when*, such as "When you eat, use a napkin." Make the same sentence with *whenever:* "*Whenever* you eat, use a napkin." Express in your voice the greater intensity of *whenever*.

where ◆ Search the classroom asking, "*Where* is my book?" Have students follow your lead. Pantomime looking for things. Lead the children in looking for things that you have hidden, such as a pencil or an eraser. Make sentences about this. —*where's* is two words squeezed together: *where* and *is*. See *where* and *is* in this glossary.

wherever ◆ Pretend that you cannot find a puppet. Say "Where is it? *Wherever* it is, I must find it. Come out, come out, *wherever* you are!"

whether ◆ Make up example sentences, such as "I don't know *whether* I want this book or this book," "I don't know *whether* I want an apple or an orange for lunch," or "I don't know *whether* I like blue or red."

which ◆ Dramatize having to make a choice between two items. Make sentences, such as "*Which* one do I want?" Lead students in similar dramatizations. Pantomime struggling over a decision such as *which* book to read first. Say "Should I read this one first or that one? I just don't know *which* one to choose."

while ◆ **1.** Contrast recess, which is a *while*, with the length of first grade, which is a long time. Mention other similar times that represent a *while* as compared to longer periods. **2.** See *taking place.* —*a good while*, check that students understand individual words in the phrase. Explain that this means "a long time." Ask to sit quietly for *a good while;* then contrast by having them sit quietly for *just a bit.* —*a while*, mention to students times when they have done things for *a while* as opposed to a long time. During a nap, they sleep a *while*. At night, they sleep a long time. During recess, they play for *a while*. On the weekend, they play for a long time.

whim ◆ Have a puppet do things on a *whim*. For example, it can stand on its head or eat a sandwich. When another puppet asks, the first puppet explains that this is his *whim*. Tell the class some things you have done on a *whim*. An example might be seeing an ice-cream truck and buying a cone. Ask students for examples of things they have done on a *whim*.

whine, whined ◆ **1.** *Whine* for students in the same way that a semi truck going up a hill would *whine*. Lead them in past tense sentences.

whip, whips ◆ Show a team of horses. Pantomime *whipping* them to go faster. Give example sentences. Lead students in sentences using *whips*.

whirl ◆ Lead students in *whirling*. Make sentences, such as "Let's *whirl*."

whirred ◆ Show a picture of a bird in flight or draw a flying bird on the board. Flap your arms like a bird's wings and blow air out of your mouth. Say "The bird's wings made a noise. They *whirred*."

whisk ◆ *Whisk* about the classroom in a breezy manner or *whisk* something out of a puppet's hand in the same breezy manner. —*whisked away*, have a puppet dance and then *whisk* itself *away*. Say "The puppet just *whisked* itself *away*. I guess it had somewhere else to go!"

whisper, whispers, whispering, whispered ◆ *Whisper* to students. Lead them in *whispering*. Talk to a student in a whisper. Ask a student to *whisper* something to a peer. Say "[She] *whispers* something into his ear."

whistle, whistling ◆ Demonstrate *whistling*. Ask, "Can you *whistle?*"

who ◆ **1.** Tell a student, "I am [say your name]." Ask, "*Who* are you?" Prompt the student to answer. Repeat with other students. **2.** Write a phrase on the board, such as, "the bird *who* sings" or "the boy *who* plays." Draw a chain to show that *who* connects the two parts of the phrase. Lead students in making up similar phrases about familiar people and objects.

Whoa! ◆ Explain to students that people say this when they want to stop or they are going too fast. It can mean "slow down" or "stop." Have students walk around the classroom and say "*Whoa!*" Use it first to mean "slow down" and then to mean "stop."

whole ◆ Draw a circle on the board. Say "*Whole.*" Erase part of the circle and say "Not *whole.*" Using a globe, point out a part of the world, then the *whole* world. Hold up a *whole* piece of paper. Then cut it into parts and point them out.

whooping ◆ *Whoop* for students and lead them in *whooping*.

why ◆ **1.** Ask a puppet to sit down. Have it ask *why.* Answer the puppet with a simple sentence, such as "It is story time." Repeat with students. Give examples of questions and answers, such as "*Why* do we go to school?" and "*Why* do we raise our hands before talking?" **2.** Explain that *why* can also be used in sentences that don't ask a question, for example "I learned *why* Marcia was late" or "I asked *why* Marcia was late."

wicked ◆ Set up a scene where two puppets are in a play. The setting is a classroom. One pupppet is sitting at its desk doing its homework while the other puppet runs about wildly. Tell the students that one puppet is showing good behavior and the other is showing *wicked* behavior.

wide, widely ◆ **1.** Cut a piece of paper that is *wide* and contrast it with one that is *narrow*. Show *wide* lines and *narrow* lines on the board. Show a *wide* stretch. **2.** Ask if everybody in the school knows the gym teacher. Say "[She] is *widely* known." Ask, "Who knows my name." Say "My name is *widely* known."

widespread ◆ On a map of the United States, show all the states with sightings of coyote (virtually all of the lower 48). Say "Coyotes are very *widespread.*" Move your hand across the map as you say this.

widow, widower ◆ Dramatize a husband and wife scene with two puppets. Have the husband die and the wife say "I am a *widow.*" Lead students in sentences, such as "She is a *widow*" and "This is *Widow* Jones." Repeat, having the wife die.

wife ⦿ Show a picture of a wedding. Point to the man and say *"Husband."* Point to the woman and say *"Wife."* They are called *husband* and *wife*. Ask for first-language names.

wiggle ⦿ Lead students in *wiggling* their fingers.

wig-wags ⦿ Lead students in making their arms *wig-wag*. Explain that this is what a dog's tail does.

wild ⦿ Show pictures of *wild* animals. Tell students that they are *wild* because they do not need to be taken care of. Contrast with a *pet*. Show pictures of *wild* animals and, in contrast, domesticated animals. —*the wild*, contrast pictures of animals in a zoo with animals in *the wild* (jungles, plains, etc.). —*wild goose chase*, explain to students that this is used when people cannot find something. Ask students to look for something in the classroom that you know they won't find. When they give up, say "I sent you on a *wild goose chase!*"

will, willing ⦿ **1.** Have each student stand up. Ask each one to decide to move to another part of the room, and have them then do it. Say "This is an exercise in using your *will*." See *unwilling*. **2.** Use *will* in sentences that express the future: "I have one doll; I *will* get another," or "I am hungry; I *will* eat a big lunch." Draw a time line on the board. Say "I am talking to you now." Move down the line to the right. Say "I *will* talk to you tomorrow." Tell students to close their eyes. Then say "You *will* see something different on my desk." Place an object on your desk, and ask students to open their eyes. **3.** Tell students, "I *will* read to you after lunch." Contrast with *will* not, such as "I *will* not read to you now." Lead students in sentences with *will* and *will* not, such as "We *will* have recess" and "We *will* not have music today." —*I'll*, write the words *I* and *will* on the board. Show how they are squeezed together to make the word *I'll*. You can also make sentences with "*I will*." Use *I'll* in sentences that express the future: "I have one doll; *I'll* get two dolls on my birthday," or "I am hungry; *I'll* eat a big lunch." —*we'll*, show on the board how the word *we'll* is two words squeezed together: *we* and *will*. —*won't*, show how *will* and *not* squeeze together and are written as *won't*. —*you'll*, show on the board how *you* and *will* can be squeezed together to make the word *you'll*. See *you* and *will*.

willed ⦿ Pretend to die. Have the puppet hand your books to a student and say "I am [Mrs. Howard's] lawyer. She told me that when she died, she wanted you to have her books. [Mrs. Howard] *willed* her books to you."

William ⦿ A boy's name.

willy nilly ⦿ Have students line up shoulder-to-shoulder and march across the room. Have students move about the room separately and haphazardly. Say "Students moved *willy nilly* around the room."

win, winner, won, winningly ⦿ **1.** Have two puppets run a race, with one being the clear *winner*. Have two puppets play a game of who can throw a paper clip the furthest. Announce the *winner* and have the *winner* announce, "I *win!*" Say "[Carlita] *won*." **2.** Set up a scene where the puppet is appealing to you for an extension of time on a homework assignment. Say "You make a good argument, [Guillermo]. You presented your case most *winningly*."

wind ❖   Show an illustration of the *wind* blowing. You can also blow breath out like the *wind* does. Draw trees on the board bowing in the *wind*.

window ❖   Have students touch a *window*. Tap on a *window*. Indicate the whole *window* so that it is not confused with the word *glass*.

window-shopping ❖   Draw store *windows* on the board with different items in each, such as toys, books, and clothes. Have students follow you in a line. Model strolling by each "*window*" and looking at the merchandise. Say "We are not buying anything today; we're just *window-shopping*."

winking ❖   *Wink* at students. Tell them that you are *winking*. Have them *wink* and make sentences.

winter ❖   Using a calendar, show the *winter* months. Show pictures of *winter* scenes. Contrast these with pictures of *spring*.

wipe, wiping ❖   Demonstrate by spilling some water on your desk and *wiping* it. —*wiping out*, Explain that when we get sick with certain diseases, medicines can kill the germs and help us get well. Say "With medicines, doctors are getting rid of some diseases; they are *wiping out* these illnesses to keep us healthy."

wires ❖   Show some *wires* and explain that putting in these *wires* and making them work is called *wiring*. Explain that there are *wires* like this in the walls.

wisdom, wise ❖   **1.** See *ignorance*. **2.** Show a picture of a person with *wisdom*. **3.** Ask students if there is someone who they think knows a lot, or someone who helps them when they have a problem. Or, perhaps you know someone who they think is *wise*. Explain that this is a *wise* person.

wish, wishing, wishes, wished ❖   Pantomime *wishing*. Hold your hands together as if praying and look up saying, "I wish for an ice cream" or "I *wish* it were my birthday." Draw on the board or show pictures of what you are *wishing* for. Cut out a star and hold it up. Have a puppet make a *wish*. Have students make a *wish*. Give examples, such as "How many pencils do you want? You can have all you *wish*." Have students express their *wishes*. Tell students, "I want a cookie; I *wish* I had a cookie" and "I do not want to watch television; I do not *wish* to watch television." Share your *wishes*. Ask students what *wishes* they have. Lead students in sentences using *wished*. —*How I wish!*, have one puppet *wish* by saying, "*How I wish* I had _____!" Have the other puppet supply the *wish*.

wispy ❖   Clap two erasers together and blow on the resulting *wispy* dust. Lead students in sentences.

with ❖   **1.** Show paper *with* lines and *without* lines, *with* a staple and *without* a staple, or *with* writing and *without* writing. Lead students in pointing *with* their finger, *with* a foot, *with* a nose, and so on. **2.** Have two students stand together and say "[Ming] is *with* [Carlos]." Repeat *with* other students.

withdraw ➤ **1.** Have students form a circle. Have one *withdraw*. **2.** Set up a scene in which students propose three candidates for class president, including one puppet nominee. Write the three names on the board. Then have the puppet erase its name.

withered ➤ Show a *withered* leaf and a *withered* flower. "If I stop watering my plants, they *wither* and die."

within ➤ **1.** Place students in a circle and have one student stand inside the circle. Say "[Felicia] is *within* the circle." **2.** Tell students that you would like them to write a sentence *within* a minute. Give them the sentence and time them.

without ➤ Show paper *with* lines and paper *without* lines. Show paper with writing and paper *without* writing.

witnesses ➤ Have a puppet steal something while students watch. Say "You are all *witnesses* to the theft."

wits ➤ Draw a big snake on the board. Walk by it and pantomime extreme fear when you see it. Regain your *wits* and walk calmly by.

woe-be-gone ➤ Draw a frowning face on the board. Model looking *woe-be-gone* and have students imitate you.

wog ➤ Explain that this is a nonsense word.

wolf, wolves ➤ Show pictures of *wolves*.

wonder, wondering, wondered ➤ Inspect something closely and pretend that you do not know what it is. Say to students, "I *wonder* what this is." Let students tell you. Repeat with other items. Then reverse it, allowing students to *wonder* about what things are, and you tell them. Dramatize *wondering* by saying, "I wonder what I'm going to get for my birthday" or "I *wonder* what is in my lunch today." Have students *wonder* about things.

wonderful ➤ Go about the room pointing to students' work and say expressively, "*Wonderful* drawing!" "*Wonderful* story!" or "*Wonderful* handwriting!"

wondrous ➤ Show a picture of a rainbow on the board. Say "The rainbow after the storm was so beautiful; it was *wondrous*."

wood-carver ➤ Using a bar of soap, carve a few shavings with a vegetable peeler. Tell students people who *carve* wood are called *wood-carvers*.

wooden ➤ Point to *wooden* things in the classroom and explain that they are made from *wood*. Show pictures of trees and lumber to explain *wood* if needed. Say that things made from *wood* are called *wooden*.

woof ➤ Show students a piece of woven fabric. Draw a picture of lengthwise and crosswise lines on the board. Explain that the lengthwise lines are called the warp threads and the crosswise lines are called the *woof* threads.

wool ➤ Show a picture of a sheep and point to its hair. Tell students it is called *wool*. Show a picture of *wool* cloth.

word, words ➤ Write a *word* on the board that students know the meaning of. Have students write a *word*. Have students touch individual *words* on a page.

work, working, worked, workers ◆ **1.** Show pictures of people who are *working*. Erase the board with exaggerated effort. Say "The teacher *worked* hard to get the board clean." Contrast *work* and *play*. **2.** Show students things that *work* and things that don't *work*. **3.** At some point, when all students are *working* diligently, say "What good *workers* you are today." —*work up the nerve*. Tell students you have to give a speech before a large audience and dramatize being very frightened. Take a deep breath, stand up tall, and say under your breath, "I can *work up the nerve* to do this." Begin practicing your speech.

workshop ◆ A place where *work* is done such as woodworking.

world ◆ Use a *globe* to explain.

worldwide ◆ Explain that this word has two parts: *world* and *wide*. Show the globe. Say that *worldwide* means "the whole world." Lead them in sentences: "There are people all over the world—*worldwide* people" and "There is hunger all over the world—*worldwide* hunger."

worry, worrying, worried ◆ **1.** One meaning of *worry* is "to bother." Pantomime one stuffed animal *worrying* another by chasing and scaring it. Dramatize how the animal being chased might feel bothered. **2.** Tell students that you have lost your chalk. Begin looking for it, and act *worried*. Ask students to help you. As you search, say things aloud that students will understand, such as "I need my chalk. I am *worried*" or "I cannot write on the board. I am *worried*." Pantomime anxiety with nail biting, fidgeting, and glancing at the clock. Say "Sometimes I get nervous and anxious when we have so many things to do and so little time. I *worry* that we won't get to finish all our work." I am *worrying* that I won't finish all my work."

worse, worsened, worst ◆ **1.** Tell students something that they would not like, perhaps not having money for a pair of expensive tennis shoes. Compare to something that would be *worse*, perhaps not having enough money for dinner. Have them give you other examples. **2.** Act out with a puppet. Have the puppet sneeze. Say "Gee, [Fluffy], it sounds like you have a little cold." Then have the puppet cough and wheeze and blow its nose. Say "[Fluffy], you sound terrible! Your little cold has *worsened*, and now you're really sick!" **3.** Write some poorly formed letters on the board and select the *worst* of them. Write some poorly formed shapes on the board and select the *worst* of them.

worship, worshipped ◆ **1.** Explain that this means "to practice your religion." Lead students in using *worshipped* in sentences. **2.** Have a puppet *worship* a superhero action figure. **3.** Show pictures of places of *worship*.

worth, worthless, worthy ◆ **1.** Have a puppet ask you how much different items are *worth*. Hold up different coins and tell students their worth. Say "This is a nickel; it is *worth* five cents," and so on. **2.** Show students the items in the trash can and tell them these are *worthless*. Show students some money and tell them this is not *worthless*. **3.** If students understand *earned*, explain that people who have earned something are *worthy* of it. Find examples among students of things that they are *worthy* of.

would ❖ Explain that *would* is a word that helps make sentences. It lets you say sentences in which something might happen, but it isn't for sure. Say "[Meg] *would* send me a present" and add "if it were my birthday." Contrast it with "[Meg] sent me a present." Make other contrasting sentences using *would*. Tell students, "I *would* like a book," then walk over and get one. Contrast with *would* not. For example, "She *would* not like a pencil." —*I'd*, show on the board how *I* and *would* squeeze together to make the word *I'd*. See *I* and *would*. —*wouldn't*, show on the board how *would* and *not* squeeze together to make the word *wouldn't*.

wrap, wrapped ❖ *Wrap* an eraser or pencil in a piece of paper and say that you *wrapped* it. *Wrap* an object in a piece of paper and explain that it is *wrapped*.

wrath ❖ Have a puppet show anger about being asked to clean up your desk. Say "You must control your *wrath*. Here, get your *wrath* out by punching this pillow."

wreck ❖ Build a tower out of blocks. Say "I am going to *wreck* the tower." Knock the blocks over. Say "This tower is a *wreck*."

wrenching ❖ Ask a student to hold something. Pull the object from the student's hand with a *wrench*. Say "I am *wrenching* that [mug] from your hand."

wresting ❖ Demonstrate *wresting* something out of a puppet's hands. You may wish to remind students that *wresting* things from people is not appropriate.

wrestling, wrestled ❖ Show pictures of *wrestlers wrestling*. Explain the sport as needed. Demonstrate by having a puppet *wrestle* with another puppet. Or, show pictures of high school *wrestlers*.

wretched ❖ Demonstrate by building a tower out of blocks. Have a puppet knock it over in a nasty way. Say "That wasn't nice! That was a *wretched* thing to do."

wriggle, wriggling, wriggly ❖ **1.** Demonstrate a *wriggle* by twisting and turning as if to get out of a tight spot. Lead students in *wriggling*. **2.** Pantomime being happy and *wriggle*. Say "I'm so happy I'm all *wriggly*." Tell students that happy, excited puppies are *wriggly*.

wring, wringing, wrung ❖ Demonstrate by *wringing* a wet cloth or sponge. Say that you *wrung* it.

wrinkle ❖ Show a *wrinkle* in paper or cloth.

wrist ❖ Show students your *wrist*. Have them point to theirs.

write, writing, written, wrote ❖ **1.** *Write* your name on the board. Lead students in writing their names. *Write* something on paper. Say "I wrote on the paper." **2.** Explain that the words are *written*.

writhing ❖ Walk across the room and pantomime stumbling. Grab your ankle, and pantomime twisting it. Turning in pain, say "I am *writhing* in pain."

wrong ❖ Contrast and dramatize things that are *right* and *wrong*, such as correctly and incorrectly done math problems or correctly spelled or incorrectly spelled words. Contrast things that are *right* and *wrong* that students will be familiar with, such as school rules. "It is *right* to come to school on time; it is *wrong* to be late." Write on the board a simple addition problem like 2 + 2 with the *wrong* answer. Correct it with the *right* answer.

wryly ❯ Draw or show a picture of a wedge of lemon. Pantomime tasting it, twisting and distorting your face to indicate distaste. Say "The teacher looked at students *wryly* when she tasted the sour lemon."

yank ❯ *Yank* on a shoelace.

Yankee ❯ Point to the Northern states on a map of the United States. Say "I have a friend who lives in Connecticut. She is *a Yankee*."

yawn, yawning ❯ Lead students in *yawning*.

year, yearly ❯ **1.** Explain with a calendar. Show students the twelve months that make a *year* beginning with January. Show them how you can make a *year* with any 12-month period. Lead students in sentences, such as "Each *year* in September, you start school" and "Every *year*, on [December 28th], you have a birthday." Show a *year* on a calendar. **2.** Write a date on the board. Set up a picnic scene with the puppets. Say "The puppets enjoy a picnic on this date every *year*. It is their *yearly* picnic." —*years ago*, explain that things that happened a very long time ago happened *years ago*.

yearning ❯ Explain that *yearning* means "wanting something very much." Lead students in sentences using *yearning*.

yell, yelling ❯ Have a puppet *yell* at another puppet. Have students tell the puppet, "Do not *yell* in the classroom."

yelp ❯ Show a picture of a puppy and explain that when puppies are hurt or scared, they *yelp*, and make a *yelping* sound. Lead students in pantomiming a puppy *yelping*.

yen ❯ Tell students that when they want something, they have a *yen* for it. Have students make sentences with both words. Examples are "I *want* an ice cream," "I have a *yen* for an ice cream" and "I *want* a new puppy," "I have a *yen* for a new puppy."

yes ❯ Ask questions of a puppet that are an obvious affirmative answer, such as "Are you a puppet?" "Am I a teacher?" and "Are they students?" Each time have the puppet answer, "*Yes*." Repeat with students.

yesterday ❯ Use the calendar or name the days of the week to explain *today* and *yesterday*.

yet ❯ Explain that *yet* is used to express the current time. Give example sentences, such as "Are you ready *yet*?" and "Are you ready now?" "May we read *yet*?" and "May we read now?"

Yiddish ❯ Look at the *Yiddish* words and explain that this is a language spoken by many Jews.

yield, yields ❯ Draw an apple tree and basket filled with apples next to it on the board. Tell the class, "This basket is the *yield* from this tree." Repeat with other fruit or vegetable drawings. Draw an apple tree on the board. Say "The apple tree *yields* apples for us to eat." Have the puppets pick fruit or vegetables from a garden. Have them show a basket of fruit to students and say "Look at what my garden *yields!*"

yip, yipping, yipped ◆▶ Show pictures of dogs, puppies, or coyotes. Make a *yipping* sound and explain that a *yip* is a sound these animals make.

yon ◆▶ Point to objects that are near and objects that are *yon*, especially *yon* objects that can be seen out a window. Explain that *yon* means "over there."

yonder ◆▶ Point out the window and say what you can see if you continue in various directions. Say "*Yonder* is a bank. *Yonder* is the playground."

you, your, yours ◆▶ **1.** Point to *yourself* and say sentences, such as "*I* am _____ [your name]." Contrast this with pointing to a student and saying, "*You* are _____ [student's name]." Contrast *I* with *you* in sentences, such as "*I* am here; *you* are there." Point to *I* and *you* as you speak. Explain that *you* means "the person *you* are speaking to." Lead students in making phrases, such as "*my* nose," "*your* nose," "*my* eyes," "*your* eyes," "*my* shoes," and "*your* shoes." **2.** Show things that belong to *you* and to the students, saying "This is *mine*, and this is *yours*." —*you're*, explain that *you're* means "*you are*." Model sentences using *you are* and then *you're*.

young, younger ◆▶ **1.** Show pictures of *young* and *old* people. Ask students if they are *young* or *old*. **2.** Draw a picture of a family on the board. Label them *youngest* to *oldest*. Tell students, "He is old, she is *young*, and she is *younger*."

yourself ◆▶ Point to the student and say "*Yourself*." Point to *yourself* and say "*Myself*." Repeat.

youthful ◆▶ Contrast pictures of *elderly* people and *young* people. Lead students in sentences using *youthful*.

Yumm-yum ◆▶ Dramatize saying "*Yumm-yum*," while acting as if you are eating something delicious.

zeal ◆▶ Use examples of people from history or present time who have devoted themselves to one cause, such as Martin Luther King, Jr. and Susan B. Anthony. Give example sentences using *zeal*.

zephyr ◆▶ Have everyone blow air into the room. Say "You are creating a wind or *zephyr*."

zigzag, zigzags, zigzagged ◆▶ **1.** Lead students in *zigging* and *zagging* through the desks. **2.** Lead students in drawing *zigzags* on a piece of paper. **3.** Lead students in past tense sentences.

zoom ◆▶ **1.** Lead students in having their hands *zoom* through the air. **2.** Push a toy car very fast. Say "*Zoom*." —*zoom in*, write something on the board. Have students *zoom in* to see it better. If you have a computer in your classroom, show students how you can *zoom in* on something on the screen.